Edited by Neil C. Cranston and Lisa C. Ehrich

Australian school leadership today

www.
AUSTRALIANACADEMIC**PRESS**
.com.au

First published in 2009
Australian Academic Press
32 Jeays Street
Bowen Hills Qld 4006
Australia
www.australianacademicpress.com.au

National Library of Australia Cataloguing-in-Publication entry

Title:	Australian school leadership today / editors Neil Cranston and Lisa Ehrich.
ISBN:	9781921513336 (pbk.)
Subjects:	Educational leadership--Australia.
	Educational leadership--Social aspects--Australia.
Other Authors/Contributors:	
	Cranston, N. (Neil), 1950-
	Ehrich, Lisa Catherine, 1964-
Dewey Number:	307.2011

Cover image source: Dreamstime.com/Magicinfoto

Contents

SECTION THREE
Professional Development and Learning for Leaders

SECTION FOUR
Leading in and for Successful Schools

SECTION FIVE
Summary and Conclusions

Preface

There is little doubt that educational leadership, and school leadership in particular, now hold centre stage in discussions about schools, their performance and student learning. Indeed, in this regard a recent Organisation for Economic Development and Co-ooperation (OECD) report (Pont, Nusche, & Moorman, 2008) noted that '[s]chool leadership is now an education policy priority around the world. Increased school autonomy and a greater focus on schooling and school results have made it essential to reconsider the role of school leaders' (p. 3). Echoing this in Australia, at the most senior governmental policy level, the 2008 *Melbourne Declaration of Educational Goals for Young Australians* (MCEETYA, 2008) noted principals and other school leaders as playing a critical role in leading their schools and shaping learners for the future.

This focus on leadership in schools is not new. Over the past few decades, there has been an increasing interest in the area evident in research, academic writings and policy statements and directives from education systems across the world. In some countries, for example England, specialised institutions such as the National College for School Leadership have been established to develop excellence in leadership through professional development programs, strategic initiatives, support and networking opportunities for school leaders. Some Australian states such as Victoria have attempted similar initiatives, albeit on a much smaller scale. Such is the plethora of material now available that some writers have attempted to synthesise out the key learnings about school leadership to make these more accessible to researchers, policymakers and practitioners. Leithwood and colleagues (2006) synthesised the key literature in the area to what they saw as seven strong claims about successful school leadership. Mulford and colleagues (2007) also focused on successful school leadership drawing on Australian research. The National College for School Leadership (NCSL, 2007) in England endeavoured to answer the question, 'what do we know about school leadership?', arriving at a position similar to that of Leithwood et al. These researchers are not alone in their efforts to seek a better understanding of school leadership today.

While Australian researchers have made significant contributions to the scholarly output on school leadership via important national and international journals, there have been few examples of collected pieces of writing from Australians focusing on school leadership. This edited collection is a response to this dearth. Our collection is distinctly Australian and focused on school leadership within an Australian context. It meets a growing interest among Australian education leadership scholars for relevant writing and research that is reflective of the social, historical and cultural contexts within which educational leadership is understood and enacted in Australia. The contributors to this collection are Australian academics who draw on their expertise, experiences and research to provide a diverse and rich set of chapters.

In reflecting on these themes and locating them in the realities of schools today, it is apparent that the complex and changing milieu in which leaders now work is fraught with paradoxes and tensions. As the reader engages with the ideas in the chapters in this book, it is important to keep these in mind so that the real-life dynamics of schools, and the challenges of leading them, are not forgotten. We have identified some of these in earlier work (Cranston, Ehrich, & Morton, 2007) where we argued that leaders needed to:

- respond to both local and system level demands/priorities when they might not always be compatible
- be seen and act as the leader while empowering others for distributed, shared, multiple leadership roles
- achieve work–life balance when the professional and personal demands of being an educational leader are significant
- drive a future-oriented sustainable vision for their schools in discontinuously changing and challenging times while managing the reality of 'the now' of schools
- continue their professional learning journey, keeping abreast of educational and related developments and trends while managing the significant competing demands on educational leaders
- allocate limited resources in effective, efficient and equitable ways to maximise the learning of all students.

As one journeys through the chapters in this book, these six paradoxes and tensions provide stark reminders of the complexities and challenges facing contemporary school today.

The book is structured around four sections:

- Section 1: Contexts and challenges facing educational leaders
- Section 2: Leadership issues and approaches
- Section 3: Professional learning and development for leaders
- Section 4: Leadership in and for successful schools.

While the book is organised around these sections, readers will soon note that many of the chapters make contributions to more than just the section to which they have been allocated. This is not surprising given the complexity and diverse nature of educational leadership and its surrounds; it is not possible to write in particular areas without being drawn into and across others. Chapters may be selected and read as stand-alone pieces, or as whole sections that provide different perspectives on the four overall themes that constitute this book.

The contributions in this edited collection provide a contemporary snapshot of writings by Australian school leadership academics. We believe they represent an excellent source of ideas that are likely to stimulate thinking and raise debate about contemporary issues relating to leadership in and of schools. Collectively, the evidenced-based findings contained within the chapters paint a picture of the Australian landscape that reveals school leadership, while not without its challenges, is a rewarding and ongoing journey.

Finally, we believe the writings in this volume should be of interest to undergraduate and postgraduate university students of school leadership, current teacher and leader practitioners, system-level educational leaders and policymakers. Our hope is that our collection of Australian writings will make a positive contribution to both school leadership thinking and practice.

Neil Cranston
The University of Queensland

Lisa Catherine Ehrich
Queensland University of Technology

References

Cranston, N., Ehrich, L., & Morton, L. (2007). Current issues in educational leadership: What is the literature saying? *Australian Educational Leader, 29(2),* 10–13.

Leithwood, K., Day, C., Sammons, P., Harris, A., & Hopkins, D. (2006). *Seven strong claims about successful school leadership.* Nottingham, UK: National College of School Leadership & Department of Education and Skills.

Ministerial Council on Education, Employment, Training and Youth Affairs. (2008). *Melbourne declaration of educational goals for young Australians.* Retrieved February 2, 2009, from http://www.curriculum.edu.au/verve/_resources/ National_Declaration_on_the_Educational_Goals_for_Young_Australians.pdf

Mulford, B., Kendall, D., Edmunds, B., Kendall, L., Ewington, J., & Silins, H. (2007). Successful school leadership: What is it and who decides? *Australian Journal of Education, 51*(3), 228–246.

National College of School Leadership. (2007). *What we know about school leadership.* Retrieved March 3, 2008, from http://www.ncsl.org.uk

Pont, B., Nusche, D., & Moorman, H. (2008). *Improving school leadership. Volume 1: Policy and practice.* Paris: OECD.

▶▶▶◀◀◀

Introduction and Chapter Summaries

Bill Mulford, Neil Cranston and Lisa Ehrich

School leadership now rightly holds centre stage in discussions about schools, their performance and student learning. However, the availability of quality evidence on school leadership in our country is scarce and what is available is scarcely used. There have been few examples of collected pieces of writing from Australians focusing on school leadership. There are a small number of research studies on Australian school leadership and there is a variable quality of the research that has been published (Mulford, 2007).

Mulford (2008, p. 49) summarises his concerns about the quality of the research as follows:

> Little of it covers more than one state, few are longitudinal and many rely on very small and unrepresentative samples. There is little resulting conceptualisation and/or model building. In addition there seems to be an aversion to building on or referencing previous research, preferring material of questionable relevance from other countries. The ability to extrapolate to larger populations, policy and practice from such a data base is severely limited.

There is a low priority in this country for the funding of educational research and, in particular, research in the area of school leadership. Limited use is made of the Australian research that is available in commissioned papers and policy documents (Mulford, 2008) or current Australian university courses in the area (Bates & Eacott, 2008).

In seeking to fill this lacuna this book commences with a section containing chapters devoted to the contexts and challenges facing educational leaders and then a second section with chapters related to leadership issues and approaches. Given these tensions, it becomes paramount for school leaders to become lifelong learners engaged in ongoing professional learning and development in order to enhance their efficacy. A third section contains chapters exploring a variety of professional development programs and approaches designed to support and enable leaders' learning and growth. A fourth section contains chapters that directly address the issue of leadership in and for successful schools.

Chapter Summaries

Section 1 on the contexts and challenges facing educational leaders begins with a chapter by Starr highlighting three contemporary issues facing school leaders today. These issues are leadership succession, leading and managing significant school change and educational leaders reclaiming a public voice in educational debates and policy making.

From her research Starr found actions that helped make school leadership more satisfying included the ability to reprioritise duties to focus on educational matters; hierarchical parity and greater collaboration with central education officers in establishing education policy, provision and practice; and the provision of timely, relevant and responsive professional learning and training. Leading and managing significant school change is see by Starr as more successful when attention can be diverted away from the day-to-day 'busyness', top-down change takes into account the complexity and dynamism of school life, clarity is achieved about goals and expectations, and time is provided for planning and professional collaboration. Finally, Starr argues that school-based educators are no longer the spokespeople for their own practice. They have lost ground to their critics, especially in the media. A key challenge is for school leaders to reassert themselves, to increase their individual and collective professional agency.

The second chapter by Ehrich, Kimber and Cranston focuses on particular challenges facing school leaders concerned with matters of ethics. In a situation where decision-making has two or more equally 'right' pathways, ethical dilemmas may arise. From an extensive review of the literature, the chapter develops and discusses a model for understanding the forces impacting upon decision-making processes faced by a school leader. The model identifies the antecedents that might typically exist prior to an ethical dilemma arising, such as the culture of the school, community expectations, and legal and policy frameworks. Also identified are the values and beliefs of the school leader. The model then outlines the potential interdependent, nonlinear pathways emanating from the choices made about the ethical dilemma and highlights that from such decisions various consequences or implications flow for the individual decision-maker, the school and the community.

Two cases developed from the authors' research are then explored via the use of the model. The model was found to provide a useful framework for better understanding the dynamics and forces at play in ethical dilemmas. Findings that emerged included the significance of values and beliefs, both espoused and practiced by school leaders, the repercussions for the school and other parties involved in a dilemma, and the professional ethics of school leaders as decision-makers with a strong sense of duty of care to young people.

The third and final chapter in this section by Matters raises several issues drawn from policy, practice and professional formation that have implications for the work of school leaders. Against a background of the standards movement for teachers and leaders, increasing evaluation and accountabilities, and high expectations on education from parents and the community, she discusses the collaborative process that led to the production of the Australian Capital Territory Educational Leadership Framework. This framework covers the areas of leadership capacity-building comprising learning-centred leadership, leading learning and teaching, leading strategic resource management, leading and working with others, and leading a quality organisation.

Matters concludes that there should be: a national set of teacher and leadership standards developed by a consortium of all interested parties and that these standards be constantly under review, adequate resourcing of formal school leadership preparation and formation programs and that these programs be evaluated in a way that would them to be compared and collated with ease across the nation, and a change to accountability mechanisms in order that the data generated can be used with equanimity for school development purposes in diverse contexts.

Section 2 examines a number of contemporary issues and approaches around school leadership. The section begins with chapter 4, a contribution by White, Ober, Frawley, and Bat who explore a range of issues pertinent to Indigenous leadership in education. They argue that to support Indigenous people to establish solid educational foundations, which will allow them to engage in quality employment and life experiences, will require a different approach, one in which leadership and education are considered within an intercultural context. Although they point out that there has been little formal research in Australia on intercultural leadership in education, they put forward an educational ideology based on the concept of 'both ways'. This concept is seen as interchangeable with multiculturalism in that both are concerned with the intersection and linking of cultural worlds, the space in which the overlap occurs and the leadership and teaching and learning that takes place within this space. Some of the competencies seen as necessary to operate with success in such a space are cultural self-awareness, awareness and acceptance of difference, knowledge of and skill in using different communication and learning styles, and skills to implement various pedagogies and curriculum to reflect the cultural diversity of students.

Chapter 5 by Neidhart and Carlin explores spiritual leadership and its contribution to school leadership. Against a background of key challenges facing education and school leaders today (including increased globalisation, constant change, uncertainty and insecurity, and increased complexity) the authors argue that thinking about, and enacting, leadership from a spiritual perspective might help us both revisit and reinforce critical values and beliefs that ought to underpin what we do in schools and shape a better future for all Australians. Spiritual leadership is not seen as just another dimension or frame; it is a core component of leaders' beliefs, values and actions. It involves an unshakeable belief in an education not only about 'doing' and 'having', but one which also addresses 'being' and becoming'. Spiritual leaders articulate and model being courageous, encouraging the use of constructive critique, endeavour to create space and energy to sustain hope and trust, and nurture healthy relationships. Ultimately, spiritual leaders aim to improve staff and student capacity to embrace the opportunities and dilemmas presented by the 21st century.

Chapter 6 by Spry and Graham introduces the important notion of parent–school partnerships and the roles parent play in school leadership. They note that transition from the traditional understanding of silent partnership to genuine parent–school partnerships remains challenging as this transition requires a significant cultural shift. The chapter supports those seeking to lead this type of cultural change by reviewing the past, present and future of parent–school partnerships. It also provides a detailed case study of the design of a genuine parent–school partnership project from Lismore (New South Wales) Catholic Education. The design of this project is based on the development of a compelling vision that linked individual and collective aspirations that created a 'pull' for change and the use of an activist approach. Individual, school and system participation, collaboration and cooperative learning through the use of public self-narrative or reflexive storytelling were at the centre of the approach, as was.

Chapter 7 by Lewis and Andrews also argues that in a context of ongoing and discontinuous change, new and different forms of leadership in schools are required. The authors posit that parallel leadership is one such frame-breaking concept that involves a process whereby teacher leaders and their principals engage in collective action to build school capacity. The frame embodies the three distinct qualities of mutual trust, shared purpose and allowance for individual expression. The IDEAS (Innovative Designs for Enhancing Achievements in Schools) project in two schools is discussed to highlight such an approach in action. In parallelism the metastrategic role of the principal is found to be crucial to a process of building capacity for improvement — improvement leading to a shared preferred future. Actions include engaging the community in a process of creating an envisioned future and aligning this vision with other organisational elements, such as community expectations, school infrastructures, pedagogical processes and professional learning. The metastrategic actions also enable teacher leadership and the engagement in collaborative action to build new ways of working.

The next two chapters, the first by Sytsma and the second by Beatty, are concerned with the emotional dimensions of school leadership. In chapter 8 Sytsma views leadership as a powerful activity. Based on a review of the literature and a study of five educational leaders who were re-examining their methods of operation, she argues that reconceptualising emotion in terms of strength, rather than stress, changes the nature of that power from disempowerment to empowerment. By engaging with emotional processing through the embodied minds of self and others, educational leaders can consciously choose reflective forms of knowing and doing. Sytsma argues that it is time to put away the educational leaders' 'toolkit' and welcome emotional ways of knowing into a 'garden' of opportunities for growing coherent and mutually empowering relationships in schools, and sustaining health-enhancing professional practices.

In chapter 9, Beatty suggests that an emotional understanding of school success is valuable. She proposes that such an understanding can be assisted by making connections among the elements of healthy collaborative professional learning communities, some of the complexities of principal succession planning problems and the transformational effects of addressing inner leadership issues in leadership preparation and development programs. Leadership is reconceived here as multidimensional, learnable and widely distributed and leaders are seen as more likely to succeed if they are humane, self-aware and open to new and collaborative learning. Unfortunately, by co-maintaining the norms of professional silence on the emotions involved with such characteristics, teachers and leaders become part of the self-replicating mechanism of bureaucratic hierarchy and contribute to society's sluggish responsiveness to pressing problems. Both Beatty's research and a case study of the Master of School Leadership program at Monash University demonstrate that going through the emotions — where educational leaders build self-awareness, foster resilience in relationships and strengthen team effectiveness for problem-solving and developing new solutions collaboratively — shows real promise. Beatty believes that leadership preparation programs would do well to acknowledge the transformational potential of leading with the emotions in mind.

In chapter 10, Cranston examines an area that has received little attention, the roles and aspirations of middle-level school leaders. Drawing on four quantitative research studies, Cranston finds that the vast majority of those holding middle-level leadership positions are satisfied in their current roles, but that only approximately one third are looking to promotion in the future. In terms of their roles, middle-level leaders perceived their 'real' week being dominated by operational matters, management and administration and staff, community and student issues rather than their 'ideal' of strategic, educational and curriculum leadership. Only about half of the middle-level leaders saw their school leadership team as highly developed (an issue taken up in chapter 16) yet rated strong interpersonal people skills the highest competency required for their role. They also saw a need to demonstrate a capacity to be able to manage and administer effectively.

Cranston's chapter concludes by raising a number of key issues when planning future programs. These issues include targeting middle-level leaders who say they are likely to seek promotion for both nurturing and professional development, providing tighter targeting as aspirants to particular schools, and providing further exploration of leadership role tensions such as those between administration/leadership and work/life.

The section concludes with a chapter that raises several important implications of Information and Communication Technologies (ICT) use for school principals. In chapter 11 Hough does not see technology in itself as the primary issue, but whether or not it adds value to the key school's processes and outcomes. He argues that in making such judgments and developing effective ICT-based schools, principals will need to assist many teachers to successfully adapt to the change that will be required. Flexible, or situational, leadership and teacher staff development will be crucial here.

Section 3 is concerned with issues relating to the professional development and learning of principals. In chapter 12, Wildy and Clarke argue the need to give greater emphasis to the preparation of principals of small schools. The area is important because of the numerical significance of small schools in Australia (a quarter of all schools in each state government system cater for fewer than 100 students), the unique context of small schools (such as being geographically isolated and in rural, conservative communities), the fact that small schools are typically led by principals (usually young, single females) at the start of their career, and the principal also tends to be a teacher. This 'double load' (teaching and leadership/administration) is increasing with moves to school-based management, expectations of being a leader of learning and requirements to attend to the same system policies and procedures as their peers in larger schools but without the assistance of deputy principals or other support staff. From four rich narratives Wildy and Clarke identify four foci that both reinforce this context and encapsulate the types of challenges faced by small school principals — place, people, system, and self. Wildy and Clarke conclude that their findings present a persuasive case for principal preparation programs that are more systematic and specialised than the ad hoc nature of many current approaches.

In chapter 13 by D'Arbon, Cunliffe, Canavan, and Jericho describe the development and evaluation to leadership development initiatives of two faith-based systems of schools, those of the Sydney Catholic Education Office and Lutheran Education Australia. Both initiatives reflect the six-step process for leadership talent development of create a culture for growth, benchmark current practice, define leadership qualities you want, identify the leadership talent pool, and assess and grow individual leadership talent. A vital feature of the programs was found to be the collegiality, sense of community and networking that they engendered.

From the evaluation of these initiatives it was found that participants generally responded positively, the programs are an effective catalyst promoting further formal study, and the programs develop leadership capacity among young teachers to the point where many now consider promotion positions (over 2 years since one program, almost half the participants have been appointed to a new leadership role). In a time of difficulties of young teacher retention, the programs also appear to have had a powerful effect in maintaining an extremely high retention rate in teaching.

In chapter 14 Dempster, Alen and Gatehouse argue that timely and targeted professional learning is essential if school leaders are to manage themselves and their leadership journeys productively over extended periods. They provide a scan of literature related to the professional learning agenda for school leaders in order to highlight its scope and recent emphases, particularly as they relate to the needs of experienced leaders. Dempster, Alen and Gatehouse worry that the emphasis in some of these reviews is too narrow (such as a concentration on just instruction and/or achievement tests) or too broad (which may result in shallow learning). They sum up the scope of the school leadership portrayed by their scan in the form of five knowledges — knowing the purpose of leadership, oneself, others, context, and the job.

Dempster, Alen and Gatehouse then describe a professional development program for experienced school leaders in Queensland (the Strategic Leaders' Program) based on a framework consisting of the five capabilities of educational, personal, relational, intellectual and organisational. The program also emphasises processes such as on-the-job and peer learning over time, coaching and establishing organisational objectives. An extensive evaluation of the program found it had the strongest effect on personal and relational capabilities, a limited effect on the educational and little effect on the intellectual and organisational. These findings lead Dempster, Alen and Gatehouse to conclude that leaders should encounter the five knowledges at different times in their careers. Aspirant and new appointees are likely to need job, or task, and context knowledge. All need reinforcement about the purposes of schooling but experienced leaders responsible for larger and more complex schools need a realistic knowledge of self and others.

The topic of formal mentoring programs is pursued by Ehrich in chapter 15. Drawing upon earlier research, she identifies the merits and demerits of mentoring programs for mentors, mentees and their organisation. Emerging from these findings is a set of critical issues that need to be considered when planning and implementing school-based mentoring programs to maximise their success. These issues include support from senior management, appointment of a coordinator, clarity in purpose, roles and expectations, careful selection of mentees, matching mentors and mentees, provision of time, training and monitoring and evaluation.

In the final chapter in this section, chapter 16, by Cranston and Ehrich concentrates on senior management teams (SMTs). In an era of distributed leadership and a focus on developing the leadership density of schools, the chapter examines the extant literature in the area, including that in the area of micropolitics, highlighting key characteristics and practices that contribute to their effectiveness. These dimensions include the clarity of SMT role and objectives, the competence and credibility of its members, the uniformity of members' values and their commitment to team work, interpersonal relations among members and with staff, and accessibility of professional development.

The chapter concludes by discussing a practical strategy employing the TEAM Development Questionnaire that can be used by teams to reflect on their practices and identify ways to develop their effectiveness. Learnings on the use of the TEAM instrument and process indicate that team building is challenging for team members and that they must be committed to making things better in their SMT. Data from the questionnaire must be accepted as a conversation starter and the start of a developmental journey. One of the major outcomes is to get people talking, sharing and trusting each other. This requires the use of quality facilitation, an acknowledgment that slow is good and a team and not just principal decision to be involved.

Chapters by Gurr and Dinham in the final section, Section 4, pick up on some of the issues running through the previous discussions. Both chapters focus on what these issues mean for schools and how we might make the connections between leadership and learning.

In chapter 17 Gurr notes that while the study of successful school leadership has attracted significant interest this decade, most of the major reviews and studies have come from research in North America and the United Kingdom. The contribution of his chapter is its focus on research in the Australian context. With a history that dates back to the mid-1960s, the chapter documents the development of this research over the last 40 years, and provides several examples of current research programs that are providing quality evidence on successful school leadership in Australia.

From major international reviews Gurr identifies that successful school leadership involves building vision and setting direction, understanding and developing people, redesigning the organisation, and managing the teaching and learning program. In addition, ongoing research in the International Successful School Principals Project (ISSPP) suggests that successful principals are good problem-solvers, can articulate worthwhile core values, build trust, focus on ensuring there is a safe and secure environment, are a visible part of the school, facilitate improvement in teaching practice, and they work well with the broader environment through coalition-building activities. The combination of these characteristics is not dissimilar to the concepts of organisational learning and professional learning communities. Finally, Gurr notes three areas of particular interest from the Australian literature — small schools, the increasing coalescing of data on each school and clearly articulated system accountability and leadership frameworks, and some evidence of what does not work.

In the final chapter, chapter 18, Dinham looks at Australian research, including his own AESOP project from New South Wales, exploring the leadership–learning nexus. While noting that this nexus is a contested and often an unclear one, he argues that what is important is the growing recognition that educational leaders (that is, distributed leadership) need to understand how students learn and what effective teaching looks like — leaders need to plan, act and evaluate on the basis of solid, empirical evidence, and not fad, fantasy, superstition or ideology. School leaders *can* play major roles in creating the conditions in which teachers can teach effectively and students can learn. In this process, principals possess and demonstrated two broad characteristics: awareness and responsiveness to people and events around them, and through high standards and expectations they are demanding, both of themselves (give a lot) and others (expect a lot).

The sections and their chapters now follow. A final chapter, chapter 19, draws some conclusions for Australian school leadership from cross-chapter comparisons.

References

Bates, R., & Eacott, S. (2008). Teaching educational leadership and administration in Australia. *Journal of Educational Administration and History, 40*(2), 149–160.

Mulford, B. (2007). *Overview of research on Australian educational leadership 2001–2005.* Melbourne, Australia: Australian Council for Educational Leaders (Monograph No. 40).

Mulford, B. (2008). *The leadership challenge: Improving learning in schools.* Camberwell, Melbourne: Australian Council for Educational Research, *Australian Education Review Series No. 53.* Available at http://www.acer.ed.au/research_reports/AER.html

▶▶▶◀◀◀

The Authors

JAN ALEN has worked in the area of educational leadership for over 20 years. She began her career as a primary teacher in Victoria and moved to Queensland in the early 1990s. In her work as a Manager, Professional Development and Leadership Institute in the Department of Education, Training and the Arts, she has been at the forefront of developing and implementing a range of successful initiatives for leaders including principal assessment centres, work shadowing for women, mentoring and coaching for leaders, building personal and relational capabilities for new leaders and working closely with leadership teams. Recently she has been involved in the development of Queensland's *Leadership Matters: Case studies for school leadership development.*

DOROTHY ANDREWS is Associate Professor in the Faculty of Education at the University of Southern Queensland. Her specialist areas include Leadership and Management, Organisational Theory, Pedagogy and Curriculum, and School Development and Change. Dorothy is the Director of Leadership Research (LRI) and IDEAS National Project Director. She was a joint recipient of the Australian Council of Educational Leaders 2003 Gold Medal for research in educational leadership in Australia and internationally.

MELODIE BAT is an academic working for Batchelor Institute of Indigenous Tertiary Education. Melodie is currently completing her doctoral research into teacher education at Batchelor Institute, with a focus on critical cross-cultural qualitative research methods. In this work, Melodie is continuing her professional commitment to both Indigenous education in the Northern Territory, begun 15 years ago as a bush teacher in Central Australia, as well as to her own continuing learning journey.

BRENDA BEATTY, an Australian Council for Educational Leadership Fellow, is designer and director of the highly regarded Monash University *Master in School Leadership*, and *Human Leadership: Developing People* programs, created for the Department of Education and Early Childhood Development in the State of Victoria. Born in Canada, and now an Australian citizen, Dr Beatty is a doctoral graduate of OISE University of Toronto, where she studied with Professor Andy Hargreaves. Her thesis, *Emotion Matters in Educational Leadership* won the Thomas B. Greenfield award for best Canadian doctoral dissertation of the year. Among her recent publications is *Leading with Teacher Emotions in Mind*, a book co-authored with Professor Ken Leithwood.

KELVIN CANAVAN is the Executive Director of Schools and is responsible for the overall leadership and management of the Catholic Education Office (CEO), Sydney. He is well known for his work on strategic planning and management in leadership succession, Brother Kelvin launched his leadership succession strategy in 1995, and he initiated the *Leaders for the Future* Program in October 2005 with a view to nurturing young teachers who aspire to educational leadership.

PAUL CARLIN currently has a part-time research position at the Australian Catholic University in the area of educational leadership. Prior to that his role at the Catholic Education Office, Melbourne, involved working with principals and deputy principals in primary and secondary schools. In the late 1990s, he spent 2 years as a project director at the newly established Australian Principals Centre, which was located at the University of Melbourne, Hawthorn.

SIMON CLARKE is a senior lecturer and currently the Deputy Dean of the Faculty of Education at The University of Western Australia where he teaches, supervises and researches in the substantive area of educational leadership and management.

NEIL CRANSTON is Associate Professor in the School of Education, The University of Queensland, Australia and Adjunct Professor, School of Education, Unitec Institute, New Zealand. He is soon to take up the position of Professor (Educational Leadership & Curriculum) at the University of Tasmania. He researches, consults and lectures in the areas of educational leadership, management and change. He is Fellow of the Australian College of Educators, and Fellow of the Australian Council for Educational Leaders. His most recent book, co-authored with Lisa Catherine Ehrich, is *What is This Thing Called Leadership? Prominent Australians Tell Their Stories* published by Australian Academic Press (2007).

ANNETTE CUNLIFFE
is Senior Lecturer in the School of Educational Leadership, based at the Strathfield Campus of Australian Catholic University. She has been involved in education for over 40 years and has held a number of senior leadership roles. Her research interests include leadership systems and frameworks, preparation of future leaders, governance, learning leadership and the person of the leader.

TONY D'ARBON is Faculty Professor in the School of Educational Leadership at Australian Catholic University. He has been writing, conducting research and teaching in the area of educational leadership, particularly in the areas of succession and succession planning. More recently he has been conducting research and writing in the area of Indigenous educational leadership in remote communities.

NEIL DEMPSTER is Professor in Education at Griffith University and former Dean of its Faculty of Education. His research interests are in leadership for learning, school governance, school improvement and the role that professional development plays in leadership, policy implementation and institutional change. Neil is an Honorary Fellow of the Australian Council for Educational Leaders, and a Fellow of the Australian College of Educators where he held the post of National President in 2006–2007. His recent publications include two edited books: *The Treasure Within: Leadership and Succession Planning* (2007); *Connecting Leadership and Learning: Principles for Practice* will be published by Routledge (London) in July this year.

STEVE DINHAM is Professor and Research Director, Teaching, Learning and Leadership, at the Australian Council for Educational Research in Melbourne. He is also Professorial Fellow at the University of Melbourne and Visiting Professorial Fellow at the University of Wollongong.

LISA CATHERINE EHRICH is Associate Professor in the School of Learning and Professional Studies, Faculty of Education, at Queensland University of Technology. She has taught, researched and published in the field of educational leadership and management for over a decade. Her research interests include school leadership, mentoring as a professional development activity for educators and other professionals, and the research methodology, phenomenology.

JACK FRAWLEY is Senior Research Fellow with Australian Catholic University's Flagship for Creative and Authentic Leadership. He has had extensive experience in intercultural education as a teacher, adult educator and researcher. He has a PhD from the University of Western Sydney and has research interests in intercultural leadership, adult education and Australian studies. He has been awarded an Endeavour Research Fellowship (2008), and Australian Research Council Post-doctoral Fellowship (2006–2008), an Ian Potter Travel Grant (2006), two Northern Territory History Grants (2002 and 2004), and an Australian Institute of Aboriginal and Torres Strait Islander Studies Research Grant (2003).

RUTH GATEHOUSE began her career as a teacher. Moving into leadership roles she worked for the Department of Employment Training and The Arts and the private sector for 17 years before joining Griffith University in 2005 as the Director of the Centre for Leadership and Management in Education. In 2009, Ruth changed roles to join the Griffith Business School and maintains her work and interest in educational leadership through its Executive Development Unit.

JOHN GRAHAM is currently Assistant Director, Catholic Education Office, Lismore, New South Wales, Australia. Prior to this appointment he taught in secondary school for several years, followed by a time at Catholic Teachers College, Sydney, where he was Senior Lecturer and Head of School. He holds postgraduate degrees in education and divinity. John has lectured widely across Australia in the area of family–school partnership. His research and publications have been in the areas of school leadership, family school partnership and student voice in religious and spiritual growth.

DAVID GURR is Senior Lecturer in Educational Leadership, Centre for Organisational Learning and Leadership, at the University of Melbourne. He coordinates the Master of School Leadership program and has research interests in school review and educational leadership. He is a member of the International Successful School Principalship Project. David is a former Vice-President of the Australian Council for Educational Leaders (ACEL), current editor of *Monograph* and past editor of *Leading and Managing*. He was made a fellow of the Victorian branch of the ACEL in 1999, a National Fellow in 2006, and awarded the National Presidential Citation for 2004.

ADRIENNE JERICHO holds the position of Executive Director of Lutheran Education Australia, a position he has held since 1995. In this position he represents Lutheran schools nationally and provides leadership in the areas of vocational formation, leadership development and overall policy development. His doctoral dissertation was in the area of principal appraisal.

MICHAEL HOUGH is a Professorial Fellow at the University of Wollongong, where he works in both the Sydney Business School and the Australian Centre for Educational Leadership. He has been National President of the Australian Council for Educational Administration, was awarded the Gold Medal of ACEA; and is a Fellow of the Australian Council for Educational Leaders, the Australian College of Educators and the Australian Institute of Management.

MEGAN KIMBER is a senior researcher. Her publications traverse Australian politics and public administration, and educational policy and administration. Megan has a particular interest in ethical dilemmas, especially those facing leaders in the public sector and in educational settings. She has examined the impact of reforms to the Australian public service on democratic government, and analysed the effect of casualisation of the academic workforce on Australian universities.

MARIAN LEWIS is a senior lecturer in the Faculty of Education, University of Southern Queensland. Her specialist areas are Knowledge Creation, Professional Learning Community, School Development and Change, and Organisational Culture. Marian is a core team member of the IDEAS National Project Team. She was a joint recipient of the Australian Council of Educational Leaders 2003 Gold Medal for research in educational leadership in Australia and internationally.

BILL MULFORD is Honorary Professor and an internationally recognised educator whose most recent book was published by the ACER in 2008 (*The Leadership Challenge: Improving Learning in Schools*). He is also editor for the Leadership and Management Section of the 2010 *International Encyclopaedia of Education*, published by Elsevier in Oxford. A former teacher, school principal, Assistant Director of Education, Faculty Dean, and Chair of a university Academic Senate, he has high legitimacy within the profession. He continues to acts as an adviser to numerous state and national departments of education including those in Australia, Singapore and England (the National

College for School Leadership) and as a consultant to international organisations such as OECD and UNESCO.

HELGA NEIDHART is currently Senior Lecturer and State Coordinator in the School of Educational Leadership at Australian Catholic University, Melbourne. Prior to this, she was a secondary school principal and teacher and so has combined both practical and theoretical levels. She has served as 'Practitioner in Residence' at the Principals' Centre, Harvard Graduate School of Education, and was a member of the teaching staff of the Harvard Leadership Academy. Helga is a researcher, lecturer in educational leadership in masters and doctoral programs, and supervises student research.

ROBYN OBER is a Murri woman from Innisfail, North Queensland. She has cultural connections to the Djiribal people through her mother and Kuku Yimithirr through her father's lineage. Robyn has a total of 22 years' teaching experience in both primary and tertiary education. At present Robyn is working as an academic researcher within the research division at Batchelor Institute of Indigenous Tertiary Education (BIITE). Robyn is involved in several projects in her current position, including Australian Research Council — 'Linking Worlds' project and Australian Teaching and Learning Council — 'Institutional Leadership Paradigm' projects with Australian Catholic University and BIITE. Other research interests include 'Both-Ways Education' and 'Leadership for Indigenous Women'.

KAREN STARR is Professor and the Chair of School Development and Leadership and Director of the Centre for Educational Leadership and Renewal at Deakin University. Prior to this appointment she was a school principal for 15 years in Victoria and South Australia. Karen was Chief Writer of the South Australian Curriculum, Standards and Accountability Framework, and in 2004 won the National Telstra Business Women's Award for the not-for-profit sector. Her research interests include the principalship, educational leadership, governance, rural education, youth engagement and the management of change and renewal in schools.

GAYLE SPRY is Senior Lecturer in the School of Educational Leadership, Australian Catholic University. Her research interests include school renewal, leadership development and schools as professional learning communities. For over a decade, she has collaborated with various educational authorities in the development of a series of leadership frameworks for school and system leaders. Most recently, she has acted as research consultant in the parent–school partnership project sponsored by Lismore Catholic Education. This project focused on the issue of parent leadership in schools and produced a leadership framework for parent partnership in Catholic schools within Lismore Catholic Education.

SANDRA SYTSMA has experience as a teacher and researcher and has worked in schools and university settings in Australia. Her publications concern the personal and professional development of leaders in education, with a current interest being sustainable leadership.

NEREDA WHITE is a Gooreng Gooreng woman from Bundaberg, Queensland. She is Coordinator of the Weemala Indigenous Unit, ACU National at the Brisbane campus. In a career spanning over 16 years, she has made a significant contribution to Indigenous higher education through her teaching, scholarship and leadership. In 2006, she received a Carrick award for outstanding contribution to student learning and in 2007 she was awarded the Neville Bonner University teaching award for Indigenous Education. Her research interests include Indigenous women's careers and leadership, learning and spirituality, and Indigenous research methodologies.

HELEN WILDY is Professor of Education and Dean of the Faculty of Education, The University of Western Australia. Her current research focuses on leadership with particular emphasis on the challenges faced by the principal in small schools. She is a co-investigator in the International Study of Principal Preparation, a cross-cultural investigation of the preparation of novice principals in 13 countries.

▷▷▷◁◁◁

SECTION ONE
Context and Challenges Facing School Leaders

Confronting Leadership Challenges: Major Imperatives for Change in Australian Education

Karen Starr

Educational leadership in Australia has undergone dramatic change over the past two decades. Structural reforms in education have been impelled by globalisation and market economy imperatives, which have created corresponding shifts in public administration, including school leadership practice. Structural reforms have embraced the neo-liberal precepts of individualism, competition, consumer choice, libertarian sovereignty and the rolled-back state, emphasising efficiency and budgetary restraint. In collusion with these dominant discourses are those supporting the new 'professionalism' based on performativity in the form of greater regulation, compliance and accountability (Ball, 2005). Quality assurance and continuous improvement have been pursued through performance indicators, standards, capabilities and benchmarks that rank 'outcomes' and 'outputs'.

In education, structural reforms have taken two distinct forms. First are those that have swept across the entire public services infrastructure: corporatisation, privatisation, outsourcing, re-engineering, and organisational downsizing in line with the philosophy of 'small government'. Social spending has been reduced as user-pays principles target costs to consumers while spending is focused on 'targeted populations'. The second form of restructuring and reform concerns the devolution of authority and responsibility to schools. These restructuring activities dovetail neatly together. For example, as education bureaucracies downsize, it is commonsense that the once centrally performed work must be conducted elsewhere, with the obvious solution being delegation to school leaders, with work overseen centrally via standardised controls.

In response to these events the role of school principals has change irrevocably (Day, Harris, Hadfield, Tolley, & Beresford, 2000; Starr,

2000). The role now equates with that of a Chief Executive Officer of any organisation, with the management of strategic planning, multi-million dollar budgets, industrial relations, facilities, marketing and public relations coming on top of the 'core business' of curriculum, pastoral care, teaching and learning. Paradoxically, however, principals perceive that their status and power in the educational hierarchy have been reduced to that of perfunctory middle management as their role entails less creativity and more external control, accountability, regulation and mandatory compliance (Starr, 2000, 2008b; Watkins, 1993). In addition, major policy decisions are made centrally for local implementation, and collaborative policy development has been replaced with limited consultation. Simultaneously, workloads have intensified with focus shifting from students, classrooms and curriculum to the business aspects of school administration. Hence, school leadership has often been hijacked by management tasks (Starr, 2008b).

Among the recent reforms has been the introduction of leadership frameworks, standards or capability statements in most Australian states and territories to guide the work and professional learning of school leaders. These latest reforms demand oversight of improvements in teaching and learning (which is what educational leadership should be about), to be demonstrated primarily through enhanced standardised test results among the school's students. These reforms indicate that policymakers recognise the substantial shift in principals' work into management and business concerns and that a rebalancing act is required to have them focus more on leading teaching and learning. Given the immensity of principals' workloads, these reforms could further contribute to issues of leadership disengagement.

This chapter addresses three major contemporary issues facing school leaders that have arisen or have been exacerbated in the context of the structural reforms and their effects described above. These issues are leadership succession, leading and managing significant school change, and reclaiming a public voice in educational debates and policy-making. While school leaders face many challenges, those chosen for discussion here not only traverse education systems and sectors across Australia, but continue to have significant consequences for educational leaders, students, schools, communities and teacher educators alike, now and into the future. Furthermore, they are likely to resonate with educational leaders elsewhere in the world.

Leadership Succession

There are over 9,800 schools in Australia and most will lose their principal due to retirement within the next 5 years (Cervini, 2003). The challenge is finding people to replace them. Too few applications are received for principal vacancies alongside a paucity of suitably qualified candidates (Barty, Thomson, Blackmore, & Sachs, 2004). Experienced principals are less inclined to seek further appointments, attrition and turnover rates are rising, and average tenure has decreased to 5 years (Lacey, 2002; Millikan, 2002). Leadership shortfalls are exacerbated by a worldwide teacher shortage.

Not so long ago the principalship was a sought-after, desirable and prestigious post, with high competition for appointments. Now it is viewed increasingly as unappealing (Hopkins, 2006; Macnamara, 2006). So what are the disincentives that are discouraging potential school leaders?

The reasons for poor attraction and retention rates in the principalship are many and complex, but the prime reason appears to be the increasingly burdensome and difficult nature of the role, and its time and task intensiveness (d'Arbon, Duignan, Duncan, & Goodwin, 2001; Myers, 2006). While 60 working hours per week is the average for Australian principals (Australian Education Union, 2007; Department of Education & Training [DE&T], 2004), at busy times of the school year and during periods of extensive reforms and restructurings, average hours often exceed 70 hours (Starr, 2000). This is greater than principal workloads in many comparable countries (DE&T, 2004; National Association of Elementary School Principals, 2003).

Many potential applicants, especially women, are eschewing possibilities of career advancement past middle management, since the principalship is perceived to come at too high a cost to personal and family life (Blackmore, 2007; Leech, 2006; Milburn, 2006). Hence, where women were once making inroads into the male dominated principalship, now fewer are applying and the earlier gender imbalance is becoming more pronounced (Blackmore, 1999, 2004).

Other disincentives include a school's location (with remote and rural schools being the least desirable), a school's size (very small or very large schools are less attractive), a school's poor reputation, an incumbent principal who is presumed to be reapplying for the job at the expiration of a contract, and the rigorous, impersonal application and interview process (Australian Secondary Principals' Association,

1999). There are perceptions about biased selection panels (Blackmore, Thomson, & Barty, 2006) and 'cloning', which favours similar types of people for the principalship, with potential believed to be outweighed by experience (Gronn, 2003). Remuneration levels are considered too low for the level of responsibility assumed (Lugg, Bulkley, Firestone, & Garner, 2002; Thomson, Blackmore, Sachs, & Tregenza, 2003), along-side a view that it is safer to remain in permanent, tenured employment in a lower paid position with good holidays than risk trading these favourable conditions for a 5-year contract, with fewer holidays, longer hours, more responsibilities and no guarantee of continuity in the job.

Some aspirants believe that disaffection arises through policy regimes that are inimical to social democratic principles (Blackmore & Sachs, 2007; Starr, 2000). Along the same lines, there is concern that principals spend too much time implementing state-mandated reforms, many of which are unpopular and perceived as unnecessary and unhelpful (Starr, 2000). Similarly, policy pressures for compliance and accountability, resource reductions and a general malaise in teacher morale are also deterrents to promotion (Blackmore, 2004). Disenchantment about 'core-periphery' power relationship between schools and central education officers is another negative factor, despite rhetoric about enhanced authority delivered through devolution and local school management (Starr, 2000).

Principals' work is subject to 'function creep' whereby tasks continually expand, further undercutting time to execute existing expectations (Goldring & Greenfield, 2002). To cope with increased workloads and the significant turnabout in foci created by structural reforms in public administration, many principals have delegated day-to-day curriculum, student-welfare and school operational activities to deputies and assistant principals. Hence, assistant and deputy principals have also assumed many new responsibilities through reforms as principals' work has been manoeuvred towards the business, compliance and strategic aspects of school management (Day et al., 2000). Principals have noticed a transformation in their relationships with staff because intensified administrative tasks, unpopular policy implementations and the greater necessity of being out of the school have made them less visible in classrooms and staffrooms (Thomson, 1998). Not surprisingly, structural reforms have had a significant impact on job satisfaction (see Hamilton, 2008).

Many new principals are shocked at what the job actually entails, and feel unprepared for the amount of work that is involved, especially in the broad range of business and compliance areas (Starr, 2008b). There is a strong sense that assistant and deputy positions are no longer sufficient training grounds for the principalship and that there is inadequate preparation for people who have progressed through the ranks of school promotion systems to acquire essential broad skills and knowledge (Starr, 2008b). Some decades ago Sarason (1982) questioned the suitability of a background in classroom teaching as preparation for school leadership, but now this case appears even stronger.

Media reports aggravate unhelpful views, accentuating principals' long hours, weekend and night work, 'dealing with conflicting demands and being pulled from one activity to another at frenetic pace' (Thomson et al., 2003, p. 5). Front-page media attention given to increasing stress levels and instances of suicide among principals exacerbate already negative perceptions (e.g., Tomazin & Waldon, 2004).

In response to the impending shortfall in principal applications, state governments are taking measures to counter the leadership supply problem. Current principals are being asked to delay their retirement; retired principals are being reemployed to work as short-term locums; mentoring schemes have been devised; and aggressive advertising, recruitment and training campaigns are underway. Higher pay for people willing to serve in 'difficult' schools is mooted, but the overseas experience indicates that this may not be the silver bullet many expect it to be (Reeves, 2008).

Principals have their own ideas, however, about how the leadership shortage can be rectified. According to practitioners (Starr, 2006), the job would be more satisfying for incumbents and increasingly attractive to aspirants if:

- principals were able to reprioritise duties to focus on educational matters, without adding to their already onerous workloads. If this does not occur, principals argue that they need more administrative support, since management impositions are incessant and becoming incrementally more time-consuming;
- the principalship attracted greater status, respect, recognition and remuneration;
- consideration was given to what constitutes a reasonable working week for school leaders. Principals often feel that their own fami-

lies suffer due to commitments and sacrifices made for other people's children;
- school leaders had hierarchical parity and greater collaboration with central education officers in establishing education policy, provision and practice;
- the rhetoric of shared leadership that redistributes both power and responsibility in schools was actually the case, with position descriptions, performance appraisal policies and employment contracts reflecting this ideal. Current employment processes and professional development programs not only fail to capture the reality of the principalship, but follow traditional hierarchical models by placing sole responsibility for educational outcomes on the principal (see Starr & Oakley, 2008);
- a comprehensive induction process were implemented;
- up-to-date, relevant and responsive professional learning and training opportunities were available, as determined by practitioners themselves;
- the benefits of being a school leader and the positive aspects of the role and its intrinsic rewards were emphasised. The most optimistic finding in 'The Privilege and the Price' (DE&T, 2004, p. 21) report is that 'principals and assistant principals almost universally love their job'. The principalship is a way of life that has an important impact on the community and especially on the lives of young people. It is these aspects of the role that require public exposure, emphasis, and be accorded adequate 'core' work time.

While some governments are implementing ameliorative strategies, not all of these ideas have been taken up. Issues such as pay, prestige, working hours and the pragmatics of shared leadership have not been addressed. Prime Minister Rudd's recent threat for principals to 'shape up or ship out' with increased external accountabilities appears to exacerbate existing concerns within the profession (Grattan, Tomazin, & Harrison, 2008; McManus & Jean, 2008). Leading schools through major change will be the rubric by which principals are appraised, and it is to this issue to which we now turn our attention.

Achieving Significant School Change and Renewal

While it is difficult to lead and manage change in any organisation, major change is often particularly hard to achieve in schools (Evans,

1996; Grey, 2005; Sarason, 1990). This is not to suggest that schools cannot and do not undertake significant change; it is to suggest that schools find it difficult to divert attention away from the day-to-day 'busyness' to undertake major change. Difficulties are exacerbated when demands for change occur simultaneously from a number of directions — the Commonwealth, the state and the district education office, in addition to any impetus for change from within the school. (Paradoxically, despite constant provocations to change, schools are also under continual pressure to revert to previous practices [Darling-Hammond, 1998], such as calls for a return to the '3Rs', which will be discussed later in this chapter.)

It is human nature to resist change, unless implementers are involved in its creation (Synnot & Fitzgerald, 2007). Practitioners are comfortable with the way things are, they are familiar with the way things work, they have established routines and organisational cultures operate to maintain the status quo. While creators of change are optimistic about the positive effects it will usher in, for implementers, the opposite is the case, with reforms often viewed as 'one damned thing after another' (Baker, Curtis, & Berenson, 1991, p. 13). Change is a political process and contestations are based on differentials of power and personal motivation (Mulford, 1998; Ridden, 1991). People feel threatened by change because they are usually being asked to give up or lose something — their identity or 'face', their feelings of comfort and security, long-held values, beliefs, relationships, territory or ways of working. Change necessitates moving from the familiar to the unknown (Bridges & Mitchell, 2002). Whatever it is, there will be some break from the past, new effort and thinking required and extra time needed to implement the new pursuit. It is easier to remain the same and hence, during initial phases of change, morale and output commonly suffer (Scott & Jaffe, 2004).

Organisational cultures influence the ability of schools to embrace second-order or major change. There is a public face of organisational cultures and an in-house view that may be very different. Cultures respond to both centripetal forces to stay the same and centrifugal forces, which demand change (Lakomski, 2004). Schein (1992) argues that organisational cultures serve two major functions: first, to safeguard a group's taken-for-granted, ingrained perceptions about itself and the environment in which it exists; and secondly, to induct newcomers into existing behaviours and belief systems. Much literature on school cultures suggests that they regularly retain outmoded workplace practices (Nadler, Shaw, Walton, & Associates, 1995), supported by a 'this is the way we do it around here' response to change initiatives as methods of self-preservation (Dennis, 1997).

Some barriers to change relate to the nature of teaching. Teachers' work is relentless — complex, demanding, requiring untold interactions each day and attention to the needs of an increasingly diverse range of students, many of whom have learning or social difficulties. Students are becoming more challenging and harder to motivate, with teachers having to perform well in order to capture and retain students' attention and cooperation (Evans, 1996). Curriculum expectations are constantly changing and expanding. On top are the daily unexpected requests, complaints, directives and queries from students, parents and others. The quotidian of schools is messy, busy, exhausting and stakeholders are many. Time for prolonged planning, reflection or problem-solving is always lacking. To make matters worse there are the endless imposed mandatory compliance agendas that are extrinsic to the school's priorities, which add to workload and hinder and steal time away from change initiatives.

The technical-rational-structural approach to change often adopted by education bureaucracies further exacerbates problems (Goldring & Greenfield, 2002). Thomson (1998, p. 47) refers to this 'test–data–outcome–report-card driven approach to education policy' as an attempt to ensure that policy is teacher and principal-proof. Change is ongoing, uncertain and time is pressured, but imposed directives regularly ignore this fact. Top-down mandatory change that assumes a straightforward, logical, predictable implementation with prescriptive procedures fails to grapple with the complexity and dynamism of school life (Leithwood, 2001). Timelines for externally initiated tasks are unrealistic (Dennis, 1997) and place enormous pressure on school personnel especially at busy periods, such as the beginning or end of the school year.

There are further criticisms about standardisation and the current pursuit of benchmarking, 'best practice' and supposedly indicative league tables that ignore the enormous contextual differences in educational settings, fail to recognise many worthwhile school achievements, and which foster emulation rather than needs-focused responsiveness (Grey, 2005).

It is common for middle-aged staff members to be the most cynical and resistant to change (Duignan, 2006; Evans, 1996), yet in many ways this observation is understandable. These staff members have other life concerns besides their work. Middle age is often the time when people's own children are going through critical times in their education or are leaving home, ageing parents make extra demands, retirement is looming and plans and adjustments have to be made. Older members of staff will not be the only ones who are less than keen to change, but they can be most confident and vocal in their dissent and have the capacity to take other members of staff with them. It is in the self-interests of dissenters to maintain the status quo. They may proclaim that they operate in the best interests of the school, but hold back its progress. Longstanding teachers are custodians of stories about the unintended, unanticipated, negative consequences or side-effects of change. Principals initiating change often hear things like 'we tried that once before and it didn't work', and quite probably it did not (see for example McKinsey & Co., 2007). The more profound the change, the longer existing arrangements have been in place and the older the people who are to make the change, the greater the sense of loss and resistance encountered (Grey, 2005). However, major change often fails because leaders do not understand or recognise the problems teachers are exposed to when asked to undertake change (Gross, Giacquinta, & Berstein, 1975). The process of change is enhanced when school leaders:

- provide teachers with school time for planning and professional collaboration
- take a strategic approach by developing common understandings and goals with stakeholders
- ensure all major change initiatives appear on the school's strategic plan
- examine current practices critically but respectfully and being explicit and truthful about the rationale for change
- explain how the change will affect people
- garner the support and involvement of key players to provide impetus, motivation and to share responsibility
- delineate clear incremental steps for change within realistic time-lines
- encourage dialogue, honest feedback and ideas during the change process

- announce the change to all stakeholders and provide progress reports at every opportunity — assemblies, staff meetings, council meetings, in newsletters — highlighting the positive effects of the change for students
- are prepared for opposition, resistance and blame while expecting unexpected repercussions and dealing with these issues through critical reflection and discussion
- are cognisant of readiness and the right time for change
- are aware of obvious signs of obstruction and noncooperation (resignations, absenteeism, lateness, sullenness, reduced productivity, sabotage), and tackling unprofessional behaviour directly and discreetly
- provide timely and responsive professional learning during school time
- discontinue any unnecessary school calendar activities
- induct new staff into the change process to ensure clarity about goals and expectations
- work alongside staff to undertake the change
- provide continuous support and optimism
- review progress and make revisions and modifications along the way
- are magnanimous with public praise and appreciation for the extra efforts that are making change happen
- celebrate and publicise successes along the way. (Starr, 2008a)

School leaders are appointed and appraised on their capacity to steer mandated policy changes within tight time frames, alongside instigating ongoing school improvement agendas. Failure to achieve second-order change spells the end of many principals' careers. However, if an audit were conducted, governments might be overwhelmed at the often conflicting change agendas with which they have lumbered school leaders. Leaders are 'key agent[s] in stimulating, shaping, and reinforcing shared meaning within a school' (Goldring & Greenfield, 2002, p. 7) and should demand and receive more professional learning and support in undertaking this most difficult aspect of their role.

I have discussed the perception among school leaders that their role has slipped in terms of power and positioning, with principals' work being open to more external control and scrutiny, with many change agendas being out of their control (Starr, 2008b). The repositioning of school leaders has seen their involvement in educational policy development and their voice in public debates about education curtailed. This issue represents a third major challenge and is the topic of the following section.

Reclaiming a Voice in Educational Debates and Policy-Making

As can be deduced from the above two sections of this chapter, school leaders have lost leverage in terms of systemic and policy impact. The challenge is to reassert the voices of school leaders in policymaking and direction-setting. Tied to this, however, is the need to manage public perceptions of schools and education, which are heavily influenced by negative media commentary from politicians and public commentators.

It is extremely rare to see a good news story about teachers, teacher education, school students, or education in general in the Australian press (Saltmarsh, 1998; Wallace, 1993). Media headlines and political outbursts suggest that schools are to blame for many of Australia's current economic and social woes. Public commentators and politicians often cite purported 'problems' in education with scathing venom to gain legitimacy for new reforms and restructurings, ostensibly smoothing the way for policy change through eroded public confidence.

Media critics embrace a very economistic and utilitarian conception of education and a lack of respect for teachers and school leaders (Wiltshire, 2008). Metaphors of war and the free market abound: we need an 'education revolution' — a 'tough approach ... to lift productivity and maintain economic growth' (Crowe, 2008, p. 1). We hear that principals of failing schools will be removed, funding will be tied to results and underperforming schools will close (Grattan et al., 2008; McManus & Jean, 2008). Consumer choice, user-pays principles, greater accountability and structural efficiencies will be the vehicles of 'improvement', while politicians argue they are responding to the wishes of parents (Beare, 2008; Ferrari, 2008). Perennially regurgitated reports suggest that student achievement and teaching standards have dropped, school leavers are ill-prepared, the curriculum has been 'dumbed down', assessment and reporting practices lack rigour, 'the basics' have been abandoned. Criticisms are generalised and underestimate complexity (see Gough, 2008; Starratt, 2008). Sadly, public commentators and policymakers choose to ignore evidence to the contrary from educational research. While apportioning blame for supposedly poor schooling outcomes to educators, there is also a failure to place the spotlight on ill-conceived policies and systemic practices and the narrow frames upon which school 'success' is defined.

The media has considerable power over public perceptions about education, since the majority of the Australian public are not in a position to discern fact from fiction or fabrication. Educators complain that the dominant recurring themes about education, especially in the print press, are distorted, partial, biased, unsubstantiated, hugely generalised or sensationalised (Reid, 2007). Moral panic is manufactured and issues escalated into crises. Homespun assumptions and alarmingly oversimplified solutions are drawn from extremely complicated issues. Critical information that would significantly alter the impact of reports is removed, and the negative, the shocking and the controversial are accentuated (Wallace, 1993). Hence, defending education, school, teachers and students is now a constant role for school leaders, although counter-commentaries from practitioners are rarely published.

Critics of current schooling use common tactics to legitimate their claims. Reid (2007) in his 'anatomy' of media attacks on education identifies some common characteristics: an educational 'problem' and its deleterious consequences are aired with no empirical evidence to back negative claims; spokespeople claim to be voicing the concerns of parents/the community/employers; 'proof' from curriculum texts or websites are taken out of context and their meanings distorted; current curriculum frameworks, pedagogies and teachers are attacked; 'evidence' may be as little as quoting a single disaffected teacher or parent; a simplistic 'solution' is provided and new 'preferred' policy measures are announced. These 'solutions' are usually theoretically incoherent, fail to grapple with the complexity of schooling and the exigencies of life in late modernity, and fail to acknowledge current research or expertise in the field. This form of educational decision-making and direction-setting is based on ad hoc processes and the least rigorous rationale for change (Reid, 2007).

Meanwhile, despite the bad publicity, Australia continues to perform very highly in international benchmarking tests. But even these good news stories are besmirched by media commentators when Australia's positioning within the top six participating countries slips by one place.

School-based educators are no longer the spokespeople for their own practice. They have lost ground to their critics. The contemporary challenge for school leaders requires, on the one hand, the need to 'manage' the agendas prioritised by politicians, journalists and policy-makers, many of which have little research legitimacy; while at the same time 'managing' the realities of their school communities, which are struggling to meet increasing demands and expectations in the midst of constant criticism.

The role for school leaders is to act collectively through professional associations to ensure they have a voice in policy and curriculum, while also forming a powerful lobby for media redress and policy proactivity. In order to achieve this, school leaders will have to work strategically and go beyond their micro contexts to embrace meso and macro arenas in education for positive purposes. While this suggestion adds a further dimension to their role, school leaders would stand to gain improved public recognition, respect and understanding of their 'insider' perspectives, greater agency over their work and a heightened sense of educational leadership.

Conclusion

The challenges discussed above are all worthy of more extensive discussion than is possible in this chapter, yet they reflect the exigencies of school leadership in highly accountable contexts where public respect is waning and where incumbent apprehension is rising (Leithwood & Prestine, 2002). They indicate a pervasive 'side-lining' of educators in their own profession.

Structural reforms have changed purposes, policies and practices in education. Multidirectional demands for change are constant and often contradictory. They usurp school-based change initiatives and provoke disgruntlement and dissatisfaction among school leaders and teachers. Yet school leaders must find pathways through such challenges as they hold significant roles in leading the education of the students in their schools.

Perhaps it is not surprising to find that principal disengagement has emerged as a problem that has never been experienced before. But governments are not always responsive to foundational problems or ideas for solutions from the field, which is perhaps indicative of the 'core-periphery' positioning that is in part responsible for inadequate leadership succession in the first place.

Leadership expectations are expanding and incessantly shifting, while external controls are proving to be too demanding and restrictive (Starr, 2008b). Despite the rhetoric of localised and devolved power and authority, governments of all political persuasions have centralised core power and decision-making while deflecting bureaucratic administration, accountability and risk to schools (Starr & White, 2008). In this hybrid governance structure (Goldring & Greenfield, 2002) the management and business aspects of schooling are prevailing over educational leadership in curriculum, pedagogy and pastoral care (Leithwood & Prestine, 2002). This fundamental policy shift has resulted in time-consuming micro exigencies that curtail practitioners' abilities to implement sustained change or involvement in meso and macro arenas. Meanwhile, public commentators on education often do not possess the experience or theoretical and practical knowledge of education to substantiate their claims and ideas for reform, despite their capacity for swaying public opinion and perceptions in unhelpful ways.

The key challenges above suggest a deep level of disrespect, neglect, oversight, undue delay and disregard for problems that are already upon educators and getting worse. Redress will entail an opening up of proper public debate, increased school resourcing, partnerships between school leaders and policymakers, and representation of the profession in its own ambit of experience, knowledge and skill. The agendas of change and influence discussed in this chapter highlight the need for renewal and change in the principalship to ensure sustainability, job desirability and effectiveness. They demonstrate the increasing need for collegial networks of influence and support. And the challenges emphasise the need for increased professional agency and autonomy for principals to be educational leaders, rather than managers whose focus and time detracts from learning and teaching.

References

Australian Education Union (AEU), Victorian Division. (2007). *State of our schools survey 2007*. Abbotsford, Victoria: Author.

Australian Secondary Principals' Association (ASPA). (1999). *School leaders: Shortage and suitability in Australian public schools*. Retrieved August 15, 2006, from http://www.aspa.asn.au/Policies/Pollead.htm

Baker, P., Curtis, D., & Berenson, W. (1991). *Collaborative opportunities to build better schools*. Chicago: Illinois Association for curriculum and Development.

Ball, S. J. (2005). *Education policy and social class: The selected works of Stephen J. Ball*. London: Routledge.

Barty, K., Thomson, P., Blackmore, J., & Sachs, J. (2004). Unpacking the issues: Researching the shortage of school principals in two states of Australia. *The Australian Educational Researcher, 32*(3), 1–18.

Beare, H. (2008, September/October). *What metaphors about the curriculum can improve how schools are run?* Discussion paper delivered at the New Metaphors for Leadership in Schools Conference, Australian Council for Educational Leadership in collaboration with the Centre for Strategic Education and the Australian Joint Council of Professional Teaching Associations, Melbourne.

Blackmore, J. (1999). *Troubling women: Feminism, leadership and educational change.* Buckingham: Open University Press.

Blackmore, J. (2004). Leading as emotional management work in high-risk times: the counterintuitive impulse of performativity and passion. *School Leadership & Management, 24*(4), 440–459.

Blackmore, J. (2007, July). *Re/positioning women in educational leadership: The changing social relations and politics of gender in Australia.* Paper written for the University Council for Educational Administration Women's SIG International Conference, Rome, Italy.

Blackmore, J., Thomson, P., & Barty, K. (2006). Principal selection: Homosociability, the search for security and the production of normalized principal identities. *Educational Management, Administration & Leadership, 34*(3), 297–317.

Blackmore, J., & Sachs, J. (2007). *Performing and reforming leaders: Gender, educational restructuring, and organizational change.* Albany, NY: State University of New York.

Bridges, W., & Mitchell, S. (2002). Leading transition: A new model for change. In F. Hesselbein & R. Johnston (Eds.), *On leading change* (pp. 33–45). San Francisco, CA: Jossey-Bass.

Cervini, E. (2003, August 17). Shortage of school principals looming. *The Age.* Retrieved from http://www.theage.com.au/articles/2003/08/16/1060936102586.html

Crowe, D. (2008, August 28). Schools shake-up tops pm's agenda. *Financial Review,* p. 1.

d'Arbon, T., Duignan, P., Duncan, D.J., & Goodwin, K. (2001, September 13–15). *Planning for future leadership of Catholic schools in NSW.* Paper presented at the BERA Annual Conference, Leeds, UK.

Darling-Hammond, L (1998). Policy and change: Getting beyond bureaucracy. In A. Hargreaves, A. Lieberman, M. Fullan, & D. Hopkins (Eds.), *International handbook of educational change* (pp. 642–667). Dordrecht, The Netherlands: Kluwer Academic Publishers.

Day, C., Harris, A., Hadfield, M., Tolley, H., & Beresford, J. (2000). *Leading schools in times of change.* Buckingham, UK: Open University Press.

Dennis, D. (1997). Managing complex workplace change through a social ecological paradigm. *Leading & Managing, 3*(4), 258–274.

Department of Education and Training (DE&T), Victoria. (2004). *The Privilege and the price.* Melbourne: Victorian Government Printer.

Duignan, P. (2006). *Educational leadership: Key challenges and ethical tensions.* Port Melbourne, Victoria: Cambridge University Press.

Evans, R. (1996). *The human side of school change: Reform, resistance, and the real-life problems of innovation.* San Francisco: Jossey-Bass.

Ferrari, J. (2008, August 28). Gillard speaking for parents and children. *The Australian*, p. 1.

Goldring, E., & Greenfield, W. (2002). Understanding the evolving concept of leadership in education: Roles, expectations, and dilemmas. In J. Murphy (Ed.), *The educational leadership challenge: Redefining leadership for the 21st century* (pp. 1–19). Chicago, Illinois: National Society for the Study of Education.

Gough, N. (2008, March). *Quality imperialism as complexity reduction in higher education.* Paper presented at a Symposium for the Chaos and Complexity Special Interest Group at the American Educational Research Association annual conference, New York.

Grattan, M., Tomazin, F., & Harrison, D. (2008, August 28). School v school: PM's rule. *The Age*, p. 1.

Grey, C. (2005). *A very short, fairly interesting and reasonably cheap book about studying organizations.* London: Sage.

Gronn, P. (2003). *The new work of educational leaders: Changing leadership practice in an era of school reform.* London: Sage/Paul Chapman.

Gross, N., Giacquinta, J.B., & Berstein, M. (1975). Failure to implement a major organizational innovation. In J.V. Baldridge & T.E. Deal, with M. Zeig Ancell (Eds.), *Managing change in educational organizations.* Berkeley, CA: McCutchan.

Hamilton, C. (2008). *The freedom paradox.* Crows Nest, Australia: Allen & Unwin.

Hopkins, G. (2006). The principal shortage: Why doesn't anybody want the job? *Education World.* Retrieved September 28, 2007, from http://www.education world.com/a_admin/admin/admin197.shtm

Lacey, K. (2002). Avoiding the principalship. *Principal Matters, November,* 25–29.

Lakomski, G. (2004). *Managing without leadership: Towards a theory of organizational functioning.* Oxford: Elsevier Ltd.

Leech, R. (2006). Through the glass ceiling. *Teacher, 170,* 6–11.

Leithwood, K. (2001). 5 reasons why most accountability policies don't work (and what you can do about it). *Orbit, 32*(1), 1–5.

Leithwood, K., & Prestine, N. (2002). Unpacking the challenges of leadership at the school and district level. In J. Murphy (Ed.), *The educational leadership challenge: Redefining leadership for the 21st century* (pp. 42–64). Chicago: NSSP, University of Chicago Press.

Lugg, C.A., Bulkley, K., Firestone, W.A., & Garner, C.W. (2002). Understanding the challenges of school and district leadership at the dawn of the new century. In J. Murphy (Ed.), *The educational leadership challenge: Redefining leadership for the 21st century* (pp. 20–38). Chicago: NSSP, University of Chicago Press.

Macnamara, L. (2006, August 23). Principals lose their job appeal. *The Australian, Higher Education,* p. 26.

McKinsey & Co. (2007, October 18). How to be top. *The Economist*. Retrieved August 6, 2007, from http://www.economist.com/world/international/display story.cfm?story_id=E1_JJRJJTQ

McManus, G., & Jean, P. (2008, August 28). Failing schools may go. *Herald Sun*, p. 1.

Milburn, C. (2006, April 10). Principal goes to court over onerous hours. *The Age*, p. 1.

Millikan, R. (2002, October). *Governance and administration of schools: The importance of stability, continuity and high quality board and school leadership* (Occasional Paper No. 77). Melbourne, Australia: Incorporated Association of Registered Teachers of Victoria.

Mulford, B. (1998). Organizational learning and educational change. In A. Hargreaves, A. Lieberman, M. Fullan & D. Hopkins (Eds.), *International handbook of educational change* (pp. 616–641). Dordrecht, Netherlands: Kluwer Academic Publishers.

Myers, T. (2006, June). Principals under pressure. *Teacher*, 12–16.

Nadler, D.A., Shaw, R.B., Walton, A.E., & Associates. (1995). *Discontinuous change: Leading organizational transformation*. San Francisco: Jossey-Bass.

National Association of Elementary School Principals. (2003). *Fact sheet on the principal shortage*. Retrieved August 1, 2006, from http://www.crpe.org/pubs/intro MatterofDefinition.shtml

Reeves, D. (2008, September 30–October 2). *Leadership at every level: Making a difference from the boardroom to the classroom*. The William Walker Oration, delivered at the New Metaphors for Leadership in Schools Conference, Australian Council for Educational Leadership in collaboration with the Centre for Strategic Education and the Australian Joint Council of Professional Teaching Associations, Melbourne.

Reid, A. (2007, Autumn). An anatomy of the attacks on Australian education'. *Principia*, 5–7.

Ridden, P. (1991). *Managing change in schools: A step by step guide to implementing change*. Gosford, Australia: Ashton Scholastic.

Saltmarsh, D. (1998, November). *Topics of interest: The reporting of education issues in the print media*. Paper presented to the Australian Association for Research in Education (AARE) annual conference, Adelaide.

Sarason, S. (1982). *The culture of schools and the problem of change* (2nd ed.) Boston: Allyn & Bacon.

Sarason, S. (1990). *The predictable failure of educational reform: Can we change course before it's too late?* San Francisco: Jossey-Bass.

Schein, E. (1992). *Organizational culture and leadership* (2nd ed.) San Francisco: Jossey-Bass.

Scott, C., & Jaffe, D.T. (2004). *Change management: Leading people through organizational transitions*. Boston: Thomson.

Starr, K. (2000). *That roar which lies on the other side of silence: An analysis of women principals' responses to structural reform in South Australian education*. Unpublished doctoral dissertation, University of South Australia.

Starr, K. (2006). Leadership disengagement. *Directions in Education, 15*(19), 2.

Starr, K. (2008a, Autumn). Leading and managing significant school change without losing sleep. *Principal Matters: Journal for Secondary School Leaders in Australia,* 26–29.

Starr, K. (2008b, November 30–December 4). *Whose risk? Managing' risk in the principalship.* Refereed paper delivered to the Australian Association of Research in Education Conference, Queensland University of Technology, Kelvin Grove.

Starr, K., & Oakley, C. (2008, Spring). Sharing leadership with teachers: A case study. *Leadership in Focus, Journal for Australasian School Leaders, 11*, 22–24.

Starr, K., & White, S. (2008). The small rural school principalship: Key challenges and cross-school responses. *Journal for Research in Rural Education, 23*(5), 1–12.

Starratt, R.J. (2008, September 30–October 2). *Learning as performance/the learner as performer.* Discussion paper delivered at the New Metaphors for Leadership in Schools Conference, Australian Council for Educational Leadership in collaboration with the Centre for Strategic Education and the Australian Joint Council of Professional Teaching Associations, Melbourne.

Synnot, B., & Fitzgerald, R. (2007). *The toolbox for change: A practical approach.* Brisbane, Australia: Danjugah Pty Ltd.

Thomson, P. (1998). *The changing role of the principal.* [Commissioned Paper]. Adelaide, Australia: South Australian Secondary Principals Association.

Thomson, P., Blackmore, J., Sachs, J., & Tregenza, K. (2003). High stake principalship: Sleepless nights, heart attacks and sudden death. *Australian Journal of Education, 47*(2), 118–132.

Tomazin, F. & Waldon, S. (2004, October 22). Stress making principals ill: Study. *The Age,* p. 1.

Wallace, M. (1993). Discourse of derision: the role of the mass media within the education policy process. *Journal of Education Policy, 8*(4), 321–337.

Watkins, P. (1993). Pushing crisis and stress down the line: The self-managing school. In J. Smyth (Ed.), *A socially critical view of the self-managing school* (pp. 85–99). London: The Falmer Press.

Wiltshire, K. (2008, October 4–5).When it comes to status, the teachers get less than top marks. *The Weekend Australian* [Inquirer section], p. 21.

▶▶▶◀◀◀

CHAPTER 2

Examining the Issues and Dynamics of Ethical Dilemmas Faced by School Leaders

Lisa C. Ehrich, Megan Kimber and Neil C. Cranston

The roles and responsibilities of school leaders in most countries across the world have become more complex and challenging in recent years. In large part, this complexity has resulted from the discontinuously changing contexts and day-to-day dynamics within which principals lead their schools. Indeed, principals are now faced with having to make a plethora of decisions in an environment of competing priorities, and with consideration for the interests of students, teachers, parents and the school and wider community. Many of these decisions present as dilemmas for school leaders, where the choices for action often involve not just choosing from 'right' versus 'wrong' alternatives but also frequently from 'right' versus 'right' alternatives (Kidder, 1995). Underlying many such decisions are issues of values, principles and ethics. Dilemmas of an ethical nature arise such that principals enter a complicated 'minefield' of decision-making (Dempster & Berry, 2003) where significant implications result not only for those at the core of the particular decision but also potentially for the wider school community and beyond.

In this chapter we explore this complex area of ethical dilemmas faced by school leaders by firstly examining some of the relevant literature of ethics and ethical dilemmas. This literature was used by the authors as a framework to develop a model for mapping and understanding ethical dilemmas faced by school leaders. Through the model (Cranston, Ehrich, & Kimber, 2003, 2006; Ehrich, Kimber, & Cranston, 2004) we can identify the 'antecedents' that might typically exist prior to an ethical dilemma arising, such as the culture of the school, community expectations, and legal and policy frameworks. Also noted here are the values and beliefs of the principal or deputy principal as key decision-makers, critical to how the response to the ethical dilemma is eventually constructed. The model then identifies the potential pathways emanating from the decision about the ethical dilemma and highlights that from such decisions, various consequences or implications flow. Notably, in many such instances, precedents are likely to be set for similar ethical dilemmas arising in the future.

The chapter then discusses the application of the model as an analytical tool to explain two case studies based around the findings of previous research undertaken by the authors of this chapter that explored the ethical dilemmas of a small sample of principals from schools in the state of Queensland, Australia (Cranston et al., 2006). All the principals interviewed for that study were from large nongovernment (independent) schools in Brisbane. The research highlighted that, as one interviewee noted, 'ethical dilemmas are the bread and butter of principals' work' (Cranston et al., 2006). Indeed, all principals had no difficulty in identifying an ethical dilemma to discuss. It is clear that school leaders do struggle regularly with decisions where ethical dilemmas are evident, many such dilemmas arising because there are equally attractive alternatives from which to choose and where the principals' own values are 'put to the test'. Importantly, the consequences of decision(s) taken in such cases also often add to the challenges. Given the commonalities across schools in many countries today, the findings of this research are likely to have wide applicability for our understandings of principals' work.

An Overview of Some Key Issues

Resolving dilemmas is an everyday occurrence for leaders in all types of organisations. It is likely, however, that they make decisions with little or no knowledge of the theoretical approaches to ethics. Although theoretical approaches cannot be applied entirely to solving dilemmas due to the abstract nature of theory and the complexity of practice, they can help leaders organise their beliefs and perspectives in a more coherent and systematic way (Freakley & Burgh 2000). Haynes (1998) suggests an approach to assist school leaders in making ethical decisions. She proposes combining 'care' — that is, educationalists often place a duty of care towards students as their primary concern and their actions are taken in response to a specific situation — with due regard for the individual and the school community (virtue ethics) and to 'consistency' (reason or rule-based ethics) so that decisions can be justified in accordance with the leader's underlying personal and professional values or modified and justified to take account of making decisions in a more ethical manner. It could be argued that Haynes is operating from the perspective of virtue ethics as relationships, care, judgment, wisdom and good or moral character appear to be important.

Ethics, Ethical Dilemmas and Educational Leadership

The moral and ethical dimensions of leadership have received increased emphasis in recent literature (e.g., Campbell, 1997, 2003; Duignan, 2002, 2006). This attention has been, in part, driven by the belief that 'values, morals and ethics are the very stuff of leadership and administrative life' (Hodgkinson, 1991, p. 11). Communities expect those who hold leadership positions to act justly, rightly and promote good rather than evil (Evers, 1992). Educational leaders are expected to view a duty of care towards their students individually and as a group as central to their work, and seek to ensure that all students are provided with the means to gain a quality education that will enable them to reach their full potential (e.g., Haynes, 1998).

The more complex and changing operational milieu (Grace, in Campbell, 1997, p. 223) in which leaders are now working is also contributing to the heightened interest in ethics within education in recent years. The advent of school-based management has generated new forms of, and competing, accountabilities (Burke, 1997; Ehrich, 2000). Indeed, the devolution and decentralisation associated with school-based management can expand not only the number of ethical dilemmas that a leader may experience but also increase the number of people exposed to such dilemmas. Several writers (Burke, 1997; Dempster, Freakley, & Parry, 2001) argue that the values underpinning managerialism and school-based management are opposed to the traditional understanding of education as a public good. These writers maintain that the focus on management arising from economic rationalist/managerialist thinking is inconsistent with the professional and personal values of school leaders and can contradict important ethics of care and justice.

A Model for Understanding Ethical Dilemmas

The model (see Figure 2.1) for considering and analysing the ethical dilemmas reported here diagrammatically represents the context, forces, and decision-making process that individuals facing ethical dilemmas are like to experience. It also highlights the implications and effects that decisions can have on the individual decision-maker, the

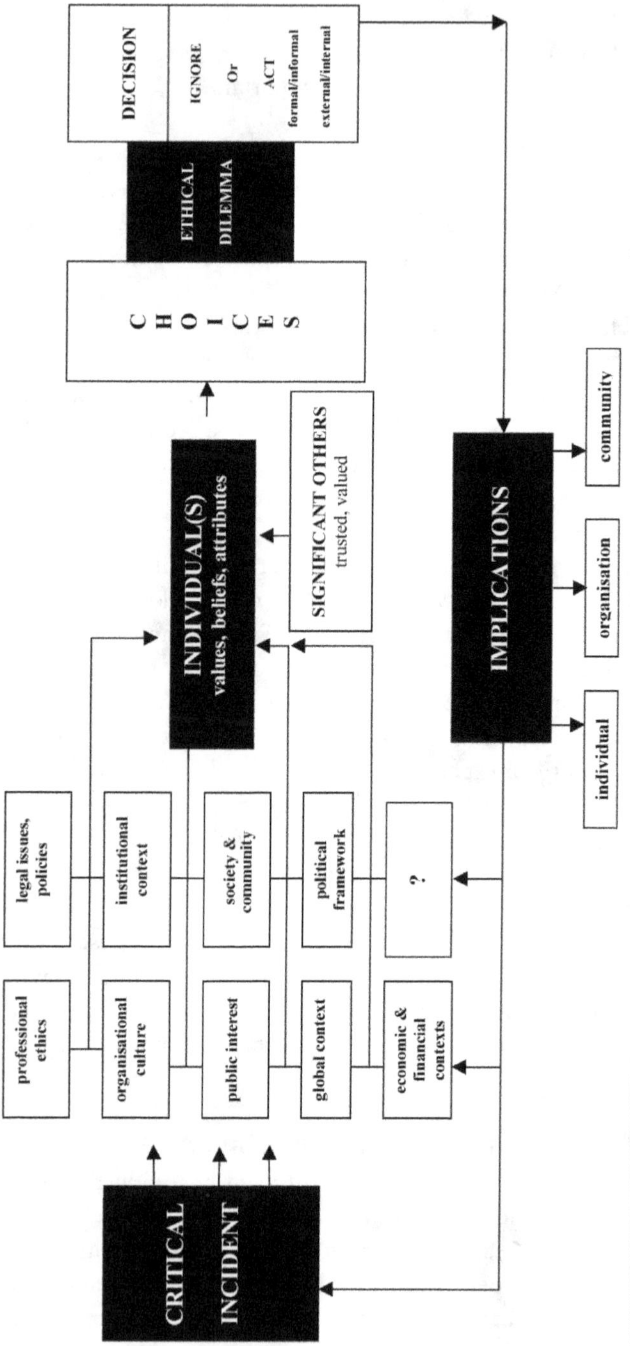

FIGURE 2.1

A model for identifying and resolving ethical dilemmas.

Source: Cranston, Ehrich, & Kimber, 2006, p. 140. Reproduced with permission.

organisation and the community. While the five components of the model can be considered separately, it is clear that there is interdependence among them. It should also be noted that ethical dilemmas do not necessarily follow a linear pattern, such that the actual decision-making process is likely to be one that revisits, revises and reacts to various forces and components in the model.

The first part of the model is the *critical incident* that triggers the ethical dilemma. Second is a set of *forces*, each having the capacity to illuminate the critical incident from its own particular basis. Clearly there may be competing tensions across these forces. There are nine competing forces — *professional ethics, legal context, organisational culture, institutional context, the public interest, society and community, political framework, global context, economic and financial contexts, and ?*. These forces are described below.

- Professional ethics can be thought of in terms of the standards, or norms, values and principles members of a person's trade or profession hold. These standards may be formal or informal, or written or unwritten. They include the ethical obligations generated by being accepted into a profession or trade (Campbell, 1997; Edwards, 2001).

- By legal context we mean legislation impacting on schools such as antidiscrimination legislation requirements (Ehrich, 2000), as well as rulings made by courts, especially when they set a precedent. Also included here is the understanding of the law as 'a consistent set of universal rules that are widely published, generally accepted, and usually enforced' (Hosmer, 2003, p. 64). In a democratic system of government, the rule of law is significant. Here, in a common law jurisdiction such as Australia, all citizens including public officials are governed by the same laws.

- The customs or 'ethos' of an institution inform its organisational culture (Edwards, 2001). Organisational culture centres on relationships among people, and on building and maintaining trust in those relationships (Preston & Samford, 2002).

- The institutional context may, for a school principal, manifest as the need to seek to reconcile multiple and competing accountabilities to students, to colleagues, to the minister and to the wider school community (e.g., Campbell, 1997, p. 225).

- The public interest is a central factor in ethical decision-making and refers to the 'expectations', needs, wants and ultimately, the wellbeing of the community as a whole (Edwards, 2001). It can be expressed through the ballot box, interest groups and ongoing debate and discussion. The public interest includes ensuring the accountability of public officials for the making and administering of laws, policies and regulations.

- Society refers to an organised system of social interaction. In this instance we refer to the key stakeholders who are served by or interact over a school. Students, teachers and parents are key stakeholders in a school.

- The global context relates to the wider global, social, political and economic context impacting on institutions. Globalisation has had a major impact upon the practices of organisations manifested, for example, in the cultural diversity of staff and the influence of market-based practices in the governance of the public sector (Currie & Newson, 1998).

- The political framework includes the structure of a polity, and the political institutions (like parties, parliament, cabinet and the High Court) and political culture that exists in it (democratic principles and practices for instance). A political framework might be derived from a written or an unwritten constitution, such as in the conventions of parliament and executive government. The Australian political system is federal in structure with each jurisdiction operating under a system of representative and responsible parliamentary government. Federalism and representative and responsible parliamentary government can conflict. In Australia, responsible government generally entails individual ministerial responsibility and collective cabinet responsibility. The political framework can also be seen to refer to the particular ideological view of key members of the government of the day that might translate into a significant force at the institutional level.

- The economic and financial contexts might emerge from managerialism whereby private sector practices are introduced into public sector organisations (James, 2003) such that concepts of the free market like competition and choice, for example, are brought to bear on schools.

- The untitled force (?) was included to signify that a significant force not identified at this time could emerge in the future. With respect to schools, it could be argued that an ethic of care could be significant here (Millwater, Ehrich, & Cranston, 2004; Haynes, 1998).

Particular forces will impact to varying degrees on the individual as he or she responds to the critical incident. It is likely that an individual's personal attributes, values and beliefs will play a major role in determining the type of decision made so that a number of possible choices emerge. Such values and beliefs might be related to the understanding of ethical theory that the individual holds. These theories include utilitarianism or consequentialism (e.g., the greatest happiness for the greatest number), nonconsequentialism (e.g., religion, or Kantian reason or rule-based), virtue ethics or institutional ethics. We have discussed these theories in greater detail elsewhere (Kimber, Ehrich, & Cranston, 2003; Ehrich, Cranston, & Kimber, 2004). The individual who is faced with the challenge of resolving the problem at hand is situated at the core of the model and constitutes its third component. The individual is in no way neutral but brings to the dilemma his or her own values, beliefs and personal attributes that have been shaped over time by a variety of sources such as religion, culture, socialisation and conscience (Edwards, 2001; Singer, 1993). Badaracco (1992) uses the term 'the commitments of private life' (p. 66) to explain the importance of an individual's personal morality in determining the outcomes of ethical decisions. As shown in the model, an individual may also be influenced by the advice of significant and trusted other(s) like a partner or a colleague.

The fourth component of the model is the *choice* that is made among the competing alternatives. It is in considering the alternatives that *the ethical dilemma* emerges. The decision might lead to either *ignoring* the dilemma or *acting* in one or more ways to resolve it. Those actions can be *formal* or *informal* or *external* or *internal*. Finally, the action (or nonaction) is likely to create particular types of *implications* for the *individual* concerned, for the employing *organisation* and for the *community* as a whole. These implications could continue generating new critical incidents, dilemmas and/or contribute to new ways of thinking about the forces involved in the dilemma.

The case studies presented below draw on the information about the prevalence and types of ethical dilemmas experienced by school leaders gleaned from semistructured in-depth interviews and document analysis. The interviews were conducted according to strict ethical guidelines and designed around a set of key issues in an aide memoir made available to participants prior to the interview process (Minichiello, Aroni, Timewell, & Alexander, 1990). As mentioned earlier, all the interviewees had no difficulty in identifying an ethical dilemma to discuss. Indeed, one observed that ethical dilemmas were 'commonplace'. Another stated that they were 'the bread and butter of what school principals do' and were 'core business' because these decisions affected not only an individual staff member or student but created a culture. These observations stressed the significance of ethical dilemmas in the work of school principals. They also indicated that principals appreciated how they managed such dilemmas had important implications for the school. This notion of implications is a feature of the model.

Many of the ethical dilemmas raised by the principals focused on similar issues including staff underperformance, student behaviour or welfare, and implementing externally imposed change. In dealing with these broad issues school leaders confronted a range of ethical dilemmas such as:

- conflicts of interest
- conflict between the individual and the community
- conflict among the dimensions of a code of conduct
- conflict between justice and mercy
- dealing with a supervisor's directive.

In considering some of the ethical dilemmas identified by the school principals, it is interesting, from a theoretical point of view, that the earlier noted ideas of Haynes (1998) seem particularly relevant, in so far as she highlights the important people side of the decision-making process and powerful notion of 'duty of care' so evident in the dynamics and culture of schools. In our study, principals stressed the need for ethical organisational cultures and significant emphasis was placed on personal and professional values, particularly where all these factors combined. The extent to which these factors were aligned appeared to often determine how the principals in this research approached and resolved a dilemma. Where the organisational culture and institutional context were strongly ethical these factors seemed to ease the principals' personal stress and trauma involved in making such decisions.

Case Studies

CASE STUDY 1: STAFF UNDERPERFORMANCE

Over the past year a teacher has received two written warnings about his work performance and has been warned that a third notice will mean automatic dismissal. These notices derive from parental and student complaints about the teacher continually being late, skipping a section of the Year 8 syllabus and being unable to discipline several classes. The teacher had been provided with professional development, and been referred multiple times to the School's Code of Conduct for teachers and to the Professional Standards set by the government's accrediting body.

The principal of the college has taken leave to attend a Church-run schools' conference, leaving the deputy principal in charge and instructions that, should this teacher be subject to a third notice, he be sacked immediately. The deputy is uncomfortable with the principal's ruling because he is friends with the teacher but knows about the notices. Part way through the class before lunch, a group of senior students approach the staff room to ask why the teacher had not come to their class. After not being able to contact the teacher, the deputy is informed and is left with no option but to take the class himself.

That evening he discusses the situation with his wife, who is a student counsellor at another school, about whether he sacks his friend or organises further professional development. She sympathises with him but reasons that, as there have been multiple instances and professional development has been provided, he probably has no choice but to sack his friend. She suggests that he obtain a list of counsellors from the union to whom the teacher could go. She also provides him with a list of the names of people she knows to be good. The deputy calls the teacher to his office to seek an explanation. As the teacher is unable to provide an explanation, the deputy reluctantly issues the notice dismissing the teacher but provides the numbers of several counselling services provided by his wife.

The *critical incident* here is a teacher, who has already been served with two notices for underperformance and been warned that a third would mean automatic dismissal, not turning for a class. The nine *factors* outlined above influence the deputy principal in resolving the dilemma with which he is confronted.

- Professional ethics is clearly a central factor impacting on the deputy principal as the decision-maker in relation to this ethical dilemma, with the teacher having been referred to both the school's Code of Conduct and the accrediting body's professional standards.
- The organisational culture of the school is likely to be centred around the values and beliefs of the church body running the school. However, the organisational culture does also seem to be one that demands high professional standards from teaching staff in the execution of their duties.
- The institutional context in this case is particularly evident in the referral of the teacher to the Code of Conduct and the seriousness with which the principal has been treating underperformance. The institutional context is also evident in the school being a church school.
- In this case, society can be defined in terms of the students, their parents and staff.
- The global context is not very prominent in this dilemma; however, it is likely that international trends in understanding and managing staff underperformance might be significant.
- In this situation the legal context might interplay with professional ethics and the institutional context. The school must uphold the standards of the teaching profession, yet might also be subject to industrial law if the teacher argues a case of unlawful dismissal.
- The political framework is evident in the professional standards set by the government's accrediting body and in terms of the supervisor's directive.
- In a church-run school the school is likely to receive funding not only from the church but from school fees and the government.
- It could be argued that there is a clear public interest in ensuring that teachers are professionally competent and diligent in performing their duties.
- It is obvious that the deputy principal cares about his friend thus it could be speculated that '?' in this case is ethic of care.

The *individual* needing to resolve the dilemma is the deputy principal, who consults a *significant other* — his wife — in resolving the dilemmas. Some of the *dilemmas* being resolved here are:

- *conflict of interest* — clearly, the deputy principal has a conflict of interest between his personal friendship with the teacher and his professional duty to sack a teacher who has consistently underperformed, particular because this duty has been sanctioned by *supervisor directive*

- *individual versus community* — this dilemma is related to the first as the deputy needs to decide between assisting the individual teacher or sacking him in the interests of the school as a whole

- *conflict between ethical principles (justice versus care* or *mercy)* — the deputy principal is required to punish a teacher who has consistently underperformed, despite being provided with considerable professional development, but he is concerned about his friendship with the teacher and how his friend will cope with losing his job.

The *decision* that the deputy principal makes — to comply with the directive to sack the teacher because a third warning had to be issued but provide a list of counsellors to assist in dealing with having been dismissed — has *implications* for the deputy principal, the school and the school community. The deputy principal might lose his friendship with the teacher. The school might have to recruit a new teacher and cover the teacher's work until that position can be filled, but is not having to provide continual warnings and professional development to an underperforming teacher. Yet there is the possibility that the teacher could take legal action against the school for wrongful dismissal. Finally, parents and teachers are not having to make complaints about the teacher to school leaders.

CASE STUDY 2: STUDENT WELFARE AND BEHAVIOUR

A teacher informs the principal that, while searching the internet at home, she found a site on which a number of students have been writing negative comments about teachers and students. She has printed off some of the pages from the site. Later that day one of the students who had contributed a comment to the site tells her form teacher about it, as she found other students had posted negative comments about her appearance. The teacher immediately alerts the principal.

In determining how to handle the situation, the principal and her leadership team consider whether or not to take action against the student who reported the site as well as against the other students and what action should be taken. One of the deputy principals is adamant that the student who came forward should not be punished because her father, as president of the P&C, had just given a large donation to the school's building fund. He does not want to risk not having further donations if the student is punished, particularly as the school has staked its future growth on the new building. This deputy also argues that the student's comments are at the lower end of the scale. The other deputy disagrees, arguing that all of the comments are distasteful and that not treating all students equally will send the wrong message to students and to parents. It would also make those teachers for whom negative comments about them were not punished feel that their colleagues did not respect them. For the principal, both deputies are correct in pointing out the importance of the building fund to the school's long-term plan and the need to show that justice is being done. The principal is concerned that, while the board has given high priority to the new building, the school has a reputation of instilling values of other-regardedness in students.

In an attempt to move the discussion forward, the principal requests that the leadership team consult school policy and departmental guidelines on technology use and bullying. One key element of both sets of documents is the need to ensure a safe environment for student learning. After much discussion, in relation to the comments about staff, the leadership team decides that the principal should call all the students known to have contributed to the site into the principal's office as a group and tell them to remove the site from the internet in the next 24-hours. From the principal's perspective, such a strategy will ensure equity and justice. In relation to the wider issue of what is placed online, the principal informs all students that these sites are wrong and students who make such comments about others in the school community are not only risking their own and the school's reputation but that they could be sued for defamation. In addition, the principal sends a general letter home to parents regarding the incident.

As the website was not removed in the specified time frame, the student administering the site is suspended for the rest of the day, ordered to remove the site and write a letter of apology. School leaders decide to block access to social networking sites. Teachers are asked to revisit the issue of bullying in with students during class time and contribute to updating the school's policy on bullying so that staff, students and parents are better equipped to deal with the online environment.

In this case, the critical incident is one of student misbehaviour and student welfare. It occurs when teachers alert the principal to the internet site where students are making negative comments about staff and bullying other students. In conjunction with the leadership team, the principal needs to decide what action is to be taken against the students and whether the student who reported the site should be treated more leniently because she reported the site, was bullied and because her father is president of the P& C. The leadership team also needs to decide whether any action — and if so what action — needs to be taken at a whole-of-school level.

It is evident from this dilemma that a variety of the nine factors influence the principal and the leadership team, but that their influence does not carry the same weight. Ultimately it is the personal values of the principal and the insights that she gains from the leadership team that assist her in resolving the dilemma.

- The professional ethics of the principal and some members of the leadership team are also apparent.
- The organisational culture is clearly one in which duty of care to students and staff, and the creation of a safe learning environment for students is significant. This aspect of the school's culture highlights the significance of relationships, which are a key element of virtue ethics. The organisational culture is further apparent in the principal's concern for the school's reputation. It could be argued that it is an ethical organisational culture because the leadership is taxed by concern around whether it is right to punish all the students or whether it is right not to punish the student who was bullied and reported the website although she also made derogatory comments about teachers on the site. Thus the principal is faced with a 'right versus right' dilemma between the individual and the community.
- The institutional context is also important here as the school leadership team consults school policies.
- Society, then, is another factor influencing the principal's decision. In the case, society is the staff, students and parents of the school. This factor is made even more significant by the influence of the P&C.
- The global context, in part, sets up the critical incident in that globalisation has been important in the diffusion of the technology the students have used.

- The legal context is a critical factor in the principal's thinking — could a student or the school be sued for the comments made by the students.
- The economic and financial factor in this case derives from the need for money for the school building.
- The political framework is evident in consulting departmental guidelines.
- It could be argued that there is a public interest in ensuring that teachers are free to teach without vilification and students are able to learn in a safe environment—including the on-line environment.
- Finally, to '?'. It might be argued that the ethics of care is a key contender here because the principal, school leaders and teachers are clearly concerned about the impact on staff and students where students have been making negative statements about staff and bullying other students. An ethic of justice is also apparent in that the principal and leadership want to do what is right by all those involved — the students who made the comments, the staff members who had comments made about them and the students who had comments made about them. Here it could be asserted that there is a dilemma between justice — treating all the perpetrators equally — and mercy — being lenient on the student who reported the site despite being one of the perpetrators herself.

Ultimately the principal and school leadership team must make a *decision and take action*. Some of the dilemmas that the principal is confronted with include those between justice and mercy, between the individual student (and father) and the school community, and between the school board's stated priority for a new school building and the school's reputation for being other-regarding. Despite the threat of not receiving any more money for the school building from the P&C because the president's daughter was punished, they decide to treat all known perpetrators equally, without singling out any student. Further, the action taken against a student is only escalated after the website is not removed in the specified timeframe. The course of action chosen also includes focusing on the school community through addressing the study body as a whole and sending a letter home to parents. These actions are both formal and informal, and are internal to the school.

The decision and actions taken by the principal have considerable *implications* for the school as an organisation. Clearly, they have set a precedent for how online bullying should be dealt with through the development of school policy on how the school should respond to online bullying of teachers and students at both a policy and a classroom level.

From this model we can see that the personal values and professional ethics of the decision-maker are critical to the way in which they approach an ethical dilemma. Indeed, it could be argued that the more clear a leader's personal values are, the easier it will be to identify an ethical dilemma. The significance of personal values and the factors that an individual leader needs to consider indicate that the virtue of practical wisdom (Kane & Patapan, 2006; Uhr, 2005) might be important for making decisions in an ethical manner and leading a school community to be more ethical in its actions. This conclusion is highlighted by the way in which the actions of leaders have implications for not only themselves but also for their organisation and their community.

This concern with the personal, professional and institutional implications of decisions taken was summarised by one head reported in the Cranston et al. (2006) study as situated in questions such as 'Can I sleep at night with this decision?' and 'Do I feel good in myself?'. The implications of decisions taken as a result of ethical dilemmas were of concern to most heads in our previous study, particularly where there was a tension between what was in the best interests of the individual and what was in the best interests of the rest of the school. In the first case described above, the deputy principal feels tension between the consequences for the teacher and the consequences for the school as whole. In the second case the principal is torn between the implications for the individual student, the school as an organisation and the community of students, staff and parents. Such ethical dilemmas rarely involve simple decisions between 'right' and 'wrong'. Rather, as Kidder (1995) points out, the 'really tough choices ... involve right versus right. They are genuine dilemmas precisely because each side is firmly rooted in ... core values' (p. 18), often around the duty of care for staff and students. In these cases there were degrees of 'right' on both sides and such complex situations rarely are amenable to simple solutions (Duignan & Collins, 2003), hence an ethical dilemma arises. Such 'tensions are usually people centred and involve contestation of values' (Duignan & Collins, 2003, p. 282).

Conclusion

This chapter presented two case studies of ethical dilemmas faced by administrators that related to student and staff issues. The model developed in earlier work by the authors and applied to the cases here, provided a useful framework for better understanding the dynamics and forces at play in such dilemmas. In this chapter, via the two cases, the findings that emerged following analysis of the dilemmas for the administrators included the significance of values and beliefs, both espoused and practised by the administrators, and the significance of the repercussions for the school and other parties involved in the dilemma. Further, the professional ethics of the administrators as decision-makers, and the strong sense of a duty of care to young people were highlighted as key contributors to decision-making in such circumstances.

It is clear that ethical dilemmas are evident in the life of school leaders and are unlikely to go away in the future. Ogawa, Crowson and Goldring (1999) go as far as saying that dilemmas within an organisational context are 'enduring and are part of the "grammar" of schooling' (p. 291). What our cases have revealed is that educational leaders, guided by their own values, their professional ethics and their institution's values, must work through and resolve such dilemmas. Following Duignan's lead, (2006), we would argue that educational leaders need to have a process of working through dilemmas facing them and our model is a step in this direction. It does this by identifying the forces impacting upon and processes characterising the decision-making dynamics facing an administrator with a dilemma. While we appreciate that no model or theory is going to provide an answer to dilemmas, being aware of the nature of the conflicting values and perspectives and the likely consequences and implications of any choices made, should help educational leaders think about the need to make informed, reflective and justifiable decisions.

References

Badaracco, J. (1992). Business ethics: Four spheres of executive responsibility. *California Management Review, 34*, 64–79.

Burke, C. (1997). *Leading schools through the ethics thicket in the new era of educational reform.* Melbourne, Australia: Australian Council for Educational Administration.

Campbell, E. (1997). Administrators' decisions and teachers' ethical dilemmas: implications for moral agency. *Leading & Managing, 3*, 245–257.

Campbell, E. (2003). Let right be done: Trying to put ethical standards into practice. In P.T. Begley & O. Johansson (Eds.), *The ethical dimensions of school leadership*. Dorderect, the Netherlands: Kluwer Academic Publishers.

Cranston, N., Ehrich, L., & Kimber, M. (2003). The 'right' decision? Towards an understanding of ethical dilemmas for school leaders. *Westminster Studies in Education, 26*(2), 135–147.

Cranston, N., Ehrich, L., & Kimber, M. (2006). Ethical dilemmas: The 'bread' and 'butter' of educational leaders' lives. *Journal of Educational Administration, 44*(2), 106–121.

Currie, J., & Newson, J. (Eds.). (1998). *Universities and globalisation*. Thousand Oaks, CA: Sage Publications.

Dempster, N., & Berry, V. (2003). Blindfolded in a minefield: Principals' ethical decision-making. *Cambridge Journal of Education, 33*(3), 457–477.

Dempster, N., Feakley, M., & Parry, L. (2001). The ethical climate of public schooling under new public management. *International Journal of Leadership in Education, 41*, 1–12.

Duignan, P.A. (2002). Formation of authentic educational leaders for Catholic schools. In D. Duncan & D. Riley (Eds.), *Leadership in Catholic education: Hope for the future* (pp. 1172–1183). Melbourne, Australia: Harper Collins.

Duignan, P. (2006). *Educational leadership: Key challenges and ethical tensions*. Port Melbourne, Australia: Cambridge University Press.

Duignan, P., & Collins, V. (2003). Leadership challenges and ethical dilemmas in front-line organisations. In N. Bennett, M. Crawford & M. Cartwright, M. (Eds.), *Effective educational leadership* (pp. 281–294). London: Sage.

Edwards. G. (2001, December). Ethics in practice. *Canberra Bulletin of Public Administration, 102*, 11–17.

Ehrich, L. (2000). Principals as morally accountable leaders. *International Journal of Education Reform, 9,* 120–27.

Ehrich, L.C., Cranston, N., & Kimber, M. (2004). Public sector managers and ethical dilemmas. *Journal of the Australian and New Zealand Academy of Management, 10*(1), 25–37.

Evers, C. (1992). Ethics and ethical theory in educational leadership: A pragmatic and holistic approach. In P. Duignan & R. Macpherson (Eds.), *Educational: A practical theory for new administrators and managers*. London: Falmer.

Freakley, M., & Burgh, G. (2000). *Engaging with ethics: Ethical inquiry for teachers*. Katoomba, Australia: Social Science Press.

Haynes, F. (1998). *The ethical school*. London: Routledge.

Hodgkinson, C. (1991). *Educational leadership: The moral art*. Albany, Australia: Suny Press.

Hosmer, L.T. (2003). *The ethics of management* (4th ed.). Boston: McGraw-Hill.

James, C. (2003). Economic rationalism and public sector ethics: Conflicts and catalysts, *Australian Journal of Public Administration, 63*, 95–107.

Kane, J., & Patapan, H. (2006). In search of prudence: The hidden problem of managerial reform, *Public Administration Review, 66*(5), 711–724.

Kidder, R.M. (1995). *How good people make tough choices: Resolving the dilemmas of ethical living.* New York: William Morrow.

Kimber, M., Ehrich. L., & Cranston, N. (2003, September). *Theorising ethical dilemmas faced by senior public servants: An excursion into Australian public sector ethics.* Paper presented to the Australasian Political Studies Association National Conference, University of Tasmania, Hobart.

Kimber, M., & Maddox, G. (2003). The Australian public service under the Keating Government: A case of weakened accountability? *The International Journal of Public Sector Management, 16,* 61–74.

Millwater, J., Ehrich, L., & Cranston, N. (2004). Preservice teachers' dilemmas: ethical or not? *International Journal of Practical Experiences in Professional Education, 8*(2), 48–58.

Minichiello, V., Aroni, R., Timewell, E., & Alexander, L. (1990). *In-depth interviewing: Researching people.* Melbourne, Australia: Longman Cheshire.

Ogawa, R.T., Crowson, R.L., & Goldring, E.B. (1999). Enduring dilemmas of school organization. In J. Murphy & K. Seashore Louis (Eds.), *Handbook of research on educational administration* (2nd ed., pp. 277–295). San Francisco: Jossey Bass.

Preston, N., & Sampford, C., with Connors, C. (2002). *Encouraging ethics and challenging corruption.* Sydney, Australia: The Federation Press.

Singer, P. (1993). *Practical ethics.* Cambridge: Cambridge University Press.

Singer, P. (1995). *How are we to live? Ethics in an age of self-interest.* South Melbourne, Australia: Mandarin/Reed Books.

Uhr, J. (2005). *Terms of trust: Arguments over ethics in Australian Government.* Sydney, Australia: University of New South Wales Press.

▶▶▶◀◀◀

CHAPTER 3

School Leaders: Issues of Policy, Practice and Professional Formation

Pam Matters

Issues of public policy and required accountability measures impact relentlessly upon the professional formation and practice of school leaders. Internationally, nationally and locally, leadership development frameworks and leadership standards have been developed and documented to ensure that current and future school leaders meet the desired requirements of their respective cultural citizenries. Government and community expectations of these measures are high, particularly in western countries where there is a dearth of suitable applicants willing to apply for school leadership positions. Implementation of each of these elements, policy decision-making, accountability mechanisms, development of leadership frameworks, documentation of leadership standards and evaluation of their efficacy generates issues that affect the continuing formation and professional progress of school leaders. The ensuing discussion aims to provoke informed debate concerning the issues that emerge by contextualising them within each element.

Current educational leadership policymakers, researchers and practitioners have directed much of their attention to the professional preparation and formation of school principals as a direct response to community dismay caused by the declining numbers of teachers willing to step forward to lead schools (Wildy, Clarke, & Slater, 2007). However, little has been achieved despite intense focus placed on the actions and effectiveness of those new to school leadership positions in order to determine where major deterrents lie, while attempting to identify the elements of their successful engagement with their roles (Blank, Hale, & Harkavy, 2005). Contested areas of formation, preparation, complex practice, reflection and refinement have been characterised as exponents of a 'one size fits all' (Lopez, Magdaleno, & Reis, 2006) approach to school leadership professional learning that permeates the globe. Not made explicit to those external to education is the profession's tacit understanding that effective progress in teaching is determined by an individual's ability to intertwine theory, practice, implementation and reflection in increasingly sophisticated and consistently effective ways, demonstrated daily to others through observable actions and incrementally improved performances. As public policy informs what is done in schools and education policy delineates requisite actions, it is only now — during a period of considerable turbulence, change and innovation — that these policies are being overtly linked to educational leadership, its development and processes, through specifically constructed frameworks. Their constituent areas have been identified as policy, accountability, standards, frameworks and evaluation. These areas are discussed in this chapter.

Policy

Public policy shapes strategic plans and actions in all organisations within its designated community of influence. Its import is noted, irrespective of whether its desired outcomes are agreed to or not. Although specific public policies such as those promulgated for education, health and social welfare are directed to the entire populace, they focus on areas of provision that draw the attention of discrete sections of relevant professions, skilled specialists, researchers, clients and the general public. In this section, transitions from public to specified policies will be examined within the contexts of their effects upon educational leadership.

Seeking legitimation from wider society, educational organisations employ comfortable illusions, dreams and imaginings that appeal to other citizens. Procedurally, they create recognisable realities and functional myths (Mulford, 2004) that serve to rationalise and explain their existence to others. Specific contexts, cultures and the shaping of education leadership and leadership development in each country (Bush, 2008) impact on their evolution and efficacy. 'Sustainable leadership and improvement efforts are interconnected and stretched out in time and space' (Hargreaves & Fink, 2006, p. 251) where the integral nature of our internal and external lives (Goens, 2005) can be observed, examined and contextualised.

For more than three decades, governments in Western societies have repeatedly used stable elements of public policy design to achieve such aims. These can be grouped within two phases, linked by clearly recognisable steps that lead to the apt formulation of policies. First, governments delineate the precise aim of any new or revised policy initiative.

Put simply, what is it that is actually desired? In phase one, the public character of a policy, its possible consequences, complexities, uncertainties and appropriateness or not to differing interests in the community is investigated (Mann, 1975). During phase two, policy analysis is conducted that interrogates its content, innovation diffusion mechanisms, outcomes and evaluation processes (Jenkins, 1978). Bobrow and Dryzek (1987) assert that for public policy and its recursive processes to be effective, it should address community values in operational and socially comprehensible forms in ways that do not trivialise its inherent complexities. Using three dimensions — timing, amount and priority — they provide clusters of policy elements that extend and expand those found in phases one and two. While noting the importance of context, stability, complexity and uncertainty, regard is addressed to feedback and its potential, control by policy actors, audience type, selection and application of appropriate approaches, interpretation of the specified problem and its performance goals, identification and collection of necessary information; and invention, stipulation, assessment and comparison of policy alternatives. All may be succinctly refined and expressed in an eight-step cycle: agenda-setting, problem recognition, issue selection, policy formulation, decision-making, implementation, evaluation and termination (Jann & Wegrich, 2007). Positing a global argument from an Australian base, Stewart (2007) argues that policy is not so cut and dried, asserting that it 'frames the game', permitting adaptation within recognisable boundaries. For instance, 21st century public policy in Australia is framed and positioned to generate

> ... active and informed citizens who appreciate Australia's social, cultural, linguistic and religious diversity and have an understanding of Australia's system of government, history and culture and who are able to relate to and communicate across cultures, especially the cultures and countries of Asia. (Ministerial Council on Education, Employment Training and Youth Affairs [MCEETYA], 2008c, p. 9)

Although public policy delineates how people are governed, Colebatch (2005, p. 86) points out the 'adjectival genre' nature of educational leadership policy dictates that the highly specific parameters of its concerns and influence be regarded in all circumstances, endorsing Biggs and Helms' (2007, p. 439) perception that government sector institutions are different to market, civil and private organisations because of 'their ability to enforce their decisions by means of legitimate coercion' (e.g., see mandatory school attendance requirements related to speci-fied student chronologies).

Schools, their organisational structures and related educational systems are well understood by personnel who are employed within them and are regarded as adaptive organisations (Segil, 2002) where the-ories, pedagogies and professional practices must be translated into peak learning performances by students and their teachers. Diverse global populations expect schools to conserve society's values, while dynami-cally reflecting constantly changing world circumstances (Gorton, Alston, & Snowden, 2007). Steadily increasing collaborative working arrangements embedded in virtual work environments (Compston, 2007) and maintained across international and cultural boundaries emphasise that knowledge is the prime resource necessary for jobs. The continuous building of capacities in individuals throughout each life span is a necessary corollary activity. This incremental improvement of social capital factors used to be the responsibility of families, now it has implications for schools as well, particularly for poor and disadvantaged individuals within them (Davies & Ellison, 2003). Cognisance of this issue is reflected in the Australian Commonwealth Government's Department of Education, Employment and Workplace Relations' (DEEWR, 2009) current cooperative alliances with state governments. DEEWR initiates strategic policy development in schools and organises delivery of programs at the national level, coordinated through the Ministerial Council on Education, Employment Training and Youth Affairs (MCEETYA), underpinned by advice documented in the *National Goals for Schooling in the 21st Century* (DEST, 1999) known as the Adelaide Declaration. The latter document specifies agreed learning outcomes for all students and although superseded recently by the *Melbourne Declaration on Education Goals for Young Australians* (MCEETYA, 2008c) its content has not changed significantly. The Melbourne Declaration provides a framework for national reporting on student achievement and for public accountability by school education authorities. Although this national framework appears sound, it encom-passes a perennially disruptive issue that needs to be resolved: Educational, social and economic policies need to be reconfigured in context so that current disadvantages are not perpetuated (Hayes, Mills, Christie, & Lingard, 2006) and minute regard needs to be directed to the political contestation and inherent dilemmas arising from how the goals and purposes of schooling are understood throughout diverse sec-tions of the Australian community.

Accountability

Until recently, public policy proposals and their introductions to their communities were subjected to trial periods where their implementation and effectiveness were monitored, evaluated and refined before final release for the use of all. Planning, documentation, trial, trial analysis, refinement, implementation, evaluation and public accountability were recognisable sequential steps in the process. Today, the politicisation of policymaking and the increased speed with which positive results are required by various governments has confined the process to three major steps: policy decision-making, implementation and accountability. In this section, the impacts of this compaction upon schools and school leadership are investigated.

Accountability defines an organisation. Although profits and dividends to shareholders continue to determine organisational success, giving clients what they want is considered essential. There are new public expectations related to social concerns, such as preservation of the environment, coping with climate change, sustainable jobs for those living in our global knowledge society and coherent public education accessible and available to all. It has become obligatory to design organisational structures to meet these needs, including the fashioning of distinctive pathways that will provide for the enhancement of employee capabilities and advanced skills development (Parston, 1997).

Heifetz (2006) argues that different personal values have the propensity to shed light on diverse opportunities and alternative facets of situations, including accountability processes. Of equal importance is their impact upon organisations, existing organisational structures and their accountability mechanisms because failure to adapt, disregard of the importance of authority within established social systems and the inability to distinguish adaptive from technical work are typical examples of debilitating organisational dysfunctions.

Generically, school leadership accountability relates directly to five areas: society and its expectations, schools and their functions, principals and decision-making, configurations of school leadership teams and classroom teachers, and typologies of student clientele.

Society expects schools to run effectively by integrating leadership and management practices and employing the key organisational functions of societal compass-setting (public policy), human development (student achievement) and organisational improvement (principal/ teacher development (Spillane & Diamond, 2007). In schools, performance imperatives are emphasised by their recurrence. In formal external domains they are policy-driven; in affective, internal domains, their impetus is described as moral (West-Burnham, 2001).

Investigating schools as organisations, Bush (1994, pp. 319–322) specifies models of accountability linked to the dominant theories to be found within them: bureaucratic, where a top-down hierarchical organisational structure is aligned with prescriptive external demands (e.g., the relationship between school leadership teams and their relevant education systems); collegial, that are teacher-defined and peer-evaluated internally; political, where power and influence are devolved to discrete subunits or faculties, but not the whole school/college and where it is assumed that conflict is resolved by the exercise of power; subjective autonomy, that relates to individual personnel where their actions are deemed to be too individual to provide reliable forms of comparison with those of other colleagues; ambiguous contexts, where uncertainty and complexity are stressed in schools and colleges characterised by problematic goals, unclear technology and fluid, indecisive participation in decision-making.

Coleman (2005) observes that present day educational leaders enjoy freedoms generated by progressive decentralisations of educational systems but such decision-making powers should be open to scrutiny from all to ensure that the exercise of power remains within prescribed system limits. Emphasising the intrusion of unprecedented levels of complexity upon modern educational leaders' actions, dimensions of accountability commonly experienced at the macro level are detailed. Areas identified comprise *political* where the use of public funds is able to be examined rigorously, cyclically and openly; appropriate *responses to market forces* where customers, stakeholders and clients are able to provide evidence of their capacities to exercise choice; evidence of *data collection and analysis* processes concerning professional formation such as the explicit documentation of norms, standards and codes of practice of the teaching profession and its leaders; and authentic *reports* of their cultural impact. Coleman posits that as education generates new insights and thereby changes societal knowledge it should acknowledge its responsibility to the community by openly disseminating its findings. Picciano (2006) adds a *bureaucratic* dimension where school leaders must remain alert to and cognisant of their formal relationships to state and federal education instrumentalities. Darling-Hammond (2004) draws attention to a *legal* dimension that mandates the compliance of educational leaders to specifically identified national and state legislature (e.g., see mandatory reporting requirements of student abuse in Australia).

Haydon (2007) provides an insightful view of current school principal accountability by asserting that while educational leaders are required to emphasise their organisational effectiveness outwards by way of their local communities and upwards through their education system hierarchies, it is critically important to their role success to simultaneously address themselves effectively to issues that emerge internally in their own schools/college and downwards through the organisational hierarchies created by their own staffs. They need to be able to distinguish between internal and external issues and bring them to satisfactory resolution, using their advanced capacities to integrate their professional core competencies (Reiss, 2007). These include demonstration of instructional vision, development of human capital, creation of organisation cultures that promote trust, collaboration and collective responsibility among colleagues and the astute procurement and distribution of resources (Spillane & Diamond, 2007). Philosophically, they need the developed capacity to critique and influence current policies and practices in educational settings (Robertson, 2008). If future school leadership is to be transformative, risk-taking and innovative, yet encompass the values and beliefs already held by their wider local communities (Heifetz & Linsky, 2002), then they must become the leaders and/or effective conduits of authentic change.

A known dilemma must be reiterated: what action must be taken to rectify the lack of teachers willing or adequately prepared to take these types of roles as school principals? In an attempt to resolve this issue early in the 21st century, documentation concerning proposed leadership frameworks outlining standards required for school leaders has begun to appear in all Australian states, territories and at the national level.

Standards

Rushing to devise and implement effective policies in education concerning improved student achievement and to emphasise their effectiveness and sustainability by providing related accountability measures, it became obvious to various governments, the teaching profession and teacher unions that an increasing number of teachers, teacher leaders, school principals and system directors working actively in the field were overloaded by competing work and community demands. Morale was rapidly decreasing. Yet a significant number of schools leaders were thriving in the same conditions. In this section, the emergence of the need for defined sets of national standards concerning educational leadership is explored.

Prompted by the provocative treatise, *A Nation at Risk–The Imperative for Educational Reform* (1983), the United States (US) Standards Based Reform Movement (SBRM) has waxed and waned for the past 30 years, growing exponentially at first with its series of summits designed to cohere shared visions, then weathering critical attacks concerning their lack of effectiveness and the disappointments caused by empty promises (Apple, 2000). Its relentless focus upon the standardisation of teaching and emphasis upon competency-based skills was perceived as actively deskilling classroom teachers and educational leaders, while denying them critical autonomy within their own profession (Morrow & Torres, 2000). Disregarding these impediments, individual US state systems were impressed with SBRM's alignment of espoused theories, focus on the professional practice of teachers and ability to demonstrate hard evidence of improved student achievement. By the early 1990s, due to its influence and support from an inquiring citizenry, many US states had embedded accountability systems comprising similar components detailing *content* standards that outlined desired student knowledge and skills at specified grade levels; *high stakes tests* regimes specifically designed to measure achievement of these content standards; explicit *performance targets* that identified criteria achievement by students; *incentives* and/or required sanctions distributed on the basis of achievement of these performance targets (Jazzar & Algozzine, 2006).

In the United Kingdom (UK), a national curriculum and testing regimen had been introduced, augmented by an inspectorial system designed to ensure the authenticity of published league tables that demonstrated the improved achievement or not of all students in all schools (National College for School Leadership, 2001). In Australia, states and territories retained control of the development and dispersion of curriculum while negotiating statewide testing at specified year levels 3, 5 and 7 in order to meet federal government demands.

Despite this ruthless pursuit of high expectations where staff and students were pushed to achieve more and more, erosion of standards by stealth was noted (Senge, 2006), particularly in relation to the lack of government fiscal support and the obvious internal decline of education systems. These deficits impacted upon initial teacher education and experienced teacher leadership preparation where weakening of standards was evidenced by increasing parent dissatisfaction, complaints, underinvestment in resources and unsustainable school structure provisions, unhappy students and undeniable evidence of a growing achievement gap between students located in different parts of states and territories within the same country and beyond. In Australia, Teese and Polesel (2003) found these substantial differences in achievement of standards affected most severely those students living in disadvantaged communities, but it was the disparities they observed between like and sometimes adjacent urban suburbs that drew most attention.

During the first decade of this century, the standards movement has arisen once again, this time driven by each country's need to compete yet cooperate with other countries in a global economy in order to guarantee equal opportunities for all students to learn thus preparing students for success in the 21st century (Drake & Roe, 2003). Emerging as a formidable group of educational entities committed to the enhancement of teaching and learning and the improvement of schooling, it is marked by its reframed purposes and clear and insistent focus on student achievement (Hessel & Holloway, 2006). Harnessing the support of policymakers, members of this reconstituted movement advocate the establishment of standards for leaders concerning professional preparation, including development of abilities and aptitudes and provisions for professional growth and development that are directly aligned with the outcomes desired of their student cohorts (Norton 2005).

Supporting this recommendation, Day (2003, p. 189) provides a description of modern leaders in education as achievement-oriented, people-centred individuals who are required to manage a panoply of tensions and dilemmas. Explicitly, he defines tensions comparatively as leadership versus management; development versus maintenance; internal versus external change; autocracy versus autonomy; personal time versus professional tasks; personal values versus institutional imperatives; leadership in small versus large schools. Dilemmas are depicted as intrusions to be resolved. For example, in the case of an underperforming employee, should there be development or dismissal; power with or power over; subcontracting or mediation?

Referring to previously encountered teacher aversion to the imposition of professional standards accountability practices, Hargreaves

(2003) warns that teacher professional standards should not be voluntary but defined and regulated through negotiated models of professional accountability. Noting that teachers have to cope with the competing pressures of improving student achievement while dealing with some of society's most disruptive elements, he observes that school leaders are dragged down further by negative market fundamentalist reactions to the costs of providing resources to effectively manage these issues. Teachers and school leaders are expected to work harder yet learn alone. In agreement and commenting caustically, Leithwood and Jantzi (2006) analogised the imperative responsibilities expected of educational leaders concerning school reform and increased accountability to equate with that of general practitioners in medicine being required to cure cancer before a cure has been discovered. In Australia, in order to maintain parity between contexts, Clegg, Kornberger and Pitsis (2008) suggest that standards should be authorised by explicit rules that are designed by independent standard-setting organisations such as Standards Australia.

The development and successful expansion of the US Interstate School Leaders Licensure Consortium (ISLLC) framework incorporated six standards — the vision of learning; the culture of teaching and learning; the management of learning; relationships with the broader community; integrity, fairness and ethics in learning; and the political, social, economic, legal and cultural context of learning. It was devised by an amalgam of ten professional associations directly involved in teacher education, educational leadership and school administration (Hessel & Holloway, 2006; Lunenberg & Irby, 2006). In the United Kingdom, the National College of School Leadership (NCSL, 2001) established similar frameworks. Using the US and UK frameworks as referential working models, Australian systems and professional associations have begun to pay serious attention to establishing sets of standards applicable to its teachers and educational leaders. It is acknowledged that proposed standards have to portray intimate links: aligning leadership with what is considered to be personal and that which is known to be professional, between the development of individuals and the contexts of their organisations, combining astute problem-solving with the management of competing forces. Therefore, advanced education training related to the standards has to provide for the introspection of personal, organisational and cultural values, supported by the acquisition of increasingly superior critical thinking capacities and the further development of intra and interpersonal skills (Day, 2003).

It is informative to compare the similarities found in standards required of UK managers that are categorised into six functional groupings: managing self and personal skills, providing direction, facilitating change, working with people, using resources, and achieving results (Davies, Ellison, & Bowring-Carr, 2005, using the HayGroup leadership and management competencies). HayGroup leadership competencies are clustered in four areas: information-seeking, conceptual thinking, strategic orientation and customer service orientation. They are presented in cohesion with an additional seven clusters deemed management competencies: achievement orientation, developing others, directiveness, impact and influence, interpersonal understanding, organisational awareness and team leadership (Teaching Australia, 2009b). Teaching Australia (2009b) and the HayGroup provide school principal training annually to a small national cohort. They operate in competition, yet collaboration, with the much larger Australian school leader development programs offered within the state, Catholic and independent school systems. Although Teaching Australia (2009a) has produced *A Charter for the Australian Teaching Profession*, marketed as an integral component of the national professional standards and described as a foundation for the detailed articulation of the knowledge and skills of teachers and principals, the latter are still under development.

For decades, the public education systems in each Australian state or territory have maintained their internal teacher leadership development programs that have progressed from single professional development activities to postgraduate courses, aligned with those offered at local universities. Reconfiguring, rebirthing and initiating state and territory institutes of teaching designed to register and monitor the progression of the teaching profession has produced a plethora of useful documents concerning required professional standards (Australian Capital Territory Department of Education and Training, 2008; Australian Education Union, 2009; MCEETYA, 2008a; Victorian Institute of Teaching, 2008), each one more developed than its predecessor. The New South Wales Institute of Teaching Professional Teaching Standards (NSWIT, 2006) explicitly delineates four key stages: graduate teacher, professional competence, professional accomplishment and professional leadership; three domains of teachers' work — professional knowledge, professional practice and professional commitment; and seven related elements encompassed within the domains that are designed as a foundation for the future accreditation of teachers. Its importance lies in its sophisticated development of teacher standards acceptable to the profession and its cognisance of educational leadership as an integral area to be addressed during teacher accreditation and/or reaccreditation.

Despite these influential moves towards firmly establishing national and state professional standards for the teaching profession, recurring dilemmas have not been resolved. Issues of social status, race and gender (Lopez et al., 2006), experienced school principal further development (Wildy et al., 2007), the reconceptualisation of schools of education in universities and their relationships to the national, states and territories systems of education (Twale & Place, 2005) and the emergence of accountability procedures such as the proposed introduction of assessment flying squads in Victoria (O'Keeffe, 2009) previously considered undesirable by the profession, have been ignored, disregarded or, worse, misconstrued as unimportant.

Frameworks

To contextualise policymaking, accountability measures and documentation of standards in education leadership, each state and territory education system in Australia has commenced or continued to document its own localised leadership framework. Discussed in this section, these activities have had a noticeable impact upon education, the teaching profession and school leaders both at national and local levels.

Each Australian state and territory has devised operational guidelines concerning the professional training and further education of its teacher leaders, principals and system managers. But in the past, these practical pathways have not always articulated into specifically designed leadership frameworks (LFs). Turbulence, change, resource cutbacks and program priority reorientations in schooling have stimulated renewed interest in the construction of LF that reflect professional and community expectations of school leadership.

Existing leadership development frameworks exhibit commonalities of purpose and content including leadership of self, collaboration with others and capacity to manage change (Australian Council for Educational Research, 2008; Department of Education and Training, New South Wales, 2008; Department of Education, Victoria 2008; Institute for Educational Leadership, 2008; Queensland Government, Department of Education, Training and the Arts, 2008). Teacher standards frameworks contain more detail but propose similar goals (National Board for Professional Teaching Standards, 2008; New South Wales Institute of Teachers, 2008; Victorian Institute of Teaching, 2008).

Leadership development frameworks link theory to practice (Hessel & Holloway, 2006), pay close attention to the interactions of leadership and management (Spillane & Diamond, 2007) and interweave everyday interactions between teachers, school leaders and others, characterised by their passion for achievement, care, collaboration, commitment, trust and inclusivity (Day, 2008). These are synthesised within a 10-point pathway comprising the following steps: define the problem, assemble evidence, construct the alternatives, select the criteria, project the outcomes, confront the trade-offs, decide, document, evaluate and disseminate outcomes — 'tell your story' (Bardach 2000, p. xiv). Dror's (1987) advice resonates today. Unexpected contingencies occur, therefore crisis decision-making (CDM) capacities need to be honed, refined and practiced within elements of educational leadership frameworks. For instance, when a scarcity of policy alternatives has become noticeable resulting in the downgrading of aspirations and expectations, consistent leadership decision-making and actions need to be employed in order to overcome constraints that may inhibit otherwise useful options. The main requirement is to invent novel policy ideas and develop them into feasible options. This essential activity depends mainly on leadership creativity and innovativeness. Just how this might be achieved is detailed in the discussion of the Australian Capital Territory, Department of Education and Training Leadership Framework Case Study (ACTDETLF, 2008) that follows.

CASE STUDY: THE ACT DET LEADERSHIP FRAMEWORK

The ACTDETLF team, comprising four ACT DET system managers, two university partners, four principals and a local representative from a large national teacher union, were challenged to produce a leadership framework that accurately represented the views of local teachers and school leaders, while meeting the requirements of its educational system. The ACTDETLF team sought advice from other groups responsible for drafting similar frameworks in Australia and overseas.

The aim of the ACTDETLF was to regenerate innovative, socially just leadership in ACT DET teachers through the production of a leadership framework that documented required professional learning standards at designated leadership levels (i.e., aspirant, new, experienced). It was important that its main focus was directed to apt leadership that would provide improved equity and high learning achievement outcomes for all students (Storms & Gonzales, 2006). From the outset, Galbraith's (2000) analysis of the advantage gained by using an organisation's formal structure and systems as a central and first lever to create ripples of change throughout the rest of the organisation was validated. These changes were managed by accepting the realities created by constant tensions between order and chaos. Uncertainties and instabilities were balanced with what was known to be stable. Tenacity and detachment were required to deal effectively with the cyclical nature of the change load that ranged from complacency, continuous improvement, intermediate movement, dramatic impetus, paradigm shifts, chaos to resolution (Conner, 1998). It was possible to redesign education by acting within an existing system to develop further a positive leadership culture (Robertson, 2008) through plausible, projective sense-making and stable identity construction (Mills, Dye, & Mills, 2009).

It was important to find the fringe, search for unusual practices, look for uncommon insights, discover the anomalies (Hamel & Breen, 2007) and respond to the challenges these activities generated by creating a democracy of ideas where human imagination is amplified. It was essential to dynamically reallocate resources and aggregate collective wisdom, taking care to minimise the drag of old mental models and give everyone the chance to opt in. Crowther, Ferguson and Hann (2009), while discussing culture-building and identity-generation in education, provided a final, prophetic clue. Leadership roles in schools might be new to their incumbents, but professional expectations and mores are not. At whatever level of influence they may now occupy, leaders in schools, and especially those in Australian schools, have been and still regard themselves as teachers, members of a coherent, recognisable international professional body of colleagues. School leadership is not their job, it is their profession (Rooney, 2008).

It was acknowledged that classroom teaching does make a difference over time to the lives of others by creating learning opportunities (Robertson, 2008), using projective sense-making and shaping individuals' interpretation of events (Mills et al., 2009). Critically, it enacts the process of teaching by linking emotions to the theories and actions needed to make it effective. Simultaneously, teachers model professional practice while developing their own skills and those of others.

Data collected and analysed from interviews and summaries derived from focus group sessions proved to be compelling because it indicated that Davies' (2005) strategic leadership model delineating actual leadership performance sequences was unknowingly the theory of choice for the majority of teachers and school leaders in the ACT. Similar combinations of strategic thinking, professional practice, followed by reliable evaluative evidence, arose time and again. Most favoured were progressions from strategic thinking to purposeful intent, while documenting cogent planning and remaining cognisant of emergent ideas and decentralised policies. Well beyond competent, professional practice was nested in the procedures and processes used. Simply stated, consistent engagement in advanced professional learning, alignment of procedures, timing of actions and the actions themselves impacted dramatically upon the quality of leadership exhibited. Interestingly, it was the repetitive references to the acquisition of wisdom through practice of strategic leadership that drew attention. Leaders reflected immediately on their own actions, then, on those of others; they created a common language among stakeholders through conversations, debates and/or discussions, they formulated mental models and subjected them to analysis and articulation. They evaluated their leadership styles and shared them with others, tacitly accepting their influence as part of their professional responsibilities. Upon further reflection, they acknowledged their culture permitted them to lead 'below the surface' (Creighton, 2005, p. 16) by bending but not breaking the rules. It required them to astutely manage political capital, overtly practise evidence-based decision-making, collaborate beyond cooperation with a diverse range of others and 'looking below the obvious', practice exemplary leadership where leadership deals with change while management copes with complexity (Kotter, 1998).

It became obvious that the developing ACTDETLDF was consistent with Yukl's (2004, p. 76) tridimensional leadership theory where school leaders are depicted as task-, relations- and change-oriented, with unmistakeable emphases devoted to consistent, excellent demonstrations of performance determinants such as efficiency and reliability, proven capacity to handle diverse human resources and relations, and repeated evidence of innovation and adaptation processes in their workplaces. Simultaneously, they are required to lead and manage situational variables while ensuring that school effectiveness is achieved. Therefore, it became vital to incorporate these factors in the LF structure from the outset. Maintenance and sustainability of professional practices were important, but there had to be room for improvement, increased effectiveness and outstanding excellence as teachers and school leaders developed and became more experienced within their chosen profession.

Using the knowledge gained and continuing to pursue regular consultations with diverse groups involved in this project, the ACTDETLF took shape, was documented, endorsed by the ACT government and released to all ACT schools in mid 2008. The ACT Educational Leadership Framework (2008) documents areas of leadership capacity-building comprising learning-centred leadership, leading learning and teaching, leading strategic resource management, leading and working with others and leading a quality organisation. Its main focus is directed to the development of learning-centred leadership within any individual employed within its organisation, encompassing exploration of its integral elements of life learning, self-awareness and acquisition/refinement of desirable leadership qualities and characteristics. The prime professional orientation of teacher leaders is acknowledged through recognition of their influential roles in classrooms where they lead teaching and learning. Integral elements of pedagogy, curriculum and reflective practice are refined to ensure that improved learning outcomes for students ensue. All teacher leaders are required to manage with integrity, be accountable and achieve results by planning, monitoring and accepting responsibility for their work. Teacher leaders must lead and work with others within and external to their classrooms, cultivating productive working relationships through open communication, diverse partnerships and enhanced capacity-building of themselves and others. As experienced teachers move on to senior leadership roles, it becomes necessary to lead a quality organisation, which may take the form of classroom teaching in addition to coordination of a large section of a school, leadership of a school, or a school district, or a state/territory program or participate as Chief Executive Officer (CEO) of a large educational system. Apt decision-making, accurate identification of cultural imperatives and the capacity to initiate and participate within learning communities are mandatory attributes. Another issue arises: how is their effectiveness evaluated?

Evaluation

Although evaluation is summative in nature, its active critique refers to present and current actions while its decision orientation points to the future. Therein lie the reasons that it is often avoided, shallowly conducted or pursued narrowly to validate sought-after positive results, while sanitising or excluding any negative findings. When linked to education, evidence of results illuminating the achievement of desired students' learning outcomes dominates most research and community interest. Teachers and schools leaders are judged to be 'good' or 'bad' with few standardised methods of evaluating such claims having been put into place. Of equal concern, there is no evidence of a commonly accepted set of school leadership standards or evaluation procedures that may accompany them. In this section, education standards in schools, their evaluation and direct relationships to employee leadership capacity-building are theorised.

Picciano (2006, p. 121) notes that there are complex differences in how people view evaluation in education, usually determined on a dichotomous basis as either an imposition on teachers and students or proper investigations of how public money is expended. Coleman (2005) examines this issue further with a discussion of internal and external evaluation in schools. Using the National Union of Teachers model (England) (NCSL, 2001), he posits that internal evaluations are intended to inform teachers and educational leaders within a particular school and the subsequent distillation of data is used for school self-evaluations. He cites items that are used to construct many internal evaluation frameworks: school climate, relationships, organisation and communication, time and resources, recognition of achievement, equity, home–school links, support for teaching, classroom climate and support for learning.

When first introduced, evaluative activities pursued by external evaluators, inspectors, employed by OFSTED, England (NCSL, 2001), were considered invasive but they evoked massive change and provided reliable comparative data over time because they provided usable information concerning the educational standards achieved in each school, the quality of education provided by the school, the quality of leadership and management of the school and the spiritual, moral, social and cultural development of its pupils (p. 163)

Gray and Wilcox (1995) found that individual schools could compare each succeeding years' performance with those that had preceded it and note their effectiveness, improvements and achievements with 'like' (similar) schools, adding their professional preference for monitoring and evaluation processes to employed on a daily basis, rather than as isolated elements submerged within 'one hit' annual inspections. Raynor (2004) concurs and argues that the educational outcomes and accountabilities of individual schools should be negotiated first with system authorities with the intention of devolving the process through successful experience to school community, principal and peer self-evaluation.

In Australia, authentic evaluations can be achieved by mapping professional standards against those found in existing leadership professional learning programs (Anderson & Cawsey, 2008) or, alternatively, to use the standards to design and develop new programs (Ingvarson, Anderson, Gronn, & Jackson, 2006). Caldwell's (2006) capacity to state topical ideas succinctly in his framework for Leadership in the School of the Future (LSF) has reminded the profession to think broadly but remain focused on issues of prime importance to school leadership during these evaluation activities. LSF is explicitly compartmentalised into interlinking elements: vision, tracks for change, values, dimensions of leadership and domains of practice. Each component integrates only two or three themes, thereby emphasising parsimoniously their strength of influence. While the suitability of Caldwell's 'new enterprise logic' for schools provokes wide debate in educational circles, its alignment and resonance with the views already held by many teacher leaders is unmistakeable. His new enterprise logic emphasises what is already known locally about educational leadership and schooling but has not been formally validated:

- students and their learning and teaching are the most important factor
- schools do not act alone, they network or federate
- leadership is distributed
- networks and federations contain various individuals, groups, agencies
- novel approaches to resource allocations are sought and used
- knowledge management is granted parity of importance alongside other management functions
- the continuing development of the intellectual and social capital of the education workforce is important
- new standards of school and education system governance are expected, leading from dependence/self-management to autonomy/self-government

- there must be provisions made/encouragement for the further adaptations of each educational institution as it participates outside its established school and/or education system
- wisdom (sagacity) of leaders is necessary because change is occurring now, it is fast paced
- educational organisations have to adapt quickly to survive and adopt refined procedures in order to progress.

Reflecting upon this cogent advice, another issue emerges: still missing are valid, accessible evaluation approaches and their accompanying research bases that connect leadership standards with student performances (Gray & Streshly, 2008). Its resolution may be achieved by using combinations of evaluation theories already in use.

For example, Grove, Kibel and Haas' (2007, p. 73) EVALULEAD framework, an open-systems approach to leadership development evaluation, proves to be of relevance and generic value to schools, their leaders, teaching staff and their communities EVALULEAD delineates benchmarks that detail more tangible, evidential approaches at one end with less tangible, evocative approaches at the other. Evidential indicators include documentation of explicitly observable societal/community/environmental improvements; notation of increased organisational capacity denoted by improved organisational outputs; and details employee review appraisals that explicate more effective job-related skills acquisition and performance. Evocative indicators delineate shifts in community norms, organisational values and describe observations of the use of new personal insights demonstrated by employees. By aligning EVALULEAD with Tyler's (2004) Learning and Capacity Building framework (LCBF) areas of further comparison emerge (see Table 3.1) that may assist evaluation processes. In this instance, the more sophisticated, incrementally improved learning of an educational organisation and its designated whole groups of individuals are aligned directly with the capacity building objectives and results desired of each of its individual employees.

Dilemmas, Issues and Next Steps

Concerning school leaders, their professional practice and formation, information and data gathered in the constituent areas of policy, accountability, standards, frameworks and evaluation should be distilled, discussed and researched further to ensure that the following

TABLE 3.1
Professional Learning and Workforce Capacity Building

Learning-entire organisation, whole groups	Capacity building – individual employees
1. Educated and capacitated individual	1. Link specific needs of individual to organisational objectives and strategies
2. Educated and capacitated organisation	2. Map specific needs of workforce to educational objectives
3. Learning intervention does not merely relate to work being done	3. Map educational objectives to individual objectives and characteristics
4. Success of intervention	4. Link workplace applications to micro context
5. Balanced relationships between the two areas of comparison describes measures of impact	5. Map congruence between micro contexts and macro contexts

Note: Adapted from Tyler (2004)

dilemmas and issues are resolved before the next wave of concerns over-takes and submerges what has been achieved. There should be

- constant review of the progress of Professional Teacher and Educational Leadership Standards to ensure that they do not become stalled at their current developmental, and therefore not formally mandated, stages
- governments' attention to long-term policy deficiencies concerning the adequate resourcing of formal school leadership preparation and formation programs at national, state and territory levels
- reviews, reconfigurations and adaptations of accountability mechanisms currently used by public, private and independent schools nationwide in order to suit all schools, so that data generated can be used with equanimity for organisational development purposes in diverse contexts
- a national set of professional teacher and educational leadership standards developed as a matter of urgency by a consortium of interested parties comprising state and territory teacher employing bodies, teacher and principal professional associations, teacher unions, independent and private school representatives and relevant associated education bodies such as Teaching Australia
- mechanisms put in place by all state and territories to ensure that all teachers employed in their locales have access to their specifically designed school leadership frameworks and their

supporting professional learning workshops in order to promote the positive practicalities of aspiring to and attaining school leadership positions

- evaluation models selected and positioned to assess established and novel school leadership preparation and formation programs in each state and territory. While individualised, they must encompass elements that permit them to be compared and collated with ease across the nation.

In conclusion, while it is frustrating that these dilemmas still exist, their resolution is entirely possible if state, territory and national governments in concert with relevant others take action without unnecessary delay. A demoralised teaching profession would be reenergised by public recognition of the standards required to attain their professional positions as teachers and school leaders.

References

ACT Government Department of Education and Training. (2008). *School leadership framework*. Canberra, Australia: ACT DET Centre for Teaching and Learning.

Australian Education Union. (2009). *Teaching standards kit*. Southbank, Victoria, Australia: Author.

Anderson, M., & Cawsey, C. (2008). *Learning for leadership*. Camberwell, Victoria, Australia: Australian Council for Educational Research.

Apple, M. (2000). Between neoliberalism and neoconservatism: Education and conservatism in a global context. In N. Burbules & C. Torres (Eds.), *Globalization and education-critical perspectives* (pp. 57–78). New York: Routledge.

Australian Council for Educational Research. (2008). *The ACER leadership development framework*. Retrieved November 14, 2008, from http://www.acer.edu.au/employment/LDF.html

Bardach, E. (2000). *A practical guide for policy analysis*. New York: Chatham House.

Belgard, W., & Rayner, S. (2004). *Shaping the future*. New York: AMACOM.

Biggs, S., & Helms, L. (2007). *The practice of American public policy making*. New York: M.E. Sharpe.

Blank, M., Hale, B., & Harkavy, I. (2005). *Engaging all leaders*. Retrieved November 18, 2008, from http://www.ciconline.org/threshold

Bobrow, D., & Dryzek, J. (1987). *Policy by design*. Pittsburgh, PA: University of Pittsburgh Press.

Bush, T. (1994). Accountability in education. In T. Bush & J. West-Burnham (Eds.), *The principles of educational management* (pp. 309–326). Harlow, England: Pearson Education.

Bush, T. (2008). *Leadership and management development in education*. Los Angeles: Sage.

Caldwell, B. (2006). *Re-imagining educational leadership*. Melbourne, Australia: ACER.

Clegg, S., Kornberger, M., & Pitsis, T. (2008). *Managing & organisations*. Los Angeles: SAGE.

Colebatch, H. (2005). *Policy*. Berkshire, England: Open University Press.

Coleman, M. (2005). Evaluation in education. In M. Coleman & P. Earley (Eds.), *Leadership and management in education* (pp. 152–166). Oxford, UK: Oxford University Press.

Compston, H. (2007). *King trends and the future of public policy*. New York: Palgrave MacMillan.

Conner, D. (1998). *Leading at the edge of chaos*. New York: John Wiley & Sons.

Creighton, T. (2005). *Leading from below the surface*. Thousand Oaks, CA: Corwin.

Crowther, F., Ferguson, M., & Hann, L. (2009). *Developing teacher leaders*. Thousand Oaks, CA: SAGE.

Darling-Hammond, L. (2004). Standards, accountability, and school reform. *Teachers College Record, 106*(6), 1047–1085.

Davies, B. (2005). Strategic leadership. In B. Davies & B.J. Davies (Eds.), *The essentials of school leadership* (pp. 10–30). London: Paul Chapman & Corwin.

Davies, B., & Ellison, L. (2003). *The new strategic direction and development of the school*. London: RoutledgeFalmer.

Davies, B., Ellison, L., & Bowring-Carr, C. (2005). *School leadership in the 21st century*. London: RoutledgeFalmer.

Day, C. (2008). Successful leadership: an intelligent passion. In B. Davies& T. Brighouse (Eds.), *Passionate leadership in education* (pp. 75–90). London: SAGE.

Day, C. (2003). What successful leadership in schools looks like: Implications for policy and practice. In B. Davies & J. West-Burnham (Eds.), *Handbook of educational leadership and management* (pp. 187–204). London: Pearson Longman.

Department of Education, Employment and Workplace Relations. (2009). *School education*. Retrieved February 16, 2009, from http://www.dest.gov.au/sectors/school_education

Department of Education, Science and Training. (1999). *National goals for schooling in the twenty-first century: The Adelaide Declaration*. Retrieved February 26, 2009, from http://www.dest.gov.au/sectors/school_education/policy_initiative_reviews/national_goals_for_schooling_in_the_twenty_first_century

Department of Education and Training, New South Wales. (2008). *The school leadership capability framework*. Retrieved November 12, 2008, from http://www.det.nsw.edu.au/proflearn

Department of Education, Victoria. (2008). *The developmental learning framework for school leaders*. Melbourne, Victoria, Australia: Office of School Education.

Drake, T., & Roe, W. (2003). *The principalship*. Upper Saddle River, NJ: Merrill Prentice Hall.

Dror, Y. (1987). Retrofitting central minds of Governments. In S. Nagel (Ed.), *Research in public policy analysis and management* (pp. 79–108). Greenwich, CT: Jai.

Galbraith, J. (2000). The role of formal structures and processes. In M. Beer & N. Nohria (Eds.), *Breaking the code of change* (pp. 139–160). Boston: Harvard Business School.

Goens, G. (2005). *Soft leadership for hard times*. Lanham, MD: Rowman & Littlefield Education.

Gorton, R., Alston, J., & Snowden, P. (2007). *School leadership & administration*. Boston: McGraw-Hill.

Gray, J., & Wilcox, B. (1995). *Good school bad school: Evaluating performance and encouraging improvement*. Buckingham, England: Open University Press.

Gray, S., & Streshly, W. (2008). *From good schools to great schools*. Thousand Oaks, CA: Corwin & NAESP.

Grove, J., Kibel, B., & Haas, T. (2007). EVALULEAD: An open-systems perspective on evaluating leadership development. In K. Hannum, J. Martineau & C. Reinelt (Eds.), *The handbook of leadership development evaluation* (pp. 71–110) San Francisco: John Wiley & Sons.

Hamel, G., & Breen, B. (2007). *The future of management*. Boston: Harvard Business School.

Hargreaves, A. (2003). *Teaching in the knowledge Society*. New York: Teachers College Press.

Hargreaves, A., & Fink, D. (2006). *Sustainable leadership*. San Francisco: Jossey-Bass.

Haydon, G. (2007). *Values for educational leadership*. Los Angeles: SAGE.

Hayes, D., Mills, M., Christie, P., & Lingard, B. (2006). *Teachers and schooling: Productive pedagogies, assessment and performance making a difference*. Crows Nest, New South Wales, Australia: Allen & Unwin.

Heifetz, R. (2006). Public leadership: Mobilising for adaptive work. In L.Budd, J. Charlesworth & R. Paton (Eds.), *Making policy happen* (pp. 234–246). London: Routledge.

Heifetz, R., & Linsky, M. (2002). *Leadership on the line*. Boston: Harvard Business School.

Hessel, K., & Holloway, J. (2006). *A framework for school leaders: Linking the ISLLC standards to practice*. Upper Saddle River, NJ: ETS & Pearson Merrill Prentice Hall.

Ingvarson, L., Anderson, M., Gronn, P., & Jackson, A. (2006*). Standards for school leadership, a critical review of the literature*. Canberra, Australia: Teaching Available at www.teachingaustralia.edu.au

Institute for Educational Leadership (2008). *Leadership competencies*. Retrieved November 17, 2008, from http://www.iel.org

Jann, W., & Wegrich, K. (2007). Theories of the policy Cycle. In F. Fischer, G. Miller & M. Sidney (Eds.), *Handbook of public policy analysis* (pp. 43–62). Boca Raton, FL: CRC Press.

Jazzar, M., & Algozzine, B. (2006). *Critical issues in educational leadership.* Boston: Pearson and AB.

Jenkins, W. (1978). *Policy analysis.* New York: St. Martin's Press.

Kotter, J. (1998). What leaders really do. In *Harvard business review on leadership* (pp. 37–60). Boston: Harvard Business Review.

Leithwood, K., & Jantzi, D. (2006).Transformational Leadership. In B. Davies (Ed.), *The essentials of school leadership* (pp. 31–43). London: Paul Chapman & Corwin.

Lopez, J., Magdaleno, K., & Reis, N. (2006, Fall). Developing leadership for equity: What is the role of leadership preparation programs? *Educational Leadership and Administration, 18,* 11–19.

Lunenberg, F., & Irby, B. (2006). *The principalship: Vision to action.* Belmont, CA: Thomson Wadsworth.

Mann, D. (1975). *Policy decision-making in education.* New York: Teachers College Press.

Ministerial Council on Education, Employment Training and Youth Affairs. (2008a). *Key performance measurement framework.* Melbourne, Victoria, Australia: Author.

Ministerial Council on Education, Employment Training and Youth Affairs. (2008b). *MCEETYA action plan 2009–2012.* Melbourne, Victoria, Australia: Author.

Ministerial Council on Education, Employment Training and Youth Affairs. (2008c). *Melbourne Declaration on educational goals for young Australians.* Melbourne, Victoria, Australia: Author.

Mills, J., Dye, K., & Mills, A. (2009). *Understanding organisational change.* London: Routledge.

Morrow, R., & Torres, C. (2000). The state, globalization and educational policy. In N. Burbules & C. Torres (Eds.), *Globalization and education: Critical perspectives* (pp. 27–56). New York: Routledge.

Mulford, B. (2004). Leadership in education: Losing sight of our interests. In N. Bennett, M. Crawford & M. Cartwright (Eds.), *Effective educational leadership* (pp. 3–13). London: The Open University & Paul Chapman.

National Board for Professional Teaching Standards. (2008). *National board for professional teaching standards: The five core propositions.* Retrieved November 19, 2008, from http://www.npts.org/the_standards/the_five_core_propositions

National Commission on Excellence in Education. (1983). *A nation at risk: The imperative for educational reform.* A report to the nation and the Secretary of Education, United States Department of Education. Retrieved February 24, 2009, from http://www.ed.gov/pubs/NatAtRisk/index.html

National College for School Leadership. (2001). *Leadership development framework.* Nottingham, England: National College for School Leadership.

New South Wales Institute of Teachers. (2008). *Professional teaching standards.* Retrieved October 13, 2008, from http://www.nswteachers.nsw.edu.au/Main-Professional-Teaching-Standards.html

Norton, M. (2005). *Executive leadership for effective administration.* Boston: Pearson & AB.

O'Keeffe, D. (2009, February). Flying squad to assess Victorian schools. *Education Review,* 3.

Parston, G. (1997). Producing social results. In F.Hesselbein, M.Goldsmith & R. Beckhard (Eds.), *The organisation of the future* (pp. 341–348). San Francisco: Jossey-Bass.

Picciano, A. (2006). *Data-driven decision making for effective school leadership.* Upper Saddle River, NJ: Pearson Merrill Prentice Hall.

Queensland Government, Department of Education, Training and the Arts. (2008). *The developing performance framework.* Retrieved November 11, 2008, from http://www.education.qld.gov.au

Raynor, A. (2004). *Individual schools unique solutions: Tailoring approaches to school leadership.* London: RoutledgeFalmer.

Reiss, K. (2007). *Leadership coaching for educators: Bringing out the best in school administrators.* Thousand Oaks, CA: Corwin.

Robertson, J. (2008). *Coaching educational leadership.* Los Angeles: SAGE.

Rooney, J. (2008). Taking hold of learning. *Educational Leadership, 66*(3), 82–83.

Segil, L. (2002). *Dynamic leader, adaptive organisation.* New York: John Wiley & Sons.

Senge, P. (2006). *The fifth discipline.* London: Random House.

Spillane, J., & Diamond, J. (2007). Taking a distributed perspective. In J. Spillane & J. Diamond (Eds.), *Distributed leadership in practice* (pp. 1–15). New York: Teachers College Press.

State of NSW, Department of Education and Training. (2008). *The school leadership capability framework.* Retrieved October 12, 2008, from http://www.det.nsw.edu.au/proflearn

Stewart, J. (2007). Academics and the public policy game. *Public Policy, 2*(1)1–9.

Storms, B., & Gonzales, S. (2006, Fall). A model for successful district-based leadership development partnerships. *Educational Leadership and Administration, 18,* 35–49.

Teaching Australia. (2009a). *Charter for the Australian teaching profession.* Retrieved February 11, 2009, from http://www.educationreview.com.au

Teaching Australia. (2009b). *School leadership.* Retrieved February 20, 2009, from http://www.teachingaustralia.edu.au/ta/go

Teese, R., & Polesel, J. (2003). *Undemocratic schooling.* Carlton, Victoria, Australia: Melbourne University Press.

Twale, D., & Place, W. (2005). Reconceptualising the school of education: Bridging the cultures. *Educational Leadership and Administration. 17,* 115–123.

Tyler, S. (2004). Making leadership and management development measure up. In J. Storey (Ed.), *Leadership in organisations: Current issues and key trends* (pp. 152–170). London: Routledge.

Victorian Institute of Teaching. (2008). *Victorian Institute of Teaching standards of professional practice for full registration.* Retrieved November 16, 2008, from http://www.vit.vic.edu.au/files/documents/787_standards.PDF

West-Burnham, J. (2001). Creating a performance culture. In J. West-Burnham, I. Bradbury & J. O'Neill (Eds.), *Performance management in schools* (pp. 15–26). London: Pearson Education.

Wildy, H., Clarke, S., & Slater, C. (2007). International perspectives of principal preparation: How does Australia fare? *Leading & Managing, 13*(2) 1–14.

Yukl, G. (2004). Tridimensional leadership theory: A roadmap for flexible, adaptive leaders. In R. Burke & C. Cooper (Eds.), *Leading in turbulent times* (pp. 75–92). Malden, MA: Blackwell.

▶▶▶◀◀◀

SECTION TWO
Leadership Issues and Approaches

Intercultural Leadership: Strengthening Leadership Capabilities for Indigenous Education

Nereda White, Robyn Ober, Jack Frawley
and Melodie Bat

In Australia, there are approximately 140,000 Indigenous students attending school, with a further 68,000 in vocational education and training and over 9,000 enrolled in university courses (Fordham & Schwab, 2007). Although educational outcomes have improved in recent years, overall the results for Indigenous students are still unsatisfactory compared to other Australian students. To support Indigenous people to establish solid educational foundations, which will allow them to engage in quality employment and life experiences, it is argued in this chapter that it will require a different approach to leadership in education, one in which leadership and education are considered within an intercultural context. In recent years, there has been a growing interest in the influence of culture on the practice of educational leadership and management (Dimmock & Walker, 2005). This challenges the dominance of western-based educational leadership theory in the leadership literature, and emphasises the need to understand educational leadership from an intercultural perspective (Blakesley, 2008). Blakesley (2008, p. 441) argues that there is an 'absence of an Indigenous cultural lens through which to examine educational leadership'. Furthermore, educational leadership studies must 'identify the particularity and diversity of cultural and contextual conditions within which leadership takes place' (Dimmock & Walker, 2005, p. 2). In the Australian context, educational leadership must take into account the perspectives and aspirations of its Aboriginal and Torres Strait Islander people.

Indigenous Leadership

To understand Indigenous leadership in education today, it must be considered within an historical and social context prior to and following European settlement. Leadership and governance in traditional Aboriginal societies were embedded in complex kinship systems, social, economic and political structures determined by the Dreaming, a framework that governed all aspects of life. Authority, wisdom and trust were distributed and shared according to role, age and skill with particular respect given to the elders.

There are numerous Dreaming stories of Aboriginal heroes and heroines, their epic journeys and achievements, which acknowledge their leadership. In the early days of first contact with Europeans, stories have also emerged about the courage of Aboriginal warriors such as Pemulwuy, Jandalmurra, Dundalli and Yagan who rose up in protest against the White invaders (Dodson, 2003). Despite many years of suppression under colonial rule, Aboriginal men and women continued to speak out against racism and the ill-treatment of their people. These notable Aboriginal activists include William Cooper, a Yorta Yorta Elder who petitioned the King of England for Aboriginal representation in parliament (Dodson, 2003); Jack Patten who organised the 1938 'Day of Mourning Conference and Protest' in Sydney; Aboriginal leader Charles Perkins, organiser of freedom rides in the 1960s; poet Kath Walker (Oodgeroo of the Noonuccal tribe); Vincent Lingiari who led Gurrindji people in the Wave Hill station walk-off in 1966 and Eddie Koiki Mabo who was instrumental in winning the landmark High Court case and overturning the legal statute of *terra nullius* in Australia. Indigenous leadership contributed to the holding of the historic 1967 referendum that gained human rights, political power and rights to self determination for Indigenous Australians. Following the referendum, there was a gradual handover of the management of former missions and settlement to Aboriginal communities. A natural outcome of that process has been the emergence of community leaders to take up the roles previously occupied by government and church-appointed managers and administrative officers.

In recent years, Indigenous issues have become more prominent within Australian society. In response to the demands for Indigenous control over Indigenous affairs, Indigenous people have endeavoured to take on a much more active role in decision-making. At the forefront since the High Court Decision (1993) and the subsequent Commonwealth *Native Title Act*

(1993) has been the negotiation of native title and land rights and asso-ciated heritage protection, which has required claimants to work with government and other parties such as mining companies to reach agreement on return of, and use of traditional land. Today, Indigenous people and communities are more involved in policy development and program implementation in areas such as housing, education and health. Their participation is now a significant aspect of Indigenous community life and community capacity-building. It has highlighted the importance of Indigenous leadership and the need to 'encourage, support and prepare more emerging leaders' (Cranney & Edwards, 1998, p. 3).

Since 2001, however, there had been growing disquiet with the current leadership in communities and representative bodies. A review of the Aboriginal and Torres Strait Islander Commission (ATSIC) con-ducted by Hannaford, Collins and Huggins (2003) raised concerns about the effectiveness of Indigenous leadership being exercised in communities and by representative bodies such as ATSIC. Many believed that the existing peak Indigenous body, ATSIC, had failed to deliver improvements in Indigenous communities and that it was engaged in nepotism and corruption (Appo, 2003c; Richardson, 2003). Despite its significant budget, it was believed that ATSIC had achieved limited success in alleviating the poor health of Indigenous Australians, the high levels of alcohol and drug abuse and the serious levels of violence in communities, the overrepresentation of Indigenous people in correctional centres, and the overall welfare dependency of Indigenous people (Appo, 2003c; Pearson, 2000). Because of concerns about the dysfunction and possible conflicts of interest within the organisation, in 2003 the federal government created Aboriginal and Torres Strait Islander Services (ATSIS), as a separate administrative body of ATSIC. With this separation, the ATSIC board was no longer responsible for the allocation of funding grants and became purely a policymaking body. The decision generated opposition from sectors of the Indigenous community, which believed it to be a regressive step in Indigenous self-determination and management. However, there were just as many who welcomed the action, saying that a change in leader-ship and management was desperately needed 'when the old ways, the old career system, fail to produce the results that we want in our com-munities' (Appo, 2003b, p. 14).

Paramount to these changes was the expressed need for the dismantlement of the 'Aboriginal industry', which had maintained the status quo of management malpractices and poor leadership that had crippled Indigenous community organisations and councils (Appo, 2003a, 2003b). A major concern was the claim that some community leaders had gained leadership positions 'through fear, favour or corruption' (Appo, 2003a, p. 14). According to Pearson (2000), the major challenge facing Indigenous communities is that current models of leadership — which have dominated governance in Indigenous communities for many years — have 'arisen from the colonial experience and the experience of institutional life in the reserves' (Pearson, 2000, p. 49). Pearson (2000, p. 37) argues that any successful new approach to community leadership must incorporate a 'shoulder to shoulder' encouragement; a sharing of, and devolution of, power that 'hands on' power to members of the community. Furthermore, Pearson advocates a system of governance that incorporates key values such as cooperation, unity, respecting rights, sharing power, taking responsibility, encouraging others; and supporting each other.

Patrick Dodson, former Chairperson of the Council for Aboriginal Reconciliation, in the Williamson Community Leadership Program Lecture (1998) emphasised the importance of community leadership when he said:

> For Aboriginal leaders, the social and moral obligation that comes with community leadership is life-long. Those who lead, who have authority, must care for and look after those who come behind. Leadership is an elusive concept, hard to describe and impossible to prescribe. It is more evident in its absence, so that when leadership is needed, its lack is sorely felt.

This calls for leadership that is able to take on the challenges of a rapidly changing world, and it requires leaders 'to work confidently and with influence in two worlds' (Cranney & Edwards, 1998, p. 5).

Indigenous Education Policy

During the late 1950s and early 1960s, attitudes towards Aboriginals were shifting amid global concerns about human rights. The 1967 referendum gave the federal government constitutional rights to implement changes for the benefit of Indigenous Australians and to legislate on their behalf. In the years following the referendum there were a number of policy initiatives that were to play a significant role in Indigenous education.

In 1968, the Aboriginal study grants scheme was implemented nationally to help meet the financial needs of Indigenous students and to encourage them to undertake post-school education. This in itself created the potential for Indigenous people to gain tertiary qualifications and, as a consequence, take up leadership roles in not only their communities but also in Australian society. However, there was insufficient take-up of the awards. The government realised that there needed to be greater support to help Indigenous students complete high school and, in 1970, introduced the Aboriginal Secondary Grants Scheme (Ngankat-kalo), followed by the Aboriginal Overseas Study award in 1974, designed to encourage community leaders to travel overseas to extend their knowledge and experience. From 1976, the Commonwealth Tertiary Education Commission agreement enabled universities to provide additional places for Indigenous students and this immediately increased the numbers of Indigenous people attending university.

Following a recommendation from the *Report to the Schools Commission* in 1975 by the Aboriginal Consultative Group, the National Aboriginal Education Committee (NAEC) was established in 1977 to provide advice to the Federal Minister for Education. This was the first time Aboriginal people had a national voice in education. The Labor government commissioned several reports that were to have significant impacts on Indigenous education across Australia.

Most Australian universities established Indigenous support units as a result of recommendations made by the Commonwealth Tertiary Education Commission (1985). Today these support units are still considered very important to the success of Indigenous tertiary students (Herbert, 2003). In the same year, the *Report of the Committee of Review of Aboriginal Employment and Training Programs*, also known as the Miller report, recommended changes to Aboriginal education and training to overcome the level of indigenous disadvantage. Similarly, the Royal Commission into Aboriginal Deaths in Custody, established in 1987 to investigate the disproportionate numbers of deaths of Aboriginal people in custody, found that there were links between the prior educational experiences and the fate of the Indigenous people who died as a result of being incarcerated.

The evidence from a number of reports was overwhelming and clearly established the severe educational disadvantage faced by Indigenous Australians. Furthermore, was the evidence that current Australian education systems had failed to rectify this situation but, more likely, had contributed to the precarious situation. Unless a cohesive approach to addressing the inequities was developed, it appeared that the gap would continue to widen between this group and other Australians to the detriment of the whole Australian community. The Miller report, together with the report of the Aboriginal Education Policy Taskforce (1988), was instrumental in leading to the development of a national Indigenous education policy.

On 1 January 1990, the federal and state/territory governments jointly implemented the National Aboriginal and Torres Strait Islander Education policy (AEP) to address the severe educational disadvantage faced by Indigenous people. The 21 goals of the AEP focused on encouraging greater participation of Indigenous people in culturally appropriate learning experiences delivered in supportive learning environments (Nelson, 2002). Five years after its implementation, the AEP was reviewed and it was found that although improvements had been made, the participation and achievement levels of Indigenous people still lagged behind those for non-Indigenous Australians (Nelson, 2002). Following the review, the Ministerial Council for Education, Employment, Training and Youth Affairs (MCEETYA) established eight priority areas for Indigenous education and training. As a further commitment to working with Indigenous people to overcome educational disadvantage, the Australian government endorsed the *National Goals for Schooling in the 21st Century*, which agreed that all children should leave school with appropriate literacy and numeracy levels (Nelson, 2002). In 2000, the National Indigenous English Literacy and Numeracy Strategy (NIELNS) was implemented specifically to 'achieve English literacy and numeracy for Indigenous students at levels comparable to those achieved by other young Australians' (Department of Education, Science & Training, 2005, p. 1).

A component of these recent educational policies is the emphasis on increasing the participation of Indigenous people in the education decision-making process. In addition, a number of leadership projects and programs have been established to encourage better leadership in Indigenous education. These include the establishment of the Cape York Institute for Leadership under Aboriginal lawyer Noel Pearson and the Institute for Educational Leadership sponsored by the Queensland University of Technology and Education Queensland under the leadership of Dr Chris Sarra, former principal of Cherbourg Community School. Both organisations have focused on building the leadership capacities of Indigenous educators and fostering improved leadership of non-Indigenous teachers and principals.

Indigenous Education: An Alternative Perspective[1]

Indigenous people in the Northern Territory have been suggesting an alternative educational ideology for many years, one that they refer to as 'both ways'. In 1976, Pincher Nyurrmiyarri from Dagaragu articulated the concept of 'both ways' (Harris 1989; McConvell, 1982). The Gurindji were worried about the schooling their children would receive. Pincher described the current school as a 'one-way school' — that is, 'only kartiya (European way)' and gave the alternative as a 'two-way' school — 'both kartiya way and ngumpit (Aboriginal) way' (McConvell, 1982, p. 62). Pincher Nyurrmiyarri developed and discussed this concept of 'two-way' schooling, which involved reciprocity and obligation, involving curriculum, knowledge, policies and power. A further aspect of the two-way schooling as explained by Pincher was 're-establishing a healthy relationship between the younger and older generations of Gurindji, healing rifts that had developed in the transmission of traditional knowledge, largely through the interference of schools in the process' (McConvell, 1982, p. 63). The younger people would bring home the new knowledge they had learned at school and the old people would be educating the young people both within the school and at home.

The implementation of bilingual education in a number of schools in the Northern Territory during the early 1970s gave a new focus to education. At this time, the 'domain separation' theory as proposed by Harris and others gained some popularity. 'Aboriginal survival history and current insight generally support the view that at least partial separation is crucial to survival' (Harris, 1988, p. 78). At this point, the term 'two-way' schooling was introduced as a way to shift discussion from centring solely on bilingual education. Harris explains this model as learning to play a role-play game, and suggests ways of living two-ways for the small culture to continue side-by-side with the majority culture (Harris, 1989, p. 174). He proposed that separating the two cultures would give the small culture a 'safe place to be itself and to grow' (Harris, 1989, p. 174) and then listed eight steps for this to happen — physical separation (e.g., outstations), maintenance of language in the home and school, Aboriginal influence in the media, economic independence, local control of Aboriginal schools, group action, social change (borrowing across cultures), and becoming highly expert in majority culture skills (at least some members).

This theorising of both-ways, while useful to promote further discussion and debate, received much criticism for its othering of Indigenous people and its oversimplification of Indigenous culture (Keefe 1989; McTaggart, 1988, 1989; Stewart 1989; Willis 1996). In the domain separation model, the cultural universals are situated within the dominant culture. Thus, while the minority culture maintains control over its own cultural specifics such as language, culture, perception and so on, there is the inherent risk that, through separation, the dominant culture retains control of the cultural universals and the members of the minority culture remain as outsiders (Stairs, 1988, p. 309). There was also concern expressed about the theorising being done by non-Indigenous academics.

> The point is here not so much whether Harris is 'right' or I am, but that both of our viewpoints are couched in terms imposed by a Western discourse about non-Western cultures. Europeans in education continually 'read back' versions of white discourse about Aborigines to Aboriginal people themselves. (McConvell, 1991, p. 21)

The domain separation theory, then, was under serious contestation and the philosophy shifted to a more interactive positioning. What emerged was a more socially critical model of both-ways practice that was represented as two overlapping circles, where the two worlds, Indigenous and non-Indigenous, intersect — see Figure 4.1.

In this model, the cultural universals are positioned in the intersecting section. 'This intrinsic development process moves towards indigenous education based not just on cultural content, but on the world-view, social roles and interactive style of the indigenous culture' (Stairs, 1988, p. 311). A graduate of the Batchelor Institute of Indigenous Tertiary Education (BIITE; formerly Batchelor College) in the Northern Territory, Wali Wulanybuma Wunungmurra, stated it clearly:

> We cannot hold back change which will happen whether we like it or not. But as a minority society we can adapt by finding common ground with the majority society. It is through an exchange of meanings that we can produce a 'two way' school curriculum. In an

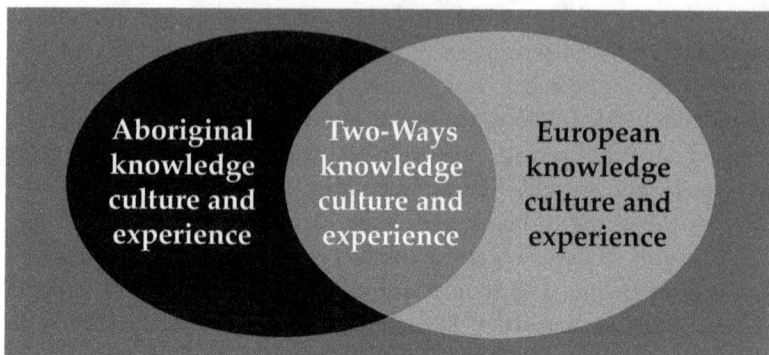

FIGURE 4.1
Two-ways model.
Source: Wunungmurra, 1989, p. 12.

exchange of knowledge both sides learn from each other instead of knowledge coming only from the Balanda side. But Yolngu and Balanda knowledge will only come together if there is respect for our knowledge and where Aboriginal people are taking the initiative, where we shape and develop the educational programs and implement them. (Wunungmurra, 1989, p. 12)

In the mid-1990s, the Yolngu people shared the metaphor of Ganma as a way of explaining the both-ways philosophy (Batchelor College, 1994; Christie, 2007; Marika, Ngurruwutthun, & White, 1992; McConvell, 1991; Ober, 2004; Willis, 1996) and is a way of exploring education and curriculum from an intercultural perspective, see Figure 4.2.

This was in contrast to the domain separation theory and gave a potentially richer image than the socially critical model. The Ganma metaphor was acknowledged as more appropriately representing the original 'two-way' education as proposed by Pincher (McConvell, 1991; Willis, 1996). A common thread, which emerged in the mid- to late-1990s, was that of identity and culture '… to live in both worlds we need to achieve a high standard in education but keep our own identity' (Ford, 1993, p. 76).

Interculturalism and Indigenous Education

The concept of 'both ways' is mutually interchangeable with interculturalism, in that both are concerned with the intersection and linking of cultural 'worlds', the 'space' in which the overlap occurs and the

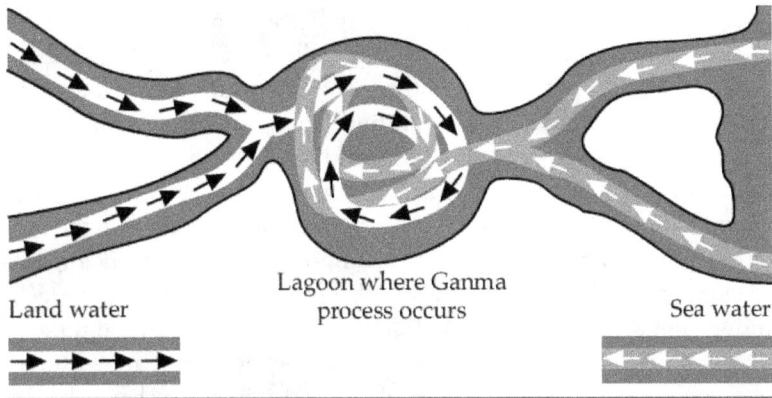

FIGURE 4.2
Ganma metaphor.
Note: Ganma is the name of a lagoon where salt and fresh water meets. Water is a symbol of knowledge in Yolngu philosophy, and the metaphor of the meeting of two bodies of water is a way of talking about the knowledge systems of two cultures working together. (Marika et al., 1992, p. 28)
Source: Ober & Bat, 2007, p. 71.

teaching and learning that takes place within this space. Like the 'both ways' focus of the interaction between Indigenous and non-Indigenous worlds, interculturalism 'is an idea that proposes an encounter between cultures that take place from fundamental characteristics, matrices, and unique aspects of each individual culture' (Coll, 2004, p. 27). To be engaged in an intercultural process 'is a releasing experience for each of the cultures involved leading to an awareness of the limits that are inherent to our own cultures and worlds' (Coll, 2004, p. 28). From this basis meaningful dialogue can occur in order to shape and negotiate the development of the intercultural space. This requires intercultural reasoning that 'emphasises the processes and interactions which unite and define the individuals and the groups in relation to each other' (Abdallah-Pretceille, 2006, p. 476). As noted above it is 'a way of talking about the knowledge systems of two cultures working together' (Marika et al., 1992, p. 28) where the 'work of analysis and of acquiring knowledge applies to others as much as to oneself' (Abdallah-Pretceille, 2006, p. 477).

There is little doubt that the context of Indigenous education, especially in remote communities has reached a critical phase brought about, to a certain extent, by incongruous government policies and decisions. On the one hand the federal government's AEP focuses on encouraging greater participation of Indigenous people in culturally appropriate learning experiences, especially in terms of educational decision-making; while on the other hand, their support for the previous Liberal government's 'intervention' policy entirely overlooks any form of consultation and decision-making with Indigenous people.[2] Similarly, in 2005 the Northern Territory (NT) Minister for Employment, Education and Training, Syd Sterling, announced that the NT Labor government was 'putting bilingual education back on the agenda' (in Purdie et al., 2008, p. 19), and yet 3 years later the new Indigenous Minister for Education, Marion Scrymgour, announced that English was to be the language of instruction for the first 4 hours of schooling each day in each school. This effectively foreshadowed the government's intention to downgrade — if not remove altogether — the 11 bilingual programs in 10 government schools, and the three remote Catholic schools bilingual education programs.

The announcement also devalues bilingual programs in remote Northern Territory schools and ignores the primacy of language and culture. Coulby's (2006, p. 246) statement 'that the need to recognise, tolerate and, at best, understand cultures other than that of the state into which people are born has never been more vital' emphasises the need for a both ways/intercultural perspective within educational systems to be supported and promoted. To paraphrase Bash and Zezlina-Phillips (2006, p. 249), if the educational experiences of Indigenous children are to be understood, contextual aspects cannot be ignored. Intercultural education needs to develop a discourse that can move from the national forces that have intervened in remote Indigenous communities, to the intricacies of an Indigenous child attending a bilingual school in a remote Indigenous community. Coulby's (2006, p. 246) view that 'if education is not intercultural, it is probably not education, but rather the inculcation of nationalist or religious fundamentalism', although somewhat extreme, has a ring of truth when posited in an Indigenous context.

As noted above, Indigenous people in the Northern Territory have been suggesting an alternative perspective on education for many years, but there have been very few real advances. There are some notable exceptions though, primarily brought about by establishment of bilingual programs in a number of remote Northern Territory Indigenous community schools from the mid-1970s and the work of BIITE, particularly its community-based teacher-training programs of the 1980s.

With the teaching of the vernacular in a number of remote Indigenous community schools, attention turned to the role of the system in supporting bilingual programs, the teachers and the students. As well as funding literature production centres, which enabled schools to publish resources in the vernacular, the education department also established additional positions for teacher linguists and local linguistic advisors. The NT Department of Education, Employment and Training (NT DEET) also published the *Handbook for Aboriginal Bilingual Education in the Northern Territory* to provide guidelines for bilingual schools and their staff. What this meant on the ground was greater involvement by the community in schooling as schools invited elders, artists and community members to teach and participate in language events. Tamisari and Milmilany (2003) provide a brief history of education at the community of Milingimbi in northeast Arnhem Land, Northern Territory from the mission times to the present. In this history they describe how the school moved from one established by the Methodist Mission in the early 1920s to its current position as a, now threatened, bilingual school. Tamisari and Milmilany (2003) state that:

> ... since the launch of the bilingual policy in the Northern Territory in 1973, Yolngu teaching staff, elders and leaders of the Milingimbi community in northeast Arnhem Land, Northern Territory have been involved in and committed to the development of a culturally appropriate education according to the social and political principles, needs and aspirations of the community. (pp. 1–2)

This meant that attention was also focussed on an Indigenous curriculum where there was an aim to integrate 50% of 'Yolngu content in the existing curriculum' with that of Balanda (whitefella) curriculum because:

> We don't want to lose our culture with too many Balanda ways of living. In other words we don't want to learn more Balanda education and less Yolngu education, or more Yolngu education and less Balanda education. We want to learn both with even understanding. (Tamisari & Milmilany, 2003, pp. 5–6)

This call for an 'even understanding' is at the core of interculturalism. While attention was given to the teaching and learning of 'both ways' education in these intercultural spaces, not a lot of thought was given to the training of teachers to be able to work interculturally, especially for non-Indigenous teachers. The community teacher education programs offered by BIITE, mentioned above, was the exception, albeit focused on only one side of the coin, that it is the Indigenous teachers, and, to a certain extent, implicit rather than explicit. Although schools like Milingimbi and organisations like BIITE have argued long and passionately for 'both ways' education, there has been very little systems thinking about the capabilities needed to work within an intercultural educational setting.

Intercultural Leadership Capabilities for Indigenous Education Systems

Shaping an intercultural space requires working with the educational system, which has the responsibility for the space, and with those who are members of it, including administrators, teachers, students, staff and community members. Systems leadership recognises the importance of connections between these key members and the whole system, and is understood as being exercised in five major domains: identity, education, stewardship, community and future focus. In each of these domains, systems leaders demonstrate a range of capabilities: personal, relational, professional and organisational (Duignan, 2006). These capabilities are founded on a value-based and ethical framework designed to integrate values and culture into future education policy and decision-making. System leaders recognise the importance of the connections between different issues, different individuals and different institutions. They understand that it is these connections that create systems, which are more than the sum of their parts. Stephenson (2000, p. 2) described capabilities as an all-round human quality, an integration of knowledge, skills, personal qualities and understanding used appropriately and effectively not just in familiar and highly focused specialist contexts but also in response to new and changing circumstances. Duignan (2006) identified capabilities as more than simply possessing particular knowledge and skills or having the potential to do something. It means demonstrating that one can actually do it. Duignan (2006) made a distinction between competency and capability-based programs as competency being about delivering the present based on past performance while capability is about imaging the future and bringing it about. Competency is about control; capability is about learning and development. Competency is about fitness for other people's purpose, while capability is about judging fitness of the purpose itself. Within Duignan's systems leadership capabilities, culture is mentioned only once, under organisational capabilities: 'Models cultural sensitivity —

shows sensitive discernment with regard to human and cultural differences, and consideration and empathy for those who may not share their perspectives or preferences' (Duignan, 2006, p. 154).

It is argued here that these categories of leadership capabilities — personal, relational, professional, and organisational — are not sufficient, in that they fail to fully embrace interculturalism; they ignore, to a certain degree, the significance of culture on leadership development and continue to privilege the western perspective. Coulby (2006, p. 246) argues that interculturalism 'needs to inform the teaching and learning of all subjects', while Abdallah-Pretceille (2006, p. 476) asks a number of questions about members of an intercultural system:

> What does one need to know about the culture of the 'Other' or, more precisely, about the 'Other', in order to be able to teach him/her or, in other words, to help him/her learn? What cultural information do educators need to become competent? Do they need to understand the cultures themselves or instead the learners through their cultures, that is, through the cultural elements expressed through their attitudes and behaviour?

In a review of literature, DeJaeghere and Zhang (2008, p. 260), identify several dimensions that are necessary for intercultural competence. These dimensions include:

> ... cultural self-awareness or consciousness-raising (Cross et al., 1989; Bennett 1993; Gay, 2000 71); awareness and acceptance of difference, and others' cultural worldviews (Cross et al. 1989; Bennett 1993; Hammer and Bennett 2001); awareness of the social-construction of race, and prejudice and discrimination in historical and contemporary societal and school contexts (Sleeter 1992); knowledge of cultural patterns and culture specific knowledge (Bennett 1993; Gay 2000); knowledge of and skill in using different communication and learning styles (J.M. Bennett 1986; Gay 2000); knowledge and skill in using diverse classroom management strategies; ability to adapt the curriculum content to reflect cultural diversity of students; and skills to implement various pedagogies, including discourse, participation and assessment, that are culturally relevant to one's students (Gay, 2000).

It has been argued in this chapter that the system of Indigenous education should be viewed as an intercultural one. Such systems function by respecting and appreciating the different cultures and allowing them to flourish with creativity and dignity. What these intercultural capabilities are is a matter of debate, discussion and further research, but it is assumed that they will focus on recognising various cultures and identities, be based on cultural values, be inclusive and harmonious, and be synergetic among other things. Duignan (2006) would argue that it is not enough to demonstrate intercultural competence, as listed above, but an intercultural leader must be able to do it. It is suggested that all educators working in an intercultural system, whether Indigenous or non-Indigenous, be viewed as working together, and not apart, and that the leadership capabilities apply to both and will be required by the 'collective leadership' (Duignan, 2006) of intercultural schools.

Conclusion

In a recent speech at the World Indigenous Peoples Conference on Education, Tom Calma, Aboriginal and Torres Strait Islander Social Justice Commissioner and Race Discrimination Commissioner, Australian Human Rights Commission, focused on bilingual education and a human rights approach to schooling. Of bilingual education he remarked on its inherent intercultural qualities stating that it is an:

> educational framework and a practice which builds a cultural bridge between Indigenous and non-Indigenous languages and knowledge systems ... (and) ... brings together the cultural richness of two worlds—teaching children to walk in both the Indigenous world and the non-Indigenous world. (Calma, 2008, p. 3).

Calma (2008, p. 12) also makes the point that there is a 'problem with accommodating diversity when education departments are monolithic bureaucracies' (p. 12) and that 'local negotiations and agreements are the only way to develop education with Indigenous students and their families to ensure there is consistency of understanding and expectation' (p. 14). Calma suggests that 'educators need to be able to reflect on their personal cultural knowledges and biases and consider the ways in which they inform professional practice' (p. 16). From Pincher Nyurrmiyarri at Dagaragu in 1976, to Tom Calma at Melbourne in 2008, there has been a range of Indigenous and non-Indigenous teachers, parents, communities and academics' voices calling for an educational system that has at its core 'an even understanding'. This requires developing the intercultural capabilities of all those engaged with it.

There has been little formal research in Australia on intercultural leadership in education, but what is emerging from current research and projects being conducted by Australian Catholic University's

(ACU) Flagship for Creative & Authentic Leadership and BIITE, is the development of intercultural capabilities to complement and extend the work of Duignan (2006) and others. Through the use of metaphor in both research and projects, interculturalism and intercultural capabilities are being explored and investigated by ACU and BIITE researchers and academics. Likewise, the continued focus of BIITE further extends 'both ways' as a philosophy that underpins its research, teaching and learning. This work continues to further advance research, discussion and debate on intercultural leadership in education. However, much more needs to done to understand the influence of culture on educational leadership. For educational outcomes to dramatically improve for Indigenous Australians, the attention must be shifted within educational leadership dialogue to an understanding of leadership from an intercultural perspective where Indigenous and non-Indigenous people, working in an intercultural space, develop an interculturally defined way of leading in education.

Endnotes

1   Much of this section was first published by Ober and Bat (2007) in *Ngoonjook: a Journal of Australian Indigenous Issues, 31*, 64–86.

2   Under the pretext of responding to a report into child abuse in some Aboriginal communities — the *Little Children are Sacred* report (Wild & Anderson, 2007) — the then Liberal federal government introduced into Australian Parliament, in August 2007, a package of five Bills that resulted in 'a comprehensive, compulsory intervention in 73 Northern Territory Aboriginal communities' (Brennan, 2007). The Bills included measures to abolish the Community Development Employment Program (CDEP); quarantine 50% of community members' welfare payments, and 100% of those whose children are truants; deploy Australian Federal Police as 'special constables' to the Northern Territory Police Force; remove the permit system that governs access to Aboriginal land; acquire 5-year leases over prescribed townships that are part of the emergency response; and negotiate with interested communities on 99-year township leases.

References

Abdallah-Pretceille, M. (2006). Interculturalism as a paradigm for thinking about diversity. *Intercultural Education, 17*(5), 475–483.

Aboriginal Education Policy Task Force. (1988). *Report of the Aboriginal Education Policy Task Force*. Canberra, Australia: Aboriginal Education Policy Task Force.

Appo, D. (2003a, July 30). Leadership qualities. *Koori Mail,* p. 14.

Appo, D. (2003b, August 13). The Aboriginal industry. *Koori Mail,* p.14.

Appo, D. (2003c, September 10). Leadership qualities. *Koori Mail,* p. 14.

Bash, L., & Zezlina-Phillips, E. (2006). Identity, boundary and schooling: perspectives on the experiences and perceptions of refugee children. *Intercultural Education, 17*(1), 113–128.

Batchelor College. (1994). *Beyond the college: Profiles of graduates.* Batchelor, Northern Territory, Australia: Author.

Blakesley, S. (2008). Remote and un-researched: Educational leadership in Canada's Yukon Territory. *Compare: A journal of comparative education, 38*(4), 441–454.

Brennan, F. (2007). The Northern Territory Intervention, the real agenda: The dream of jobs and real services for northern Australia. Retrieved March 12, 2008, from www.acu.edu.au/data/assets/pdf file/0007/55879/NDA_Talk_Aug_2007.pdf

Calma, T. (2008, December). *Indigenous education in the 21st century — Respecting tradition, shaping the future.* Keynote address at the World Indigenous Peoples' Conference on Education [electronic version]. Retrieved December 18, 2008, from http://www.hreoc.gov.au/about/media/speeches/social_justice/2008/20081209_world.html

Christie, M. (2007). Yolngu language habitat: Ecology, identity and law in an Aboriginal society. In G. Leitner & I. Malcolm (Eds.), *The habitat of Australia's Aboriginal languages: Past, present, and future* (pp. 57–58). Berlin: Mouton De Gruyter.

Coll, A.C. (2004). *The intercultural challenge.* Bangalore, India: Pipal Tree.

Commonwealth Tertiary Education Commission. (1985). *Support systems for Aboriginal students in higher education.* Canberra, Australia: Australian Government Publishing Service.

Coulby, D. (2006). Intercultural education: Theory and practice. *Intercultural Education, 17*(3), 245–257.

Cranney, M., & Edwards, D. (1998). *Concept study into an Australian Indigenous leadership development program.* Canberra, Australia: Australian Institute of Aboriginal and Torres Strait Islander Studies.

DeJaeghere, J.G., & Zhang, Y. (2008). Development of intercultural competence among US American teachers: Professional development factors that enhance competence. *Intercultural Education, 19*(3), 255–268.

Department of Education Science & Training. (2005). National Indigenous English literacy and numeracy strategy (NIELNS), Supporting statement [Electronic Version]. Retrieved November 14, 2008, from http://www.dest.gov.au/sectors/Indigenous_education/policy_issues_Reviews/national

Dimmock, C., & Walker, A. (2005). *Educational leadership: Culture and diversity.* London: Sage.

Dodson, M. (2003). *How an Indigenous leader should sound today.* Speech given to the Lord Mayor's Charitable Fund [Electronic Version]. Retrieved February 7, 2008, from http://www.theage.co.au/cgi-bin/common/popupPrintArticle.pl?path=/articles/2003/0

Dodson, P. (1998). *On leadership.* Williamson Community Leadership Program Lecture [Electronic Version]. Retrieved February 10, 2006, from http://www.leadershipvictoria.org/speeches speech_dodson.html

Duignan, P. (2006). *Educational leadership: Key challenges and ethical tensions.* Cambridge: Cambridge University Press.

Ford, M. (1993). Involving Aboriginal people in course development. *Ngoonjook: A Journal of Australian Indigenous Issues, 9*, 70–81.

Fordham, A.M., & Schwab, R.G. (2007). *Education, training and indigenous futures. CAEPR policy research: 1990–2007.* Canberra, Australia: Australian National University.

Hannaford, H.J., Collins, H.B., & Huggins, J. (2003). *Review of the Aboriginal and Torres Strait Islander Commission: A Public Discussion Paper.* Canberra, Australia: Department of Immigration and Multicultural and Indigenous Affairs.

Harris, S. (1988). Culture boundaries, culture maintenance-in-change, and two-way Aboriginal schools. *Curriculum perspectives, 2*, 76–83.

Harris, S. (1989, September). *Coming up level' without 'losing themselves': The dilemma of formal tertiary training for Aborigines.* Paper presented at the national conference on Adult Aboriginal Learning, Western Australian College of Advanced Education.

Herbert, H.J. (2003). *Is a success of a matter of choice? Exploring Indigenous Australian notions of success within the context of the Australian university.* Melbourne, Australia: Royal Melbourne Institute of Technology.

Keefe, K. (1989). Curriculum development in Aboriginal studies: A Yanangu case study. *Australian Aboriginal Studies, 1*, 36–44.

Marika, R., Ngurruwutthun, D., & White, L. (1992). Always together, yaka gäna: Participatory research at Yirrkala as part of the development of a Yolngu education. *Convergence, 25*, 23–39.

McConvell, P. (1991). Cultural domain separation: Two-way street or blind alley? Stephen Harris and the neo-Whorfians on Aboriginal education. *Australian Aboriginal Studies, 1*, 13–24.

McConvell, P. (1982). Supporting the two-way school. In J. Bell (Ed.), *Language Planning for Australian Aboriginal Languages.* Alice Springs, Northern Territory, Australia: ALA/IAD.

McTaggart, R. (1988). Aboriginal pedagogy versus colonization of the mind. *Curriculum Perspectives, 2*, 83–92.

McTaggart, R. (1989). Aboriginalisation implies empowerment and disempowerment. *The Aboriginal Child at School, 17*, 37–44.

Nelson, B. (2002). *National report to parliament on Indigenous education and training.* Canberra, Australia: Department of Education Science and Training.

Ober, R. (2004). Reflections on both-ways at Batchelor Institute. *BiiteN, 13*(8–9).

Ober, R., & Bat, M. (2007). Paper 1: Both-ways: the philosophy. *Ngoonjook: A Journal of Australian Indigenous Issues, 31*, 64–86.

Pearson, N. (2000). *Our right to take responsibility.* Cairns, Australia: Noel Pearson & Associates.

Purdie, N., Frigo, T., Ozolins, C., Noblett, G., Thieberger, N., & Sharp, J. (2008). *Indigenous languages programmes in Australian schools: A way forward.* Canberra, Australia: Department of Education, Employment and Workplace Relations.

Richardson, P. (2003, August 15). An embarrassment to us all. *Koori Mail,* p. 15.

Stairs, A. (1988). Beyond cultural inclusion: An Inuit example of Indigenous educational development *Multilingual Matters, Series 40 (Minority Education: From Shame to Struggle),* 308–327.

Stephenson, J. (2000). *Corporate capability: Implications for the style and direction of work-based learning.* Sydney, Australia: Research Centre for Vocational Education and Training, University of Technology Sydney.

Stewart, I. (1989). *Community based teacher education: The logic of restructuring the Batchelor College teacher education program.* Batchelor, Northern Territory, Australia: Batchelor College.

Tamisari, F., & Milmilany, E. (2003). Dhinthun wayawu–looking for a pathway to knowledge: Towards a vision of Yolngu education in Milingimbi. *The Australian Journal of Indigenous Education, 32,* 1–10.

Wild, R., & Anderson, P. (2007). *Ampe akelyernemane meke mekarle' Little children are sacred: Report of the Northern Territory Board of Inquiry into the Protection of Aboriginal Children from Sexual Abuse.* Darwin, Northern Territory: Department of the Chief Minister.

Willis, C. (1996). A critical review: S. Harris (1990) Two-way schooling: Education and cultural survival. *The Australian Journal of Indigenous Education, 24,* 6–11.

Wunungmurra, W. (1989). Dhawurrpunaramirr—finding the common for a new Aboriginal curriculum. *Ngoonjook: A Journal of Australian Indigenous Issues, 2,* 12.

▷▷▷◁◁◁

CHAPTER 5

Spiritual Leadership in Australian Schools: Can it Enhance School Leadership Today?

Helga Neidhart and Paul Carlin

> We yearn for strong leaders so we can borrow their strength. We want leaders with integrity because we know their example can inspire us and expand our own capacity for honesty and moral clarity. We admire leaders with passion because they radiate the kind of commitment, the charisma, the emotional force and courage we wish we had. (Mackay, 1999, p. 138)

In recent decades, the global world has undergone significant and complex change. This change has been characterised by constancy, uncertainty and insecurity. Instant communication has expanded rapidly, climate change threatens our world and the continuing challenge of poverty, civil war and terrorism has resulted in homelessness and displacement of people and nations. For increasing millions of people the search for meaning, security and hope has never been greater (Carlin & Neidhart, 2004; Furedi, 2006; Gilbertson, 2006; Kriger & Seng, 2005). This is a context demanding leaders with courage, integrity and, above all, solid values (Duignan, 2006).

The growth of globalisation has changed the way in which people live and relate to each other; how businesses and industry, and also employment structures operate. The speed, volume and complexity of transactions across continents have led to a continuous compression of time and space, and a massive change in the nature of human interaction. Despite the rhetoric about how reflective practice can provide critical insights, the notion of reflection itself is in danger. The prevalence of e-mail and mobile telephone technology has enabled work to become a 24/7 reality, with adverse consequences for families and quality of life in many western countries (Birch & Paul, 2003; Eckersley, 2005; OECD, 2007).

The crucial issues of trust and hope have been the subject of considerable examination in recent years, not only in families, but also in institutions and workplaces (Bates, 2003; O'Neill, 2002; Goleman, Boyatzis, & McKee, 2002). In addition to the challenges of a rapidly changing world, the increased outbreaks of terrorism such as in September 2001 in New York, and the London bombings in 2005 have seriously threatened the ordinary citizen's sense of trust, stability and security. The last two decades have witnessed a growing emphasis and concern about issues like wellbeing, security, quality of life, and work–life balance (Australian Public Service, 2006; Birch & Paul, 2003; OECD, 2007). Consequently, the search for meaning, identity and security has become more urgent and challenging. Not surprisingly, schools, together with families, play an important part in helping children and young people to sustain purpose and hope in these uncertain times.

Schools have been identified as one of the more potentially effective agencies to address the important life issues for children and adolescent youth. Social policymakers nominate schools as important centres of formation and social hubs for the delivery of significant social services (Edgar, 2002). Many would agree that in much of the western world, including Australia, postmodernity has resulted in increasing disenchantment and scepticism about most traditional institutions, and their influence on society has declined sharply (Edwards, 2008; Putnam, 1996). Schools and churches are not exempt. At the same time, governments are demanding rigorous reporting and accountability and more is expected of schools. Their priorities, national curricula and testing, outcomes and standards, have become highly contested and given rise to continuing and increasing tensions. The complexity of school leadership in the 21st century is spelt out in a recent OECD report: 'The role of school leaders has changed radically as countries transform their education systems to prepare young people to function in today's world of rapid technological change, economic globalisation and increased migration and mobility' (Pont, Nusche, & Hopkins, 2008, p. 1).

In the midst of such turmoil, individuals and nations need anchors or reference points to rely on (Mackay, 2005). Such trusted reference points might range from the core beliefs of a particular faith, to an inner conviction shared and nurtured by even a small number of trusted friends or colleagues (Covey, 2008). For many, human life has a larger purpose and their confidence in key reference points helps sustain them through turbulent times and assists them to navigate pathways towards a better and more secure future. Sociologists have reported that increasing numbers of people are finding their traditional anchors no longer helpful and reliable, and many are turning back to the existential questions (Angel, 2004; Mackay, 2005). 'As our world grows more chaotic and unpredictable', suggests Wheatley, (2002, p. 1), 'we are forced to ask questions that have, historically, always been answered by spiritual traditions. How do I live in uncertainty, unable to know what will happen next?' In this chapter, spirituality is understood broadly as part of human evolution. It can have its source in various domains: religious faiths, the environment, tribal cultures and humanism, and has been described as seeking the ultimate purpose in life and trying to live it accordingly (Mitroff & Denton, 1999).

Even in the world of business and industry, spirituality is increasingly referred to: 'The spiritual dimension has been part of leadership since time immemorial; but in today's global economy, it is undergoing an historic universal transformation' (Filson, 2006, p. 1). The 2007 World Economic Forum in Switzerland, reported on the emergence of a 'culture of transcendent leadership', which was described as a 'willingness by those with company or country responsibilities to make decisions that benefit those far beyond the decision maker's own organization or nation' (Useem, 2007, p. 1).

Some employees however, express deep concern that the same employers who use the language of spirituality and corporate social responsibility, are also those who, in the name of competition, reduce employee benefits, entitlements and job security. Such practices contradict the rhetoric and arouse suspicion, damaging relationships and trust. In schools, this is manifested in teacher quality being judged simplistically by the test scores of their students and their remuneration and, in some cases, their future employment being dependent on those scores.

This chapter will look at ways in which this changing environment is impacting on schools, both locally and globally, and explore how the incorporation of the spiritual dimension can more effectively provide for human hope and flourishing through what we call courageous school leadership.

Some Insights Into Spirituality

Spirituality has been an integral part of the human story of evolution for almost 70,000 years, whereas formal religion did not come into existence until about 5,000 years ago. Some recent writings discuss spirituality in relation to religion, secularism and fundamentalism (Chittister, 2006; Sunderland, 2007; Tacey, 2002). Spirituality has been described variously as:

> ... an ancient and primal search for meaning that is as old as humanity itself and, ... belongs — as an inherent energy — to the evolutionary unfolding of creation itself. (O'Murchu, 1997, p. vii)
>
> ... a certain awakening to life that relates us more deeply to life. ... There are dimensions of life yet to be explored, all of which offer greater depth, connection, centredness and wholeness. (Ransom, 2002, p. 17); and also as
>
> ... a project of life integration, which means that it is holistic, involving body and spirit, emotions and thought, activity and passivity, social and individual aspects of life. (Schneiders, 1989, p. 675)

Neidhart (2000, p. 88) refers to 'authentic contemporary spirituality' not as something additional, but rather as something that should ... 'give depth, meaning and resonance to the ordinary in daily life; all human experience has some, greater or lesser, spiritual value'.

According to a number of writers, there is an important difference between religion and spirituality. Religion is about '... what we believe and why we believe it. It is about the tradition, the institution, the system. Constructed over centuries religion draws for the world a portrait of creation and relationships' (Chittister, 2006, p. 2); whereas spirituality is: '... a commitment to immersion in God, to the seeking that has no end. It is a consciousness of engrossment in God that lives beyond convention that eclipses convention' (Chittister, 2006, p. 3).

Schneiders (2000) explores the relationship between spirituality and religion in terms of the metaphors 'rivals', 'friends' and 'partners', strongly suggesting that the ideal relationship should be partnership, as both religion and spirituality have the capacity for mutual enrichment. As the focus of the current chapter is on spirituality framed more, but not exclusively, in the western tradition, the partnership relationship will not be further explored here.

From the early days of the Christian Church, there was only a single spirituality: that of Christ. According to Christians, Christ, as part of the Trinity, was the origin and the source of spirituality. Spirituality challenges people to be not only the best they can be, but also to advocate and work for the entitlements of all, particularly the disadvantaged or disenfranchised. One writer claims that Christian spirituality is built on four nonnegotiable pillars: private prayer and private morality, social justice, mellowness of heart and spirit and community, as a constitutive element of true worship (Rolheiser, 1998).

Those whose spirituality is based on a faith in a superior being or God may see faith as an integral part of life, rather than one that is separate from their being. They do not conceive the existence of a dualism. Some writers link spirituality to the notion of soul which, according to Moore, (1992, p. xi) 'lies midway between understanding and unconsciousness, and has imagination as its instrument'. For religious people, faith has at its core a soul, an inner essence that provides direction and purpose (Ransom, 2002). By following a particular faith, participants are invited to learn about the teachings of their God or prophet so that they can live according to those teachings. They learn to accept that pain, loss and lack of peace are part of the journey, but they can also come to know and appreciate the place of wonder and mystery in human life: 'Care of the soul is not solving the puzzle of life; quite the opposite, it is an appreciation of the paradoxical mysteries that blend life and darkness into the grandeur of what human life and culture can be' (Moore, 1992, p. xvii).

Buddhist spirituality, while sharing some essential similarities with Christianity, is also significantly different. It is not based on doctrine or belief, but rather is focused on living and practice. Its spiritual practices are, 'all oriented towards ultimate freedom from suffering and the cultivation of wisdom and compassion' (Muesse, 2002, p. 1). Buddhism acknowledges and respects other religions, accepting that they too are pathways to salvation. In much the same way as other religions advocate service for a greater good, Buddhism asserts that living compassionately involves living a life that puts the wellbeing of others ahead of self. The basis of spiritual training is the 'Noble Path', which is built around eight interrelated disciplines: four that focus on moral behaviour and compassion; and four that are intended to nurture and reinforce wisdom. A central component of the development of wisdom is 'to cultivate the mind to see reality clearly' (Muesse, 2002, p. 5).

Buddhism asserts it has much to offer those struggling or anxious about the intensity and rapid rate of change of the 21st century world. The cultivation of the mind and the search for truth offer enlightenment and equanimity.

Like Christianity, Islam teaches that each human being comprises two components: one is physical, derived from this earth, and destined to return to earth after death; the other is the 'soul', which comes from Allah and will return to Allah (Bayakly, 2002). Each person is responsible for taking care of both dimensions — the physical and the spiritual. The spiritual dimension is deemed to be metaphysical, 'it is alive in our conscience and reflected in our manners, behaviour and character' (Bayakly, 2002, p. 1). Spirituality is informed by the Quran, the Word of God. Five pillars underpin Muslim spirituality: declaration of faith, five daily prayers, fasting in the month of Ramadan, annual poor-dues, and, once in a lifetime pilgrimage to Mecca.

There are also a number of nonfaith spiritualities including ecospirituality and secular spirituality. Some environmentalists contend that the sacred is an essential dimension of the environmental movement. This is sometimes expressed in the urge to protect particular sites from destruction by developers, construction companies and agribusinesses. In some respects this response resembles indigenous spirituality, which proclaims the earth as sacred Mother and indigenous people see their identity rooted in their land. The underpinning inspiration and common teaching of many spiritualities and religions is the basic and variously expressed message, 'Do unto others as you would have them do unto you' (Jeffrey, 2003, p. 1), and a shared key premise underpinning the environmental movement is that human nature is an integral part of our environment, and not its master.

Some writers caution against confusing spirituality and spiritualism, 'Without intellectual accountability, "spirituality" is adrift and free to meander into "spiritualism" …' (Ransom, (2002, p. 16). The notion of each person caring for the soul referred to above is reinforced as: '… a certain attentiveness to life — an attentiveness which contains within itself a certain desire, certain hopefulness, a certain anticipation. Spirituality is attention combined with intention' (Ransom, 2002, p. 17).

This perspective suggests that spirituality, as described above, shares some of the components of an intellectual discipline. It possesses elements of tradition, mystery, reflection and the search for understanding and wisdom and acknowledges the complementary processes of 'being' and 'becoming'. Thus spirituality in its various forms can exist as an integral and pervasive essence for setting life directions and values, and for the way we lead our lives, irrespective of the precise source of the particular kind of spirituality. Spirituality, unlike religion, has its origins in our humanity: it is an essential aspect of being human.

Perspectives on Leadership

During the last decade much has been written about leadership in general and educational leadership in particular (Carlin & Neidhart, 2004; Cranston & Ehrich, 2007; Duignan, 2006; Kriger & Seng, 2005; Sinclair, 2007, Starratt, 2003; Wheatley, 2006). Many writers stress the belief that leadership emerges from the person's inner core (Australian Principals Association Professional Development Council, 2007; Covey, 1992; McCrimmon, 2008). Leadership is not merely a package of competencies; rather it is 'a transformative way of thinking, feeling, and functioning, a way of life, a way of being' (Parikh, 2005, p. 3). A number of authors have distilled the attributes and practices of successful leaders. Kouzes and Posner summarise these as:

- challenging the process, refusing to accept the status quo
- inspiring a shared vision, with the emphasis on sharing
- enabling others to act (leaders shun the word 'I' in favour of 'we')
- modelling the way (their behaviour exhibits integrity)
- encouraging the heart (they empower and celebrate). (2002, p. 9)

Some writers isolate a special capacity of effective leaders that seems to give life to an institution or organisation: '… so spiritual dimensions of leadership are its very life-breath …' (Filson, 2006, p. 1). The 'word "inspire" means "to breathe" or "breathe life into" and it seems a powerful metaphor for the day-to-day work that educational leaders do' (Cawsey, 2008, p. 5). A related characteristic is 'presence', described as an aura, occasionally powerful, more often subtle, that many notice. Leadership as 'presence' calls forth the best in every employee and provides the context for its manifestation: 'A response-full life provides the spiritual and intentional roadmap not only for relationship health, but because of that, for organizational health and profit' (Rock & Smith, 2004, p. 4).

Sergiovanni, (2005) and Mant (1997) contend that effective leaders construct their leadership philosophy and practice around particular virtues. Sergiovanni (2005) goes so far as to identify the promotion of virtues as an essential component of a school's culture: 'Teachers and students alike seek frameworks and norm systems that help them sort out how they fit into a school's culture. Cultural frameworks are sources of sense making and meaning that all of us need' (p. 112).

Virtues are a significant area of leadership research and practice. Some writers describe leadership as a question of 'character' (Havard, 2007), others refer to the notion of personal and communal 'human flourishing' (Aristotle, in Brookshire, 2001), and Greenleaf (2002) promotes the practice of 'servant leadership'. Virtues are not just dispositions, they are a source of intentional, consistent action: '... virtues are more than simple values, they are real dynamic forces — notice the word's Latin root, "virtus", meaning strength or power. Each, when practised habitually, progressively enhances one's capacity to act' (Havard, 2007, p. 2).

While there are several classic lists of virtues, the following virtues are the more common: courage, justice, prudence, self-discipline, humility, generosity and hope (Sergiovanni, 2005). It is through modelling, practice and reflection on these virtues that the culture of institutions is observed, experienced and sustained. Leaders at all levels have the responsibility to promote and reinforce the virtue constituents of a school's mission and culture.

Differences in leadership approaches — autocratic, democratic, transactional, transformational, and more recently, transcendental — have also been a key focus of leadership research. These characteristics are not mutually exclusive but, rather, represent a repertoire of leadership capabilities that leaders mix and match according to the situation, in order to achieve intended outcomes effectively, while at the same time upholding core values and promoting healthy relationships: 'The metaphors of transactional, transformational and transcendent leadership provide a map to understanding the evolution and theory of practice of governance' (Gardiner, 2006, p. 62).

While transactional leadership focuses on the effective management of the status quo, according to Burns (1978, p. 462), transformational leadership is ennobling, 'lifting people into their better selves'. Advocates of transcendental leadership claim that spirituality is a key characteristic (Thompson, 2000). Transcendental leaders tend to be reflective, work out of core values, encourage meaningful dialogue, and invite others to work with them for a better world. Transcendental leadership seeks to renew society: '... what matures is a system or framework within which continuous innovation, renewal and rebirth can occur '(Gardner, 1963, p. 5).

Leadership in faith-based schools is informed by the key teachings of the particular faith, '… the fundamental beliefs, values and relationships of the faith tradition' (Statnick, 2004, p. 14).

The rapidly changing context of many western countries has become increasingly complex and challenging for school leaders:

> … the perceived decline over the last 20 years of the Church, neighbourhood and family has led to the expectation that schools take on more responsibilities and adopt a more holistic approach to education, embracing the social, spiritual, pastoral and moral dimensions. (Gipson, 2003, p. 1)

The introduction of 'self-management' in schools and the requirement of increased accountability for student learning outcomes (Gunter & Fitzgerald, 2007), in the late 1980s and early 1990s, has also created ever greater challenges. The policy of self-management significantly increased the managerial responsibilities of school leaders (Walker, 2002). Many felt unprepared for this role and many others simply did not want the responsibility (Smyth, 2003). With increased emphasis on assessment and reporting, rather than on teaching and learning, many teachers also saw their roles as different to earlier times. To many principals and teachers alike, this was yet another imposition on top of numerous others. Some authors described policies like self-management as 'cultural agents' whereby 'whole populations can be constructed as new kinds of "citizens" and subjects of power, often in ways of which they are not fully conscious' (Shore & Wright, 1997, p. 24).

Many school leaders and teachers believe that these policy changes, with their emphasis on management and accountability, threatened collegial relationships and created divisions between leaders (managers) and teachers. The workplace called school has come to be characterised by a managerial climate with staff as producers of human capital, rather than an educational institution staffed by professionals with a high level of trust, cooperation and imagination (Ball, 2004). The policy has also helped to increase parent, social and political leader expectations and demands on schools. Government policy reinforces education as a central platform for building a strong national economy within a competitive global world. This has resulted in the intellectual and human capital dimensions of education allocated higher priority (Dawkins,

2007; Turner & Seemann, 2004), and a lower priority assigned to aspects of a more liberal education focusing on the whole person.

Such perceptions threaten the key fundamentals of effective leadership relationships. Experienced leaders understand that, while authority and coercion may sometimes achieve compliance, they are unlikely to be conducive to a positive work environment, where staff feel valued and supported and consequently, are willing to make a deep commitment to the mission of the school. (The authors' use of 'mission' includes terms such as 'charter' and 'philosophy'.) It is clear that disenchantment exists in many areas of contemporary leadership (Wheatley, 2006; Sinclair, 2006). Consequently, there is a longing for a new kind of leadership — one that recognises the various and complex dimensions of human beings as people with the capacity to seek deep meaning and a desire to work for a better world for all. Today, above all, 'there is a widespread longing for leaders of substance, leaders with a touch of nobility, vision, and transcendence about them, leaders with soul' (Beare, 2006, p. 5).

However, school leaders are generally walking very tense tightropes. Within the policy framework of individualism and competition, and with schools being regarded as a primary agency for social change by governments, employers, and even families, leaders are continually confronted and expected to deal with, and even to resolve, complex dilemmas that frequently involve a choice between two rights or entitlements (Duignan, 2006). Given the increasing number and diversity of students' needs in most of today's schools, as well as the responsibility of leaders to support and enhance the capacities of teachers, demands on leaders have probably never been greater. To build cohesive, sustainable school communities under these circumstances remains an ongoing challenge.

In recent years, system authorities to support today's leaders and assist in the development of leaders for the future have constructed various leadership frameworks. These frameworks attempt to map the range of complex tasks, which are part of school leadership in the 21st century. Bolman and Deal (2003) claim that, to effectively deal with the complexity and scope of modern schools, today's leaders must understand and be able to work across four frames of reference — structural, human resource, political and symbolic. Of particular relevance to this discussion is the 'Symbolic Frame', which focuses on '... how humans make sense of the messy, ambiguous world in which they live. Meaning, belief and faith are its central concerns. Meaning is not given to us; we have to create it' (p. 240).

The Department of Education Victoria (2007) recently developed a leadership framework, which was based on Sergiovanni's (1984) hierarchy of leadership forces. It comprises three major components: leadership domains (technical, human, educational, symbolic and cultural), capabilities and profiles. In 2004, the Queensland Catholic Education Commission also developed a leadership framework particularly suited to Catholic schools. This framework comprised six leadership dimensions: (inner, interpersonal, organisational, educative, faith and community); and four capabilities: (personal, relational, professional, missional). All these frameworks recognise what may be called a spiritual dimension in school leadership today. Drawing on the frameworks described above, it is clear that the spiritual dimension of leadership is confirmed as an integral and respected element of school leadership, and one which might make an important contribution that enables education to work towards the creation of a more compassionate and tolerant world.

The Continuing Development and Review of the Spiritual Dimension of School Leadership

Spiritual leadership, irrespective of its source, is not just another dimension or frame; it is a core component of leaders' beliefs, values and actions (Neidhart, 2000; Ransom, 2002; Schneiders, 1989). Many leaders who seek to make a difference and to leave the world in a better state than when they arrived, have a sense of vocation or calling, even though they may not recognise it as such. Vocation is an ongoing quest of learning: '... a lifelong process of discovering who you are, who you desire to become, and how you want to live your life' (Braskamp & Wergin, 2008, p. 1). This quest is very much an inner journey of reflection on one's values and purpose and how these can be used to improve the life chances and wellbeing of particular groups; and how giving a large part of one's life to leadership, can enable the enactment of servant leadership. It is the complementary process of 'being' and 'becoming'; what some writers call 'formation of the authentic self' (Duignan et al., 2003, p. 14).

Like teaching, leadership is an intentional process. It involves articulating and living the core values that underpin the school's mission. The way leaders operate, show respect, and resolve disputes and dilemmas communicates who they are and what is important to them. There must be a strong and consistent level of alignment between rhetoric and practice. When working with staff, students and parents, leaders must regularly name the values articulated in their school mission, which has informed their decisions and guided their actions. Thus the mission, with its purpose and expressed core values, becomes the leadership compass guiding their decision-making and that becomes their reference point for evaluating integrity. In this way the entire school community can gain deeper insights into the process of living the mission. Unfortunately, judgments and decisions are often made in the midst of 'hot action' when several decisions compete for quick resolution and relevant information is incomplete, 'Skills and competencies are thus at the heart of these holistic human experiences, but although they are necessary for successful practical judgements, by themselves they are an insufficient account of such judgements' (Beckett, 2005, p. 2).

This is the reason Duignan (2006) and others argue that leaders need capabilities in order to develop, review and validate practical real-time decisions according to a specific mission and context. Reflection and analysis of key practical judgments and critical incidents in context is imperative, for the purpose of learning as well as to ensure alignment between mission, values and practice. However, scheduling and protecting time for these processes is a challenge in the busyness of today's schools. Wheatley (2004, p. 2) agrees:

> We are not learning from all the experiences we are having. I think a major act of leadership right now, call it a radical act, is to create the places and processes so people can actually learn together, using our experiences.

Intentional leadership gives priority to reviewing all major decisions, checking for integrity, consistency and alignment with core values. These review processes, which reflect on practical judgments and decisions over time, are a very effective investment in the development of leadership skills and insights, and ensure consistency across the school. Scheduling priority time to reflect on relevant evidence can be a very powerful tool to identify the relationship between effective practice and improved outcomes. These processes can also help to highlight practices and outcomes that are not working as intended, and/or are not well aligned with the school's mission and culture. It is this process of deep and purposeful analysis and reflection on structures, programs, pedagogy and culture that engages leaders in applying their leadership frameworks to ensure decisions are aligned with, and communicate, the school's core purposes and values. In a study of Catholic head teachers in Britain, Grace (2002) comments that they have '… in the main, attempted to maintain the mission integrity of Catholic schooling in the face of many external pressures which could compromise that integrity' (p. 237).

A context of competition, markets and individualism can make the exercise of spiritual and authentic leadership extremely challenging (Duignan, 2006; Grace, 2002). Because spiritual and authentic leaders are mindful of the needs and entitlements of all students and their families, they work purposefully to ensure the educational experience will assist students to overcome barriers and to develop the capabilities and resilience needed to become competent and discerning learners and citizens. Leaders at all levels are encouraged to explore, refine and clarify their own inner leadership as a basis for working with all constituents to shape a mission not only informed by relevant government policies but also reflecting local needs and preferences. In this way, spiritual leadership seeks to redress disadvantage and restore voice and capability. In this way spiritual leadership aims to work in pursuit of a more just society.

Conclusion

This chapter has explored the concept of spiritual leadership and how it can contribute to Australian schools at the beginning of the 21st century. Many writers have commented that, in today's rapidly changing and increasingly challenging world, there appears to be a loss of trust, hope and meaning, so essential to wellbeing for individuals and for society. Traditional institutions like families and churches are no longer adequate anchors or guides for many people trying make sense of the world. Consequently, the capacity to build and sustain trusted relationships has diminished, and has resulted in governments, churches and families expecting schools to take increasing responsibility for functions, which in the past were largely theirs. This has occurred simultaneously with governments imposing higher workloads and demanding more rigorous accountability. The cumulative effect of this movement has threatened the enthusiasm and resilience of teachers and leaders alike and, above all, the general wellbeing of the school workforce.

Spiritual leaders encourage the use of constructive critique. Such critique, based on the values that underpin the just society, sets out to question current practice and build a sense of renewal, seeking better ways to manage challenge and tension. Spiritual leaders endeavour to create space and energy to sustain hope and trust, and nurture healthy relationships. The emphasis on the spiritual complements other leadership dimensions, enhancing transformation and discernment. Ultimately, it aims to improve staff and student capability to embrace the opportunities and dilemmas presented by the 21st century. Thus 'spirituality and consciousness are not irrational, "far out" beliefs but, rather, the core of dynamic evolutionary systems and, this, must be included in analysis and practice of organizational design, change and management' (Banner & Gagne, 1995, in Korac-Kakabadse, Kouzmin, & Kakabadse, 2002, p. 166).

Spiritual leaders are committed to developing a legacy with students and staff for their life journeys. In this way, they reinforce the holistic nature of education — intellectual, physical, emotional, ethical and spiritual development. In short, such leaders emphasise an unshakeable belief in an education not only about 'doing' and 'having', but one which also addresses 'being' and 'becoming'. Spiritual leaders not only articulate this belief, but model it in their practice.

References

Angel, R.B. (2004, November). *Educational leadership frameworks: Looking to archetypal images for twenty-first century wisdom.* Paper presented to the University Council for Educational Administration Convention, Kansas City, Missouri.

Australian Principals Association Professional Development Council. (2007). *Learn: Lead: Succeed.* Canberra, Australia.

Australian Public Service Commission. (2006). Work–life balance in 'Equity and diversity' (Ch 5). *State of the Service Report.* Canberra, Australia: Author.

Ball, S.J. (2004, June). *Education for sale! The commodification of everything.* Kings Annual Education Lecture, University of London.

Bates, R. (2003, October). *Can we live together? The ethics of leadership and the learning community.* Paper presented at the BELMAS Annual Conference, Milton Keynes, UK.

Bayakly, N. (2002). An overview of Muslim spirituality. From a series presented by the Center for Spiritual Growth, Memphis, Tennessee. Retrieved April 17, 2008. from http://www.explorefaith.org/living_spirituality/following_a_sacred_path/muslim_spiritual

Beare, H. (2006). Leadership for a new millennium. *Australian Council for Educational Leadership Monograph, No. 38.* Hawthorn, Victoria, Australia: Australian Council for Educational Leaders.

Beckett, D. (2005). *Being human, and human beings: Agency at work.* Draft paper for PESA (Philosophy of Education Society of Australia), Hong Kong, July. Retrieved June 20, 2008, from www.pesa.org.au/html/documents/2005.../Paper-50__Beckett.doc

Birch, C., & Paul, D. (2003). *Life and work: Challenging economic man.* Sydney, Australia: University of New South Wales Press.

Bolman, L.G., & Deal, T.E. (2003). *Reframing organizations: Artistry, choice and leadership* (3rd ed.). San Francisco: Jossey-Bass.

Braskamp, L.A., & Wergin, J.F. (2008). Inside-Out leadership. *Liberal Education, 94*(1), 30–35.

Brookshire, M.S. (2001). Virtue, ethics and servant leadership. Centre for Ethics, Emory University. Retrieved August 11, 2008, from http://www.ethics.emory. edu/news/archives/ 000165.html

Burns, J.M. (1978). *Leadership.* New York: Harper & Row.

Carlin, P., & Neidhart, H. (2004, October). *A framework for the moral development of professional educators.* Paper presented at the Leadership and Values Conference, Barbados.

Catholic Education Commission of Victoria. (2005). *Leadership in Catholic schools: Development framework and standards of practice.* Melbourne, Australia: Author.

Cawsey, C. (2008). I think I would rather inspire than expire. *The Australian Educational Leader, 30*(2), 5–7.

Chittister, J. (2006). In the garden of spirituality. *The wild reed.* Retrieved August 21, 2008, from http://thewildreed.blogspot.com/2006/12/in-garden-spirituality-joan.html

Covey, S.R. (2008, July 17). *Voices on leadership* [Video series]. Online with The Washington Post. Retrieved May 23, 2008, from www.washingtonpost.com/ wpdyn/content/discussion//2008/07/16/D12008071602427.html

Covey, S.R. (1992). *Principle-centred leadership.* London: Simon & Schuster.

Cranston, N.C., & Ehrich, L.C. (2007). *What is this thing called leadership? Prominent Australians tell their stories.* Brisbane, Queensland, Australia: Australian Academic Press.

Dawkins, P. (2007, November). *Human capital and early childhood development.* Address to CEET 11th Annual National Conference, Monash University, Melbourne.

Department of Education. (2007). *The developmental framework for school leaders.* Melbourne, Australia: Office of School Education.

Duignan, P. (2006). *Educational leadership: Key challenges and ethical tensions.* Port Melbourne, Victoria, Australia: Cambridge University Press.

Duignan, P., Burford, C., Cresp, M., d'Arbon, T., Fagan, M., Frangoulis, M., et al. (2003, February). *Contemporary challenges and implications for leaders in frontline human service organisations.* The SOLR Project Executive Summary, Flagship for Catholic Educational Leadership, Strathfield, Australia.

Eckersley, R. (2005). What is wellbeing? *Wellbeing manifesto*. Retrieved May 9, 2008, from http://www.wellbeingmanifesto.net/wellbeing.htm

Edgar, D. (2002). *Early childhood development and education*. Australian Fabian Society, Autumn Lectures. Retrieved August 26, 2008, from www.fabian.org.au/default.asp?pageId=932

Edwards, B. (2008). *The decline of NZ societal organisations*. Retrieved August 23, 2008, from http://liberation.typepad.com/liberation/2008/04/third-parties-3.html

Filson, B. (2006). Leadership, tribal spiritual wisdom and the leadership talk. *Buzzle.com*. Retrieved March 4, 2008, from http://www.buzzle.com/editorials/5–16–2006–96348.asp

Flagship for Catholic Educational Leadership. (2004). *A framework for leadership in Queensland Catholic schools: A report*. Brisbane, Australia: Australian Catholic University.

Furedi, F. (2006). Five years after 9/11: The search for meaning goes on. *Spiked*. Retrieved March 6, 2008, from http://www.spiked-online.com/index.php?

Gardiner, J.J. (2006, Spring). Transactional, transformational and transcendent leadership: Metaphors mapping the evolution of the theory and practice of governance, Kravis Leadership Institute *Leadership Review*, 6, 62-76.

Gardner, J.W. (1963). *Self-renewal: The individual and the innovative society*. New York: The Free Press.

Gilbertson, G. (2006). *Citizenship in a globalised world*. Washington, DC.: Migration Policy Institute.

Gipson, S. (2003). *Issues of ICT, school reform and learning-centred school design*. Research Associate Report, Nottingham, UK: National College for School Leadership.

Goleman, D., Boyatzis, R., & McKee, A. (2002). *The new leaders: Transforming the art of leadership into the science of results*. London: Little & Brown.

Grace, G. (2002). *Catholic schools: Mission, markets and morality*, London: RoutledgeFalmer.

Greenleaf, R.K. (2002). *Servant leadership: A journey into the nature of legitimate power and greatness*. New Jersey: Paulist Press.

Gunter, H., & Fitzgerald, T. (2007). Leading learning and leading teachers: Challenges for schools in the 21st century. *Leading and Managing*, 13(1), 1–15

Havard, A. (2007). *Leadership for everyone. Interview with author by Miriam Diez I Bosch*. Retrieved June 5, 2008, from http://www.zenit.org./article-21334?1

Jeffrey, S. (2003, August). Spirituality and the environment. *Gatherings: Seeking Ecopsychology*, 8.

Korac-Kakabadse, N., Kouzmin, A., & Kakabadse, A. (2002). Spirituality and leadership praxis. *Journal of Managerial Psychology*, 17(3), 165–182.

Kouzes J.M., & Posner, B.Z. (2002). *The leadership challenge*. San Francisco: Jossey-Bass.

Kriger, M., & Seng, Y. (2005). Leadership with inner meaning: A contingency theory of leadership based on the worldviews of five religions. *The Leadership Quarterly, 16,* 771–806.

London, S. (2008). *The new science of leadership: An interview with Margaret Wheatley.* Retrieved April 8, 2008, from http://www.scottlondon.com/interviews/wheatley.html

Mackay, H. (2005, March). *Social disengagement: A breeding ground for fundamentalism.* Annual Manning Clark Lecture, National Library of Australia, Canberra, Australia.

Mackay, H. (1999). *Turning point: Australians choosing their future.* Sydney, Australia: Pan Macmillan.

Mant, A. (1997). *Intelligent leadership.* St Leonards, NSW, Australia: Allen & Unwin.

McCrimmon, M. (2008). Kouzes and Posner on leadership. *Ezine @rticles,* 13 January. Retrieved June 27, 2008, from http://EzineArticles.com/?expert=Mitch McCrimmon

Moore, T. (1992). *Care of the soul: How to add depth and meaning to your everyday life.* London: Piatkus.

Mitroff, I. I., & Denton, E. (1999). A study of spirituality in the workplace. *Sloan Management Review, 40*(4), 83–92

Muesse. M.W. (2002). *What does it mean to lead a spiritual life? Insights from different faith traditions.* Retrieved June 2, 2008, from http://www.explorefaith.org

Neidhart, H. (2000). Leadership spirituality in the context of Catholic education. In P. Duignan & T. d'Arbon (Eds.), *Leadership in Catholic education: 2000 and beyond.* Canberra, Australia: National Catholic Education Commission.

O'Murchu, D. (1997). *Reclaiming spirituality,* New York: The Crossroad Publishing Company.

O'Neill, O. (2002). *A question of trust.* Reith Lectures, BBC Radio. Retrieved July 30, 2008, from www.bbc.co.uk/radio4/reith 2002/

OECD (2007). *Babies and bosses–Reconciling work and family life: A synthesis of findings for OECD Countries.* Paris: Directorate for Employment, Labour and Social Affairs.

Parikh, J. (2005). The Zen of management maintenance: Leadership starts with self-discovery. *Working Knowledge for Business Leaders.* Harvard Business School. Retrieved May 9, 2008, from http://hbswk.hbs.edu/

Pont, B., Nusche, D., & Hopkins, D. (2008). *Improving school leadership: Case studies & concepts for systemic action.* Executive Summaries. OECD, Directorate for Education, Education & Training Policy Division. Retrieved October 10, 2008, from http://www.oecd.org/edu/schoolleadership

Principals Australia. (2007). *Learn: Lead: Succeed. A resource to support the building of leadership in Australian schools.* Retrieved March 18, 2008, from http://www.leaderslead.edu.au/servlet/Web?s=1890876&p=LeadersLead_LLS

Putnam, R.D. (1996). *The decline of civil society: How come? So what?* The John L. Manion Lecture, Canadian Centre for Management Development, Ottawa, Canada.

Ransom, D. (2002). *Across the great divide: Bridging spirituality and religion today.* Strathfield, New South Wales, Australia: St Paul's Publication.

Rock, M.E., & Smith, B. (2004, November 1–7). The new balance sheet: Leadership as presence. *Magazine,* Canadaone, November. Retrieved June 5, 2009, from http://www.canadaone.com/ezine/nov04/ leadership_presence.html

Rolheiser, R. (1998). *Seeking spirituality.* London: Hodder & Stoughton.

Schneiders, S. (1989). Spirituality in the academy, *Theological Studies, 50*(2), 676–697.

Schneiders, S. (2000). Religion vs spirituality: Strangers, rivals or partners. *Spiritus: A Journal of Christian Spirituality, 6*(2), 163–185.

Sergiovanni, T.J. (1984). *Handbook for effective department leadership: Concepts and practices in today's secondary schools.* Boston: Allyn & Bacon.

Sergiovanni, T.J. (2005). The virtues of leadership. *The Educational Forum. 69*(2), 112–123.

Shore, C & Wright, S. (Eds). (1997). *Anthropology of policy.* London: Routledge.

Sinclair, A. (2006). *Leadership for the disillusioned: Moving beyond myths and heroes to leading that liberates.* Crows Next, NSW, Australia: Allen & Unwin.

Sinclair, A. (2007). *Leading with spirit.* The Australian Women & Leadership Forum, October. Retrieved April 20, 2007, from http://www.womens forum.com.au/ index

Smyth, J. (2003). A High school teacher's experience of local school management: A case of the 'system behaving badly towards teachers. *Australian Journal of Education, 47,* 265–282.

Starratt, R.J. (2003). *Centering educational administration: Cultivating meaning, community, responsibility,* Mahwah, NJ: Lawrence Erlbaum.

Statnick, R.A. (2004). Elements of spiritual leadership. *Human Development. 25*(4), 14–24.

Sunderland, S. (2007). Post secular nation: or how 'Australian Spirituality' privileges a secular, white, Judeo-Christian culture. *Transforming Cultures eJournal, 2*(1), 57–77.

Tacey, D. (2002, January). *The rising interest in spirituality today.* Extract of a presentation given at the Convention of the Theosophical Society in Australia, Adelaide.

Thompson, M.C. (2000). *The congruent life: Following the inward path.* San Francisco, CA: Jossey-Bass.

Turner, A., & Seemann, K. (2004, December). *Innovation education.* Proceedings of the 3rd Biennial International Conference on Technology Education Research 'Learning for Innovation in Technology Education'. Surfers Paradise, Queensland, Australia.

Useem, M. (2007). The world economic forum: A call to exercise global leadership, not just self interest. *The Huffington Post.* Retrieved April 22, 2008, from http://www.huffingtonpost.com/michael-useem/the-world-economic-forum_b_40743.html

Walker, E.M. (2002). The politics of school-based management: Understanding the process of devolving authority in urban school districts. *Education Policy Analysis Archives, 10(33)*, Retrieved 18 July, 2008, from http://epaa.asu.edu/epaa/v10n33.html

Wheatley, M.J. (2002). Leadership in turbulent times is spiritual, Retrieved April 18, 2008, from www.margaretwheatley.com/articles/turbulenttimes.html

Wheatley, M.J. (2006, Summer). Leadership lessons for the real world. *Leader to Leader Magazine.* Retrieved July 29, 2008, from http://www.margaretwheatley.com/articles/ leadershiplessons.html

Wheatley, M.J. (2004, March). Is the pace of life hindering our ability to manage? *Management Today*, Australian Institute of Management. Retrieved July 29, 2008, from http://www.margaretwheatley.com/articles/thepaceoflife.html

▶▶▶◀◀◀

CHAPTER 6

Leading Genuine Parent–School Partnerships

Gayle Spry and John Graham

Traditionally, there has been a clear demarcation line between parents and schools. Parents, as the first educators of the child, took primary responsibility for the social and moral development of the child, with the school being primarily responsible for the development of academic knowledge and work-related skills. Accepting this demarcation line, parents become 'the teacher's ideal silent partner — pushing the pupil to work harder at home, while maintaining a respectful distance from the teacher and his or her expertise at school' (Hargreaves, 1999, p. 2). Yet, this silent partnership approach became increasingly untenable over the last quarter of the 20th century, as educational researchers identified the vital role of parents in schooling. For example, an Australian study, drawing on the case-studies of 61 schools, identified that partnerships between families and schools can:

- improve educational outcomes for students
- contribute to the building of social capital in the community
- positively alter school culture
- simulate self-growth among parents
- enhance the professional rewards for principals and school staff. (Saulwick Muller Social Research, 2006, p. 14)

At the same time, this study also identified just how 'embryonic is the implementation of family–school partnerships' (p. 6). Consequently, it concluded that the parent–school partnership:

> … is a bold concept requiring substantial cultural change, both within schools and in attitudes to schools. Generally speaking, this cultural change is only just beginning. A long journey lies ahead if it is to be accomplished widely, but the educational and social goods demonstrated by many of the projects examined here suggest that the journey is well worth making. (p. 6)

To support this 'cultural change' and the 'journey' ahead, this chapter will explore the past, present and future of this partnership. In short, we will reflect on the journey so far in terms of policy and practice, review theoretical developments along the way, examine a practical initiative in the field and, finally, consider a way forward.

The Journey So Far in Policy and Practice

It seems that we have been on this journey towards genuine parent–school partnerships for some time, at least 30 years. The conversation regarding the role of parents in Australian schools was stimulated by the report titled *Australian Schools: Report of the Interim Committee for the Australian Schools Commission* (Karmel, 1973). Seeking to ensure the application of democratic principles to education provision, this committee determined that 'opportunities will need to be open to parents and to the community at large to increase their competence to participate in the control of schools' (p. 11). Consequently, the practical reform initiatives (e.g., *Disadvantaged Schools Program, Innovation Program, Participation and Equity Program*) that followed 'aimed to empower parents by involving them in making decisions aimed at promoting equity, equality and social justice' (O'Donoghue & Dimmock, 1998, p. 19).

Around this time, parent–school partnerships were described in terms of *parent involvement* and *parent participation*:

> [Parent] involvement refers to the process which guarantees a role for the community, especially parents in school, but where the nature and the extent of this role is defined by the professional group in the school. Individuals and groups involved in the school are not given responsibility for initial decisions ... The term [parent participation] refers to the process in which members of the school community have an active role in decision-making over a wide range of issues, including policy, staffing and staff development, budget, grounds and buildings, management of resources, and the school curriculum. (Beazley, 1984, pp. 257–258)

Making this distinction between 'parent involvement' and 'parent participation' is significant as these two terms continue, even today, to describe how the notion of parent–school partnerships may be interpreted in practice.

Interest in parent involvement and parent participation continued into the 1980s and 1990s. However, the forces behind the push for this participation began to change. For example, *The Strengthening Australia's Schools* Report (Dawkins, 1988), in the section headed 'Maximising Our Investment in Education', called for 'stronger links between schools, the community, the labour market and other educational agencies' (p. 6). This view of the relationship between school and the community was justified on economic grounds rather than democratic principles (Marginson, 1997). A decade on, in 1999, *The Adelaide Declaration on National Goals for Schooling in the Twenty-First Century* (Ministerial Council on Education, Employment, Training and Youth Affairs, 1999) called for 'further strengthening schools as learning communities where teachers, students and their families work in partnership with business, industry and the wider community' (p. 1). This time the emphasis was on student learning and there was a keen interest in achieving quality education in response to the demands of the economy.

To fully appreciate the significance of this policy direction, we need to situate this development within the broad reform and restructuring movement that swept through the public sector, including public education, in the 1980s and 1990s.

> Since the 1980s, every feature of the public sector in Australia has undergone extensive reform; cultures, structures and processes bear little resemblance to those of earlier change initiatives. These reforms are based on the assumptions that the application of market theory and private sector management principles, procedures and structures to the public sector will result in increased efficiencies, improved quality of service and greater accountability. (Sachs, 2003, p. 20)

Here there is a firm belief that 'good management could solve any problem' and 'that practices which are appropriate for the conduct of private sector enterprises can also be applied to the public sector' (p. 26). Here 'management is inherently good, managers are heroes, managers should be given room and autonomy and other groups should accept their authority' (p. 26).

Thus, Sachs (2003) argues that the educational reforms and restructuring of the 1980s and 1990s have encouraged the emergence of 'managerial professionalism' (pp. 25–27). This development assumes a 'professional who clearly meets corporate goals set elsewhere, manages a range of students well and documents their achievements and problems for public accountability purposes' (Brennan, 1996, p. 22). Consequently,

> Teachers are placed in a long line of authority in terms of accountability … that stretches through the principal, the district/regional office, to the central office. [Furthermore] principals have moved from the role of senior colleague to one of institutional manager. (Sachs, 2003, p. 27)

Logically, in this managerial environment, parent–school relationships become another aspect of school life for the professional to 'manage'. While the role of the parent in school life was guaranteed, the nature and the extent of this role are defined by the professional group in the school and education system. In this way, Karmel's concern for equity, equality and social justice is put aside as the inherent goodness of the parent–school partnership is replaced by a 'corporate form of devolution' (Marginson, 1997, p. 167).

Into the new century, the notion of parent–school partnerships continued to be popular with politicians and central agencies and, in line with this understanding, the Minister for Education, Science and Training approved a new category for the *2007 National Awards for Quality Schooling*, namely, *Family–School Partnerships*. In 2008, the Australian Council of State School Organisations (ACSSO) and the Australian Parents Council (APC) in collaboration with the Commonwealth Department of Education, Employment and Workplace Relations established the Family–School and Community Partnership Bureau. The stated aim of this bureau is to 'help Australian schools, families and communities to build sustainable, collaborative, productive relationships' (Family–School and Community Partnership Bureau, 2008).

So this is where we have come to. Genuine parent–school partnerships are now described in terms of sustainable, collaborative and productive relationships. To fully appreciate the possibilities for moving towards this understanding of parent–school partnerships, we now examine some of the theoretical developments around this topic.

Theoretical Developments

When it comes to studying the role of parents in schools, the most systematic research and development around this topic has been conducted by Epstein and her colleagues (2001). Based on this research and development, Epstein (2001) argues that:

> Research suggests that 'partnership' is a better approach. In partnership, educators, families, and community members work together to share information, guide students, solve problems, and celebrate

successes. Partnership recognizes the shared responsibilities of the home, school and community for children's learning and development. (p. 4)

Thus Epstein (2001) advances a 'model of overlapping spheres of influence' (pp. 27–31) that illustrates the overlapping relationship between family, school and community. Focusing in on the role of parents within this relationship, Epstein (2001) groups school–family partnership activities into a typology consisting of six categories, including parenting, communicating, volunteering, learning at home, decision-making and collaborating with the community. To further describe each of these categories, she offers sample practices for each type of parent involvement. In addition, she proposes that family–school partnerships 'can be built intentionally'(p. 408) and recommends that teachers and school administrators design 'a comprehensive program of partnership' (p. 414) that includes opportunities for six types of parental involvement. Finally, she recommends the establishment of 'action teams' of teachers, parents and school administrators, that 'take responsibility for assessing present practices, organising options for new partnerships, implementing selected partnerships, implementing selected activities, evaluating next steps, and continuing to improve and coordinate practices for all six types of involvement' (p. 416).

While not directly focusing on the role of the parent in schools, other researchers (see for example, Hargreaves, 1999; Sachs, 2003) offer insights that both complement and extend Epstein's theoretical work. Motivated by a concern to challenge the dominance of managerial professionalism within education, Hargreaves (1999) argues for a new form of principled, transformative professionalism for educators:

> … transformative professionalism promotes high teaching standards that are used for moral purposes to advance the public good of all children; it stimulates and supports professional learning and collegial interaction to help clarify the moral purposes of teaching and to keep pushing standards higher in order to achieve them; it is open to, inclusive of and actively learns from others (especially parents) who have a stake in children's education and children's futures. (p. 9)

This more principled, transformative professionalism allows for the inclusion of parents in a parent–school partnership to support student learning. For Hargreaves (1999) it is in the 'teachers' own interests' to engage parents as partners as parents represent 'the important allies teachers have in serving those parents own students and in defending themselves against political assaults on their professionalism' (p. 7). Consequently, he calls for 'activist partnerships' (pp. 8–12) in which professionals and parents both individually and collectively act as change agents in support of student learning.

In presenting this idea, Hargreaves draws on Sachs's (1999) notion of the profession taking an 'activist stance' (Hargreaves, 1999, p. 9) in support of student learning. According to Sachs (2003) this activist stance is founded on the traditional moral purpose of teaching and follows the intention of 'changing processes and structures that inhibit democratic impulses, making resources available, and developing net-works to sustain the commitment and energy for educational change' (p. 147). Importantly, Sachs alerts us to the micropolitics and the messiness of particular social relationships and advances the twin concepts of 'active trust' (pp. 140–144) and 'generative politics' (pp. 144–146) as the way forward. Here active trust refers to working rela-tionships in which there are strong 'obligations towards and responsi-bility for' (p. 141) one's colleagues; generative politics encourages individuals and groups to be proactive 'to make thing happen rather than to let things happen to them in the context of overall social con-cerns and goals' (p. 144).

In this way, Sachs (2003) challenges contemporary managerialist professionalism that 'segments education interest groups and hinders rather than facilitates dialogue among them' (pp. 145–146). As an anti-dote to managerialism, she recommends a commitment to the five activist principles of 'learning', 'participation', 'collaboration', 'coopera-tion' and 'activism' (pp. 31–33). Learning, in this instance, has 'per-sonal, professional and political dimensions' (p. 31) and is about building capabilities in support of personal and professional transforma-tion as well as political activism. Participation is evident when profes-sionals see themselves as active agents/leaders/people of influence in the school and the wider community. Collaboration is linked to working collegially with those with an interest in education, including parents. Cooperation requires the development of common language and tech-nology that enables professionals to discuss and document their practice. Finally, activism is associated with moral purpose and professionals entering the public domain and taking up issues that directly and indi-rectly relate to student learning and sustainable education.

As a precursor to taking an activist stance, Sachs (2003) recommends that professionals assume an 'activist identity' (p. 130) that inspires the professional to be 'collaborative, socially critical, future oriented, strategic and tactical' (p. 134). This activist identity stands in direct contrast to the 'entrepreneurial identity', associated with managerial professionalism that is 'individualistic, competitive, controlling and regulative, externally defined and standards-led' (p. 130). Noting the challenge of developing an activist identity in an era of managerial professionalism, Sachs (2003) argues that the formation of an activist identity requires 'a sustained effort to shed the shackles of the past, thereby permitting a transformative attitude towards the future [as well as] overcoming the legitimate or the illegitimate domination of some individuals' (p. 131). To this end, she recommends two interconnecting strategies. Firstly, there is a recommendation for professionals to engage the reflective tool of 'self-narrative' (p. 132) or reflexive storytelling that relates experience with assumptions, values and beliefs. Secondly, there is a recommendation in support of the establishment of 'communities of practice' (p. 133) or action learning projects that support the development of practical knowledge by grounding theoretical knowledge in a specific social, political and professional context.

As this review of the literature shows, there has been significant theoretical development in respect to the role of parents in schools. As a consequence, we now understand the overlapping nature of the relationship among home, school and the community. We also recognise the need to develop conceptual frameworks to describe parental involvement as well as comprehensive programs, action projects and action teams to develop these parent–school partnerships. Finally, we have a deeper appreciation of the possibility for activist partnerships that include parents, as an antidote to the development of managerialist professionalism and managed parent–school partnerships. In this way theoretical developments point the way forward in respect to the role of parents in schools. However, does the theoretical work examined here have practical as well as theoretical significance? Are these theoretical developments meaningful to practitioners? With these questions in mind, we now turn to examining a practical initiative by one education system designed to strengthen parent–school partnerships.

A Practical Initiative

The Catholic Education Office, Lismore, New South Wales, serves 34 primary schools with over 9,000 students and nine secondary schools with over 16,000 students in an area that extends from Tweed Heads in the north, to Laurieton in the south, and west to the foothills of the Great Dividing Range. This system of schools is characterised by relatively decentralised administrative arrangements. Consequently, individual parishes through the parish priest, principal and parent bodies are given a significant degree of autonomy and local responsibility. The principal, with the consent of the parish priest and after consultation with the Catholic Education Office, offers employment to teaching staff on behalf of the Bishop and his trustees. Capital programs for school building projects are initiated and managed at parish school level with support from the Catholic Education Office. Within this decentralised system of schools, the Catholic primary school principal has a leadership role with wide-ranging local community accountability. Within these decentralised administrative arrangements, the Catholic Education Office fulfils a 'service' role to local school communities.

In 1990, the Catholic Education Office appointed a consultant with oversight of the family, school and community services provided by the Catholic Education Office. Within this role, this consultant deployed a wide range of initiatives to develop schools as inclusive communities. These initiatives included the establishment of class parents, a prekindergarten parent induction program, Parish Schools Forum to engage parents in the life of parish school communities, a Diocesan Catholic Schools Parent Assembly organisation to expressly serve the role of parents in Catholic schools. By the mid-1990s, the vision statement for the Lismore Catholic Education clearly stated that Catholic schools were in partnership with parents. On a positive note, at the 1998 and 1999 Annual Principals Conferences, principals expressed their interest in developing parent–school partnerships to support student learning. However, there were also reservations, as these principals felt that they lacked the time and resources to support this innovation. Moreover, they wondered whether the majority of parents really wanted to participate and there were concerns about dealing with demanding parents. A few years on, research (Graham, 2007) confirmed an operational impasse with regard to building genuine parent–school partnership. In particular, this research found that principals wanted partnerships with parents but primarily saw it in terms of a silent relationship in which parents maintained a respectful distance and gave unquestioning support for the work of the professionals in the school.

In the light of this research, in 2008, Lismore Catholic Education sponsored a parent partnership project in support of a transition from silent partnerships to genuine parent–school partnerships. In brief, this parent partnership project was conducted by a project team made up of parent representatives, Catholic Education Office personnel and an academic from Australian Catholic University. Taking note of theoretical developments in respect to parent–school partnerships (Epstein, 2001) the project team accepted that parent–school partnerships 'can be built intentionally' (p. 408) provided there is a commitment to designing 'a comprehensive program of partnership' (p. 414). Moreover, sharing Hargreaves's (1999) and Sachs'(2003) concern that activist partnerships act as an antidote to managerial professionalism, the project team was interested in designing a parent partnership project that was informed by the five activist principles of learning, participation, collaboration, cooperation and activism.

The project moved through a number of stages (Figure 6.1). Here the intention was to develop a conceptual framework for parent partnership that recognised the educational, social and political agendas of key stakeholders (i.e., parents, school personnel, Catholic Education Office staff and clergy) in Lismore Catholic Education. It was understood that the transition to genuine parent–school partnerships would be a long-term commitment with this parent partnership project being the first of many projects to come. For example, at this point, it was accepted that, after the development and publication of a parent partnership framework document, there would need to be a series of projects to support the implementation of this framework document.

- **Stage 1** involved gathering parent wisdom on the role of parents in Catholic education. During this first stage, 34 parent representatives from 21 schools met at the annual 2-day Diocesan Catholic Schools Parent Assembly Conference in order to develop an initial draft of a parent partnership framework. During this conference, parents identified their role in the school in terms of parent leadership and their relationship with school administrators and teachers as co-leadership. Initially, this parent leadership was associated with formal parent positions in their schools, the region and the diocese. However, after reflecting on self-narratives

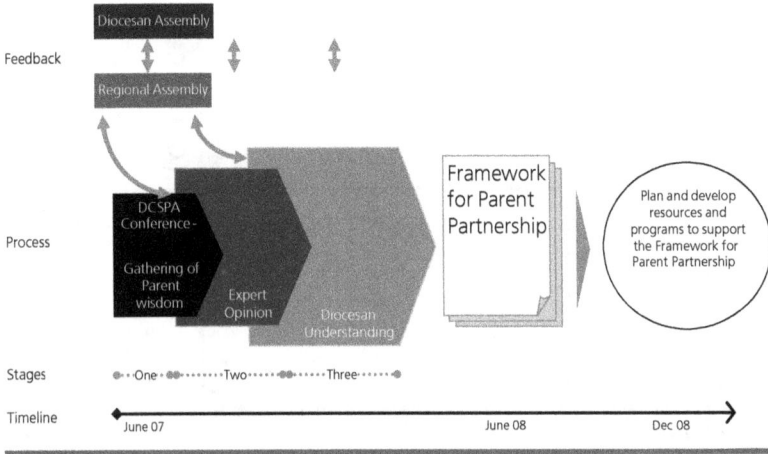

FIGURE 6.1
The design of the parent partnership project.

around their experience as parents in the school, they came to appreciate that parents are leaders, with or without formal parent positions, because they are a major influence in terms of the success of the school and student learning. At the same time, they recognised that parent leaders and school leaders (i.e., school administrators and teachers) shared mutual concerns and needed to work together in a strong partnership in which the capabilities of both parties are respected. This understanding of the nature and purpose of parent–school partnerships is reflected in a figure developed in the course of the conference (Figure 6.2).

In describing the nature and purpose of the parent–school partnership in this way, these parents forecast their desire to act as activist partnerships with professionals. This figure is consistent with descriptions of the 'activist partnership' (Hargreaves, 1999, pp. 8–12) that included notions of parent engagement, leadership, decision-making and moral purpose as well as a commitment to working with professionals.

In addition to describing the nature and purpose of parent–school partnerships in this way, these parents also identified the key domains (i.e., action areas) in which parent leaders are able to work in partnership with professionals. In short, they associated the role of parents within the parent–school partnership with parent leadership in the home, classroom, school as organisation and the local church commu-

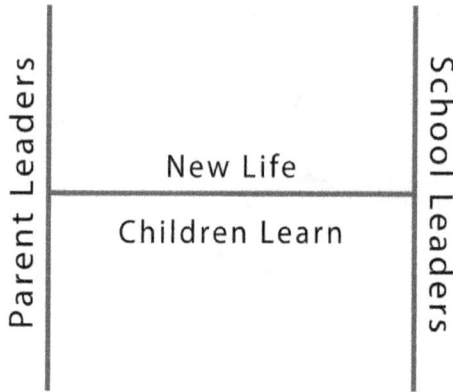

FIGURE 6.2
The nature and purpose of the parent–school partnership in Lismore Catholic Education.

nity. Moreover, they also identified an extensive list of capabilities (i.e., knowledge, skills and attitudes) that parent leaders would require to effectively lead in each of these domains or action areas.

- In **Stage 2**, there was an opportunity to refine the ideas gathered during Stage 1 by listening to 'expert' opinion. Here the project team collected this 'expert opinion' through a review of relevant literature as well as seeking advice around specific questions regarding the domains of parent partnership and the capabilities required of parents working within the parent–school partnership. During this stage there were also opportunities for further feedback from parent participants in Stage 1 with regional parent assemblies acting as the communication conduit. In this way, the project team facilitated a conversation between expert opinion and parent commonsense wisdom and, subsequently, the domains and capabilities of parent partnership were further refined (Figure 6.3).

As Figure 6.3 illustrates, this understanding of the parent–school was informed by a theological appreciation of the role of parents in the Christian family. Flowing out of this understanding, this figure describes the role of parents within parent–school partnerships in terms of four domains or action areas of 'home life', 'school life', 'organisational life' and 'faith life'. In addition, this figure identifies the capabilities (i.e., knowledge, skills and attitudes) required of parents if they are going to be effective in each of these domains. Here it is assumed that

> "The family has the mission to guard, reveal and communicate love , and this is a living reflection of and a real sharing in God 's love for humanity and the love of Christ the Lord for the Church his bride ...
>
> Pope John Paul II (Familiaris Consortio, #17)

	Forming a community of persons	Serving life	Participating in the development of society	Sharing in the life and mission of the Church
Four General Tasks for the Christian Family				
Domains of Parent Partnership	*Home life:* towards a community of persons	*School life:* towards a learning community	*Organisational life:* towards an authentic and sustainable parish school community	*Faith life:* towards the fullness of life
Capabilities of Parent Partnership	Builds a community of love in the home	Serving educational life	Participates in direction setting and responds to the resource needs of the school	Shares in the life and mission of the Church
Knowledge	The characteristics of a good marriage and good parenting	School operations and procedures; the education program and curriculum	Diocesan and parish school policies as well as relevant legislation and regulations	Catholic beliefs and practices
Skills	Parenting skills and relationship building	Able to work collaboratively with teachers	Organisational skills such as prioritising, goal setting and budgeting	Sharing of a faith perspective
Attitudes	Humility, selflessness and commitment	Patience and sensitivity to classroom needs	Openness to alternative views, respect for authority and accountability and a commitment to the stewardship of resources	Openness to the Catholic faith and willingness to participate in the faith life of the parish and its school

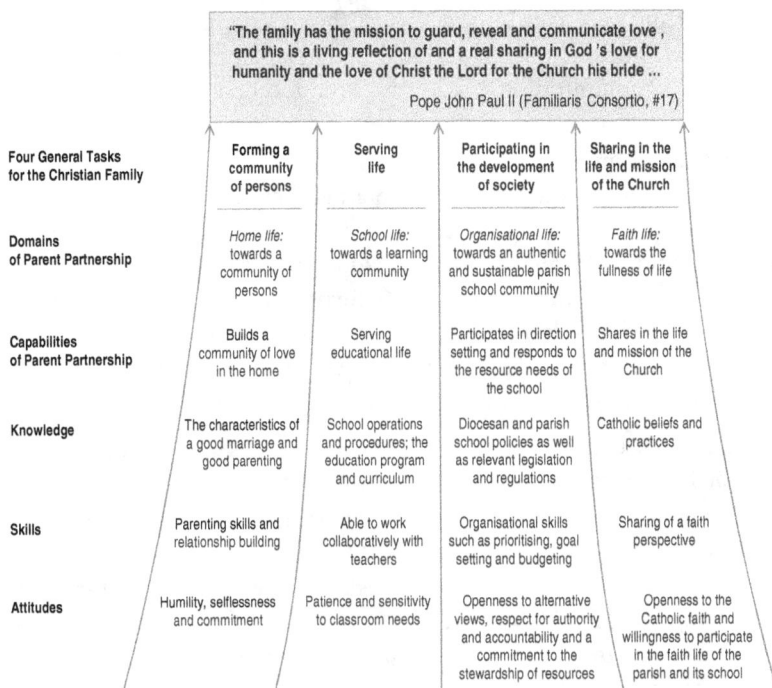

FIGURE 6.3
Parent Partnership Domains and Capabilities (Catholic Education Office, 2008, p. 9).

parents as partners require relevant knowledge, skills and attitudes in order to 'build a community of love in the home', 'serve the educational life' of the school, 'participate in direction-setting and respond to the resource needs of the school' and, 'share in the life and mission of the Church'. In outlining the domains and capabilities of parent leadership in this way, the project team understood that it was impossible to be too specific. Consequently, it was decided to present general descriptors with the intention of inviting further conversation across this educational system.

- **Stage 3** involved collecting the 'diocesan understanding' on the role of parents in the school. At this point, a draft parent partnership document was prepared that included a rationale, vision and strategic directions for parent partnership. An extensive consultation period followed with the clergy, principals and Catholic Education Office staff being consulted. As in the previous stages, parents were kept informed of further developments to the framework document with regional parent assemblies again acting as the communication conduit between local parent groups and the project team.

- **Stage 4** involved taking the consolidated comments from the previous consultation and incorporating them into a further revision of the draft *Framework for Parent Partnership*. This draft contained a rationale, vision and strategic directions for parent partnership. In addition, there is a role statement that identifies the domains (i.e., action areas) for parent partnership as well as the capabilities (i.e., knowledge, skills and attitudes) required of parents working in each of the domains.

At the 2008, Parent Assembly Conference this draft was further revised on the basis of comments by the participating parents.

- **Stage 5** The draft parent partnership framework document (Catholic Education Office, 2009) is now available for further consultation and it is anticipated that the framework document will be signed off by the Director of Catholic Schools in late 2009. To date, the framework document has been well received across the system.

However, these are early days and the parent partnership framework document will be tested as the various school communities move into the next phase of implementation and demonstrate their capacity to institutionalise the parent participation framework document. Planning for this implementation phase, the project team has identified three strategic directions. First, it is recognised that this parent–school partnership approach will require new capabilities (i.e., knowledge, skills and attitudes) on the part of all stakeholders. Consequently, there are plans for various education programs for parents to raise awareness of the possibilities for parent–school partnerships in local schools. In addition, school communities will be encouraged to establish action learning projects or communities of practice to supplement theoretical understanding of parent–school partnerships with practical knowledge in support of this project. Beyond these activities within local school communities there will be a comprehensive process for reviewing various system and school policies and programs to ensure consistency with the parent partnership framework. Moreover, consultants employed by the Catholic Education Office will provide both support and challenge for parent–school partnerships through professional development programs, forums for dialogue around the practical issues of parent–school partnerships and, resources to support actions learning projects.

The Way Forward

As we have noted, the idea of parent–school partnerships is not new and, for over 30 years, policymakers, educational researchers and school personnel have shown interest in enhancing the relationships among the home, school and community. During this time, powerful arguments have been advanced in support of a vision of genuine parent–school partnerships. However, research continues to suggest a need for substantial cultural change in order to see the vision of such partnerships widely in evidence. Recognising the need for such change, in this chapter, we have reflected on the journey so far in terms of policy and practice, reviewed theoretical developments in support of parent–school partnerships and examined a practical initiative in the field. Now we consider a way forward for those seeking to lead genuine parent–school partnerships. In doing so, we will directly focus on the Lismore parent partnership project discussed above and reflect on what this project teaches us about leading genuine parent–school partnerships.

Recognising the need for substantial cultural change in support of genuine parent–school partnerships, those responsible for leading the Lismore parent partnership project (i.e., the project team) saw the need to develop a compelling vision for parent–school partnerships. It is generally accepted in the literature (Senge et al., 2000) that a compelling vision that links individual and collective aspirations creates a 'pull' for change. Here it was recognised that while parents and professionals potentially wanted more collaborative relationships, they could not see the possibilities and were not confident in initiating it. Consequently, those responsible for leading this parent partnership project sought to design the project in a way that would enable both parents and professionals to see the possibilities for genuine parent–school partnerships and, perhaps, be inspired to take action.

However, it was soon recognised that coming up with a compelling vision was challenging. An initial review of the literature (e.g., Hargreaves, 1999; Sachs, 2003) revealed different conceptualisations of parent–school partnership, including silent partnerships, managed partnerships and activist partnerships (Table 6.1).

TABLE 6.1
Conceptualising Parent–School Partnerships

	Parent–school Partnerships		
Vision	Silent partnership	Managed partnership	Activist partnership
Assumptions about parents	• respectful • limited capacity • acknowledges teachers' expertise • teachers' aide	• mostly disinterested • vocal minority concerned for own child at the expense of the group, • unreasonable • threatening teaching profession	• engaged • co-leaders • decision-makers • motivated by a moral purpose (i.e., all students learning), • willing ally of the teaching profession
Nature	Passive relationship	Supervised relationship	Reciprocal relationship
Purpose	To maintain a clear demarcation line between the home and the school	To control parents in order to protect the vision and mission of the school	To ensure school sustainability and learning for all students

In mapping the different conceptualisations of the parent–school partnership, the project team came to appreciate that in advocating for genuine partnerships they were, in fact, recommending an activist approach. In accepting this conceptualisation of parent–school partnerships, the project team was confident that an activist approach was consistent with the vision and mission of Lismore Catholic Education. In addition, they were aware that the literature (Hargreaves, 1999; Sachs, 2003) offered strong arguments for activist partnerships in which professionals and parents individually and collectively act as change agents in support of student learning. In practice, they also knew that there was growing interest in this activist model of parent–school partnership as new policy initiatives recommended building 'sustainable, collaborative, productive relationships' (Family-School and Community Partnership Bureau, 2008). Finally, the project team was reassured that their judgment was sound when participants in Stage 1 of the project developed a model for parent–school partnerships (Figure 6.2) that was consistent with activist notions of parent engagement, leadership, decision-making and moral purpose, as well as a commitment to working with professionals.

In line with this vision of activist parent–school partnerships, the project team settled on a project design (Figure 6.1) informed by a suite of activist principles. Here the project team had accepted Sachs's (2003) recommendation that, when applied together, the five elements of learning, participation, collaboration, cooperation and activism offered a platform for rethinking activism in schools. Thus *learning* was at the core of this project and this learning occurred for the individual, the school community and the system. Individuals (i.e., parents and professionals) through the use of the strategy of self-narrative or reflexive storytelling became aware of the assumptions, values and beliefs that influence their behaviour in respect to parent–school partnership. By making self-narrative public they contributed to the development of the collective identity of the school community and the system. *Participation* was evident as parents and professionals were encouraged to contribute to the development of the parent partnership framework document. *Collaboration* and *cooperation* were evident within the project as the project design encouraged interaction between parents and professionals that resulted in the development of shared perspectives and cooperative action. Finally, this project was informed by the principle of *activism*. Parents and professionals were encouraged to see themselves as active agents and from the outset the project was designed to access this agency.

To date, the Lismore parent partnership project has successfully reached its first target, namely, the development of a framework document that offers a clear rationale and vision as well as strategic directions for the future. So far, the framework document has received virtually unanimous approval from the various stakeholders including parents, principals and clergy. In particular, the idea of parent leadership/activism in the context of parent–school partnerships is well received. Moreover, there is considerable support for the identification of the domains and capabilities of parent partnership as people can see the practical advantages of naming the parent partnership role in this way. In other words, the framework document is helping parents and professionals to see the possibilities for activist parent–school partnerships.

Beyond these practical outcomes, the design of the project has also well received by participants. Within this project, professionals and parents demonstrated that they can work together in reciprocal relationships. Here the expertise of all parties was recognised and there was evidence of an environment of trust and mutual respect. Participants were also able to put aside self-interest and proved to be responsive and responsible in terms of reading strategic possibilities. In addition, there was a commitment to learning along the way as participants appreci-ated the need for new capabilities in support of parent–school partner-ships. In short, this project provides a tangible example of genuine parent–school partnerships in operation. Consequently, there seems to be a strong emotional commitment to the project, a 'pull' towards living the vision parent–school partnerships. In other words, parents and professionals are inspired to take action.

Conclusions

Acknowledging that it is early days in respect to living the vision of genuine parent–school partnerships in Lismore Catholic Education, we believe that there are lessons here for those seeking to lead genuine parent–school partnerships. Firstly, given that there are different con-ceptualisations of parent–school partnerships, leaders should expect conceptual confusion in respect to what constitutes a genuine parent–school partnership. Consequently, developing a shared vision should be a priority for leadership. Secondly, in developing this shared vision, leaders should consider the possibility of moving towards an activist model of parent–school partnership. Finally, if leaders believe activism represents a compelling vision for parent–school partnerships, leaders need to consider the application of Sachs's five elements of learning, participation, collaboration, cooperation and activism in future parent–chool projects. What if professionals and parents as leaders looked for opportunities for activist parent–school partnership and, then made a commitment to learning, participation, collaboration, cooperation and activism within the context of action teams? Would we see evidence of the transition to genuine parent–school partnerships?

References

Beazley, K. (1984). *Education in Western Australia: Report for the committee of inquiry.* Perth: Government Printer.

Brennan, M. (1996). *Multiple professionalisms for Australian teachers in an information age.* New York: American Education Research Association.

Catholic Education Office. (2008). *Framework for parent partnerships in the apostolate of Catholic education Draft 3, Version 1.* Lismore, New South Wales, Australia: Catholic Education Office.

Catholic Education Office. (2009). *Framework for parent partnerships in the apostolate Catholic education Draft 5, Version 2.* Lismore, New South Wales, Australia: Catholic Education Office.

Dawkins, J. (1988). *Strengthening Australian schools: A consideration of the focus and content of schooling.* Canberra, Australia: Australian Government Publishing Service.

Epstein, J. (2001). *School, family and community partnerships: Preparing educators and improving schools.* Boulder, CO: Westview Press.

Family-School and Community Partnership Bureau. (2008, August 12). *Bureau takes off* [Press Release]. Retrieved November 5, 2008, from http://www.familyschool.org.au/?m=200808

Graham, J. (2007). *An exploration of primary school principals' perspectives of the concept of community as applied to Catholic schools.* Unpublished doctoral thesis, Australian Catholic University, McAuley, Brisbane, Australia.

Hargreaves, A. (1999, April). *Professionals and parent: A social movement for educational change.* Paper presented at The Times Educational Supplement Leadership Seminar, University of Keele, Keele, United Kingdom.

John Paul II. (1982). *Familiaris consortio.* Sydney, Australia: St Paul Publishing.

Karmel, P. (1973). *Australian schools: Report of the interim committee for the Australian schools commission.* Canberra, Australia: Australian Government Publishing Service.

Marginson, S. (1997). *Markets in education.* Sydney, Australia: Allen & Unwin.

Ministerial Council on Education, Employment, Training and Youth Affairs. (1999). *The Adelaide Declaration on National Goals for Schooling in the Twenty-First Century.* Retrieved February 20, 2004, from http://www.mceetya.edu.au

O'Donoghue, T., & Dimmock, C. (1998). *School restructuring: International perspectives.* London: Kogan Page.

Sachs, J. (1999, January). *Towards an activist view of teacher professionalism.* Paper presented at the International Conference on the new professionalism in teaching: Teacher education and teacher development in a changing world, the Chinese University of Hong Kong, Shatin, N.T.

Sachs, J. (2003). *The activist teaching profession.* Maidenhead, England: Open University Press.

Saulwick Muller Research. (2006). *Family-school partnership project: A qualitative and quantitative study* (A report prepared for the Department of Education, Science & Training; The Australian Council of State Schools Organisations; Australian Parents Council). Canberra, Australia: Commonwealth of Australia.

Senge, P., Cambron-McCabe, N., Lucas, T., Smith, B., Dutton, J., & Kleiner, A. (2000). *Schools that learn: A fifth discipline fieldbook for educators, parents, and everyone who cares about education.* New York: Doubleday.

▶▶▶◀◀◀

CHAPTER 7

Parallel Leadership: Changing Landscapes for Principals

Marian Lewis and Dorothy Andrews

Undoubtedly, the 21st century has brought new and significant challenges to schools, and in particular to principals. In facing these challenges there is a recognition that change is ongoing, discontinuous, and that responsiveness to change requires new and different forms of leadership in educational organisations. Morgan (1997, 2006) indicates that old styles of organisation and management no longer work. We have to find alternatives (Morgan, 1997, p. xxviii), we need to create new insights and find innovative ways to deal with challenges (Morgan, 2006). We have to find creative ways of organising and managing that allow us 'to go with the flow', using new images and ideas as a means of creating shared understandings that will allow us to do new things in new ways (Morgan, 1997, p. xxix). 'We are not passive observers interpreting and responding to events and situations … we play an important role in shaping those interpretations and thus the way events unfold' (Morgan, 2006, p. 365).

Complexity and diversity place huge demands on the capacity of one person to lead and manage an organisation (Duignan & Gurr, 2007; Gurr, 2008). Mulford (2008) indicates that successful school leaders 'adapt and adopt their leadership practice to meet changing needs of circumstances in which they find themselves' (p. 65). Further, he states that:

> The major challenge is for school leaders to be able to understand and act on the context, organisation and leadership of the school, as well as interrelationship between these three elements. Successful school leadership will be contextually literate, organisationally savvy and leadership smart. Successful school leadership links the context, the organisational frame and the role of leaders. (p. 67)

Leading in Times of Change:
The Need for a New Cultural Landscape

The pressure for ongoing change within the educational system is relentless. The 21st century is the age of an information revolution and schools are becoming self-managing, partly self-funded, networked and global (Beare, 2001, 2006). Drucker (1994) argues that as the world moves into the post-corporate world of discontinuous change where the main form of work is knowledge creation, 'education will become the centre of the knowledge society and the school its key institution' (p. 9). Recent literature has indicated that if schools of the 21st century are to become knowledge generating (Drucker, 1994; Senge, 1994) then new conceptualisations of professional knowledge and new forms of school leadership are required. Linking new forms of school leadership, including teacher leadership, to the enhancement of school outcomes through successful organisational learning has been outlined by a number of writers (see e.g., Hargreaves, 2000, 2002; Harris & Muijs, 2003; Lambert, 2003).

Dinham (2007, p. 263), defines leadership as 'the influence exercised by leaders and the functions and processes performed by leaders'. Furthermore, no leader can accomplish change and renewal on his or her own (Dinham, 2007; Owens, 2004). Therefore, leadership emphasises the importance of relationships both personal and professional (Dinham, 2007, p. 265). The challenge of leading in times of change is to create new frames or landscapes (Morgan, 2006; Owens, 2004).

Creating a new landscape for principal leadership requires a rethinking in terms of concepts of power and influence. Establishing a new landscape requires new interactions of human activity, new practices, beliefs, concepts and traditions of those who live within the landscape:

> ... new and different working relationships need to be established between teachers and administrator in order for any new leadership role to make a positive and lasting contribution to the improvement of teaching and learning in a given setting. (Wasley, as cited in Sherrill, 1999, p. 57)

Parallel leadership is one such frame-breaking concept. Parallel leadership is defined as 'a process whereby teacher leaders and their principals engage in collective action to build school capacity. It embodies three distinct qualities — mutual trust, shared purpose and allowance for

individual expression' (Crowther et al., 2008, p. 53). This conceptualisation unlocks the leadership potential for building the capacity to
respond to change in schools.

Parallel leadership is both powerful and challenging for principals.
Teacher pedagogical leadership has been investigated in some detail
(e.g., Crowther, et al., 2008; Murphy, 2005) and there has been some
exploration of the meta-strategic role of the principal (Crowther et al.,
2001; Crowther & Andrews, 2003; Morgan, 2008). Such action
includes aligning organisational elements, articulating shared direction
and values, developing trust (Bryk & Schneider, 2002; Louis, 2007)
and networking beyond the school (Mulford, 2007). Also crucial to the
principal's role is the task of building leadership capacity within the
professional community. This task includes enabling the growth of
leadership skills and of the particular group of teachers within the
school — a group that changes as staff come and go. There is both flexibility and fluidity implicit in this aspect of the work of the principal
within parallel leadership.

As indicated in the definition above, teachers and their principal
engage in collective action. What implications does this have for the
principal? For parallel leadership to emerge, teachers' leadership must be
enabled (Crowther et al., 2008). For collective action to be sustained,
new ways of working must be developed for both the principal and the
teachers. This is the area explored in detail in this chapter. Further
insight will be provided through the exploration of the experiences of
principals working within the reality of parallel leadership. The two
cameos provided illustrate the power and the challenges of working in
parallel with teachers where shared purpose, trust and mutualism are
valued and there is clearly allowance for individual expression.

Creating a New Landscape

School systems have changed in response to the wider global restructuring (Beare, 2001; Hargreaves, 2002). Significant restructuring initiatives such as devolution and site-based management have involved
teachers in school-based decision-making and increased the expectation
that they will operate on a more collaborative, collegial basis (Beare,
2001; Kalantzis & Harvey, 2002). This increasing involvement of
teachers in whole-school matters represents a different focus for teachers, one beyond the classroom (Harris & Muijs, 2003; Lambert, 2003;
McLaughlin & Talbert, 2001).

Society has expectations for continual responses to an ever increasing pace of change. The demands of the 21st century external to the school often motivate little to no response from those within schools (Stoll, 1997). Crowther et al. (2008) argue that leading schools today needs to be conceptualised as an organisation-wide process that recognises:

> [that] today's leaders can come from many places and assume many forms; acknowledges leadership capabilities throughout organisations and centres leadership away from positional authority and onto core organisational processes. (p. 33)

Crowther et al. (2008) then assert that:

> Leadership for school improvement is a process whereby Principals and Teacher-Leaders engage in collective action to build school capacity for improvement ... [and the nature of the relationship] will vary with contextual influences and the personalities of each parallel leadership team. (p. 68)

Crowther's model connecting the influence of leadership on capacity-building for school improvement is captured in Figure 7.1. The activation and sustaining of three processes, namely, the development of vision and school-wide pedagogy, culture-building and organisation-wide learning, are dependent on leadership.

To illustrate this model in action, in particular the role of the principal, this chapter reports on the experiences of two principals of schools who engaged with a whole-school revitalisation process, called Innovative Designs for Enhancing Achievements in Schools (IDEAS; Andrews, Conway, Dawson, Lewis, McMaster et al., 2003). This process of school improvement is conceptualised from an understanding of successful school revitalisation as articulated in the Crowther and Andrews model (2003; see Figure 7.1). The IDEAS program enables a recognition of the need for new ways of working and hence influence (and power) to mobilise the community towards a preferred future that does not reside solely with the principal. The three core processes that build capacity for improvement are interrelated and developed co-jointly and each process requires strong principalship (meta-strategic development) and strong teacher leadership (pedagogical development).

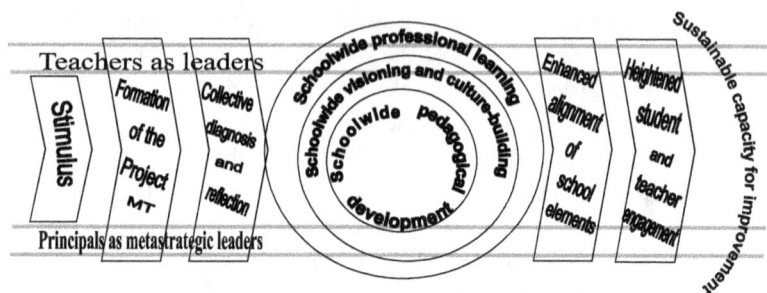

FIGURE 7.1
Enhancing school outcomes through holistic school reform: The IDEAS way.
Source: Crowther & Andrews, ARC Research Report (2003). Reproduced with permission.

The IDEAS Program for School Improvement

IDEAS is an approach to school revitalisation that is distinguished by use of four interdependent components, namely, (1) the image of a successful school (the Research-based Framework for Enhancing School Outcomes); (2) an organisation-wide and individual learning process, the *IDEAS* process; (3) images of teacher work, three dimensional pedagogy (3D.P) and (4) parallel leadership. Each of these components is now discussed.

THE RESEARCH-BASED FRAMEWORK FOR ENHANCING SCHOOL OUTCOMES

The Research-Based Framework for Enhancing School Outcomes (RBF) synthesises significant current research to build the framework of a successful school. Working with IDEAS, schools are challenged to create an image of what they want their school to become (Morgan, 2006) and collectively work towards building this envisioned future. When schools commence working with IDEAS they collect a comprehensive dataset made up of a 70-question survey of the perceptions of teachers, parents and students. The survey (called the Diagnostic Inventory) provides information about each element of the RBF and their interrelations.

As a conceptual model for school revitalisation the RBF has been developed in full cognisance of significant global research findings about successful organisational reform (Cuttance, 1998; Hill & Crevola, 1999; Kaplan & Norton, 1996; King & Newmann, 2000; Newmann & Wehlage, 1995). It comprises five contributory elements:

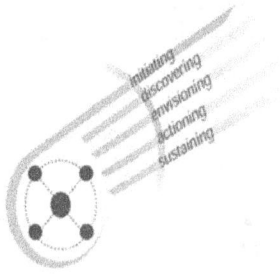

initiating: resolving to become an IDEAS school, establishing a management team (Ideas School Management Team - ISMT) and appointing an IDEAS school-based facilitator (s);

discovering: revealing your school's most successful practices and key challenges and sharing collective responsibility for the situation in a no blame environment;

envisioning: picturing a preferred future for your school - an inspirational vision, and an agreed approach to pedagogy;

actioning: implementing plans to align school practices and structures with your school's revitalised vision;

sustaining: keeping the revitalisation process going by building on successes and embedding processes into organisational operations and management structures.

FIGURE 7.2
The IDEAS process.
Source: Crowther, Andrews, Dawson and Lewis, (2002). Reproduced with permission.

strategic foundations, cohesive community, infrastructural design, schoolwide pedagogy (SWP; Andrews & Crowther, 2003), professional supports, along with school outcomes. When administered in a school community the survey provides relevant data as a starting point in generating an image of a preferred future. Enhanced school outcomes (student achievement, knowledge creation, development of community relationships and sustainability) come as a result of alignment between the contributory elements.

THE IDEAS PROCESS

The IDEAS Process (Figure 7.2), as an approach to school revitalisation, comprises five phases: initiating, discovering, envisioning, actioning and sustaining (IDEAS). Journeying through these phases enables groups of professionals to work together to create understandings that could not easily by created by individuals. In conceptualising IDEAS four sources have been used, namely, Meta-strategy (Limerick, Cunnington, & Crowther, 1998); Appreciative Inquiry (Cooperrider & Whitney, 1996); Action Learning (Argyris & Schon, 1974; Zuber-Skerit, 1990) and Organisational Capacity Building (Newmann, King, & Youngs, 2000).

As a process of organisational and individual learning, IDEAS enables the creation of an envisioned future for the school developed through a collective commitment to building this future. The professional community develops a shared approach to pedagogy (Andrews & Crowther, 2003) that enables a schoolwide approach to teaching, learning and assessment, that focuses the work of teachers and the infrastructure and professional development that supports their work. The creation of the new image of the organisation is the result of leadership of the professional community in mutual relationship with the strategic work of the administration, that is, parallelism and that re-images roles and responsibilities in the organisation — pedagogical leadership and a meta-strategic leadership (Crowther et al., 2008).

THREE-DIMENSIONAL PEDAGOGY

Three-Dimensional Pedagogy (3D.P) — IDEAS conceptualises the work of the 21st century teaching professional as 3-dimensional pedagogy (3-D.P). In proposing this construction of teacher professionalism we have stated elsewhere that:

> ... 3-D.P teachers develop their personal pedagogical self at the same time as they engage with their school's SWP [schoolwide pedagogy] and explore the potential of relevant authoritative theories of teaching and learning to both their personal pedagogy and their SWP. (Andrews & Crowther, 2003, p. 101)

The concept of 3-D.P provides a framework that, it is presumed, enables IDEAS program teachers to engage in dialogue where deeply embedded pedagogical practices are shared and new levels of pedagogical insight can be generated. It presumes a professional learning community as articulated by writers such as Hord (1997) and Kruse, Louis and Bryk (1995).

PARALLEL LEADERSHIP

Parallel Leadership in IDEAS schools engages teacher leaders and administrator leaders in collaborative action, while at the same time encouraging the fulfilment of each individual's capabilities, aspirations and responsibilities. Based on the characteristics of mutualism, a sense of shared purpose and allowance for individual expression, it leads to strengthened alignment between the school's vision and the school's teaching and learning practices (Andrews & Crowther, 2002; Crowther, Ferguson, & Hann, 2008). It facilitates the development of a professional learning community (Hord, 1997), culture-building (Schein, 1992) and schoolwide approaches to teaching and learning (Andrews & Crowther, 2003). It makes possible the enhancement of school identity, teachers' professional esteem, community support and students' achievements in the quest for enhanced action and sustainability. Unifying and underpinning the school improvement process is a leadership relationship based on parallelism. This leadership construct acknowledges the diversity of roles of people in a 21st century school organisation and, in particular, the changing roles and relationships of principals and teachers.

Crowther et al.'s (2008) concept of the role of the principal in parallelism is based on Meta-strategy. Meta-strategy (Limerick et al., 1998) related to parallelism comprises five functions:

- envisioning inspiring futures
- aligning key institutional elements (i.e. vision, stakeholders expectations, school infrastructures, pedagogical processes and professional learning)
- enabling teacher leadership
- building synergistic alliances
- culture-building and identity generation.

Crowther et al. assert that:

> this five-part framework ... recognises the expanding duty of care functions of educational managers at all levels; is linked ... to emerging forms of teacher leadership; and is responsive to the growing reality of the school as a fundamental cog in networked communities. (p. 71)

The IDEAS program also provides a set of 'rules' or 'principles' of practice. These include: teachers are the key and teachers' learning is the key to school improvement and enhanced student outcomes, successes breeds success, and adopting a principle of 'no blame'. The final principle, alignment of school processes is a *collective* responsibility and assumes a whole-school approach to school improvement (Crowther et al., 2002).

The Research Data Source

The cameos presented in this chapter emerge from two of the many schools that have been involved with IDEAS. The principals' stories recount their actions around rethinking their role and building a new landscape for leadership and broader relationships. The two stories selected come from state primary schools (student age: 5–12 years) in Queensland, Australia. The selection was deliberate in an attempt to illustrate the operation of parallel leadership within two different contexts. One cameo comes from a small rural school (Merryvale State

Primary School) and the other comes from a large primary school in a regional city in Queensland (Forestville State Primary School). The name of the school and the informants used in the cameos have been changed.

The two principals interviewed had been involved with IDEAS for more than 2 years and had reported that they and their communities had had considerable success in rethinking school and leadership. In-depth interviews were held with principals and significant others (other staff such as teachers and teacher aides) in the respective schools. Therefore, even though the cameos presented refer to the principals' voice, the verification of a 'different place now' has come from the significant others as well as the principals themselves.

Cameo 1: Merryvale State Primary School

Merryvale State Primary School has 51 students housed in two double classrooms. The students are drawn from families associated with rural or service industries. The school is well resourced, and the old school building houses the library. A number of visiting specialist teachers service the school providing drama, music, physical education, LOTE (German), learning support and a guidance officer is available as required. The current enrolment is continually growing, which demon-strates community confidence in the quality of the school's learning environment. The school is staffed by a teaching principal, one full-time classroom teacher, a part-time teacher, a teacher's aide and several part-time general staff. The school website artefact (see Figure 7.3) clearly articulates the co-created vision, values and schoolwide pedagogy.

The principal's initial experience was typical of many small school principals as reported in the literature (Lester, 2003; Mulford, 2008): '… where a female, first-time principal, [is facing] multiple demands as well as high teaching loads … building reciprocal relationships with the community was found to be difficult' (Mulford, 2008, p. 59).

PARALLEL LEADERSHIP AT MERRYVALE SCHOOL

Merryvale, a small state primary school, sits in a beautiful rural setting, close to a prosperous regional town, west of Brisbane in Queensland. The size of the school belies the significance of its achievements over the last 3 years. Here, parallel leadership has become deeply embedded in the internal operation of the school and has changed the relationship between the school and its community.

Our vision was developed as a result of several workshops and meetings over 18 months
The vision is:

Each word in the vision is important and carries with it a background meaning and understanding. An explanation of the vision is as follows:

Growing

Growing is a nurturing word that suggests care. The children are growing –
physically, intellectually, emotionally.

Beautiful

Our school is in a beautiful setting.

We value creative, artistic and beautiful things.

We feel positive and inspired by beauty

Futures

We are preparing our children for their futures–for each individual child.

In the Valley

Our school is situated in the Merryvale Valley.

Of Opportunities

Children who attend our school will be given many opportunities to succeed.
This includes academic, sporting, creative and social fields.

FIGURE 7.3
Merryvale State Primary School Statement of Purpose.
Reproduced with permission.

The development of parallel leadership can be explored though the experiences of Alison, the principal, Julia, an experienced teacher, and Lorraine, a long-serving teacher aide, with strong links into the community. Arriving in the school as the new principal 4½ years previously, Alison had faced a number of challenges. The staff, taking a fairly critical stance, stood back waiting to see what the new principal intended to change to put her mark on the school. The community, meanwhile, looked on with suspicion and some mistrust, regularly engaging in carpark gossip about aspects of the school's operation.

Alison saw IDEAS as a way of building the relations of trust and respect — of bringing everyone on board and developing a clear sense of common purpose. Through the process of collaboratively developing the vision and the values, she helped people to understand that the school was 'really grounded in the community ... [the school] belongs to the community not to the principal'. There is evidence that this understanding has taken root — the Parents and Citizens (P&C) group no longer opposes the principal's suggestions 'as an almost "knee-jerk" reaction' and is now leading a move to promote the school in the broader community to increase enrolments. Alison no longer needs to 'second-guess' what the P&C wants. The unwillingness to engage with the principal has been replaced with dialogue that recognises shared responsibility for the future of the school. The level of parent involvement in the school has increased considerably.

Over time, as the school engaged with IDEAS, there were many conversations about creating the school vision, the values they shared and pedagogy that really worked for their students. 'Now we have our vision — how things have changed for us — how we feel about ourselves and where we are heading — we have a plan now'. In Julia's words, the contributions come from everyone, 'we are constantly talking about different things ... bouncing ideas off each other, all the time'. As a result, not only does everyone have a say, everyone is also very well-informed. This degree of mutual knowledge and understanding has many benefits. As an example, it has allowed a rapid response to be made when parents were upset about the reorganisation following a reduction in staffing. A complete plan of action was prepared and presented to parents — addressing and allaying their concerns.

With a strong sense of shared purpose came the potential for a different way of working. Strengths could be identified to build on and new contributions made. It was no longer necessary for the principal to keep track of all that was happening in the school. With the shared purpose and mutual understandings that had been developed, others could lead — occasionally 'checking in' with Alison, to keep her informed. It is a change from 'can I do this?' to 'this is what I've done'. Reflecting on this new experience, Lorraine reported that the recognition of her strengths and her ability to make decisions increased her feelings of self-worth. No longer was she 'just a teacher aide' — she was now trusted to lead in certain areas, like the organisation of the annual Book Fair, a responsibility that she relishes. In the classroom, too, Lorraine is very much part of the team. No longer 'living in the staff room, preparing materials ... a bystander wondering what we are going to do each week', Lorraine is knowledgeable and valuable contributor in the classroom, 'an integral part of the team'. Another of Lorraine's obvious strengths is her ability to connect with the community and to be listened to. She has been able to convey a sense of positive change out into the community, where she is both respected and well known — a contribution that has been welcomed and used by Alison. Every effort is made to identify and build on individual strengths. If a staff member refuses to work collaboratively towards achieving the shared vision, this is not tolerated. In one such instance the principal exercised her authority and the person ceased employment at the school. The use of 'power' was a deliberate in that situation, 'I have exercised that power. I had to. I have used that power and it was a conscious choice'.

Respect plays an important part in the collegial relationships in the school — but the trust within this team is such that Julia feels she can put her ideas forward, make suggestions for change, have a say. The team is 'on the same wavelength' as a result of all the conversations they have had. Where there is a problem to be solved, Alison does not feel responsible for coming up with the solution. Everyone may have a different perspective and between them create a solution. Power differentials do not come into play. This is a new experience for Julia who left her previous school because her suggestions for change were perceived as threatening the authority of the principal. Interestingly, all the ideas and suggestions from others are welcomed by Alison, who says, 'I feel more relaxed knowing that I can share the problem and I am not here alone having to deal with it ... I know that everyone will support me or that we can share the problem and work together to get through the issue'. Alison is aware of her power but chooses to exercise it through these forms of shared leadership in order to achieve her goals for the school.

Alison acknowledges that previously, trust was lacking at Merryvale. Working with IDEAS was appealing to Alison as she was 'searching for a way to build that trust, to build the realisation that I am just not here to change everything because of a whim — this change is genuine and grounded in the community'. Trust is a word used frequently in school conversations. For Alison it means confidence that you are not going to be undermined. It is about feeling safe to say what you think. It is about believing that people will do what they say they will. Mistakes will be acknowledged and then addressed without great fuss. Trust is about integrity, respect, honesty, fairness, and your contribution to the collective effort being valued.

After describing how in the past she had gone home and cried when things went wrong at work, Lorraine says she is now confident about speaking up. As she says, the way of working in the school now, 'actually gives you a lot of confidence to express yourself. You know where you stand and you say what you feel'. This created 'a superior work environment and greater productivity', a stark contract to the 'strict confines' she has worked in for so long.

For Alison, parallel leadership at Merryvale is about team work 'where everyone is a respected member of the team and we are all valued equally'. This is her preferred way of working to achieve her aims as principal. Everyone has an equal say — a *genuine* say — and everyone's ideas are respected. There is a genuine ownership of what happens. Alison believes in trusting, in respecting ideas and not pulling rank, unless it is absolutely necessary. There is recognition that leadership relationships, like the culture of the school, have evolved over time. New ways of working within the school have been developed and the relationship between school and community is increasingly positive. But can what has been created be sustained if the current principal leaves? Julia and Lorraine both recognise that a change in principal could threaten what has been created in the school. At the same time they have gained in confidence to the extent where they would not stand back and see what changes the new principal wanted to implement. Lorraine, as teacher aide, recognises that there is power in her voice too and it would be important to convey to the new person all the benefits of how the school was operating. The groundswell of support from within the community for the vision and values that guided that way of working is also important. If the ways of working are more deeply embedded in the culture of the school, the signage and visual

Our vision *Growing Together – Learning Forever* is a guide and evaluation filter to ensure that any action within our school is enhancing what we truly believe in as a school community. Students can easily relate to the simplicity of this vision and embrace it and the symbolism associated with it. Our 'Vision' and 'Values' songs reflect the metaphorical image of the Jacaranda tree which plays an integral part in articulating elements of classroom practice and positive behaviour management strategies. The vision is for the present and the future while being linked to our past through the symbol of the Jacaranda tree. It is based around growth as individuals, as a school community and as an integral part of the wider community. Our School Wide Pedagogy is a direct expansion of our vision as it adds the other important aspect that characteristics our school which is that we each support the other in our strive for personal success (Statement on school website).

FORESTVILLE STATE SCHOOL
Supporting Each Other

FIGURE 7.4
Forestville State Primary School Vision.
Reproduced with permission.

representation of the vision and values capture and hold meaning — all that has been done cannot easily be ignored.

Cameo 2: Forestville State Primary School

Located on the outskirts of a major Queensland regional centre catering for the rapid growth in population in the area, Forestville grew rapidly from small beginnings to its present population of around 440 students. The campus includes a primary school, doubleunit preparatory year (with separately fenced playground area) and a special education program centre. The school covers six hectares, with areas around the buildings landscaped and 'the many beautiful jacaranda trees provide a source of inspiration for our community through our vision, school emblem and the visual metaphors used in our social skills and positive behaviour program There is a large oval and a native bush area with seating and native shrubbery. Bird and possum breeding boxes have been erected in the trees and water dragons abound' (School web site: see Figure 7.4).

The principal, an experienced, reputedly competent principal, had come from another IDEAS school to take up an acting position. At this stage, IDEAS had already commenced. Subsequently she applied and was appointed to the position.

PARALLEL LEADERSHIP AT FORESTVILLE STATE PRIMARY SCHOOL

As the principal of Forestville, Christine has a clear understanding of the kind of leadership she wants in the school. She conceptualises this as parallel leadership. Although fully acknowledging her responsibility and accountability as principal, Christine leads in parallel with all her staff as this 'allows you to espouse that we are here as a team, working together … and that includes everyone'. Positive relationships are at the core of this way of working.

The building of positive relationships is central to Christine's work as principal. She has an open door policy, 'inviting people to come in at any time' and is regularly out and about in the school, being visible, talking to teachers and students, taking an interest, acknowledging and getting to know people — always building relationships. All of this takes time and so she does her principal's (desk) work 'before and after school … because if I just sat in here doing work, work, work and gave [the staff] things to develop, that would not be meaningful and it wouldn't happen'. As principal, Christine sees herself as the driver who empowers teachers to take on leadership roles. She encourages, providing opportunities and the structures that enable this. Christine's availability and her willingness to be involved in the daily life of the school (her 'visibility'), is appreciated by teachers who report feeling well supported in their work.

Christine finds it exciting to keep on discovering the different strengths that the teachers have — things 'you never would find that if you're stuck in your office'. When new teachers come into the school Christine loves getting to know them and identifying their particular talents. She appreciates working with people who have a similar philosophy and core beliefs, but if people are different, her approach is to acknowledge the difference and say 'let's work together to be able to mesh that difference into a unified approach'.

While clearly 'the principal', Christine's leadership does not rely on the authority that comes with her position. She trusts that people will work alongside her, as a team, working towards agreed goals. Structures are put in place to check progress along the way, to keep track of 'what *we* have done'. Christine believes that you have to be willing to let go and to trust teachers, not setting people off on a task and checking on them later, but 'working alongside them … coming in and out all the time, helping, supporting, redirecting, talking, enhancing … or whatever, and by doing that it is easier to let go of that "power"'. David, a longstanding teacher in the school, reflected on his experience with this approach and confirmed that it worked very well. Christine's support, respect and, above all, her honesty were appreciated. Further evidence of how the staff respond to Christine's approach to leadership comes from an unlikely source. Applying for confirmation of her position, she gave the staff the selection criteria and asked for honest anonymous feedback about her leadership. She knew she was making herself vulnerable but was delighted with the feedback — the valuing of relationships, the unexpected insights and perspectives offered.

Christine readily acknowledges that there are things in the school that she wants to develop. She often identifies issues to be addressed, taking these to the staff, asking for their thoughts. Issues identified by teachers are also brought to the table. In either case, everyone can join in the debate about what is to be done. Christine relishes the range of perspectives, even welcoming the 'blockers' because of the richness they can bring to the discussion. As the protocols of skilful discussion are used, although the debate can be robust, everyone's viewpoint is valued and everyone has the opportunity to contribute. Christine summarises the discussion, checking that it represents what was agreed, and uses that to guide the direction she subsequently takes. One of her particular passions is students as leaders — as demonstrated by the contribution that students have made in enriching understandings of schoolwide pedagogy. Students have been involved in an examination of the school-wide pedagogy (SWP) and have presented their views to the staff and to some of the parents.

Christine is intentionally building a culture that centres on relationships, and through that, one that achieves better and more sustainable outcomes. She believes the principal has to be strong, as achieving those outcomes through parallelism may take longer and there will be detractors. If you can persevere and be patient though, 'when it does come, it's wonderful because it mushrooms and you are getting more quality'. It is very powerful as in the end the staff and the students have ownership and they request better outcomes: 'so it's not *you* dictating to them, and that is scary for you as leader, but you have to reflect and say, well, *I* haven't got to provide that, *we* are going to provide that'. Christine acknowledges that it is 'not all rosy, because there are lots of personalities out there where you've got lots of people vying for power'.

Christine sees parallel leadership as confident leadership — but also as leadership that needs to be authentic and consistent. It is not possible to say that you embrace parallel leadership and then become a hierarchical leader because you believe your authority or credibility is being questioned by teachers. Christine recognises that some situations are really confronting but if you have built the trust and the relationships, it is not necessary to revert to that 'old leadership style' of 'I'm in charge'. She adds that if someone questioned her leadership — she'd talk to them about it, find out what was behind it and work it out. Christine does not feel the need to have all the answers. Recognising the ability and the talent of her staff, she seeks to draw on that pool of knowledge and experience to meet challenges. This is not diminishing her leadership as principal, but enhancing her leadership style by 'recognising that *we* as a group are here to solve this'. Christine acknowledges that IDEAS gave her the confidence and the power to lead as she wanted to. In addition, working in the way she does, allows her to prioritise systemic initiatives coming into the school, embracing those that enrich the schools pedagogical framework, and not implementing others on the grounds that they are already embedded in the school, in context relevant ways. David reflected on the strength of Christine's leadership — acknowledging that her way of giving opportunity and providing direction had the effect of drawing people in, building momentum and the positiveness to keep the initiative moving.

The principle of *no blame* is very important in the school and Christine firmly believes that she has to be able to model that all the time — not blaming teachers, not blaming the parents, not blaming the students. If something is not working then a solution has to be found. She will not rant and rave but say 'look I'm not really happy with that. What can we do?' Christine says that she does not like, but can manage confrontation. She has a bottom line about acceptable behaviour, for all the school community, including parents, who can be quite aggressive. Sometimes she has to confront this and finds people respond. For Christine, though, while she has her bottom line she 'always has to value the person and you can never lose it … you have got to be able to model what you want them to be able to do'.

Discussion

The next part of the chapter considers several common features of the actions and practice of the principals captured in the cameos.

LEADERSHIP RELATIONS

Both of these principals have sought to establish the kind of leadership relations that help them to successfully carry out their roles. For Christine, this was a way of working that she had previously aspired to but had not been confident enough to take on. Parallel leadership gave her a framework for understanding and enacting the type of leadership she wanted. For Allison, IDEAS was the vehicle for creating mutualism and shared purpose and, significantly, for building trust. The creation of trusting relationships and mutualism within school communities has been well documented (Bryk & Schneider, 2002; Crowther et al., 2008; Louis, 2007; Mulford, 2007) and has been of central importance in enhancing outcomes in both schools reported on in this chapter. Christine reflected on the challenge that this provided for her on a daily basis — often referring to the need for constant modelling of practice and managing confronting situations in a way that 'it is not necessary to revert to that old leadership style of I'm in charge'.

WORKING TOWARDS A SHARED PURPOSE

Both of these principals are strong leaders but both work mutualisti-cally (Crowther et al., 2008) to build a better school. Both seek to build from the strengths of their staff but with a view to contributing to the collective effort — the shared purpose. There is a clear under-standing that outcomes will be better if everyone works as a team — building on their strengths. Both have built cultures that value what individuals can contribute to the development of the school. Teamwork is a key feature of both schools, where individuals are respected and valued and everyone has a *genuine* say.

NEW WAYS OF WORKING

In both schools new ways of working have evolved and the develop-ment of positive relations has been significant. Alison recognised the importance of building a culture of trust and respect and developing a clear sense of common purpose. For Christine, the building of positive relations and trust is the priority. The development of respect, her authenticity as a leader who genuinely values each person required a significant investment of her time and emotional energy.

As evidenced in the literature, Bryk and Schneider (2002), Louis (2007) and Mulford (2007), the development of relational trust was crucial. Developing new ways of working requires rethinking in terms of power and influence (Morgan, 2006; Owens, 2004) and new human interactions, new practices, concepts and traditions with those that operate within the school (Sherrill, 1999).

RAISED EXPECTATIONS

In both of these schools, shared responsibility for success is at the heart of the principal's way of working. Expectations are high that teachers will contribute positively to the agreed preferred future of the school. Both these principals clearly seek to work 'alongside' their staff — still being principal, but as part of the team. The focus for change is identified by the principal or other members of staff and generally the solution is reached through collaborative processes — though the principal may need to provide additional resources.

SHARED RESPONSIBILITY

Both the principals are concerned with the sustainability of the ways of working in the school. By establishing shared responsibility and a broad-based ownership of the current success and future development of the school, they are building a culture in which the principal is not the 'one' responsible for the school or for finding a solution to problems. It is a culture where everyone, from their position/role, plays a part in taking the school forward. At Forestville this may not be everyone (certainly not everyone to the same extent) but it is broad-based. As people are actively involved in making changes, they have ownership and are actively concerned with improving the quality of school outcomes.

ARTICULATING A POSITION

Both of these principals consistently value parallelism, particularly in the larger school context; credibility would be lost if hierarchical relations of power were invoked in response to teacher questioning of leadership. Both though use the power of their position when necessary as they have a clear bottom line and will stand firm where people are working against building the desired future.

PROFESSIONAL CONVERSATIONS

Both schools have built the capacity to share and converse through ongoing professional conversations — more formally conduced in the larger school context. The sharing brings together divergent views. For Christine, this is through her capturing the essence of the discussion and using that as the basis for further action. Building common ground (shared understanding) through discussion is important in both schools. In both schools the staff are well informed because they contribute to many of the decisions made. At Merryvale there is also strength in unifying divergent views — different views coming together to create a solution that no one member of the team would have come up with when working alone.

RELATIONAL CAPACITY

Trust, respect and professional confidence (Bryk & Schneider 2002; Louis, 2007) were evident in the relationships between and among members of the staff in both schools. Trust that people will do the right thing was a common feature of both stories. Both principals had a way of checking progress that was not construed as 'checking up' on people. Trust allows people to take initiative and to develop their skills individually and in collaboration with each other. Respect is also vitally important in both cameos. In both, the principal is open to suggestions for improvement. They have no feelings of defensiveness. Building confidence to be the professional you want to be is also a feature of both stories — for example, Christine at Forestville and for Lorraine (a teacher aide) at Merryvale — and, as such, has created a better and more productive work environment.

Limitations of the Study

This chapter has reported on experiences of two principals engaged with the IDEAS program. This program uses the leadership construct of parallelism and assumes that as the principal and their school communities engage with ideas, the principal will use the leadership framework provided and the processes provided to work towards reimaging the school and relationships therein — the metastrategy of parallelism (Crowther et al., 2008). The engagement by principals in metastrategy reflects experiences of other principals as reported in other cases (Andrews, 2008; Andrews & Crowther, 2002; Crowther et al., 2008). While parallel leadership is not the only form of leadership for school improvement, for these principals, in these schools, it has provided a way of thinking and acting that has enabled their preferred way of working to be achieved.

Concluding Comments

'The heart of the matter is power and how it is exercised' (Owens, 2004, p. 260). Leadership deals with exercising influence on others through social interaction. Parallelism is conceptualised as the process of leadership relationships that acknowledges diverse roles of people in

21st century schools (Crowther et al., 2008). Christie and Limerick (2004, p. 3) commenting on discourse in leadership, state:

> Seldom is leadership probed in ways that reveal the condition of its own construction. The ethics of its power dynamics are often glossed over. The interplay of unconscious as well as conscious, of irrational as well as rational dynamics in human relationships, is often overlooked.

The cameos presented in this chapter attempt to do just that. That is, describe the changing landscape constructed as the principal, staff and the broader community involve themselves in transforming processes that underpin IDEAS. In particular, the filter has been the role of the metastrategic actions of the principal. Using different sources of power available to them, each principal has engaged others in a process that has enabled these spheres of influence to be used in positive and fulfilling ways for all involved. Empowerment techniques, such as, shared decision-making, developing trust and openness to create growth, and enhancing the school culture were used. Owens (2004) has captured this process so aptly when he asserted:

> ... creating this mutually shared vision cannot be done without sharing some of the power that was traditionally closely held by those in the administrative hierarchy ... power, for example, in the form of information about the organisation, authority to participate freely in making decisions, recognition of the legitimacy of followers as stakeholders in the enterprise, and creating an environment that facilitates the development of trust and open communication that is essential to collaborative group effort. This is the basis for the empowerment of teachers, parents, students, and others who were formerly shut out of decision making of the organisation. (p. 277)

In parallelism, the metastrategic role of the principal (Crowther et al., 2008) is crucial to a process of building capacity for improvement — improvement leading to a shared preferred future (refer Figure 7.1). Actions include engaging the community in a process of creating an envisioned future and aligning this vision with other institutional elements such as community expectations, school infrastructures, pedagogical processes and professional learning. However, it is also the metastrategic actions that enabled teacher leadership, and the engagement in collaborative action to build a new way of working around here (Schein, 1992) that are most evident in the actions of the two principals depicted in the cameos.

References

Andrews, D. (2008). Working together to enhance school outcomes: An Australian case study of parallel leadership. *Leading and Managing, 14*(2), 45–60.

Andrews, D., Conway, J., Dawson, M., Lewis, M., McMaster, J., Morgan, A., & Starr H. (2003). *School revitalisation: The IDEAS way.* ACEL Monograph Series, No. 34. Winmalee, New South Wales, Australia: Australian Council for Educational Leaders.

Andrews, D., & Crowther, F. (2002). Parallel leadership: A clue to the contents of the 'black box' of school reform. *The International Journal of Educational Management, 16*(4), 152–159.

Andrews D., & Crowther, F. (2003). 3-Dimensional pedagogy: The image of 21st century teacher professionalism. In F. Crowther (Ed.), *Teachers as leaders in a knowledge society* (pp. 95–111). Deakin West, ACT: Australian College of Educators.

Argyris, C., & Schon, D. (1974). *Theory in practice: Increasing professional effectiveness.* San Francisco: Jossey-Bass Publishers.

Beare, H. (2001). *Creating the future school.* London: Routledge/Falmer.

Beare, H. (2006). *How we envisage schooling in the 21st century.* London: Specialist Schools and Academies Trust.

Bryk, A., & Schneider, B. (2002). *Trust in schools: A core resource for improvement.* New York: Sage.

Cooperrider, D.L., & Whitney, D. (1996). *Appreciative inquiry consultation workbook.* Chagrin Falls, OH: Taos Institute.

Christie, P., & Limerick, B. (2004). Leadership as a field of study: Editorial. *Discourse: Studies in the Cultural Politics of Education, 25*(1), 3.

Crowther, F., Andrews, D., Dawson, M., & Lewis, M. (2002). *IDEAS facilitation folder.* Toowoomba, Australia: Leadership Research Institute, University of Southern Queensland and Education Queensland.

Crowther, F., & Andrews, D. (2003). *From conceptual frameworks to improved school practice: Exploring DETYA's Innovation and Best Practice Project outcomes in Queensland schools.* ARC SPIRT Grant Report to Australian Government Department of Education Science and Training: Canberra. Retrieved April 8, 2008, from http://www.dest. gov.au/highered/respub.htm

Crowther, F., Ferguson, M., & Hann, L. (2008). *Developing teacher leaders: How teacher leadership enhances school success* (2nd ed.). Thousand Oaks, CA: Corwin Press.

Crowther, F., Hann, L., & McMaster, J. (2001). Leadership. In P. Cuttance (Ed), *School innovations: Pathways to the knowledge society* (pp. 123–142). Canberra, Australia: Australian Commonwealth Department of Education, Training and Youth Affairs.

Dinham, S. (2007). How schools get moving and keep improving: Leadership for teacher learning, student success and school renewal. *Australian Journal of Education, 51*(3), 263–275.

Duignan, P., & Gurr, D. (2007). *Leading Australia's schools.* Winmalee, Australia: Australian Council of Educational Leaders.

Cuttance, P. (1998). *Flexible schools project, research proposal.* Sydney: University of Sydney.

Drucker, P. (1994, November). The age of social transformation. *The Atlantic Monthly*, 1–19. Available at http://www.theatlantic.com/issues/a5dec/chilearn/drucker.html

Gurr, D. (2008). *Principal leadership: What does it do, what does it look like, and how might it evolve?* ACEL Monograph No 42. Winmalee, New South Wales, Australia: Australian Council of Educational Leaders.

Harris, A., & Muijs, D. (2003). Teacher leadership and school improvement. *Education Review, 16*(2), 39–42.

Hargreaves, A. (2000). Four ages of professionalism and professional learning. *Teachers and teaching: History and practice, 16*(2), 151–182.

Hargreaves, A. (2002). Sustainability of educational change: The role of social geographies. *Journal of Educational Change, 3*(2), 189–214.

Hord, S. (1997). *Professional learning communities: Community of continuous inquiry and improvement.* Austin, TX: Southwest Educational Development Laboratory.

Hill, P., & Crevola, C. (1999). Key features of whole-school, design approach to literacy teaching in schools. *Australian Journal of Learning Disabilities, 4*(3), 5–11.

Kalantzis, M., & Harvey, A. (2002). Preparing educators for the twenty-first century. *Professional Educator, 1*(1), 8–9.

Kaplan, R., & Norton, D. (1996). *The balanced scorecard: Translating strategy into action.* Boston: Harvard Business School Press.

Kruse, S., Louis, K., & Bryk, A. (1995). Analysing school-based professional community. In K.S. Louis & S.D. Kruse (Eds.), *Professionalism and community: Perspectives on reforming urban schools* (pp. 23–42). Thousand Oaks, CA: Corwin.

King, B., & Newmann, F. (2000). Will teacher learning advance school goals? *Phi Delta Kappan, 81*(8), 576–580.

Lambert, L. (2003). *Leadership capacity for lasting school improvement.* Alexandria, VA: Association for Supervision and Curriculum Development.

Lester, N.C. (2003). Primary leadership in small rural communities. *Leading and Managing, 9*(1), 85–99.

Limerick, D., Cunnington, B., & Crowther, F. (1998). *Managing the new organisation* (2nd ed.). Sydney, Australia: Business and Professional Publishing.

Louis, K.S. (2007). Trust and improvement in schools. *Journal of Educational Change, 8*(1), 1–24.

McLaughlin, M., & Talbert, J. (2001). *Professional communities and the work of high school teaching.* Chicago: University of Chicago Press.

Morgan, A. (2008). The principal in a process of school revitalisation: A metastrategic role. Unpublished doctoral dissertation, University of Southern Queensland, Australia.

Morgan, G. (1997). *Imagin-i-zation: New mindsets for seeing, organizing and managing.* Thousand Oaks, CA: Sage.

Morgan, G. (2006). *Images of organisation.* Thousand Oaks, CA: Sage.

Mulford, B. (2007). *The leadership challenge: Improving learning in schools.* Victoria, Australia: Australian Council for Educational Research.

Mulford, B. (2008). The leadership challenge: Improving learning in schools. *Australian Education Review No. 53.* Melbourne, Australia: Australian Council for Educational Research.

Murphy, J. (2005). *Connecting teacher leadership and school improvement.* Thousand Oaks, CA: Corwin Press.

Newmann, F.M., King, B., & Youngs, P. (2000). *Professional development to build organizational capacity in low achieving schools: Promising strategies and future challenges.* Madison, WI: Centre on Organisation and Restructuring of Schools, University of Wisconsin-Madison.

Newmann, F., & Wehlage, G. (1995). *Successful school restructuring: A report to the public and educators.* Madison, WI: Centre on Organization and Restructuring of Schools, University of Wisconsin-Madison.

Owens, R.G. (2004). *Organizational behaviour in education* (8th ed.). New York: Pearson.

Schein, E.H. (1992). *Organizational culture and leadership* (2nd ed.). San Francisco: Jossey-Bass.

Senge, P. (1994). *The fifth discipline fieldbook.* London: Nicholas Brealey Publishing.

Sherrill, J. (1999). Preparing teachers for leadership roles in the 21st century. *Theory into Practice, 38*(5), 583–595.

Stoll, L. (1997). *Successful schools: Linking school effectiveness and school improvement.* (Seminar Series No. 66). Melbourne, Australia: Incorporated Association of Registered Teachers of Victoria.

Zuber-Skerrit, O. (1990). *Action learning for change and development.* Aldershot, England: Gower-Avebury.

▷▷▷◁◁◁

CHAPTER 8

Coming to Terms With Emotions in Leaders: From Stress to Strength

Sandra Sytsma

> Emotional growth is the end result of putting yourself on the line. I believe that emotional growth and strength is the best asset we can have. [School leader] (Sytsma, 2007, p. 251)

Leading is a powerful activity in education. In taking people on journeys, it positions leaders to affect the lives of themselves and others. Leadership in schools engages emotional states in leaders as they respond to their lived experience in relating to teachers, students and other members of school communities. How these states may be understood and applied to developing leaders' strength, resilience and sustainability in their professional practice is the focus of this chapter.

The literature on emotions in educational leadership indicates that leaders feel required to manipulate their emotional states for a variety of personal, professional and political reasons (Beatty, 2002; Crawford, 2007). Their struggle in the workplace to overcome self, often for the interest of another, led to the identification of terms such as 'emotional labour' and 'emotional work' (Hochschild, 1983). These constructs reflect an expenditure of emotional energy in forced ways, following the physical definition of work as an application of force to move a body. Emotions do move a body — the leader's mind–body — but adopting 'labour' and 'work' metaphors to describe that process implies force, rather than unfoldment in emotional expression. Leaders' tales of burnout express work both *on* leaders' emotions by external, coercive power and *by* leaders in managing their emotions in response to it. This kind of work may eventually leach leaders' personal power and potentially result in debilitating stress.

A different perspective of emotional processing is generated here, with a view to leaders' empowerment. Rather than using metaphors of stress to come to grips with the challenges of forced, mechanistic 'work/

labour' on self and emotion, alternative metaphors of strength are proposed in reshaping emotional responses as opportunities for natural, organic 'growth/healing' within the self and with others. Reconceptualising and embodying leaders' emotional meaning-making as a process of transforming the self and others reclaims personal power.

In this chapter, a brief contextualisation of the term 'emotion' will be followed by an examination of emotion in educational leadership, including the management of emotion in professional practice and the ways in which it is put to work. Some alternative ways of understanding are introduced through exploring the function and system of emotion in the mind–body and the sociocultural shaping of emotions. Finally, some parameters for educational leaders' emotional growth are considered in proposing new and transformative ways of coming to terms with emotion in self and others and generating an emotionally integrated professional practice.

The Term 'Emotion'

Interpretation of the term 'emotion' has changed over time. In western usage in English, Harper (2001) specifies the ancient Latin roots of *emovere* as 'move out, remove, agitate' as *ex* 'out' and *movere* 'to move'. In the early modern era, emotion was understood as a disturbance moving out from the body. By late modern times, however, the term 'emotional' described overt displays that were socially unacceptable. Now, emotion is most often constituted and controlled 'inside' in the mind. When considering emotion in educational leadership, there is more likely to be disembodied, conceptual talk *about* feelings than surrender to the physical display of emotional states.

Tracing western epistemologies of consciousness adds to understanding the evolution of emotion. Reason (1994) outlines successive phases describing human consciousness. Initially, human consciousness was 'undifferentiated from the natural world and people lived in deep unconscious communion with their surroundings' (p. 17). Emotional processing was embodied but insignificant to consciousness awareness. In a second phase, human beings differentiated themselves from their environment and developed a separation between self and others. Emotion as a phenomenon separated from the body and moved to the head. Eventually, human consciousness became alienated and lost any sense of intentional and aware personal participation in world-making. We shall see later how such a separated consciousness and the negation of overt emotion play out in the professional practice of educational leaders.

Looking forward, Reason's (1994, p. 2) belief is that 'the Western world-view is … changing towards a realization that our existence is based on participation and communion rather than separation and competition'. In future consciousness, the body could reintegrate with the mind and become Varela, Thompson and Rosch's (1993) 'embodied mind'. Healing the mind–body rift could engage emotion in conscious and self-reflexive forms of knowing. Rather than modelling human consciousness on nonliving things, with its emphases on quantity and cause/effect, it may be modelled on living process where quality and patterns of information flow are important (Bateson, 1979; Reason, 1994). Terms of emotion can also move from the factory model of work and labour to growth models of resilience and capacity development. In such a future, leaders in education may consider emotional processing as self-and-other 'gardening' rather than 'labour', and as a generative activity rather than 'work'. Before using recent advances in understanding emotion to explain how this move might be made, we will first examine the current state of emotion in educational leadership.

Emotion in Educational Leadership

Recently, in an educational forum I attended, a school principal of 2 years' experience spoke about the stress of his work. He anticipated he would be a victim of burnout before another 3 years had passed. In reflecting on his comments, I wondered if 5 years was a reasonable and healthy span for the development, implementation and embedding of an initiative like becoming an educational leader, but if it was seen as an unavoidable totality, as for this principal, I felt concern. He was convinced that educational leadership would break him.

His incident had parallels in the experiences related by the group of educational leaders who participated with me in a study of the changing meanings of their leading (Sytsma, 2007). The five leaders created an interstitial cyberspace (a space between the normal 'spaces' of their lives) to engage in an email-based dialogue in which they explored a range of themes in their leadership. Being concerned with meaning-making and the restorying of meaning, emotional states were often involved. In some of these leaders' stories work felt 'forced … with all the strain and energy sapping effort that entails', 'like being locked in a Groundhog Day', 'like an empty lunch box', and that it was difficult to not let the 'emotional bucket' run dry. These leaders were also proactively involved during the study in self-healing and the development of emotional resilience, but many have to struggle alone. In my experience in schools, for example, I have encountered a leader/colleague who split himself emotionally so he had an outer school face to deal with the people who needed him, and an inner side in which he tried alone to process his feelings of frustration and grief that school situations engendered. Through other collegial relationships, I have witnessed leaders' high degrees of emotional stress precipitating burnout followed by stress leave, resignation or illness, including heart disease and cancer. This loss of personal and professional potential demands attention when considering the sustainable practice of educational leadership.

Emotion in Professional Practice

The concept of 'profession' is next examined. Traditionally, an individual who professed to have high levels of knowledge, skills and attitudes in a specific area gained the trust and respect of others to whom these attributes were applied. This was achieved by demonstrating a long and scholarly apprenticeship to his or her profession, acquiring specialised knowledge and developing advanced standards of performance. Professionals were accorded, by virtue of their value and esteem in the community, autonomous and self-responsible practice.

The notion of 'profession' has today been commandeered by corporate organisations to reflect a set of practice standards that are inscribed at a systemic level, rather than by individual discretion. In terms of educational leadership, where 'rationalist, behaviourist and cognitivist conceptions of leadership dominate the literature', 'matters of emotion have largely been marginalised in the mainstream discourse of educational leadership research, theory and practice' (Beatty, 2002, p. 4). The advent of systemic frameworks for professional standards of practice has effectively hidden or even silenced emotional meaning-making as a valid aspect of professional practice (Beatty, 2002; Beatty & Brew, 2004). In public service positions, such as the case with many principals in schools, there is a 'highly socially-engineered "professionalism"' (Hochschild, 1983, p. 14) in operation. With professional identity now owned, to a large degree, by systems rather than individuals, and professional practice inscribed externally with little regard for the individual professional's moral purposes and values or health and wellbeing, the emotional aspects of leadership are notably absent. A professional image does not include the inherent messiness of emotional display. Emotions, properly being 'embodied sensations', are seen as the 'antithesis of reason and rationality' and are considered impediments to judgment and intellectual activity (Lupton, 1998, p. 3). They are too subject to lack of control to be professionally appropriate to display. They are, in Reason's (1994) sense, a product of separated consciousness where minds and bodies are alienated. Before reflecting on the cost of apparently emotionally-cleansed professionalism in educational leadership, we look in more depth at what lies beneath the professional 'act' where emotional states are not only hidden or denied, but subverted, manipulated and put to work in the service of professional practice.

'Emotion@Work'

Hochschild (1983, p. 189) makes the observation that 'estrangement from display, and from what feeling can tell us is not simply the occupational hazard of a few. It has firmly established itself in the culture as permanently imaginable'. Bourdieu's (1990) term of 'habitus' reflects this normalisation of disembodied emotion where physical display is, as a matter of course, hidden or masked in the workplace. In such separated consciousness, emotional responses are kept inside and negotiated in the mind. From the examination of the term emotion above, this conceptual excision of embodied emotion from a holistic sense of being can be seen largely as a product of the modern, industrial era. That the western social taboo on unbridled emotional states has become entrenched in professional practice may be related to the increased emphasis, in the information era, on the production of services more than goods. As Hochschild (1983, p. 9) points out, 'nowadays most jobs call for a capacity to deal with people rather than with things'.

In this service orientation, organisational representatives must attend to relationships with customers and clients such that their service maximises use of the service–product, and hence the generation of profit from productivity. The ability in service providers to display or restrict certain emotional expressions in themselves and to cultivate or manipulate them in others, so as to enhance service–product use and profit, is often a job requirement. The play of countenances and charade is used to create a specifically desired state of mind in others, that is, one of desire to use the service–product. Such purposeful adjustment of emotional 'image' to meet organisational 'feeling rules' and purposes is described by Hochschild (1983) as emotional labour, and in being a required 'part of the job', becomes a saleable commodity. As Hochschild (1983, p. 7) explains:

> I use the term emotional labour to mean the management of feeling to create a publicly observable facial and bodily display; emotional labour is sold for a wage and therefore has exchange value. I use the synonymous terms emotion work or emotion management to refer to these same acts done in a private context where they have use value.

Educational leaders are not exempt from such labour in the workplace. In the corporate/educational world, a leader's duty of emotional labour has exchange value in that it is employed to manage and control teachers and students as emotional beings. It also has professional survival value in the sense that it supports required standards for professional practice. However, its value in personal survival is doubtful when it contributes to the loss of emotional honesty, the compromise of moral purposes, and burnout. A detachment of 'real self' from an 'on-stage self' performing emotional labour, as mentioned with the leader/colleague who maintained a divided self with a public face over his private self, could occur. When consciously used as a strategy in clearly separating self from role, this could be seen as a 'healthy' estrangement (Hochschild, 1983), although involving tension. In extremity, the sociocentric, other-directed 'false self' might become so entrenched as to become the 'real self' with resulting identity confusion. On a more positive note, Hargreaves (2000) urges a return to the private context of emotional work that has *use value* for the individual leader. He suggests that, at its best, 'emotional labor ['work' in Hoschchild's definition] ... can be pleasurable and rewarding — when people are able to pursue their own purposes through it, and when they work in conditions that allow them to do their jobs well' (Hargreaves, 2000, p. 814).

Orienting to New Terms With Emotions

For educational leaders, there are personal and professional costs in practice that denies or manipulates emotion. Apart from the individual burnout described earlier, Beatty (2002, p. 2) argues that:

> The endorsement of a rubric of professionalism that requires one to be and/or seem to be unemotional — as if contrived unemotionality were more rational than integrated emotionality — relegates one of the most powerful meaning making systems of the mind to the role of a pesky interloper.

This indictment of professionalism as it is commonly practiced today, and of leaders who accommodate to it and thus perpetuate and 'ritually seal' (Hochschild, 1983, p. 10) the current feeling rules and cultural hierarchies of education, serves notice to concerned practitioners. School leaders need to consider their moral purposes and their health by stepping away from coercion to grow more authentic and integrated approaches to emotional processing that support resilient and adaptive practice.

To offer a way forward, Feldman (2006) argues that emotion does matter in leaders' professional meaning making. Beatty (2002, p. 4) is also adamant that, 'implicitly ... all ... leadership models are foundationally emotional. Leaders affect us emotionally. They move us'. Despite this, and what Beatty and Brew (2004, p. 330) describe as the 'inextricable links among emotion, learning and leading', 'the effective integration of emotional meaning-making as professional practice remains outside the norm in most schools'. In proposing a range of emotional epistemologies that provide a framework for bringing emotions into professional dialogue and practice, Beatty and Brew advocate that proactive educational leaders move from emotional silence and emotional absolutism, where emotional authority is externalised and mandated by organisational standards, to the recognition that inner emotional realities are crucial to professional practice. In developing what is termed 'resilient emotional relativism', leaders openly engage with emotional ways of knowing and creatively collaborate with others in reclaiming an embodied professional practice (Beatty & Brew, 2004). While also noting that the relational aspects of school leadership, which require emotional skills in leaders, are beginning to be recognised, Beatty (2006, p. 22) poses the wider challenge that 'leadership sustainability and principal well-being depend on breaking the silence on emotions in leadership'. This challenge will be taken up later in this chapter when we look at how emotions can be voiced through leaders' wounding and healing. In moving beyond political and economic issues of emotion in professional leadership practice, we will first explore how leaders' personal and social empowerment as active and open emotional meaning-makers might move the metaphors and the fact of emotion from terms of *stress* to *strength*. To understand how such a change can happen, we will consider how emotions work in the mind–body.

Emotion in the Mind–Body

The following explanations draw on neurobiologist Damasio's (1999) work. Emotions contribute to the human body's self-maintenance in the constantly changing environment within and around it. The body has a narrow range of tolerance to change in its state. Body functions are thus directed towards keeping it within the boundaries that support life. They achieve this through maintaining a steady state with minimal fluctuation, known as homeostasis. Without our conscious intention, some parts of the brain continuously monitor the body state, note an array of altered circumstances, and adjust the processes in the body to achieve stability.

Emotions are a basic part of this body maintenance system and serve two biological functions, that of registering a change in the body's external or internal environment, and regulating the body in preparing an appropriate reaction to the change. They are simple bio-regulatory devices directed to supporting our overall organism's stability. However, when *emotions* are linked to the bodily *feelings* they give rise to and to the mental *knowledge of feelings*, the sophisticated mind–body system that results enhances our adaptivity and enables creativity and dynamism in maintaining our steady state. For leaders in education, understanding and working with this system develops an integrated future consciousness that informs a new appreciation of emotional processing in generating strength instead of stress in their personal lives and professional practice.

Emotional Processing

When attention is aroused, the brain deploys regulatory processes towards building conscious, adaptive responses to changes. Without consciousness, an *emotion* is induced by a stimulus to register a change. The emotion triggers a preset neural system whose effect prepares the body for a response. Some preparations can be observed externally as emotional display. A mapping of the stimulus–body relationship establishes what Damasio (1999) calls a *feeling*, a 'private, mental experience of an emotion' (Damasio, 1999, p. 42). A brief, conscious sense of self arises and becomes aware of the feeling. We *know we have a feeling* and properly realise a 'mind–body'. All this happens so rapidly that 'emotions and feelings appear to be a functional continuum' (Damasio, 1999, p. 43). If attention continues, a stronger self-consciousness emerges to shape a response to the stimulus. The brain is engaged in reasoning, the 'complex, flexible, and customized plans of response [that] are ... executed as behaviour' (Damasio, 1999, p. 55), the consequence of which restores mind–body stability.

Superficially, it appears that emotional processing locks us into a kind of habitus of self. 'Groundhog Days' of being stimulated, triggering emotions, forming feelings, becoming conscious of them, and often consciously making decisions about how to respond, all serve homeostasis and survival. Although this 'tyranny of emotion' (Damasio, 1999, p. 58) is based on the 'fundamental stereotypicity, automaticity, and regulatory purpose of the emotions' (p. 51), the system as a whole offers human beings a chance of thriving. The ongoing emergence of a conscious and knowing self adds a creative dimension. As Damasio (1999, p. 303) concludes, '[c]onsciousness is valuable because it introduces a new means of achieving homeostasis'. In knowing the self in reasoned thinking as well as feeling, the mind–body can adaptively refine, or learn, its responses to stimuli. While *emotions* and *feelings* themselves are below the level of consciousness, there are adaptations that can be made once we *know how we feel*. In generative practice, educational leaders can consciously *choose* how to deal with emotionally-laden situations.

In observing others, it is easy to identify the rapid bodily expression of primary emotions such as fear and anger, but we are also adept at detecting subtle tones of background emotions such as 'stress' or 'strength'. These are most often induced internally, that is, by emotions triggering emotions, and by ongoing 'processes of mental conflict, overt or covert, as they lead to sustained satisfaction or inhibition of drives and motivations' (Damasio, 1999, p. 52). (While emotional 'strength' exemplifies the 'high' of sustained satisfaction, 'stress' is indicative of the 'low' of sustained inhibition from emotional labour.) The continuity and intensification of background emotions can lead to identifiable internal states, like the knot in the abdominal muscles from heightened stress or a sense of buoyancy from resilient strength. For educational leaders, too often their mental and body states reflect the background emotion of stress. Here, we will take advantage of the conscious self to assist leaders to choose emotional states of strength.

Tinkering With the System

As a first step in examining the leader's conscious ability to master the mind–body, we need to consider the limitations of the body maintenance system. We cannot control emotions by will, that is, through conscious intention (Damasio, 1999). The preset automata of emotions are so entrenched in human evolutionary biology that, across a lifetime, certain classes of stimuli will cause certain emotions, such as happiness and sadness, in one individual, in individuals with the same sociocultural background, and often across cultures (Damasio, 1999). However, although emotions are induced nonconsciously and the stimulus may or may not be attended to, there can be partial control of 'whether a would-be inducer image should be allowed to remain as a target of our thoughts' (Damasio, 1999, p. 48). The leader has some choice over continuing to focus on, or to ignore, a stimulus that she or he is aware of attending to, for example, verbal put-downs from colleagues.

Once the relationship of the stimulus to the mind–body is established, there is little chance of inhibiting the emotion because the change has been registered by the emerging conscious self. The outward emotional display, however, can be partially controlled, as we commonly see in intentional emotional labour. Damasio (1999) cites the suppression of anger and masking of sadness as examples, but also notes that these are rarely effective, as is trying to fake an emotional expression through mimicry. Trying to appear in another state is often patently obvious to others. Additionally, partial control of outward expression does not, in general, extend to altering the automated changes in the overall internal body state. The 'knot in the stomach', for example, can be persistent. The interior feelings that arise are also not altered. If fear is induced, a stressed leader may project an outer simulacrum of calmness but the inner mind–body and self is feeling frightened and preparing for flight.

Developmental conditioning can also predict a partial control over the unfolding of emotions. Consistently choosing not to attend to an inducing stimulus known to provoke the emotion of anger is one form of self-conditioning. Similarly, experience and subsequent association between stimuli can affect emotional expression. For example, a happiness response to one situation may be extended to other similar situations. One form of conditioning useful to educational leaders in increasing control over emotional expression is what I call 'wait time'. To use the processing of fear as an exemplar, the instinctive flight or fight response is the result of emotion triggering an entrenched neural pattern that uses an old part of the brain to allow rapid, crude, broadbrush processing (LeDoux, 1996). This is a quick and dirty, low road in emotional processing. The stimulus that evokes fear is also processed, albeit slightly more slowly, via a complementary high road through a newer part of the brain to provide greater detail and accuracy in representing the situation (LeDoux, 1996). Although emotional expression has already commenced as a result of the direct, quick and dirty representation, the representation in the newer brain (sensory cortex) can refine the response, for example, by suppressing a response less appropriate than another.

Low road processing is old in evolutionary terms, and effective when an individual is physically threatened in producing fear responses such as 'freezing', increasing blood pressure, the release of stress hormones such as cortisol and adrenaline, and the startle reflex (LeDoux, 1996). However, in today's professional practice, danger often comes in social forms and, for educational leaders, high road processing can be particularly useful in overriding responses that are less personally or socially advantageous. In emotional labour, however, it can also be disadvantageous in being applied to creating responses to emotions that are professionally but not personally of benefit. In conditioning themselves to take a moment of 'wait time', leaders can not only suppress basic, primitive low road responses, but can make conscious and reasoned choices about which sophisticated high road responses are really most appropriate to their needs. Thus, tinkering with the system aside, the real advantage of the tripartite system of emotion, feeling and consciousness for thriving more than surviving lies in the ability to alter cognition and behaviour. Consciousness allows leaders to think and reflect on feelings and their effect. We will return to this later in negotiating a high road to emotional strength and resilience for leaders.

The Cultural Shaping of Emotional Processes

Regardless of the degree to which the body maintenance system that includes emotions is preset biologically, development and culture are highly influential in how this unfolds in our lived experience. Damasio (1999) proposes three primary fields of social and cultural shaping of emotional processes. The first concerns the *shaping of inducers of emotions*. External and internal stimuli mostly work directly to trigger emotion, but indirect induction can happen. This occurs when an inducer blocks the progress of an ongoing emotion and produces a different response. In a school situation, for example, a leader may be involved in an interaction that sparks his or her anger but, working across that, the professional norm of controlling emotional display might inhibit the outer physical expression of anger. Internal responses continue to occur and may be observed outwardly, such as in flushing of the face, but the leader may be able to control a tendency to large body movement, and also use breath control to settle the body.

The second field of social emotional shaping concerns *emotional expression*. Attempts at preventing emotional expression are only ever partially successful because of the limited control of automated, internal changes. Cultural influences however, as cross-inducers, enable us to become adept at disguising outer expression. In emotional labour, while educational leaders in professional practice may become quite effective dissemblers in the service of cultural norms about emotional display and organisational profit or advancement, their acting does not extend to significantly changing the internal bodily expressions of emotion or of the feelings that result. Surrender to emotional stress from continually working against emotional expression, may seem inescapable for leaders.

In the third field of shaping emotional processes, being conscious of the feelings generated in emotional states allows the taking of the high road of mental processing and choosing adaptive over accommodative responses. The knowing self can move beyond reflexive responses to reflect on emotional situations and use reasoning to consider the most appropriate response. In other words, self-consciousness allows us to *shape our thinking processes or cognition (metacognition) and our behaviour following an emotion* (Damasio, 1999). Thinking about feeling draws on experience through reference to socially and culturally shaped memories. What leaders choose as appropriate responses, therefore, has some form of social and cultural bias. The self (as individual) and other (as social, cultural and wider environmental conditionings) are implicit in the mind–body's emotional system and in the emotional epistemologies (Beatty, 2002) we develop to enhance our functioning. Although the quality of that function is related to the fundamental values of homeostatic regulation (Damasio, 1999), leaders, in particular, should also consider that function in terms of adaptability as individual and social beings. Let us look at how that ability for selective response to emotion plays out in lived experience.

The Power of Emotion

As Lupton (1998) observes, the power of emotions can make leaders feel passive and helpless, and that 'we often find ourselves submitting to them or overpowered by them despite our better judgement or our best efforts' (p. 84). Added to this is the socially conditioned sense of trying to feel what we *should* be feeling, according to the norms that make for emotional labour and work. Educational leaders may feel they are swimming against the tides of emotionality, even to the degree of denying their true feelings. Like respondents in Lupton's (1998) study of perceptions of emotions, they are likely to feel that natural expression of emotion is an authentic human need. Allowing others to know internal feelings is a way of facilitating relationships with them. Constraining and repressing emotion may feel dishonest and harmful to physical and mental health. Yet, like others, leaders in education are enmeshed in an experience of emotion which, as explained above, 'involves the interpretation of physical sensations mediated through a body image that is culturally contingent' (p. 167). Lupton argues that one's being-in-the-world and 'location as an embodied subject in a particular socio-cultural milieu' (p. 167) qualifies the physical display of emotion to be viewed as not natural or inherent, but a located product of acculturation. Her explanation is that while a feeling may be internal, its conscious interpretation as evidence of emotion is always a social product. In adjustment, I propose that the inclusive emotion–feeling–consciousness system is natural and inherently culturally modulated because it incorporates consciousness of self, and by extension, of other. Feelings and the actions that follow are indeed socially interpreted (Denzin, 1984), courtesy of self-consciousness and the memory of culturally mediated life experiences. Further, as already noted, inducers and display are also culturally shaped.

As the biology and sociology of the emotional system are inseparable, the leader is always dependent on, and responsive to, the physical *and* social environment. Emotional meaning-making is intersubjective (Denzin, 1984) and thus, emotional management is part of our 'habitus'. The tide of emotion and coming to terms with its power is natural and necessary to wellbeing, rather than something to be fought. As educational leaders accept that sociocultural factors are entailed by the biological, embodied human emotional system, the way is open for engaging with the adaptability that the consciousness of feeling and thinking, and subsequent behaviour, from a position of strength brings. In considering emotion, it is time to move past binaries that work to separate consciousness, such as mind or body, biology or sociology, physical nature or social nurture, thinking or feeling, subject or object, and self or other, and recognise the intrasubjective and intersubjective whole of human being. Leaders in education need to lead themselves, that is, to turn and swim with the tide in generatively using emotional states and feelings to enhance personal life and professional practice. As the educational leader whose words open this chapter indicate, making healthy and empowering choices about responses to emotion puts one 'on the line' and develops the 'best asset' of emotional growth and strength.

Emotional Growth
Choosing the High Road

Living with emotion in more aware, self-chosen ways will involve the educational leader in change. One way to take the lead is to reclaim the emotional aspects of professionalism. Beatty (2002) proposes moving beyond an image of leaders as merely influential. Her alternative view of professional practice for leaders posits emotional experience 'as valuable and informative, important to share, generative and potent for creating connections and making new meanings together' (p. 5). In being 'emotionally connected, contextual knowers who support and respect their own emotions as much as everyone else's' (p. 5), educational leaders' professed assets include a valuing of emotion in leading and a commitment to openly engage in emotional meaning-making in self and with others. Such a change moves professionalism from inscription through 'working on emotion', such as in emotional labour to influence people, to an emotionally integrated professional practice wherein 'growing with emotion' is enabling and empowering for both leaders and followers. Thus, the leader's authentic and emotionally mediated self is engaged in leadership that is less a role than a way of being and his/her new professionalism, in being emotionally situated, is essentially creating a future consciousness of embodied mind.

Changing one's mind–body about emotions in leadership can be a challenge or an opportunity. The latter view is taken here because growing with emotional experience is adaptive and thus about change. Change and emotion are inseparable. Self-initiated change generates pride and satisfaction in accomplishment, as well as trust and excitement (Hargreaves, 2004). As leaders choose to overcome a resistance to change, they accept that, while passive accommodation is a comfortable strategy in managing emotional matters, adaptive strategies that consciously make use of thinking and feeling reasoning have growth outcomes that are satisfying rather than frustrating. However, knowing that positive outcomes can come of emotional engagement may provide insufficient motivation to take up the opportunity of choosing change.

What often lifts motivation to the level of committing to change is a leadership crisis, or 'wounding' experience that elevates states of dissonance to a degree that impels adaptivity. Ackerman and Maslin-Ostrowski (2004, p. 313) propose that 'interpersonal and intrapersonal experience of leadership wounding is itself a defining characteristic of leaders, an important source of emotional and social learning, and a critical opening to the exercise of leadership.' This position is supported here, based on experiences with leaders in crisis (Sytsma, in press). The crisis point provides an opportunity for choice between accommodating to emotional dissonance, with its implications for health, and adaptively *moving* the mind–body through consciously reinterpreting feeling, critically reflecting on patterns on thinking and affirming new ways of being and doing to achieve a sense of emotional integrity. The learning is that emotional dissonance and crisis in leadership can have the positive outcome of engaging the whole of the leader, including feelings, attitudes and authentic relationships, in changing meaning and facilitating a self-and-other integrated professional practice (Sytsma, 2007).

In reflecting on such metachange as a form of emotional healing, and a repair of the divided self, this leadership is true-to-self in being coherent with the values framed by memory, and is in essence about leading or empowering the self. The leader is researching his/her own leadership, seeing experience for what it genuinely is and reflectively witnessing the self as situated within that whole (Sytsma, 2008). Through iterative reasoning, this leadership heightens self-awareness, sharpens moral purpose and commits leaders to ongoing integration through the development of an intersubjective emotional understanding of self and others. In changing the leader's being, it changes the leader's doing and lifts the veil on the habitus of hidden and silenced emotion. Such a 'complex affective paradigm for leadership' is, as Crawford (2007, p. 529) believes, beyond the range of the competencies of emotional intelligence (Goleman, 1996), such as managing moods. The emotionally aware leader is always consciously in motion — cognitively, affectively and physically — and adapting to experience as it is presented and lived.

With Lupton (1998, p. 3) suggesting that, in today's postmodern world, 'emotional responses are viewed as important sources of human values and ethics and as a proper basis for political action', it is time to come to new terms with emotions. Beyond the binaries that have previously characterised emotion, it is also time to choose new metaphors of emotion. Mechanical metaphors have been popular throughout the modern industrial era, as Lupton (1998) indicates. In a world dominated by separated consciousness, hidden and silenced emotions have been of hydraulic concern because they 'build up pressure', or even as dam-buster material when they build up and are 'held back', causing stress. Leaders who are proactively healing recognise that emotional integration develops a strong and resilient sense of self. In allowing emotion to move the mind–body, there is no build up or holding back as a sense of flow (Csikszentmihalyi, 1992) is engendered. Trusting in self and others, the leader is confident that her or his embodied mind can respond creatively, almost momentarily, to emotional situations. In shaping such mind–body participation in future consciousness, adopting metaphors of emotion that speak of human beings rather than machines names a new path in emotional meaning-making and voices a new way of knowing emotion. In coming to new terms with emotions, leaders may come to profess learning, growing and empathetic caring as their fields of developing expertise.

Growing New Metaphors of Emotion

In the earlier mentioned study (Sytsma, 2007) where leaders explored their changing meanings of leadership in a closed mailing list, the themes they generated to describe their various understandings of leadership contained no hint of mechanical metaphors. The first theme, *organic gardener*, immediately demonstrated the group's choice to identify with leadership as a growing process. They saw it as beginning 'at home', in a natural, close-to-the-heart way, unfolding through cycles of change and maturing as a multifaceted constant in relationships. In expressing comfort with the language of growth and development, they noted that, in contrast to relationships in their professional settings, it was satisfying to be connected and have a sense of relational texture among themselves. Despite the group being newly formed, these leaders displayed a considerable level of emotional maturity in their openness and trust of others. That these leaders self-nominated for an exploratory study, albeit in a closed environment, also demonstrated self-awareness and a willingness to engage with emotional others in disclosing and mediating self.

Three weeks into the study, as the leaders negotiated their collaborative sense of self and other, *cooking* emerged as a complementary theme to growing. Just as Hargreaves (2004) suggested a 'slow movement' in educational leaders' reform practices, these leaders would not be hurried by the current norms of professional practice in their cooking up of new recipes of leading. They reflected on the quality of ingredients, how they mixed together and how much time and heat was needed for a delicious outcome. They loved the taste of growing their own agenda and the richness that their profession, in the original sense of the word, as leaders brought to their mix. In reclaiming themselves emotionally in the space of the study, these leaders were able to claim new understandings of what they thought and felt about themselves and their practice.

By the seventh week, they were engaging with stories and dreams of their becoming as leaders. They spoke of their innocence as they grew into adults, feeling like 'a "nakey" babe growing up in the jungle, miraculously unafraid' and 'child-like yet [wanting] to be authentic/"honest", not overapplying the rules'. They wanted to carry the practices of compassion and empathy, modelled to them when younger, into the workplace but found there were issues in being open. They wondered if 'in schools, we become so habituated to referring problems to positionally authorised leaders, or accepting problems as parts of authorised leaders' roles, that we both develop and sustain rigidity in responses'. As wounding and 'pain … taught lessons about transparency in self', it was time to 'starting thinking about world instead of just reacting'. In changing meaning, they came to recognise that 'little life-changing or life-affecting learning takes place until the affect is mobilised, until passion is engaged' and that 'joy [was] found in better appreciating where others are at'. These leaders found their personal power and strength in authentic emotional meaning-making with others, and came to variously name their true selves in leading as a papa bear, the leading duck in a flight, and a glowing dragonfly, 'a magnificent, larger-than-life, ancient, and darkly iridescent creature, with power, grace and speed'.

Over the 7 months of the study, the unfolding themes continued to reflect the group's emotional growth in exploring their evolving meanings of leadership in a safe and confidential space. Other early themes were about the importance of sensitivities and feelings, and about permaculture as representative of sustainable leadership. Themes in the middle months directed related to engagements with primary, secondary or background emotions, such as confidence, conflict, love, hate and fear. Towards the conclusion of the study, themes reflected the emerging emotional integration of the group, with terms such as resilience, chords or 'harmonic resonance', and 'heart and soul' being used. All of these terms reflect the importance that the leaders had begun to place on emotional processing. The space and time of being together effectively supported these leaders' emotional meaning-making such that it, as one leader admitted, 'became a self-help group in which we shared ourselves with each other. That was probably it at its richest'. These leaders demonstrated that, in consciously engaging the whole self in intersubjective knowing, the outcome is that new terms of emotion are declared. The next step for these leaders was to continue to be 'on the line' in courageously translating their changing meanings and learnings in their workplaces.

In another study of principals exploring the emotions of school leadership, also using an online methodology, Beatty (2006) identified common themes in the principals' stories as reflecting a self under siege in the professional workplace. Emotional labour, hidden feelings, isolation and loneliness were what leaders were used to, but the advent of the study group enabled the personal and intimate development of emotionally grounded, relational realities that empowered those involved. Beatty concluded that 'in the face of the isolation and emotional labour inherent in principals' work, they need the regular opportunity to re-integrate with peers, so that they don't literally and figuratively dis-integrate' (p. 32). Remen (1999, p. 35) reminds us that education, at root, is meant to *'to lead forth the hidden wholeness, the innate integrity that is in every person'* [emphasis in original]. She sees educators as healers who bring together ways of thinking and feeling about self and others in wholeness. Educational leaders, in engaging with peers in the processes of wounding and making whole, model an emotionally integrated practice. In coming to terms with emotions themselves and in using new metaphors of emotion, they give permission for feeling and emotional ways of knowing to be visible and valued in educational settings.

New Terms of Emotion

In shaping new terms of emotion in their personal and professional experiences, educational leaders interrupt the habitus. In accepting the embodied-mindedness of the emotion–feeling–consciousness system, there is a shift away from separated consciousness and towards future consciousness. Beatty (2002) expected that the emotionally integrated practice of leadership would require a 'newfound willingness to entertain alternative understandings of mind, body, and self, to rationalist views which have dominated the Western world' (p. 6). We now understand that emotion, the conscious interpretation of feeling in reasoned thinking, and individual and social action are integral aspects of a holistic, mind–bodied sense of human being (Beatty & Brew, 2004; Hargreaves, 2000; Pitt & Rose, 2007).

I now return to the origins of the term emotion to highlight its sense of movement and change. Lupton (1998, p. 4) relates how sociological views of humanity as 'fixed' or 'biological' have been surpassed such that 'emotional states serve to bring together nature and culture in a seamless intermingling in which it is difficult to argue where one ends and the other begins'. While the integrated biology/ sociology of emotion is primarily about homeostasis, it is never about fixedness. Rather, the dynamic balance created to maintain the human life system within acceptable limits is always moving and adjusting. The emotion–feeling–consciousness system, in forming part of this self-regulation, gives human beings a unique advantage in that it enables the adaptive generation of new responses to the inducers of emotion. At the outset, it uses automatic routines in case of danger, but then engages sophisticated new brain systems to modulate reflexive responses or even to cleverly generate completely new ones that give better advantage in the context.

In awake and aware states, this body maintenance system enables us to be always 'on the move', constantly fine-tuning our personal and social senses of self within lived experience. It is in this constancy of motion, its 'now-ness' and its 'flow', that emotional processing (especially when 'wait time' is added) engenders an expanded sense of the moment and of the passage of time. Leaders attuned to this sense, as Beatty and Brew (2004) relate, an emergent quality in the constant recreation of relational integrity through the self-and-other adventures of emotional storying. Such holistic feeling/thinking mind–bodiedness 'emphasises immediate, subjective experience and perspectives' and deepens the 'emotional experience of leadership' (Ackerman & Maslin-Ostrowski, 2004, p. 312). More than this, Zorn and Boler (2007) suggest that a viable conception of emotion and educational leadership needs not only the holistic sense of emotional processing as developed here, but a leadership that is seen 'as an enacted, emergent phenomenon rather than socially expressed or constructed' (p. 137). This implies that emotional ways of knowing cannot be trained or predicated as 'best practice' habits of mind through emotional intelligence skilling but are emergent and responsive in the moving moment. We are thus aiming to move from a professional practice of hiding and silencing emotion into a proactive practice of moving fully into emotional situations with others and engaging collaboratively, as did the leaders in the studies above, in conscious emotional processing to shape adaptive and mutually advantageous responses, all in an expanding and unfolding moment in time.

Conclusion

At the outset, I noted that leadership is a powerful activity. It has been demonstrated here that reconceptualising emotion in terms of strength rather than stress changes the nature of that power from disempowerment to empowerment. In unfolding this chapter, we have moved from emotions being seen as a covert field of labour and work to emotions 'coming out' as growth potentials in educational leaders' integration, resilience, and self-determined personal and professional practices. In engaging with emotional processing through the embodied minds of self and others, educational leaders consciously choose reflective forms of knowing and doing.

To shape such emotionally integrated meanings and actions, it is time to move past the separation of mind and body, and of self and other, towards a future consciousness. Mechanical metaphors for emotion, like stress, can be left to rust while organic metaphors such as nurture, cultivat, and care can be chosen as the seeds of new 'terms of emotion' such as strength and resilience. It is also time to put away the educational leader's 'toolkit' and welcome emotional ways of knowing into a 'garden' of opportunities for growing coherent and mutually empowering relationships in schools, and sustaining health-enhancing professional practices.

References

Ackerman, R.H., & Maslin-Ostrowski, P. (2004). The wounded leader and emotional learning in the schoolhouse. *School Leadership & Management, 24*(3), 311–328.

Bateson, G. (1979). *Mind and nature: A necessary unity.* New York: E.P. Dutton.

Beatty, B. (2002, April). Emotional epistemologies and educational leadership: A conceptual framework, *Annual Meeting of the American Educational Research Association*. New Orleans, LA: American Educational Research Association.

Beatty, B. (2006, April). Principals explore the emotions of leadership. *Redress*, 26–33.

Beatty, B., & Brew, C. (2004). Trusting relationships and emotional epistemologies: A foundational leadership issue. *School Leadership & Management, 22*(3), 329–356.

Bourdieu, P. (1990). *In other words: Essays towards a reflexive sociology*. Stanford, CA: Stanford University Press.

Crawford, M. (2007). Emotional coherence in primary school headship. *Educational Management Administration Leadership 35*, 521–534.

Csikszentmihalyi, M. (1992). *Flow: The psychology of happiness*. London: Random.

Damasio, A. (1999). *The feeling of what happens: Body and emotion in the making of consciousness*. New York: Harcourt Brace & Company.

Denzin, N. (1984). *On understanding emotion*. San Francisco: Jossey-Bass.

Feldman, P. (2006, November). *Emotion matters: Professional meaning making*. Paper presented at Conference of the Australian Association for Research in Education. Adelaide, South Australia.

Goleman, D. (1996). *Emotional intelligence: Why it can matter more than IQ*. London: Bloomsbury.

Hargreaves, A. (2000). Mixed emotions: Teachers' perceptions of their interactions with students. *Teaching and Teacher Education, 16*, 811–826.

Hargreaves, A. (2004). Inclusive and exclusive educational change: Emotional responses of teachers and implications for leadership. *School Leadership & Management, 24*(3), 287–309.

Harper, D. (2001). *Emotion*. Retrieved January 24, 2008, from http://www. etymonline.com/index.php?search=emotion&searchmode=none

Hochschild, A.R. (1983). *The managed heart: Commercialization of human feeling*. Berkeley, CA: University of California Press.

LeDoux, J. (1996). *The emotional brain: The mysterious underpinnings of emotional life*. New York: Simon & Schuster.

Lupton, D. (1998). *The emotional self: A sociocultural exploration*. London: Sage.

Pitt, A.J., & Rose, C.B. (2007). The significance of emotions in teaching and learning: On making emotional significance. *International Journal of Leadership in Education: Theory and Practice, 10*(4), 327–337.

Reason, P. (Ed.). (1994). *Participation in human inquiry*. London: Sage.

Remen, R. (1999). Educating for mission, meaning and compassion. In S. Glazer (Ed.), *The heart of learning: Spirituality in education* (pp. 33–50). New York: Tarcher/Putnam.

Sytsma, S. (2007). *The leading way of changing meaning*. Brisbane, Australia: Post Pressed.

Sytsma, S. (2008). Leaders as seers and witnesses: A changing way of researching leading. *Journal of Spirituality, Leadership and Management, 2008*(01).

Sytsma, S. (2009). The educational leader's alchemy: Creating the gold within. *Management in Education, 23*(2), 78–84.

Varela, F., Thompson, E., & Rosch, E. (1993). *The embodied mind: Cognitive science and human experience.* Cambridge, MA: The MIT Press.

Zorn, D., & Boler, M. (2007). Rethinking emotions and educational leadership. *International Journal of Leadership in Education: Theory and Practice, 10*(2), 137–151.

▶▶▶◀◀◀

CHAPTER 9

Toward an Emotional Understanding of School Success: Connecting Collaborative Culture Building, Principal Succession and Inner Leadership

Brenda Beatty

The Call for Collaborative Cultures: A New Lingua Franca for School Leadership

From sector to sector, state to state, current policy documents, principles and frameworks are increasingly calling for schools to become professional learning communities engaged in dynamic, collaborative inquiry and ongoing refinement of teacher practice. Correspondingly, leadership is being reconceived as multidimensional, learnable and widely distributed. To foster collaborative cultures in their schools, leaders who are humane, self-aware and open to new learning are more likely to be successful. Whatever the nomenclature, systems are beginning to embrace the notion that shared language goes hand-in-hand with shared understanding.

To illustrate this direction, at the national level the federally funded entity, *Teaching Australia's* 'Leading Australia's Schools' course includes topics addressing planning and implementing change, understanding self and relationships with others, developing capability in their own teams, operating strategically and having a professional impact beyond their own school. The Victorian state school system's developmental learning framework for school leaders endorses Sergiovanni's (1994) human, cultural, educational, symbolic and technical leadership forces and helps build participative leadership capacity across the system. In the same state, the Catholic Education sector's leadership development framework (Catholic Education Commission Victoria, 2009) features a clear moral purpose, building relationships, understanding and managing change, creating and sharing knowledge, and ensuring coherence and alignment of structures in various areas of action. The Association of Independent Schools, also in Victoria (AISV, 2008) features many of the same elements in short courses: the changing nature of the principalship, leading and managing change; technical details including media relations and human resource management; improving student outcomes through attention to best practices, diversity, positive learning cultures and commitment to continuous improvement.

At the national level, the Australian Principals Association Professional Development Council (APAPDC) offers its L5 Leadership Framework based on five propositions (APAPDC, 2007):

- leadership starts from within
- leadership is about influencing others
- leadership develops a rich learning environment
- leadership inspires leadership actions and aspirations in others.

Indeed, the call for a shift from school cultures characterised by disconnected silos of specialty to ones that enjoy collaborative interdisciplinary inquiry and ongoing professional learning is strengthening. Reflected in these approaches is the demand for nothing short of a redefinition of principals' ways of working. What is needed is a shift away from the prototypical bureaucratic, hierarchical figurehead, who operates from a position of disconnected positional authority.

Tomorrow's leader is relationally attuned, an interdisciplinary thinker and a collaborative learner. S/he has equal humility, and is fully engaged as a cooperative participative inquirer in the project of making schools smarter (Leithwood, Aitken, & Jantzi, 2006). These authors invite us to imagine the nature of nonbureaucratic educational organisations: '[s]uch organisations embrace rather than eschew overlapping responsibilities, collective accountability, open-ended tasks, imprecise goals, and evolutionary planning' (p. 16). They remind us that, '[t]aking action in an organization is like firing a cue ball into a complex and large array of billiard balls' (Leithwood et al., 2006, p. 16). The premises of learning organisation theory inform the recommendations of most leading educational leadership theorists.

Shifting the Culture: Rediscovering the Love of Learning Together

School reform is essentially dependent on teacher learning. Collaborative teacher learning in schools is a teacher preference among the various professional development modalities on offer (Flores, Rajala, Simao, Tornberg, Petrivic, & Jerkovic, 2007), one that requires a commitment to inquiry and the development of communication skills (Ball & Cohen, 1999; Lampert, 1999; Lieberman, 1995). Yet, if educators are to engage in daily collaborative professional learning, teachers and leaders need strong resilient relationships and open lines of communication. 'Some disequilibrium is needed for professional learning ... they should be able to puzzle about things together, disagree about aspects of the grounded practice they are debating and reach their own conclusions'. (Groves & Wallace, 2007, p. 4)

In contrast, contrived collegiality (Hargreaves & Dawe, 1990), restricted lines of communication and even distance and disconnection are common. The all important trust factor for healthy resilient working relationships remains underdeveloped (Tschannen-Moran, 2007). Thus, despite these encouraging trends in policy, in practice there emerge several critical issues:

- What are the opportunities and challenges in a policy environment that is inviting these kinds of changes in focus and emphasis in school leadership?
- How do leaders and teachers come to recognise and extricate themselves from the limitations inherent in influential cultural traditions of the past?
- What is required for leaders and teachers to embrace a different way of working together?
- How can programmatic approaches assist leaders and teachers to prepare themselves for creating the collaborative professional learning communities they need to meet the demands of the day?

Shifting the culture involves going deeper to build trusting reliable relationships through which professionals can work supportively and interdisciplinarily, sharing real concerns and celebrating successes as well as addressing weaknesses in their practice. For the leadership class, when the challenge to distribute authority is met, their schools can enjoy an ethic of shared responsibility (Blase & Blase, 2001). This means letting go of hierarchical command and control tactics and adopting instead, a far more respectful, caring, supportive, transparent style. This is a tall order for those who have become wedded to well-rewarded ways of the past.

Indeed, if policies could 'make it so', the harvest of collaborative professional learning communities that is the all-important improved learning opportunities for students would already be in every classroom. For some schools who have done the hard yards of changing their ways and learning to trust and learn together, there is evidence that the effort has been well worthwhile (e.g., Bryk & Schneider, 2002) as student performance is predictably linked to the level of trust among adults in schools. However, the inertia of traditional professional cultures in schools, the persistent norms of the teacher–leader relationship characterised by professional silence and apparent obedience combined with covert resistance and outright antagonism (Starratt, 1991), are unlikely to change merely in response to new policy imperatives. Cultures have their own inertia.

Another important trend to consider across institutions generally is the increasing requirement for accountability implemented through regular evaluations. This is evident in school systems through student performance data and staff surveys. As the saying goes, that which gets measured gets valued. Thus one might argue that it could be influential to both value and evaluate signs of a healthy school culture. In the Victoria state school system for instance, among a suite of yearly measures provided to all schools are the results from a staff survey that considers some of these themes. Schools are encouraged to make sense of these data as they direct their energies for strategic improvement. Also in Victoria, to receive accreditation as a 'Performance and Development Culture' state schools get feedback on data that explicitly pertain to teacher perceptions about the level of professional collaboration and shared leadership in their schools. While some might question the validity of the results of these surveys, given the implicit and sometimes explicit pressure to select '4s' and '5s'(anecdotal), the trend toward putting a specific label on the qualities of high performing and well developing schools is arguably a step in the right direction. The measurement of progress toward the cultural underpinnings of leading edge school reform deserves attention.

While we may have entered a time of transition, and there are signs that things are shifting as noted above, if the vision is to become a reality that lasts and not just a data point from a one-off survey, the success of school improvement initiatives will depend on the power of new collaborative cultures to sustain their momentum. With the call for major school reform, high stakes national testing and league table comparisons among schools, principals and teachers are finding themselves in the middle of an emotional maelstrom (Jeffrey & Woods (1996); this, in times when principal succession planning issues are becoming acute. Could the 'problem' pressures of today's demands on educators hold within them, the seeds of their own solutions?

To answer this question, it is important to look not only at the quantity but also at the quality of these demands. If for instance, 'Understanding self and relationships with others' is required, how does a traditional school leader begin to accomplish this? Often through sustained isolation in the role and the perpetual emotional labour of masking real feelings and projecting others (Hochschild, 1983), leaders become emotionally numb, and dis-integrated, cut off from their inner meaning-making processes and personally and emotionally disconnected from their colleagues (Beatty, 2002a). With their inner resources depleted in this way, understandably leaders become dispirited with correspondingly deleterious effects upon their own wellbeing and that of their staffs and their families (Beatty, 2002a). The problem is persistent and well worth exploring.

Not only is leadership inherently taxing, even though it may be highly rewarding, to lead one must disturb the status quo. Understandably, in response, people regularly resist and push back, even lash out. Woundings are to be expected (Ackerman & Maslin-Ostrowski, 2002) — it is the nature of the beast. Yet there is little in the dominant traditional culture of school leadership to remediate the personal fallout from these inevitable events. Over time, to manage the pressure, typically in isolation, if leaders become hardened in order to cope they find their inner emotional meaning-making processes less and less accessible. This is a dangerous phenomenon when one's moral and ethical centre (Margolis, 1998) and capacity for empathy and relational connectedness are so reliant on retaining access to one's emotions (Denzin, 1984). The question emerges: What difference could a focus on the emotions of leadership make? Over the past decade, the results of my research with teachers and leaders who have been deliberately and explicitly encouraged to go through the emotions to access and reintegrate the multidimensions of mind indicate that this can be a fruitful approach.

There is much to be done to help educators, and especially school leaders, work through the outmoded traditions of denying emotion's place in their inner professional lives. In part this is really a matter of reclaiming their entitlement to be human. When leaders become more comfortable with their own emotional meaning-making processes they also begin to accept their imperfections and their entitlement to consider themselves 'a work in progress'. From this perspective, it is a natural progression to confer the same entitlement upon others. Such leaders find it easier to recognise and respect a wider diversity of perspectives, seeing them more as a rich resource than a threat (Beatty, 2007a). By going through the emotions, in collaborative reflection with trusted others, leaders and teachers are finding they can heal from old scars and release new energies (Beatty, 2007a, 2007b). In effect, they are 'growing stronger in broken places' (Leask & Beatty-Leask, 2003). A return to this theme follows a consideration of some of the complexities of leadership succession planning.

Leadership Succession Planning 'Crisis': Understanding Dangers and Opportunities

Success is literally and figuratively inherent in 'success'ion planning. Australia, like most Western nation states, is facing the danger of its schools becoming captain-less ships. Statistics on applicants as a ratio to positions on offer suggest a steady decline in applications for principalship positions, albeit more intensified in some schools and some areas and some sectors than others (Gronn & Lacey, 2004, 2006; Lacey, 2001, 2002, 2003, 2004). Coupled with the demographic reality that most principals are (now) 5 years or so from retirement, this makes the imminent danger of the crisis quite evident (Pyke, 2002; Rowe, 2000).

Lacey (2003) identified a number of disincentives among teachers with respect to applying for the principalship: too much stress, too little time, negative impact on family, deleterious impact of society problems and lack of budget. Studies of the acute lack of applicants in the NSW Catholic Education system (e.g., D'Arbon, Duignan, & Duncan, 2002) identified similar disincentives with perceived negative impact on personal and family life the most frequently represented. Even so, as Gronn and Lacey (2006) note, it is still not appropriate to infer simple disinterest. There are other factors that obstruct access to the principalship in Australia.

In their study of aspirant principals, Gronn and Lacey (2006) asked focus group participants to identify supports and blockers to their career aspirations. Blockers outweighed supports and the most frequently cited blocker was school-based appointment and selection; a pattern these authors call cloning — the tendency to hire who you know — was reported to act as a significant disincentive to prospective applicants along with other 'application mechanisms, interview treatment of candidates, and postinterview experiences' (Gronn & Lacey, 2006, p. 106).

Perceptions of the position as unattainable, principal work–life balance as unachievable and conditions of the job untenable all help to explain why many teachers are simply eliminating this option from their career plans. They see the toll that the job takes on their own leaders and, for many, that is evidence enough that they are best to steer clear. This is a pity, as principals are almost unanimously enthusiastic and passionate about their work and usually say they would not want to do any other job in the world (Beatty, 2005).

But do teachers get all of their impressions about the principalship directly from their own professional experiences? North American media representations of the principalship are argued by Thomson, Blackmore, Sachs, and Tregenza (2003) to be skewed toward the negative as they reflect the political and policy push of the sources for these articles. We see the same pattern in the Australian media. Thomson et al. note that what is less well-represented, but very important to communicate is '… the satisfying emotional–intellectual nature of principals' work and the importance of being part of a team working on a common endeavour' (p. 127). This view is echoed by the Deputy President of the Australian Secondary Schools Principal Association, Wendy Teasedale-Smith (2007, http://www.aspa.asn.au/content/view/147/38/), who challenges that the workaholic hero principal prototype is dysfunctional. She notes that while stress issues persist and more support is needed, '[t]here is another story out there and it needs to be told … There are large numbers of principals who find their jobs rewarding, challenging and fulfilling'.

Indeed we know much more now about both the 'privilege and the price' of this important position (Saulwick & Muller, 2004), as health and longevity issues have been directly linked to the conditions of the job. Contributing importantly to the national awareness of school leader wellbeing issues, the Australian Primary Principals and Australian Secondary School Principals Associations track principal wellbeing in national surveys each year. The findings from these surveys have for some time signalled the definite dangers of the work (e.g., Carr, 2000), along with the need to look after principals, rather than leaving them to manage the myriad complexities and high stress levels (Thornton, 1996) alone. Thomson and Blackmore (2006) call for a major redesign of the work of school principals.

Another factor that contributes to the succession planning challenge, one that is particularly pertinent to the Australian context, is that the pathway to the principalship is not clear. While there are various aspirant leader programs offered in most states and their respective school sectors and there are master's courses that pertain to leadership, Australia does not have a national- or a state- level certification requirement for principals. There is no 'sheep dip' through which one may become officially anointed as ready for the job. Instead, traditions of internal promotions and old boys' networks have led many teachers, irrespective of gender, to put their would-be aspirations for the principalship into the 'too hard basket'; the perceived challenges for female aspirants can be particularly daunting (Lacey, 2004).

Along with the challenges to aspirants, principals themselves may be unwittingly contributing to the succession planning problem. As Hargreaves warns (Hargreaves & Fink, 2006), it is difficult to imagine the organisations we lead as going on without us. But principals must do this, if they are to mitigate rather than exacerbate the succession planning challenges ahead. 'Effective educational leaders are strategic about building leadership in the school, to sustain the school and education generally into the future' (D'Arbon & Dormon, 2004, http://www.leeds.ac.uk/educol/documents/00003655.htm). Principals who model shared and collaborative leadership provide opportunities for subordinates to learn new leadership ropes. Without sufficient opportunities to try these new ropes, however, teachers are less likely to be able to imagine themselves in the role of school leader.

The style of school leaders is profoundly influential. Leaders who exhibit closed transactional styles engender lower engagement and a greater likelihood of emotional malaise in their teachers (Blase & Anderson, 1995). While one might hope that the best do eventually join the leadership team, we also need to be aware of research that has informed us of a disquieting pattern whereby the brightest and the best can become victims of mistreatment, marginalisation and bullying (Blase & Blase, 2003). One interpretation of this research is that principals who lack the emotional preparedness to manage their feelings of insecurity, may feel threatened by a gifted articulate teacher and become defensive, protectionistic, even deliberately damaging, in order to silence the voice of dissent and/or to avoid being overshadowed. It is a slippery slope from wounded to wounding (Beatty, 2004); abuse tends to beget abuse. Teachers in school cultures with leaders who rule by fear experience models of the role that are anathema to trust, nonconducive to collaborative culture-building and less likely to experience healthy leadership development opportunities.

Thus, we can appreciate the dangers of the succession planning crisis, in terms of both perceptions and realities.

- *Realities*: The wave of greying baby boomers is leaving the scene. There is a dwindling number of applicants. Pathways are less than clearly defined and encumbered by traditions suggestive of favouritism and cloning (Gronn & Lacey, 2006). Stress levels and health threats abound due to the questionable manageability of the complexity and sheer volume of the work. Little support for stress management is provided. Many principals are suffering in silence.
- *Perceptions*: Leadership positions are inaccessible. Hiring practices are unfair and even corrupt. Due to unaddressed woundings from being bullied and marginalised, or knock-backs with disrespectful or non-existent debriefs, highly capable aspirants infer they are unwelcome or unsuitable for the job. The role is considered unattractive and a danger to one's family, one's health and one's happiness.

We need to understand how the traditional bureaucratic culture is so inclined to persist. Once we understand this, we can design support for leaders to become well prepared to reduce stress, foster wellbeing and at the same time provide the necessary conditions for creating collaborative cultures.

Transcending the Iron Cage of Bureaucracy

Organisational cultures have an amazing capacity to persist. The norms of bureaucracy have a particularly powerful inertia that is a matter of emotion. According to social theory philosopher, Max Weber, bureaucracies' iron cage qualities can be directly attributed to depersonalisation.

> … the more fully realized the more bureaucracy 'depersonalizes' itself, that is, the more completely it succeeds in achieving the exclusion of love, hatred, and every purely personal, especially irrational and incalculable, feeling from the execution of official tasks. In the place of the old-type ruler who is moved by sympathy, favor, grace, and gratitude, modern culture requires for its sustaining external apparatus the emotionally detached, and hence rigorously 'professional' expert. (Weber, as cited in Coser, 1977, p. 230)

The dangers and difficulties are clear, but the opportunities begin to emerge when we start to understand the deleterious effects of de-emotionalised 'professionalism'. While some might argue that bureaucracies are time-honoured and have served us in the past so why not in the future, bureaucracies are built to move slowly and change very little. They are not suitable for adjusting nimbly to the pressing challenges facing the world today (Rischard, 2008). By co-maintaining the norms of 'professional' silence on emotion, teachers and leaders unwittingly become part of the self-replicating mechanism of bureaucratic hierarchy (Beatty, 2000c) and contribute to society's sluggish responsiveness to pressing problems. A different, more efficient, synergistic approach to understanding problems and working together to solve them needs to emerge now. Schools are the ideal places to model these new ways of seeing and being. The key is to interrupt the cycle. Successful school leadership can do just that by transcending the traditional cultural imperative for depersonalised practices that deny emotion's important place in our lives and its influence upon our experiences of self and others.

In the educational discourse the call for a departure from traditional bureaucratic hierarchies has been heard for some time; for instance in the advocacy for teacher empowerment in shared decision-making (e.g., Blase & Blase, 1994; Malen & Ogawa, 1988; Peterson, Gok, & Warren, 1995; Short & Greer, 1997) and the associated necessity of different, more collaborative relationships (e.g., Dunlap & Goldman, 1991). Yet the focus on the emotional dimension of leader teacher relationships is a relatively recent arrival. Blase and Blase (1994/2001) note some of the emotional effects on teachers from the process of being empowered. Desirable qualities of leaders who employ transformative, facilitative styles that involve engaging in 'power with' their teachers are reflected in positive emotional indicators, conceptualised as micropolitical phenomena by Blase and Anderson (1995). But a primary focus on emotions per se, especially the emotions of leaders, is new to education. Going through the emotions — to build self-awareness, foster resilience in relationships and strengthen team effectiveness for problem-solving and developing new solutions collaboratively — is showing real promise (Beatty, 2007a, 2007b).

With the increasing emphasis on instructionally focused school leadership, teachers and leaders need to acknowledge each other's expertise and engage in developmental processes together (Glickman, Gordon, & Ross-Gordon, 1998). The professional domain of the classroom is emotionally sensitive territory for teachers. Understandably then, attunement to these matters of emotion is foundational to effective instructionally focused leadership.

The need to build a more humane and interpersonally connected professional cultures in schools has been well-argued by others, including Nias, Southworth and Yeomans (1989); Lieberman (1996); Hargreaves (1998a, 1998b) and Fullan (1999, 2008). When such relationally grounded collaborative cultures are developed, they are enjoyed and celebrated as sources of support for improved teaching and learning. Such professional cultures are characteristically more emotionally comfortable (Nias et al., 1989).

Yet, despite the encouraging evidence from a minority of exemplary collaborative schools, in the main, the teacher–leader relationship remains problematic (Blase & Anderson, 1995; Blase & Blase, 2003) and the resulting systemic tensions undermine the ability to trust. While we may be able to envision school cultures with teachers and leaders within them energised by the spirit of cooperation, creating dynamic learning communities together, if an ethic of depersonalisation persists, the envisioned evolution is unlikely. To reculture schools as vibrant learning communities we require a reconceptualisation of the role of leadership and a reframe of the parameters for developing a healthy professional leadership identity.

Inner Leadership: Getting to the Heart of School Renewal
Leaders, Put Your Own Oxygen Mask on First ...

Schools that are dynamic learning organisations can improve continuously and sustain their own momentum. Such schools are a pleasure to work in and to lead. Even so, as accountability pressures mount, and leaders disturb the status quo and inevitably become wounded, they need to become prepared to embrace the potential for deep emotional learning in these occasions (Ackerman & Maslin-Ostrowski, 2002, 2004). Conversely, without sufficient support for processing the pain and repairing the damage, isolated leaders are likely to become less effective at doing what they need to do to keep themselves and their professional learning communities healthy. This can become a vicious circle, one that deserves our attention.

With school leadership reconceptualised in terms of placing a top priority on the inner work that helps keep leaders well, educators can envision and co-create a different future, one that is far more appealing and accessible to aspirant leaders and sustainable for incumbents. Like the imperative to put one's own oxygen mask on first in a mid-air crisis, principals who understand, value and have well-grounded experiences in

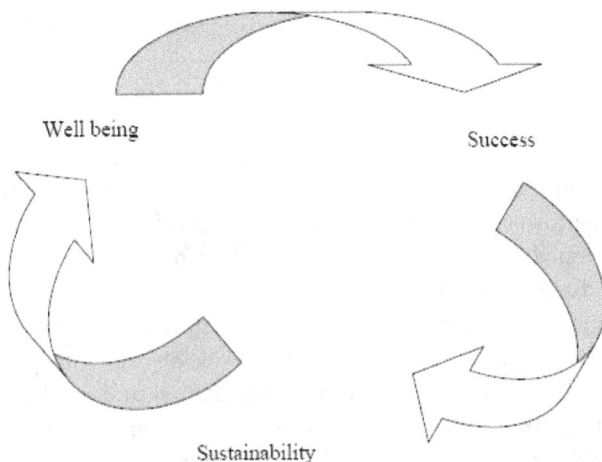

FIGURE 9.1
Wellbeing success and sustainability.

reflective, emotional meaning-making, are also better prepared to collaborate authentically (Beatty, 2006), even in the midst of increased performativity pressures (Ball, 2000; Blackmore, 2004). Such leaders are also more likely to be able to work with each other to create a unified expression of their concerns and make a difference at a system level if they are not silenced by their own fears and disempowered by their isolation from one another. Emotional wellbeing, school improvement and the sustainability of success are inextricably linked. Instead of a 'vicious' circle, together they can create a positive reinforcing spiral of cause and effect that is generative and self healing (see Figure 9.1).

> To create successful schools, leaders, teachers, students and parents need to develop new, more effective ways of working, communicating and learning together. To overcome the traditional antagonism between teachers and leaders (Starratt, 1991), teachers and parents, and even teachers and students, new mental models are needed that acknowledge the role of trusting relationships in learning, teaching and leading. (Tschannen-Moran, 2007, p. 107)

Exploring the Importance of Trust

Research with young people demonstrates that the greatest risk factor for developing a life of crime is the detachment from school altogether.

The presence or absence of social protective factors is well-known to be predictive of pro- or antisocial behaviours and learning outcomes (Dean, Beatty, & Brew, 2007). Yet we are just beginning to explore how intertwined are the relationships among adults in schools with the social emotional conditions for student learning. The level of trust among adults in schools has emerged as an important predictor of student performance outcomes (Bryk & Schneider, 2002). In a study that developed and validated an instrument to measure student sense of connectedness with school (Beatty & Brew, 2005), structural equation modelling provided evidence of plausible connections among student trust in leaders, trust in teachers, sense of belonging with peers, academic engagement, confidence in self at school and academic optimism. The suggestion of a shadow effect from perceived leader trustworthiness through teacher trust by students, to student engagement, underscores the importance of the principal in creating conditions of trust. School leaders set the tone and shape the culture that is reflected in student learning. The principal is a deciding factor. 'Quality school administrators lead their schools by transforming their culture into one that emphasises cooperation, trust, openness, and continuous improvement' (Hoy & Miskel, 1996, p. 237).

Teacher openness to new learning and creativity in the classroom is connected to the sense of social emotional and professional safety that engenders or fails to engender the willingness to trust. Understanding trust involves an appreciation of emotional risk. The trustworthy principal makes a commitment to relationship.

In a disposable society known for revolving door relationships, trustworthy principals stand for something different. They let all their constituencies know that conflict and even betrayal are not necessarily the last word. They hold out the hope of reconciliation and the repair of trust. But it is not enough to just lift up a vision; trustworthy leaders must also play the role of mediator when trust breaks down (Tschannen-Moran, 2007).

Awareness of the emotion factor in the teacher–leader relationship (Beatty, 2002a) and the leader's influence upon teacher emotions (Leithwood & Beatty, 2008) are among the most important keys to school success. Ken Leithwood and I in our recent book, *Leading with Teacher Emotions in Mind* (2008) address some of the ways leaders can make a difference in teacher working conditions, so that they can get on with their most highly prized work — making a difference in students' lives.

What's Good for the Goslings ... Connecting Adult and Student Learning Conditions

The need for a secure foundation from which to reach out and grow by experimenting and taking learning risks is as important for adults as it is for children. In commenting on his latest book, *The Six Secrets of Change: What the Best Leaders Do to Help their Organizations Survive and Thrive*, Michael Fullan (2008) noted that it all boils down to relationships, relationships, relationships (Fullan, 2007). By influencing the sense of safety and cooperation experienced by adults in the cultures of their schools, leaders influence the learning conditions of students (Silins & Mulford, 2002) and teachers (Leithwood & Beatty, 2008).

When leaders demonstrate humility, respect, self-reflection and genuine interest in others and in learning and inquiring together, they model and teach trustworthiness. In such schools all adults can have a positive impact upon each other as well as on the children and parents, through flow-on effects that are most accurately envisioned in exponential terms.

Pressures Upon Leadership Preparation and Development: Yes We Can!

School leadership preparation and development programs are becoming the next place to put the onus for the fulfilment of society's needs. However, Leithwood and Levin (2008) argue convincingly, that research into program effectiveness is highly complex.

> ... formal development experiences are just one of many influences on leaders' actual behaviors and they are less powerful than others such as leaders' internal states, existing skills, beliefs, values and dispositions. Internal states constitute the perceptual filters and meaning-making 'tools' through which all other potential influences must pass if they are to change leaders' behaviors. In order to change leaders' behaviors, other types of influences must actually change some aspect of a leader's internal states. (p. 289)

Given the profound influence of principals upon their school cultures (Silins & Mulford, 2002; Leithwood, Aitken, & Jantzi, 2006) and through the trust factor upon teaching and learning (Beatty & Brew, 2004, 2005), we can no longer ignore the importance of linking leader learning and development with social and emotional wellbeing. A starting place is inside the leader her/himself.

Highlighting that it is these inner states of leaders that must change, Leithwood and Levin (2008) note, however, that there are other powerful influences including the social, cultural and historical contexts of leaders' work. These authors appreciate that power, respect, hierarchy and the place of diversity may play very differently in different parts of the world, and for that matter in different school regions. This internal state domain, they argue further, composes an enormous storehouse of tacit knowledge that they consider to be, by definition, inaccessible. On the other hand, Polanyi (1962), who coined the expression tacit knowledge, was more interested in tacit knowing processes, a more dynamic image if you will. Let us imagine these pools of tacit knowledge and consider the renewing generative potential that lies beneath the surface of these waters.

Importantly, the conscious exploration of tacit ways of knowing, such as emotional meaning-making processes, can be very successful, but it requires inner work, and personal contact, ideally with trusted peers. We *can* make the tacit explicit. As Barth (2004) recommends, and I too have found, reflection works best when it is written, shared and discussed. To enliven our reflective powers, leaders may tell their stories and listen deeply to each other, using various frames for listening and providing feedback (e.g., the facts, the emotions, the values, the holistic impression etc.). As leaders do this, they begin to story and restory themselves (Beattie, 1995), discovering and rediscovering their ways of knowing and experiencing firsthand how to create similar opportunities for others (Beatty, 2006).

Yet this notion of sharing one's inner experiences is distinctly counter to the traditional leadership culture's norms of projected certainty, pseudorationality and professional silence on emotion. The reintegration of the multiple inner dimensions of one's socially situated self represents a tall order, especially when custom has it that leaders are traditionally required to leave their emotional and even their moral integrity at the door in order to gain entry to the principal class (Marshall, 1992; Marshall & Greenfield, 1987). Yet, to handle the challenges facing schools today, we need nothing less than emotionally grounded leaders; this so that healthy resilient authentic relationships can become the strongest links in the learning chain.

Programmatic Approaches

A progression of design iterations for leadership preparation programs has ensued between the 1940s and the present day. North American universities began by championing models based on industry with a focus on compliance and passivity in the ideal worker. Dominant were technicist managerial orientations with an explicit focus on hierarchy and control, wherein '[e]fficiency, rationality and precision became the watchword as educational leaders worked to build a stable, predictable and reliable hierarchy for teachers and students'; whereas today the 'limits of the bureaucratic regulatory model have been reached' and '[s]chools will need to flatten out the hierarchies' as principals become

> prepared to create the conditions for a professional teaching force by sharing planning and decision-making responsibilities with staff … The idea that answers to school problems cannot be fixed from the top requires a fundamental reordering of the very fabric of the relationship between administrators and teachers. (Mulkeen & Cooper, 1992, p.17 & 22).

Like the trend in current Australian policies, a recent study of leadership preparation programs in the United States has signalled the critical need for principals to learn how to support teachers and develop collaborative learning communities (Davis, Darling-Hammond, LaPointe, & Meyerson, 2005). These authors found that cohort structures, mentoring and collaborative support networks also need to be embedded in programs that ideally include internship/practica, such as leading change action research projects, as core to their assessment protocols.

In response to the much needed support for principal wellbeing, the Australian Principals Association Professional Development Council under the leadership of Jeremy Hurley and in collaboration with a committee of professional and academic consultants, created a nationally available workshop entitled *Leaders Lead*, in which the L5 framework is used. Participating school leaders are coached to reconsider, reframe and reintegrate their view of themselves and their work in terms of the potential confluence among personal, professional and organisational dimensions (also see Beatty, 2000a). The workshop promotes reflective practice, puts an emphasis on emotional ways of making sense of the work, and nurtures collaborative processes while encouraging leaders to value and seek out peer support networks to help them overcome the isolation of the job.

Other programs will no doubt be discussed in other chapters in this volume. The remainder of this chapter will focus on one Master in School Leadership[1] (MSL) course in the state of Victoria, which has given prominence to the role of emotion with promising results.

Putting Emotion on the Agenda

Over the past 10 years of working with incumbent and aspirant leaders in various programs and award courses, both in the United States (see Beatty & Brew, 2004) and Australia, I have found that the most effective way to foster personal and professional growth — transformation if you will — is by acknowledging and working with the emotions, rather than stepping around them, denying them, silencing them, rationalising them and even shunning them as pesky interlopers (Beatty, 2000b). I reject the proposition that we should feel shame that we have emotions. Emotions are not optional. It feels counterintuitive to acknowledge them and is countercultural to speak of them, but I believe our new mental models for leadership need to be grounded in the explicit acknowledgment of the role of emotions.

Breaking the silence and putting emotions on the agenda (Beatty, 2000b) has provided a highly successful 'way in' to addressing the serious challenges of leader wellbeing and, at the same time, fostering the development of emotional preparedness for collaborative culture-building, school improvement and sustainable success. Aspirant leaders begin the MSL course often expressing fear they may lose themselves by taking on the borrowed robes of leadership. In this course and other professional development programs of the same ilk,[2] participants soon discover that leadership can be redefined in terms of finding yourself and helping others do the same. This reconception of leadership as a journey to centredness and authenticity, as unleashing rather than controlling others, is both inviting and exciting.

By fostering the reintegration of the personal professional and organisational 'self' (Beatty, 2000a) and deliberately disturbing the traditional professional culture of silence on emotion, leaders learn to recognise and mitigate the usual side effects of perpetual emotional labour (Hochschild, 1983). They begin to reform their schemas for leadership.

In my earlier emotions of leadership research, through the grounded theory analysis of qualitative data from 50 Canadian teachers and 35 principals from six Western nation states, I gained some valuable insights. These included the toll that emotional labour and the isolation of the role were taking on principals and head teachers. We also explored some of the corresponding deleterious effects that professional isolation and emotional silence were having on their relationships with teachers. An emotional epistemologies theoretical framework emerged from this research, along with evidence of the transformational effects of breaking the silence on emotion (Beatty, 2002a, 2002b).

The resulting framework presents four perspectives or stances: (1) *emotional silence* within which emotions are denied or shunned as too difficult or dangerous, which is the traditional norm; (2) *emotional absolutism*, within which emotional knowledge authority remains externally defined by organisational norms or feeling rules that reward and punish displays of approval and disapproval; (3) *transitional emotional relativism*, in which the transformational power of emotional meaning-making is discovered and recognised and (4) *resilient emotional relativity*, in which reflective and collaborative emotional meaning-making becomes a regular modus operandus. (See also Beatty & Brew, 2004.)

Among the results from interviews with graduate MSL participants to consider the flow on effects if any from their emotions focused work in the course, are the following (Beatty, 2006):

- facing fears affirms the place of authentic curiosity and acknowledging vulnerability transforms it into a strength
- making emotions explicit creates inner change
- redefining leadership as the entitlement to imperfection helps in transcending the need to direct and confront: moving toward relationship
- reframing conflict as an opportunity to build trust and strengthen relationships helps overcome tendencies to be defensive or aggressive
- discovering the role of emotional reflection for understanding self and others helps close the gap on the teacher–leader relationship
- by embracing a pedagogy of discomfort (Boler, 1999) and applying the power of reflection it becomes possible to seek support from trusted others and affirm the importance of safe spaces for collaborative learning
- This 'new breed' of leader
  - challenges the culture of silence on emotion and positions emotional meaning making as critical to her/his own wellbeing, and the well being of others
  - embraces diversity of perspectives with confidence and respect
  - uses emotional meaning making to build and maintain healthy relationships that provide a strong foundation for the leadership of change.

Looking Back on the Dynamics of Some Key Programmatic Processes[3]

Increased awareness of the role of emotions emerges through the collaborative reflective practices in the course. All MSL students write their own and respond to peer reflections designed to demonstrate the conscious integration of personal/emotional, professional, organisational and scholarly meaning-making processes. This is not an easy transition, from a position of emotional silence to one of openly sharing and exploring inner experiences. 'I had trouble finding an emotionally reflective voice. It was a valuable experience in the end'.

However, the effort creates a critical springboard to experiencing firsthand, some new mental models for leadership based on alternative perspectives and practices:

> The most powerful opportunity to consider the emotions of leadership for me occurred through participation in the on-line forum ... Through interacting with others & sharing our stories ... we were able to build a trust with each other that meant we were in a safe place to share our true emotions about our experiences.

Together we deliberately break the 'emotional silence', challenge the norms of the traditional feeling rules (Hochschild, 1983) that demand masking and feigning of feelings and acceptance of the norms of external rewards and punishments that dictate what is 'right' to feel, (emotional absolutism) (Beatty, 2007a). We reposition this ongoing activity of recognising the external feeling rules and reflecting upon inner emotional meanings and their complex derivations as pivotal to sustainable professional leadership practice. School leaders soon begin to experience 'transitional emotional relativism' (Beatty, 2007a).

> The four stances [from the emotional epistemologies framework] have underpinned all that we do in the course and in the opportunities to make sense of our professional and personal learning.

> When we shared that [vulnerability and fears] together and online and others validated or affirmed that they too felt this way, it opened up a community of trust and acceptance that I had not previously experienced in Education apart from two of my mentors.

Through an exercise conducted early in the course, the relevance to leadership practice emerges.

> The most powerful experience of recognising the power and usefulness of emotions in our work was to collect data on a negative and

positive experience with leadership. This helped us to recognise what wounding does in terms of the emotions never disappearing and therefore being the cause of us wounding others.

Going through the emotions helps leaders strengthen their reflective practice as they make meaningful personal professional and scholarly connections.

> The best thing for me has been the reflective writing. Making connections between my scholarly, personal and professional life and thinking and connecting and exploring the feelings behind it. The emotional meaning-making helps me to understand my motivations and why sometimes that intuition about a situation kicks in.

> By being encouraged to integrate the importance of emotions during my tertiary study I think I connected with the course and the course material on a much deeper level [and] significantly developed my reflective self ... continually reflecting on how the readings connected to my own experience both personally and professionally.

In evidence is the importance of consciously embracing a pedagogy of discomfort (Boler, 1999), wherein emotional discomfort is recognised and reframed as a source of learning rather than something to fear and avoid: 'the journey of discovering myself was empowering, and scary'. As well this emotional journey acts as a catalyst for developing resilience which is the cornerstone of wellbeing and sustainability.

> Finally, after two years I feel a resiliency of spirit and heart that I haven't had before. It's permission to accept your whole self and share that with others. I feel like I have made many mistakes in my leadership but now more than ever they are learning opportunities rather than shameful. The power of reaching out and working through a wounding has forged bonds with staff members I have not previously been able to reach.

Emerging throughout these several studies of MSL graduate experiences are links among emotions, self-acceptance, wellbeing and greater effectiveness in the practice of relational leadership, even when the person does not consider themselves to be particularly empathic.

> I have had the opportunity to use my learning in the workplace. I am not a very empathetic person. The awareness of my emotional state within my work place has made me more aware of the emotions of the people I work with.

I have become more conscious of following up with people … to thank … for support … A staff member was angry about a couple of things but deep down was grieving about leaving. I consciously went and spoke with her to let her work thru her anger then talked with her about my experiences when I left a school. The conversation finished with her tears, a hug and thanks. I think she felt happier.

I am much more willing to acknowledge emotions in my day to day work. While prior to the course I believed I was a good manager, my greater knowledge of emotions has developed my understanding of what good leadership is. That is, good leaders not only acknowledge the emotions that are connected to day-to-day work but also actively encourage the recognition of emotions in the workplace.

Leaders who learn to work in this way become more aware of the impact of emotional silence and emotional absolutism by observing and reforming the treatment of emotions in their school cultures.

I've become more aware of how other leaders try to squash recognition of the emotions in the decisions they make and how this affects those they work with.

I am aware that my actions and attitude can have a profound effect on the people that I work with and that I can change the overall feeling of the school, for better or worse.

They make the connection between emotional meaning-making, offering of self and lessening their need to control, as they become open to new kinds of collaborative learning opportunities.

While I was busy being worried about being the one with all the answers I blocked the learning of others. My need to be in control, because I felt insecure about my gifts and my areas of need, often led me to assume the motivations of others instead of our learning being constructed together.

Leaders who recognise the role of emotions have success in leading change by developing an emotional understanding (Denzin, 1984) of resistance:

I have come to realise that leaders who do not have a good understanding of emotions and how they may impact on a person are not as effective as those who do. For me, good leaders model the recognition of emotions — particularly when it comes to implementing any type of change. When these leaders make decisions that are likely to have negative emotions attached then they acknowledge this and try to minimise the negative impact as much as possible.

The awareness of emotions has caused me to stop and view those on staff traditionally labelled as 'blockers' in a new way and I am beginning to develop a better way of working with them … I am better able to implement change in a school situation … because of my increased awareness of emotions in leadership I am often seeking out conversations with others who have the same awareness—particularly when I'm looking for a sounding board or advice on leadership decisions I need to make.

Since becoming a principal and participating in the Masters program I have become much more active in dealing with my emotions and considering others.

Emotions are positioned as a catalyst for managing the workload with greater ease. The sense of membership coupled with the ability to disagree without fear, figure prominently in the following account, which illustrates the participant's associations among wellbeing, relationships and workload management.

Our work is so huge, unending and, at times, overwhelming that there needs to be that emotional hook that creates the sense of flow so that the workload appears to minimise. Building relationships built on mutual respect where conversations are about meaning-making is that hook for people. You can achieve great things if you feel you are part of a team that values your contribution, that you can disagree without fear of retribution and that learning is a process.

The importance for leaders to establish their own base of support emerges clearly in the following participant statement:

[S]taff do not necessarily reciprocate with a similar understanding. It is as if you are the leader and you are not supposed to have … issues in terms of stresses, coping, workload. And so once they have worked thru an issue with me, they feel better and I feel unloaded on! I therefore have learnt how important it is that I have someone to work thru things with — in my case it is the other AP in my school. We support each other, unload to each other and have become critical friends who offer support, constructive feedback etc. It is a growing honest relationship — I think all leaders need one.

I could not agree more. Collaborative reflection holds the most healing and transformational power: Leaders need to seek out, establish and maintain a base of safe support for themselves, so that they can maintain their own inner wellbeing. By breaking the silence on their own emotions with trusted others they overcome the traditional isolation of the role. When fears are identified and faced and wounds addressed, they find it far easier to achieve a genuinely nonanxious presence (Friedman, 1985) from which they can be present to others and avoid becoming defensive or aggressive, even in the face of opposition. Signs of resilient emotional relativity emerge clearly in these leaders as they apply their emotional preparedness to get on with the tough work of leading change.

> I think I have learned not to be afraid of opposition. Although I am really well prepared for the things we need to do I am more prepared now because I am open to people and their fears. I spend a lot more of my time listening to the hopes and dreams of others for kids and our school and through talking we build that picture together.

Associated with this approach is a greater comfort with and openness to a wider diversity of perspectives:

> My message of making a difference shines now because I am able to tap into the passion I feel about people and not be afraid to share it. [As a new principal] I came to understand my school community much faster by listening to all voices than by blocking those that might have been a danger. In recognising all voices and being able to model learning from mistakes, we are on the way to building a strong team … I don't have to be a cool cucumber … I don't have to build a brick wall to protect myself.

There were signs that the acknowledgment of emotions was playing a role in helping these leaders stay morally centred and connected with their values, which reflects Sergiovanni's (1992) call to moral leadership through relationally connected communities of learning, and Margolis' (1998) notion that the emotions are essential to the ethical fabric of the self.

> Through this [MSL course] I feel like I reached an inner core of myself where I was firmly placed in my value system. I feel a strong emotional resilience now that used to waver all over the place depending on where I was and what I thought others thought were important. The course helped me immensely in being a better leader and helped me articulate my leadership and share it with others … As a result I was able to apply and secure a Principal position. While

I am on a steep learning curve, many of the emotional meaning-making lessons and ability to reach out and connect with people are standing me in good stead. I think it has made me understand myself more fully and value my own contributions as well as others in the leadership of a community.

Summary and Conclusions

While the call for collaborative professional learning communities is emerging clearly in policy documents, and evaluative frameworks such as those used presently in the Victoria state school system offer needed emphasis, there is still much to be done. Heralding the transition to a different style of leadership, the policy requirement to foster such communities cannot simply be added on to the seemingly endless list of principal responsibilities. There is a qualitative issue here. Instead of seeing this mandate as just one more thing to work on in the same old fashion, leaders need to become emotionally prepared to lead in entirely new ways.

The work of going through the emotions to enliven inner leadership dynamics and deepen the capacity for integrative ways of seeing and being, holds promise. Leadership preparation and development programming would do well to acknowledge the transformational potential of leading with the emotions in mind (Beatty, 2009). When emotional meaning-making becomes second nature to educational leaders, the new collaborative shared leadership culture envisioned may be able to emerge quite naturally. In the process, teachers will have all the opportunities they need to try leadership 'on for size' and experience firsthand, ideal models of shared authority and cooperative learning across a wide spectrum of positional responsibility. It is less likely in such cultures that so many of the brightest and best teachers will find themselves bullied and marginalised. Instead, the infectious excitement of collaborative professional learning may become pervasive and even one of the best perks of the job!

Positioning emotional meaning-making as standard professional practice simply makes pragmatic, albeit (un)common, sense. Leaders need to come to terms with the emotional work of looking after their inner selves, for the very important reason that in so doing they will be far better able to look after others. In the coming years, as classroom instruction and student relationship management receive greater emphasis, those who are emotionally prepared for leading with not only their own, but also teacher emotions in mind, cannot help but be better suited for the important collaborative work that lies ahead. With the principalship redefined in these terms, and leader wellbeing, collaborative culture-building and sustainable school success going hand in hand, I expect soon there will be no shortage of applicants for the job.

Endnotes

1   The Monash Master in School Leadership was established in 2004 in response to the Department of Education and Training Victoria's tender call for places in a master's course that was designed to prepare aspirants and practicing principals and assistant principals to lead culture change and school reform through the creation of collaborative professional learning communities. The experiential approach embedded a carefully sequenced series of units was tailor-made for this purpose: Understanding self and others; Leading Learning Communities; Understanding Environments and Leading Change: Professional Action Research. With a sufficiently high grade point average the course provides a direct pathway to PhD studies at Monash.

2   A professional development program entitled *Human Leadership: Developing People* was commissioned in 2006 by the Victorian Department of Education and Early Childhood Development to foster similar transformational learning effects for leaders.

3   All of the comments cited in the following section were derived from research involving interviews and open-ended surveys with MSL graduates who hold substantive positions in the principal class.

References

Ackerman, R., & Maslin-Ostrowski, P. (2004). The wounded leader and emotional learning in the schoolhouse. *School Leadership and Management, 24*(3), 311–328.

Ackerman, R., & Maslin-Ostrowski, P. (2002). *The wounded leader: How real leadership emerges in times of crisis.* San Francisco: Jossey-Bass.

Australian Independent Schools Victoria. (2008). *Leadership development short course offerings.* Retrieved November 14, 2008, from http://www.ais.vic.edu.au/

Australian Principals Association Professional Development Council. (2007). *Learn: Lead: Succeed.* Retrieved February 26, 2009, from http://www.pa.edu.au/servlet/Web?s=157573&p=LLS_INDEX

Ball, S. (2000). Performativities and fabrications in the education economy: Towards the performative society. *Australian Educational Researcher, 27*(2) 1–25.

Ball, D., & Cohen, D.K. (1999). Developing practice, developing practitioners: Toward a practice-based theory of professional education. In L. Darling-Hammong & G. Sykes (Eds.), *Teaching as the learning profession: Handbook of policy and practice* (pp. 3–32). San Francisco: Jossey-Bass.

Barth, R. (2004). *Learning by heart.* San Francisco: Jossey-Bass.

Beattie, M. (1995). *Constructing professional knowledge in teaching: A narrative of change in professional development.* New York: Teachers College Press, Columbia University, and Toronto: Ontario Institute for Studies in Education Press.

Beatty, B. (2009). Developing school administrators who lead with the emotions in mind: Making the commitment to connectedness. In T. Ryan (Ed.), *Canadian Leadership Paradigms* (pp. 161–185). Calgary, Alberta, Canada: Detselig.

Beatty, B. (2007a). Feeling the future of school leadership: Learning to lead with the emotions in mind. *Leading and Managing, 13*(2), 44–65.

Beatty, B. (2007b). Going through the emotions: Leadership that gets to the heart of school renewal. *Australian Journal of Education, 51*(3), 328–340.

Beatty, B. (2006). Becoming emotionally prepared for leadership: Courage, counter-intuition and commitment to connectedness. *International Journal of Knowledge, Culture and Change Management, 6*(5), 51–66.

Beatty, B. (2005). Emotional leadership. In B. Davies (Ed.), *The essentials of school leadership* (pp. 122–144). Thousand Oaks, CA: Sage.

Beatty, B. (2004). Book review of J. Blase & J. Blase, *Breaking the silence: Principal mistreatment of teachers*; R. Ackerman & P. Maslin–Ostrowski, *The wounded leader. Educational Administration Quarterly, 40*(2) 296–312.

Beatty, B. (2002a). *Emotion matters in educational leadership: Examining the unexamined.* Unpublished doctoral dissertation, Ontario Institute for Studies in Education, University of Toronto, Canada.

Beatty, B. (2002b, April). *Emotional epistemologies and educational leadership: A conceptual framework.* A paper presented at the American Educational Research Association, New Orleans.

Beatty, B. (2000a). Teachers leading their own professional growth: Self-directed reflection and collaboration and changes in perception of self and work in secondary school teachers. *Journal of In-Service Education, 26*(1) 73–97.

Beatty, B. (2000b). The emotions of educational leadership: Breaking the silence. *International Journal of Leadership in Education, 3*(4) 331–357.

Beatty, B. (2000c, September). *The paradox of emotion and educational leadership.* A keynote address presented to the British Educational Administration and Management Annual conference, Bristol, UK. Available at http://www.shu.ac.uk/bemas/beatty2000.html

Beatty, B., & Brew, C. (2005). Measuring student sense of connectedness with school: The development of an instrument for use in secondary schools. *Leading and Managing, 11*(2) 103–118.

Beatty, B., & Brew, C. (2004). Trusting relationships and emotional epistemologies: A foundational leadership issue. *School Leadership and Management, 24*(3) 329–356.

Blackmore, J. (2004). Leading as emotional management work in high risk times: The counterintuitive impulses of performativity and passion. *School Leadership and Management, 24*(4), 439–459.

Blase, J., & Anderson, G. (1995). *The micropolitics of educational leadership.* New York: Cassell.

Blase, J., & Blase, J. (2003). *Breaking the silence: Overcoming the problem of principal mistreatment of teachers.* Thousand Oaks CA: Corwin Press.

Blase, J., & Blase, J. (2001). *Empowering Teachers: What successful principals do.* Thousand Oaks, CA: Corwin Press.

Blase, J., & Blase, J. (1994). *Empowering teachers.* Thousand Oaks, CA: Corwin Press.

Boler, M. (1999). *Feeling power: Emotions in education.* New York: Routledge.

Bryk, A., & Schneider, B. (2002). *Trust in schools: A core resource for improvement.* New York: Sage.

Carr, A. (2000). *State principals' welfare needs: Annual survey.* Sydney, Australia: New South Wales Principals Association.

Catholic Education Commission Victoria. (2009). *Leadership in Catholic Schools: Development Framework and Standards of Practice.* Retrieved February 26, 2009, from http://lsf.vic.catholic.edu.au/

Coser, L.A. (1977). *Masters of sociological thought: Ideas in historical and social context* (2nd ed.). New York: Harcourt Brace Jovanovich.

D'Arbon, T., Duignan, P., & Duncan, D. (2002). Planning for future leadership of schools: An Australian study. *Journal of Educational Administration, 40*(5), 468–485.

D'Arbon, T., & Dormon, J. (2004, September). Career aspirations and succession planning of potential applicants for leadership positions in Australian Catholic schools. Paper presented at the *British Educational Research Association Annual Conference*, University of Manchester. Retrieved 18 January, 2009, from http://www.leeds.ac.uk/educol/documents/00003655.htm

Davis, S., Darling-Hammond, L., LaPointe, M., & Meyerson, D. (2005). *School leadership study: Developing successful principals.* Stanford, CA: Stanford Educational Leadership Institute.

Denzin, N. (1984). *On understanding emotion.* San Francisco: Jossey-Bass.

Dean, S., Beatty, B., & Brew, C. (2007) Creating safe and caring learning communities: Understanding school based development of social capital. *ACEL Yearbook, 2007.* Melbourne: Australian Council for Educational Leadership.

Dunlap, D.M., & Goldman, P. (1991). Rethinking power in schools. *Educational Administration Quarterly, 27*(1), 5–29.

Flores, M., Rajala, R., Simao, A., Tornberg, A., Petrivic, V., & Jerkovic, A. (2007). Learning at work: Potential and limits for professional development. In J. Butcher & L. McDonald (Eds.), *Making a difference. Challenges for teachers: Teaching and teacher education* (pp. 141–156). Rotterdam, The Netherlands: Sense Publishers.

Friedman, E.H. (1985). *Generation to generation.* New York: The Guilford Press.

Fullan, M. (2008). *Six Secrets of change: What the best leaders do to help their organizations survive and thrive.* San Francisco: Jossey-Bass.

Fullan, M. (2007). Interview podcast *New imagery for schools and schooling*. ACEL Annual International Conference Oct 1–3. Retrieved November 12, 2008, from http://www.acel.org.au/index.php?id=792

Fullan, M.G. (1999). *Change forces: The sequel*. Bristol, PA: Falmer Press.

Glickman, C., Gordon, S., & Ross-Gordon, J. (1998). *Supervision of instruction: A developmental approach*. Needham Heights, MA: Allyn & Bacon.

Gronn, P., & Lacey, K. (2006). Cloning their own: Aspirant principals and the school-based selection game. *Australian Journal of Education, (50)*2, 102–121.

Gronn, P., & Lacey, K. (2004). Positioning oneself for leadership: Feelings of vulnerability among aspirant school principals. *School Leadership and Management, 24*(4) 405–424.

Groves, R., & Wallace, J. (2007, November). *The nature of teacher learning: Talk about teaching among video study club participants*. A paper presented at the annual conference of the Australian Association for Research in Education, Fremantle, Australia.

Hargreaves, A. (1998a). The emotional practice of teaching. *Teaching and Teacher Education, 14*(8), 835–854.

Hargreaves, A. (1998b). The emotional politics of teaching and teacher development: with implications for educational leadership. *International Journal of Leadership In Education, 1*(4), 315–336.

Hargreaves, A., & Dawe, R. (1990). Paths of professional development: Contrived collegiality, collaborative culture, and the case of peer coaching. *Teaching and Teacher Education, 6*(3), 227–241.

Hargreaves, A., & Fink, D. (2006). *Sustainable leadership*. San Francisco: Jossey-Bass.

Hochschild, A.R. (1983). *The managed heart: The commercialization of human feeling*. Berkeley: University of California Press.

Hoy, W.K., & Miskel, C.J. (1996). *Educational administration: Theory, research, and Practice* (5th ed.). New York: McGraw-Hill.

Jeffrey, B., & Woods, P. (1996). Feeling deprofessionalised: The social construction of emotions during an OFSTED inspection. *Cambridge Journal of Education, 26*(3), 325–343.

Lacey, K. (2001, September). Succession planning in education. Australian Council for Educational Administration. *Hot Topics, 4*, 1–2.

Lacey, K. (2002). *Succession planning in education*. Retrieved November 10, 2008, from http://www.apapdc.edu.au/2002/downloads/2002/Lacey_succesion_planning.pdf

Lacey, K. (2003). *Factors that impact on principal-class aspirations*. Unpublished doctoral dissertation, University of Melbourne.

Lacey, K. (2004). Women in teaching: Factors that impact on their leadership aspirations. *IARTV Seminar Series* (No. 131). Melbourne, Australia: Incorporated Association of Registered Teachers of Victoria.

Lampert, M. (1999). Knowing teaching from the inside out: Implications of inquiry in practice for teacher education. In G. Griffen (Ed.), *The education of teachers: 98th Yearbook of the National Society for the Study of Education, Part 1* (pp. 167–184). Chicago: University of Chicago Press.

Leask, D., & Beatty-Leask, M-E. (2003). *Strong in broken places.* Song lyric in *Tightrope of Dreams.* David Leask/Jeddart Music (SOCAN).

Leithwood, K., Aitken, R., & Jantzi, D. (2006). *Making schools smarter: Leading with evidence.* Thousand Oaks, CA: Corwin Press/Sage Publications.

Leithwood, K., & Beatty, B. (2008). *Leading with teachers' emotions in mind.* Thousand Oaks, CA: Corwin Press/Sage Publications.

Leithwood, K., & Levin, B. (2008). Understanding and assessing the impact of leadership development. In J. Lumby, G. Crow & P. Pashiardis (Eds.), *International handbook on the preparation and development of school leaders* (pp. 134–157). New York: Routledge.

Lieberman, A. (1996). Networks and reform in American education. *Teachers College Record, 98*(1), 7–45.

Lieberman, A. (1995). Practices that support teacher development. *Phi Delta Kappan, 76*(8), 591–596.

Malen, B., & Ogawa, R.T. (1988). Professional-patron influence on site-based governance councils: A confounding case study. *Educational Evaluation and Policy Analysis, 10*(4), 251–70.

Margolis, D.R. (1998). *The fabric of self: A theory of ethics and emotions.* New Haven: Yale.

Marshall, C. (1992). *The assistant principal: Leadership choices and challenges.* Newbury Park, CA: Corwin Press.

Marshall, C., & Greenfield, W. (1987). The dynamics in the enculturation and the work in the assistant principalship. *Urban Educatio, 22*(11), 36–52.

Mulkeen, T.A., & Cooper, B.S. (1992). Implications of preparing school administrators for knowledge work organizations: A case study. *Journal of Educational Administration, 30*(1) 17–29.

Nias, J., Southworth, G., & Yeomans, R. (1989). *Staff relationships in the primary school.* London: Cassell Education.

Polanyi, M. (1962). *Personal knowledge.* Chicago: University of Chicago Press.

Peterson, K.D., Gok, K., & Warren, V.D. (1995, August). *Principals' skills and knowledge for shared decision making.* Washington, DC: US Department of Education, Office of Educational Research and Improvement.

Pyke, N. (2002, February 9). Counting Heads. *The Tablet,* 18–20.

Rischard, J. (2008, September/October). High noon: The urgent need for new approaches to global problem-solving and the role of education institutions. Keynote address ACEL *New Metaphors for Leadership in School* Annual International Conference Melbourne.

Rowe, R. (2000, January 14). Shortage of school principals looming. *New Zealand Education Review.*

Saulwick, I., & Muller, D. (2004) *The privilege and the price. A study of principal class workload and its impact on health and wellbeing.* Melbourne, Australia: Department of Education and Training. Retrieved 18 January, 2009, from http://pandora.nla.gov.au/tep/46027

Sergiovanni, T. (1994). *Building community in schools.* San Francisco: Jossey-Bass.

Sergiovanni, T. (1992). *Moral leadership.* San Francisco: Jossey-Bass.

Short, P., & Greer. J. (1997). *Leadership in empowered schools.* New Jersey: Prentice Hall.

Silins, H., & Mulford, W. (2002) Leadership and school results. In K. Leithwood & P. Hallinger (Eds.), *Second international handbook of educational leadership and administration* (pp. 561–612). Dordrecht, The Netherlands: Kluwer Academic Press.

Starratt, R.J. (1991). Building an ethical school: A theory for practice in educational leadership. *Educational Administration Quarterly, 27*(2), 185–202.

Teasedale-Smith, W. (2007). *We don't need another hero.* Australian Secondary Principals Association Online. Retrieved February 26, 2009, from http://www.aspa.asn.au/content/view/147/38/

Thomson, P., & Blackmore, J. (2006). Beyond the power of one: Redesigning the work of school principals and schools. *Journal of Educational Change, 7*(3), 161–177.

Thomson, P., Blackmore, J., Sachs, J., & Tregenza, K. (2003). High stakes principal-ship — Sleepless nights, heart attacks and sudden death accountabilities: Reading the media representations of the United States principal shortage. *Australian Journal of Education, 47*(2), 118–132.

Thornton, P. (1996). The physiological, psychological and work stress of primary school principals. *International Journal of Educational Management, 10*(6), 42–55.

Tschannen-Moran, M. (2007). Becoming a trustworthy leader. In *The Jossey-Bass reader on educational leadership* (2nd ed., pp. 99–114). San Francisco: Jossey-Bass.

▶▶▶◀◀◀

CHAPTER 10

Middle-level School Leaders: Understanding Their Roles and Aspirations

Neil C. Cranston

Middle-level school leaders (e.g., deputy principals, assistant principals, associate principals) have received considerably less attention by researchers in recent years compared with their principal colleagues. This is despite several decades of self-managing school trends and more recent arguments for distributive leadership models in schools. As a result of this research dearth, there are few documented understandings of how their roles and responsibilities have been evolving under the plethora of changes impacting on schools. Further, in a context of a potential growing demand for principals in the near future to replace retiring baby-boomer principals, the intentions (or otherwise) of such school leaders to seek principal positions are of interest. This chapter draws on a number of recent studies that looked specifically at just what such middle-level schools leaders did in their roles, what attitudes they held regarding various aspects of their roles and what their views of the principalship were in a context of possible future career aspirations. The chapter concludes with some issues for schools and school systems to consider.

Background and Context

Increasingly, designated school leaders other than the principal, with various titles such as deputy principals, assistant principals, heads of school (e.g., junior, middle), deans of study and so on, have started to attract research interest in various countries (National College of School Leadership [NCSL], 2003). This is in a context where the vast bulk of research into school leadership in recent decades has focused almost exclusively on the principalship. In this vain, the NCSL noted 'that the international literature pertaining to assistant and deputy headteachers is substantially smaller than that relating to headteachers or principals' (p. 2). Other writers, such as Harvey and Sheridan (1995), saw the deputy principalship as remaining 'one of the least understood roles in the schools of contemporary education systems' (p. 90).

Indeed, Harvey (1994) suggested the possibility of an interest growing in Australia in such positions, but it was not until a study by Cranston, Tromans and Reugebrink (2004) that any in-depth work in one system (Queensland) and type of school in Australia, at least, was available. The situation is similar in New Zealand, although Fitzgerald (2004) did look at gender issues in middle management in schools. Despite the dearth of research in this important area of school leadership, there is broad acceptance that deputy principals hold key leadership and administrative positions in schools (Webb & Vulliamy, 1996) and would certainly have been impacted upon by the various reforms, devolution and accountability agendas of recent decades. However, some observers believe the roles of such leaders have emerged 'without a proper philosophical basis, and its development … has continued to be more a matter of expedience than an end product of careful planning (Golanda, 1991, p. 266). Indeed, Garrett and McGeachie (1999) identified that there was a considerable lack of clarity about the role, certainly for primary deputies in the United Kingdom. Harvey's (1994) work in Australia was more critical, describing positions such as deputy principals as a wasted educational resource. His research revealed that deputy principals were struggling for a greater involvement in instructional leadership and management of school level change.

In the United States (US), Porter (1996) reported assistant principals as seeing their role as the 'daily operations chief', with their major foci being on staff and student issues. West (1992) in the United Kingdom (UK) used an aircraft analogy, describing such positions as a 'co-pilot' compared with the head as the 'pilot'. Weller and Weller (2002) noted the role as one of ensuring stability and order. That is, it was a role concerned with maintenance rather than leadership or development. Garrett and McGeachie's (1999) research supports this, revealing that primary school deputies thought of their role more in operational terms, with very few able to develop more strategic perspectives in their schools.

It is this set of leaders 'below' the principal — deputy principals, assistant principals, heads of school, deans of study and so on — which is the focus of interest in this chapter. Many in this middle-level leadership group are at what Hopkins (2001) described as at the cusp of entry to the headship. The chapter acknowledges the importance and positive contributions of distributed, shared and multiple leadership models in schools (Cranston, 2000; Crowther, Kaagan, Ferguson, & Hann, 2002; Gronn, 2000, 2003; Katzenmeyer & Moller, 1996) and other organisations (Limerick, Cunnington, & Crowther, 2002). Typically, however, while the leadership roles and responsibilities of principals, middle-level leaders and teachers may change under these models, it is the principal who remains in the 'hot seat' and who, under self-managing school models, essentially is now responsible and accountable for almost everything that happens in the school. Not surprisingly, then, there is now a plethora of research reporting that the roles of principals have changed significantly in recent years (see for example, Cranston, 2002; Cranston, Ehrich, & Billot, 2003; Gronn, 2003; Leithwood, Jantzi, Early, Watson, Levin, & Fullan, 2004). Not only are they expected to be the educational leader of their school, but under the increasing managerialistic models of school operations, their role has emerged into one akin to a CEO in the private sector (Cranston, 1999; Gronn, 2003). Indeed, as our conceptualisations of schools and schooling for the future change (Beare, 2001; Caldwell, 2005), the complexities and demands of the principalship are likely to increase. What must not be overlooked in discussions about such issues is that the complexities and demands on those in middle-level positions are also likely to change and intensify.

As well as a need to deepen our understandings of the roles of such school leaders, their intentions regarding career moves into the principalship are of interest as the literature (see for example, Barty, Thomson, Blackmore, & Sachs, 2005; D'Arbon, 2003; Lacey, 2002) is increasingly pointing to a crisis of sorts in attracting and keeping quality people in principal roles as the retiring baby-boomer phenomenon (Healey, 2003) starts to have an impact. It may be that this group of middle-level leaders, the natural set of next generation leaders, may not be as large as might be expected. At least two factors have emerged to create closer interest in this aspirant pool, the first of which is the age profile of current principals (D'Arbon, 2003; Lacey, 2002). Consistent with the baby-boomer retirement phenomenon evident in most western countries, the next few years are likely to see a significant increase in the number of retirees from the principalship in many these countries. The replacement demand of itself would perhaps not be a matter of major concern were it not for the second factor, that there is increasing evidence that the aspirant pool is not all that large — that is, the number potentially wanting to move into the principalship is smaller than expected (Preston, 2002). One of the key drivers in determining whether talented principal aspirants actually decide to move into the principalship will be what they actually think about school leadership, and the principalship in particular.

Within this dynamic, in examining the career decision-making of aspirant principals in Scotland, Draper and McMichael (2003) reported a declining interest in the principalship. James and Whiting (1998) earlier noted a similar trend in the United Kingdom. In the United States, a 1998 survey commissioned by the National Association of Elementary School Principals (NAESP) and the National Association of Secondary School Principals noted that half of the school districts surveyed reported a shortage in the labour pool for K-12 principal positions they were trying to fill that year regardless of location (NAESP, 2003), noting that 'qualified professionals are not seeking the position of school principal' (p. 1). The concern about such issues is widespread, with Brooking, Collins, Court and O'Neill (2003) reporting principal recruitment problems in primary schools in New Zealand and Williams (2003) looking at the principal shortage in Ontario, Canada. In the United Kingdom, the appeal of school leadership to prospective leaders was a key focus of research commissioned by the Department of Education and Skills (Earley, Evans, Collarbone, Gold, & Halpin, 2002). It captured the negative view of the principalship held by many:

> Leaders in schools are de-motivated by over-bearing bureaucracy and excessive paperwork and also by 'constant change' in the education system. Balancing work and home life is an increasing concern and more work is needed to make school leadership both an attractive and do-able task. (p. 1)

In Australia, research (see, e.g., Barty et al., 2005 — Victorian and South Australian states & Lacey, 2002 — Victoria) has revealed similar trends, which are also evident in the Catholic school system, with a major study commissioned to look at the issue (D'Arbon, Duignan, & Duncan, 2001, 2002; D'Arbon, 2003; Dorman & D'Arbon, 2003). In response to this concern, some systems such as the Catholic and Lutheran sectors have mounted specifically targeted leadership programs for their potential future leaders (details of these programs are examined in Chapter 5). What the various studies into the aspirants are highlighting is that we need deeper understandings about just what they — our middle-level school leaders — actually do in their roles and what their views are about the principalship from a career aspiration perspective.

The chapter draws on four research studies to examine some of the issues raised above: three from Australia (Cranston, 2006, 2007a, 2007b, 2007c; Cranston et al., 2004) and one from New Zealand (Cranston, 2007b). The New Zealand study is included as it provides additional data from a country and education system not too different from Australia. The chapter provides a scan across the data from the four studies in an effort to look more strategically at some of the important findings regarding what the middle-level school leaders think about their roles and responsibilities, what their leadership career aspirations might be and how these might be developing.

The Four Research Studies

The four research studies providing the basis for the discussion are:

- *Study 1*: respondents included middle-level school leaders from non-state (i.e., nongovernment) primary and secondary schools in Brisbane and Sydney (Australia) — research reported in Cranston (2006);
- *Study 2*: respondents included secondary middle-level leaders from schools in the Auckland (New Zealand) area — research reported in Cranston (2007b, 2007c);
- *Study 3*: respondents included secondary middle-level school leaders in state (i.e., government) schools across Queensland (Australia) — research reported in Cranston et al. (2004).
- *Study 4*: respondents included primary and secondary middle-level leaders in state schools across Queensland — research reported in Cranston (2007a). This study is drawn on to specifically investigate the career aspirations of middle-level leaders.

Each of the first three studies was focused around the following set of questions:

- How satisfied are middle-level school leaders with their current position?
- What are some of the general characteristics surrounding their roles, such as degree of pressure, time spent and variety of work done?

- Is there role alignment between what they actually do in their role (the *Real*) and what they would like to do in a preferred situation (the *Ideal*)?
- What capabilities do middle-level school leaders see as critical to carrying out their roles?

The fourth study was concerned with questions about:

- What are the views of potential aspirants, in particular deputy principals in primary and secondary schools, about the principalship?
- What are the intentions of potential aspirants in seeking promotion (or otherwise) to the principalship, and the reasons driving such intentions—encouraging, discouraging?

The data were collected via the *Roles of School Leaders Questionnaire* (RSLQ) — Studies 1 and 2, and the *Secondary Deputy Principal Questionnaire* (SDPQ) — Study 3, both of which have significant commonalities in structure and questions and also both of which drew, in part, on an instrument used in earlier research into the principalship in Australia and New Zealand (Cranston, Ehrich, & Billot, 2003). The instrument contained mainly closed items, about half of which contain several subsections within each item; several open-ended items linked with closed items providing the opportunity for explanation of responses; one specially targeted open-ended item; and one general open-ended item. Most of the closed items were in a Likert format, with 5 response options, examples of which included *very satisfied* to *very dissatisfied* or *very important* to *not important* (Kerlinger & Lee, 2000). It was anticipated the questionnaire would take about 15 to 20 minutes to complete. It was completed anonymously, although respondents could add their name and contact details if they so wished with a view to potential participation in follow-up interviews at a later time. The fourth study draws on data from the *Aspiring Principals Questionnaire (APQ)* administered to deputy principals in state primary and secondary schools in Queensland across 2005–2006. (A fuller discussion of the development and structure of the *APQ* is available elsewhere [Cranston, 2007a].) The *APQ* was especially developed for the study from concepts synthesised from the literature, as well as ideas from the three studies noted above. It was similar in format, structure and response mode to those noted above for the RSLQ and SDPQ.

Details of the research participants are provided elsewhere (see, Cranston et al., 2004; Cranston, 2006, 2007a, 2007b).

Findings and Discussion: Examining the Middle-Level School Leader

The findings across the first three sets of data are presented under a number of headings, consistent with the various foci of the questionnaires. Findings from the fourth study (see later) provide deeper insights into the career aspirations of these middle-level leaders. It is to be noted that no statistical comparative analysis of the data was undertaken — this was not the original intention and as a result the design was not developed along such lines. Rather, overall general qualitative comparisons are made.

The respondent samples in all four studies drew on male and female middle-level school leaders, with females more heavily represented in each. Groups represented a fairly even spread of leadership experience in terms of years in such roles and the numbers of schools in which they had held such positions.

SATISFACTION IN THEIR CURRENT ROLE

Respondents were asked to indicate their level of satisfaction with their current role as a middle-level school leader. Table 10.1 summarises this data.

These data suggest similar trends in levels of satisfaction, although the nonstate respondents are somewhat more *satisfied*. These levels of satisfaction certainly appear high when one combines the *satisfied* and *very satisfied* categories. Clearly, the vast majority of those holding middle-level leadership positions are satisfied in their current roles. This trend is of interest when one considers responses to questions about whether they might consider seeking promotion in the future, with about 30%, 43% and 40% for Studies 1, 2, 3 respectively indicating they would. From the perspective of an aspirant future principal

TABLE 10.1
Satisfaction in Current Role

Study satisfaction %	Study 1 (Nonstate, Australia)	Study 2 (Secondary, New Zealand)	Study 3 (State Secondary, Australia)
Overall (very satisfied + satisfied)	90	81	80
very satisfied	32	32	25

pool, this represents a relatively positive picture. Not only are middle-level school leaders satisfied with what they are doing currently, but a good number are looking to promotion in the future. However, it is instructive to reflect on the reasons offered as to why they might not seek a principal position in the future. In this regard, and these data are similar across the three studies, the main reasons were related to the principal's role being too demanding, their degree of satisfaction in their current role, and related to both these, lifestyle decisions related to achieving work–life balance. These issues are examined in more depth later in the discussion of Study 4.

SENIOR MANAGEMENT-LEADERSHIP TEAM DEVELOPMENT

Respondents were asked to comment on the notion of team development among the senior leadership–management team in their school, this has significance in a climate of shared decision-making and distributive leadership notions. Ratings of team being highly developed ranged from 30%, 52%, 55% respectively across the three studies. The majority of the remainder indicated it was still evolving. Key influences in team development — again consistent across the three studies — were reported to be related to the attitude and skills of the principal, interpersonal skills and relationships among team members, and the attitudes and skills of team members

GENERAL ASPECTS OF ROLES AND RESPONSIBILITIES

Respondents were asked to comment on a number of general aspects of their roles, including hours worked, pressure they felt and the variety of things they were expected to do. There are similar trends across the three sets of data suggesting that these middle-level school leaders from different schooling sectors were working quite long hours, were feeling a deal of (increasing) pressure and increased workload in their roles and were experiencing changes in those roles. A variety of reasons were offered as to why these changes were being felt. While there were idiosyncratic reasons among these relating to the particular sector (e.g., nonstate leaders noted the influence of school boards, while state leaders noted systemic/departmental pressures), a number of common key 'forces' underlying the changes can be synthesised including:

- expectations of schools had changed and hence this flowed over onto their schools generally and thus through to their particular roles; and

- internal school changes, such as changes in personnel (e.g., principal), changes in the culture and/or direction of the school.

Specific Aspects of the Role of Middle-Level School Leader

In an endeavour to identify what middle-level school leaders actually did in their role (i.e., their *Real* role), the respondents in the three studies were asked to indicate the time dedicated in a typical week to a number of key aspects/categories of activities. They were then also asked to reflect on, and indicate how they might *like* to spend their time in an *Ideal* or preferred situation relative to the same aspects/categories. These data are summarised in the following tables showing those receiving the highest responses (in terms of the amount of time — *great deal* + *some* categories combined). Table 10.2 is for a *Real* week, Table 10.3 for an *Ideal* week.

TABLE 10.2
Time Dedicated to Various Aspects of the Role of Middle-Level School Leader (*Real*)

In a real week	Study 1 (non-state Australia)	Study 2 (secondary New Zealand)	Study 3 (State secondary, Australia)
Strategic leadership			
Educational/curriculum leadership			
Management/administration	P	P	P
Student issues	P	P	P
Parent/community issues			P
Staffing issues	P	P	P
Operational matters			P

Note: (P = high priority > 85% of respondents indicating *great deal* + some)

TABLE 10.3
Time Dedicated to Various Aspects of the Role of Middle-Level School Leader (*Ideal*)

In an ideal week	Study 1 (non-state Australia)	Study 2 (Secondary New Zealand)	Study 3 (State secondary, Australia)
Strategic leadership	P	P	P
Educational/curriculum leadership	P	P	P
Management/administration			
Student issues			
Parent/community issues			
Staffing issues			
Operational matters			

Note: (P = high priority > 85% of respondents indicating *great deal* + some)

The summary data provided in the tables illustrates remarkably similar trends across the three studies. Respondents across the three sectors reported their Real week being dominated by operational matters, management and administration and staff, community and student issues. Significantly, strategic leadership and educational/curriculum leadership was less evident in their week. However, those two aspects were the two dominant activities/aspects preferred all three respondent groups in their Ideal week. It is important to note, that even though they would prefer a higher profile in strategic and curriculum leadership in their Ideal week, the data for all three groups indicated they did not ignore their responsibilities for staff, students, parents and general management matters. What they were clearly less enthusiastic about were operational matters or what many in the open-ended questions termed lower level tasks. What these data demonstrate is that there is lack of role alignment between what middle-level school leaders are actually doing and what they would prefer to be doing.

Respondents in each of the studies were asked to identify the key factors or pressures they saw as mitigating against moving to their preferred or Ideal roles. The main factors reported — again these are consistent across the studies — were that there were just too many demands on their time to do any more (the major factor), the expectations set by the principal, and flow-on effects to them as a result of changes in roles and responsibilities of the principal and/or others. Importantly, the vast majority of respondents indicated they thought they had the skills to carry out their preferred leadership roles.

Capabilities Identified as Important to the Role of Middle-Level School Leader

The middle-level school leaders in the three studies were asked to identify and rate the degree of importance of the key skills and competencies they considered important in undertaking their roles and responsibilities. These data are summarised in Table 10.4 following. While all were rated highly, those rating the highest (> 90% — *very important* + *important* categories combined) are highlighted in bold.

These school leaders across the three sectors clearly emphasised a very similar variety of both leadership and management capabilities as being critical to their role. Clearly, all the capabilities identified in the survey items were considered to be important to the roles of these school leaders. Especially noteworthy were *interpersonal skills* and *being an effective and*

TABLE 10.4
Skills and Competencies Required of Middle-Level School Leaders

Capabilities important to role	Study 1 (Nonstate Australia)	Study 2 (Secondary New Zealand)	Study 3 (State Secondary, Australia)
Inspiring, visioning change for school	(88%)*	≥ 90%	≥ 90%
Demonstrating strong interpersonal, people skills	≥ 90%	≥ 90%	≥ 90%
Capacity to delegate, empower others	≥ 90%	≥ 90%	≥ 90%
Managing uncertainty for self and others	≥ 90%	≥ 90%	≥ 90%
Managing change for self and others	≥ 90%	≥ 90%	≥ 90%
Capacity to develop supportive networks among colleagues	≥ 90%	≥ 90%	(85%)*
Being an effective and efficient manager and administrator	≥ 90%	≥ 90%	≥ 90%

Note. * = just short of the 90% cut-off criterion

efficient manager and administrator, which received the strongest '*very important*' percentage responses. Notably, *demonstrating strong interpersonal, people skills* rated the highest of all. Notwithstanding this, it seems apparent that they have to be both a competent manager as well as a leader to satisfactorily carry out their roles and responsibilities.

VIEWS OF THE PRINCIPALSHIP AND CAREER ASPIRATIONS

Study 4 provides an in-depth look at middle-level leaders in terms of their career aspirations and their views about the principalship; views that, in large part, might be expected to shape their interest in applying for such a position in the future.

With respect to their current position as deputy principals, and in a similar vein to the earlier studies, the vast majority of respondents reported being *satisfied* (82%), with over a quarter *very satisfied*. Only about one in ten was *dissatisfied* — of this, only 1% was *very dissatisfied*. Almost 4 in 5 report thinking about doing another job — 6% *very often*, 20% *often* and over half, *sometimes*. About a half saw an alternative job as one not in schools or education, with about a third seeing the alternative in schools, and 20% in education but not in schools. These data suggest that while overall they appeared to be a satisfied group with respect to their current position, a good number of them were thinking about career alternatives outside schools, and in some cases, away from education altogether.

Just over a half of the respondents reported that they intended to seek promotion to the principalship in the future, 16% would not, and about a third was unsure. One in five had sought promotion three or more times previously and a further one in ten, twice before. Notably, males indicated they had applied more often than females in the past, with one in four males applying three or more times in the past (unsuccessfully). Of those indicating they would seek promotion, over two-thirds said they would do so within 2 years, with the bulk of the remainder planning to do so in 3 to 5 years. This suggests that a good number of this potential aspirant group will be actively seeking principal positions across the next few years.

Respondents were asked to rate the importance (from very important to not important) of various factors they saw as influencing their desire to become a principal. These factors related to their personal driving forces or reasons in wanting to be a principal and what might be achieved once they became a principal. The main reasons identified were:

- capacity to influence the lives and learning of young people;
- capacity to have a more strategic influence on education; and,
- opportunity to work with diverse individuals and groups.

The potential status associated with the position of principal and a desire simply for promotion were rated the least important. Respondents had the opportunity to add their own comments for this item. The following illustrate some of the main reasons identified above.

> An educator is what I am by training and inclination. Principals have the capacity to influence education. I am at a point where I want to lead, not follow. (Primary principal)

> Being able to motivate and inspire others. (Secondary principal)

Respondents were asked to rate the level of importance of various factors that might act as positive influences and those that might be barriers for them in making a decision about seeking promotion to the principalship. The four main factors acting as *potential incentives* for those considering seeking promotion are:

- capacity to achieve work–life balance
- school location acceptable to family
- good work conditions
- good remuneration.

These four can be clustered under two broader concepts of *work–life balance* and *work conditions*. Aspects related to professional learning opportunities once in the role or to any potential status one might attract in holding the role of principal rated the lowest. Of note is that female respondents saw *access to quality professional development and secondments* as more important than males, while males reported *professional reputation and status* as more important than females in deciding whether to apply for the principalship.

Respondents had the opportunity to add their own comments regarding positive factors with regard to their seeking promotion. These tended to reinforce the concepts noted above and highlight the fact that aspirants may not be looking for just any school were they to seek promotion, but that school location, educational opportunities for their own children and family issues were important in their decisions regarding seeking a position as principal:

> I would not consider the principalship until my children have completed secondary education. (Primary principal)

> Work/life/family balance is critical to my decisions having been a principal and relinquishing to accept a deputy principal role. (Secondary principal)

The open-ended comments also added important additional concepts relating to aspects of support one might seek/require once appointed to the principalship. That is, these potential aspirants identified that there would be ongoing support/developmental needs once they had successfully been promoted, indicating that they were not necessarily fully prepared for the principalship at the moment. Mentoring and general support from colleagues and senior officers were featured here.

> Good role models and capacity to be mentored by principal colleagues who are experienced and good at what they do. (Primary principal)

> Support from personnel higher up the 'food chain' when the hard calls are made. (Secondary principal)

The main factors acting as *potential barriers* were:

- work–life balance being easier to manage in the (current) deputy principal position — extra remuneration as a principal is not worth the extra responsibilities

- high satisfaction in current role — a role that allows closer contact with teaching and learning.

Female respondents rated the perceived demands of the roles and responsibility of being a principal as a barrier higher than their male counterparts. An important factor, apart from those rated high by respondents, related to the negative perceptions about the recruitment and selection process. What is significant in all of these data is that the aspirant deputy principals have perceptions of the principalship as a role somewhat different from their current one. It is seen as one charac-terised by impacting more on their work–life balance, holding higher levels of responsibilities and accountabilities and moving them away from a teaching and learning focus.

Respondents had the opportunity to add their own comments regarding factors acting as potential barriers to their seeking promo-tion. These tended to reinforce items already noted.

> Principals are currently very exposed in their role. In my view they hold massive accountability and do not receive a great deal of support from District/Central Office. They are expected to imple-ment systemic initiatives but have limited control over much of the implementation eg staff selection, funding allocations etc. when dif-ficult issues arise. (Secondary principal)

> Principals I have known work tirelessly with little thanks, too smaller remuneration and little sleep due to the magnitude of the job. (Primary principal)

The recruitment and selection process attracted many comments from respondents, several of whom suggested that the process was unfair for some and unclear for others.

> Trying to understand the game. Shouldn't be a secret. Subjectivity is still a characteristic of the selection process- what one panel thinks is good another rejects. (Primary principal)

> I have, as have many of my DP colleagues observed many anomalies in the selection processes throughout the state. Until the aspect of 'recruitment' is addressed … many highly effective leaders will remain without principal opportunities. (Primary principal)

Discussion
This review of related studies into middle-level school leaders across different sectors (non-State schools in Australia, secondary New

Zealand, State secondary Australia) suggests that the life of the middle-level school leader is typically a busy one, traversing a wide range of roles and responsibilities, thus requiring a variety of skills and competencies to be demonstrated by the incumbents. Their world is characterised by change, with many having experienced school management, structural and curriculum changes in recent times. While the three sets of middle-level school leaders were somewhat different in that they were drawn from different schooling sectors, there are many similarities in the way they described their roles (both *Real* and *Ideal*), the capabilities they believed were important in effectively carrying out those roles, and the nature of the 'forces' impacting on their roles.

Of note is the high level of satisfaction of these school leaders in their roles across all the three different sectors. Such findings present as real positives for the schools in which they work. They are consistent with those reported by Hausman, Nebrasker, McCreary and Donaldson (2002) who noted that the vast majority of assistant principals described their worklife in positive ways. While a good number indicate they are thinking about promotion, the majority of the logical pool for the next generation of principals has no intention of seeking promotion or is, at least, uncertain about this. In part, this may reflect the comment from the NCSL (2003) that many headteachers found their deputy principal experiences frustrating as they did not have the opportunities for leadership to the extent they had hoped.

Notwithstanding the reported positive job satisfaction of these groups of school leaders, many respondents reported working quite long hours and under considerable pressure. This is consistent with the findings reported by Hausman et al. (2002) where assistant principals were working an average of 55 hours per week. The increase in pressure on middle-level school leaders as identified here has been noted earlier by Campbell and Neill (1994) who described both internal and external school pressures increasing. Kaplan and Owings (1999) also noted increased stressors on assistant principals, including different and wider responsibilities, increased planning, organising and coordinating, more problem solving and more interaction with adults, such as parents and staff. They effectively needed more time to do the job, reflecting Porter's (1996) observation of 'overwhelming time constraints' on them (p. 25).

Noteworthy are the generally positive findings reported here regarding the notion of the senior team and the extent of its development, which have been identified as important ingredients of schools operating under devolved decision-making regimes. For example, Ribbins (1997) has suggested heads and deputies, along with other senior staff, need to be able to work in partnership as a management team, and share the roles and responsibilities of leadership of the school.

A major and important finding emerging from these studies is that middle-level school leaders desire a greater leadership role in their schools: strategic and curriculum/educational leadership. However, as it stands, this group's current roles have less to do with leadership than with management; although, like Harvey and Sheridan's (1995) findings, these school leaders acknowledged that there are expectations on them regarding administrative routines and staff management. The overall discrepancies between the *ideal* (preferred) and *real* (actual) roles have been described here as a lack of *role alignment.* In considering this lack of role alignment, it would be interesting to compare the *real* and *ideal* as reported by the respondents with the stated/expected roles evident in their position descriptions, raising the question as to whether they are in fact doing what they were employed to do, or has their position been changed. It is likely, that similar to others in schools, their position is an evolving one, subject to a number of influences of change, such as the principal, individual capacities and school-level change processes.

What might be considered operational matters and dealing with staff and students appears to be significant time consumers for these school leaders. This finding is consistent with that of Hausman et al. (2002) who noted that assistant principals reported spending considerable time working on student and staff issues, raising concerns about the minimal time they spent on other matters, such as instructional leadership. Garrett and McGeachie (1999) noted a similar situation, with deputies in their study thinking of their role mainly in operational terms, with few being able to develop more strategic perspectives.

The participants in these three studies identified a number of barriers working against greater involvement in leadership roles in their schools. These barriers — and again, these were generally consistent across the three studies — included that there were too many things to do in their role already, and the expectations placed on them by the principal. These are similar to those reported by Celikten (2001) and Hausman et al. (2002) that such school leaders often needed to react to matters as they arose that prevented them from attending to higher levels of engagement in the curriculum and, further, that changes in the school as noted above almost invariably impacted heavily on their roles.

In consideration of the *leadership* versus *management* tension evident in the role common across these three groups, Rutherford (2002) and Southworth (1995) have argued, that in relation to leadership responsibility, the headteacher essentially determines the extent of the involvement of deputy heads, a key point made by this group. Further, what is also important as Rutherford identified, is that the leadership capacity of middle-level school leaders was not being fully accessed by many schools — nor were their leadership capabilities being developed. This latter point is clearly being expressed by those in these studies, who desired a more significant leadership role. Failure to take up this opportunity is potentially a lost opportunity; for as Kaplan and Owings (1999) have argued, by assistant principals effectively sharing instructional leadership roles the school's potential success as a learning organisation for students and educators can be enhanced.

The findings generally support the argument that school leaders today require a broad range of capabilities to carry out their increasingly diverse and pressured roles. In this regard, it is worth highlighting the important, albeit not surprising, finding that interpersonal/people skills are critical to carrying out the role of a middle-level school leader. Morrison (1997) saw this as the 'need to attend to people, personalities, interactions — the human dimension' of such roles (p. 68). This need for good interpersonal skills was also noted by Johnson (2000) who saw that between 80 and 90% of assistant principals' time was spent communicating. This reflects the essential people-nature of both the leadership and management aspects of the roles of these school leaders. Notwithstanding this strong people-orientation of the role, these middle-level school leaders also need to demonstrate a capacity to be able to manage and administer effectively.

The research reported in the fourth study adds valuable insights into what potential aspirants, or what might be termed next generation school leaders, think about the principalship and their intentions and motivations in seeking promotion to this position. On a positive note, the vast majority of the respondents from across Queensland state primary and secondary schools reported being satisfied in their current position, despite many of them thinking about doing another job in the future. For some this is in the principalship, as over half indicate they will seek promotion in the future. For the education system that can be expected to look to this group of middle-level school leaders as the promotional pool for the principalship in the future, this ought to provide some encouragement; although this needs to be balanced by the responses of about half of this group, who indicated they thought about working in roles not in schools or education. This represents a leakage of potential aspirants from the pool of next generation school leaders. It may be that some of this leakage is due to concerns over the recruitment and selection process, a factor identified earlier by Gronn and Lacey (2004), who noted candidates were 'often unclear about the rules of the selection game' (p. 416), a sentiment reflected in the comments of some aspirants in the fourth study.

The view of the respondents that they would like to see the principal's role focusing more on strategic and educational/curriculum leadership and less on operational matters, management and administration is significant and is consistent with what principals themselves say about the reality of their roles (Barty et al., 2005; Blackmore, Thomson, & Sachs, 2002; Cranston et al., 2003). It also parallels the tensions they noted in their own roles, where management often dominates. Much of the contestation principals feel in managing increasing systemic and local accountability demands shapes as a key driver in just what principals want, can and actually do as principals. Clearly, there are elements of Gronn's (2003) notion of 'greedy work' at play here, such that there are some real policy and practice implications evident. For instance, it is likely that more rigorous investigations of alternative conceptualisations of the principalship will be required in the future (Blackmore et al., 2005; Gronn, 2003). Some work on this has been initiated already (see D'Arbon et al., 2001; D'Arbon, 2003) albeit without widespread success or acceptance.

In considering any such reconceptualisation, a number of issues require close attention. Work–life balance continues as a dominant struggle for principals against a backdrop of intensification of their roles (Thomson, Blackmore, Sachs, & Tregenza, 2003), at least in the eyes of these aspirants as they observe their principals firsthand. Tied up with this is accepting a principal's position in a school suitable for the aspirant's family, a parallel notion of seeing family and work as interdependent, and not independent. Limerick et al.'s (2002) notion of 'lifestreaming' emerges as a critical factor for consideration. Issues of work conditions and remuneration are also factors for deliberation. .

The reasons deputy principals identify as influencing them to aspire to the principalship are based on what might be considered highly laudable principles, including wanting to positively influence the lives and learning of young people. It could be argued they are looking to the principalship for the 'right reasons'. The tension, however, will be to try to catalyse such notions into practice and not allow them to be swamped by the accountability and managerial demands already noted. This possible distancing from teaching and learning, were they to move into the principalship, is reported by some as a potential disincentive in seeking promotion. In seeing school and educational leadership as key goals one might strive for in the principalship, these deputy principals identify strong interpersonal and people skills, visioning and inspiring change among the school community and acting ethically and fairly as key capabilities principals would need to hold to make them a reality. Such 'leadership capabilities' are evident in statements about the principalship now promulgated by many education systems across most western countries (see for example, Department of Education and Skills, 2004; New South Wales Department of Education and Training, 2004). Importantly, many respondents also identified ongoing learning and professional development needs to achieve these, noting mentoring and observing quality principals as means to developing these.

Conclusions

This review of the findings of the four studies of middle-level school leaders provides important insights into these critical, yet underresearched positions in our schools, positions that are of increasing importance in an era of significant and rapid change. Deeper understandings of both the dynamics of the roles in action and their potential to contribute to the leadership capacity of schools in these challenging times present as issues of interest. While middle-level leaders are clearly very busy people who work long hours under considerable pressure in roles that have changed and are changing, there is a strong suggestion that they may well be an underutilised resource for the school, particularly from a leadership perspective. How schools might develop and unleash this resource, while at the same time addressing the roles they currently carry out, present as real challenges if such positions as deputy principal, heads of schools, directors of studies and so on are to move beyond mainly managerial responsibilities. It is more than a decade since Harvey (1994) argued for a reconceptualisation of the role of deputy principal to one embracing both leadership and management. It would seem that progress in this regard has been slow, and that for many in the role, the challenges of Kaplan and Owings (1999) to reduce the crisis-oriented, reactive nature of the assistant principal's daily routine have not been taken up.

These studies point to some critical issues for consideration by schools and systems as they seek the leaders of their schools for the future, many of whom can be expected to be drawn from those currently in middle-level school leadership positions. These issues can be summarised as follows:

- Potential aspirants indicating that they are likely to seek promotion to the principalship in the future, particularly in large education systems, could be targeted for both nurturing and professional development to minimise future leakage from the pool as well as better placing and preparing aspirants for taking up principal positions when they are ready to make the move into such roles. The strong educational drivers identified in the aforementioned research studies as likely reasons for aspirants to seek promotion are significant positives on which to capitalise in this regard. It is to be noted that some systems are indeed doing this (see the discussion about the Catholic and Lutheran sectors in Chapter 13).

- In consideration of this first recommendation, the career cycles and preferences of potential aspirants may need to be more carefully considered, such that tighter tailoring of aspirants to particular schools is taken into account. In other words, the personal and professional characteristics of aspirants may need to be taken into account in different and more fine-grained ways than currently; such that high quality potential aspirants do not feel excluded from the promotional process because, for example, the schooling of their own children is currently taking priority (a factor identified in this research for many), but that rather they continue to be nurtured and mentored such that they are ready for the transition when they, and their circumstances, are appropriate.

- The contestation and tensions surrounding leadership versus management aspects of the role of middle-level leaders (and indeed principals) needs discussion and debate at both school and system levels. While there may be no easy resolution to the currently perceived state of the domination of management aspects inherent in the role, in the longer term alternative conceptualisations of the principalship seem worthy of serious exploration if leadership potential is to be unlocked, and the strengths of, and opportunities for, such school leaders are built upon.

- The work–life balance tensions evident in leaders' roles is not unique to schools and abounds across all types of work sectors and organisations; nor are related issues of work intensification and accountability demands. Again, while there are no easy solutions to such challenges, the power of such factors as barriers for potential aspirants looking to the principalship emerges as a matter of serious debate among system-level decision-makers and not dismissed as simply a fact of life today for leaders of busy organisations as it not only impacts negatively on those aspiring to higher level leadership positions (such as principals) but it also impacts negatively on those already in such positions.

- Concerns over recruitment and selection processes, in so far as they are seen by some applicants as not to be fair and well understood, need attention. It is clear that unsuccessful applicants need frank and detailed feedback such that they clearly understand (and accept) that the process is not at fault, but that either they 'lost out' to a better applicant or perhaps that they were not suitable for the position. Currently, many applicants hold quite different views, negatively impacting on perceptions of the selection process and affecting the likelihood of their applying again in the future.

- The final issue urges systems and schools to look for, and nurture aspirants from wider pools than those presenting as the most natural pool. In this study this was deputy, assistant and associate principals moving to principals. Some initiatives in this regard warranting careful monitoring are occurring already and may provide some useful directions in the future. For instance, the initiatives by the Catholic and Lutheran systems explored in Chapter 13 of this book.

There is clearly some cause for optimism as we examine this key segment of school leaders. While there are tensions and struggles evident around their roles and responsibilities, there appears to be a potential aspirant principal pool who express strong educational drivers as the main incentives that might see them applying for principal positions in the future. This optimism, however, needs to be balanced by a level of pessimism about promotion, underpinned by concerns about work-life balance and work intensification for principals deriving in part from the dominant accountability and managerial agendas impacting on many principals at the moment. It also needs to be underpinned by an acknowledgment that being appointed as a principal is not the end of the journey. As one secondary school deputy noted:

> Many newly appointed principals lack relevant skills in financial management and other operational duties. A more intensive course for newly appointed principals or aspiring principals would ensure quality service. The development of new leaders should be seen as a worthwhile investment, not a budgetary hindrance. The cost of unsatisfactory leadership in schools would outweigh the cost of providing better leadership development courses.

References

Barty, K., Thomson, P., Blackmore, J., & Sachs, J. (2005). Unpacking the issues: Researching the shortage of school principals in two states in Australia. *Australian Educational Researcher, 32*(3), 1–18.

Beare, H. (2001). *Creating the future school.* London, New York: Routledge Falmer.

Blackmore, J., Thomson, P., & Sachs, J. (2002, December). *'Silly us' of course the grid doesn't work: Reading methodologies and policy texts on principals' work.* Paper presented at the Australian Association for Research in Education Conference (AARE). Brisbane.

Brooking, K., Collins, G., Court, M., & O'Neill, J. (2003). Getting below the surface of the principal recruitment 'crisis' in New Zealand primary schools. *Australian Journal of Education, 47*(2), 146–158.

Caldwell, B. (2005). *Re-imaging the self-managing school.* London: Sage.

Campbell, R.J., & Neill, S.R. (1994). *Primary teachers at work.* London: Routledge.

Celikten, M. (2001). The instructional leadership task of high school assistant principals. *Journal of Educational Administration, 39*(1), 67–78.

Cranston, N. (1999). CEO or headteacher: Challenges and dilemmas for primary school principals. *Leading & Managing, 5*(2), 100–113.

Cranston, N. (2000). Teachers-as-leaders: a critical agenda for the new millennium, *Asia Pacific Journal of Teacher Education, 28*(2), 123–131.

Cranston, N. (2002). School-based management, leaders and leadership: Change and challenges for principals. *International Studies in Educational Administration, 30*(1), 2–12.

Cranston, N. (2006). Leading from the middle or locked in the middle? Exploring the world of the middle-level non-state school leader. *Leading & Managing, 12*(1), 91–106.

Cranston, N. (2007a). Through the eyes of potential aspirants: Another view of the principalship. *School Leadership & Management, 27*(2), 109–128.

Cranston, N. (2007b). What do we know about middle-level school leaders in New Zealand? An exploratory study of Auckland secondary deputy and assistant principals. *New Zealand Journal of Educational Leadership, 22*(1), 16–30.

Cranston, N. (2007c, December). *Middle-level school leaders in Australia and New Zealand: An emerging picture from recent research.* Paper presented at the New Zealand Association for Research in Education (NZARE) Conference, Christchurch.

Cranston, N., Ehrich, L., & Billot, J. (2003). The secondary school principalship in an Australia and New Zealand: An investigation of changing roles. *Leadership & Policy Studies in Schools, 2*(3), 159–188.

Cranston, N., Tromans, C., & Reugebrink, M. (2004). Forgotten leaders: What do we know about the deputy principalship in secondary schools? *International Journal of Leadership in Education: Theory & Practice, 7*(3), 225–242.

Crowther, F., Kaagan, S., Ferguson, M., & Hann, L. (2002). *Developing teacher leaders: How teacher leadership enhances school success.* Thousand Oaks, CA: Corwin.

D'Arbon, T., Duignan, P., & Duncan, D.J. (2001). *Leadership succession in Catholic schools in New South Wales.* A research report on behalf of the Catholic Education Commission NSW (Final Report). Sydney, Australia: Australian Catholic University.

D'Arbon, T., Duignan, P., & Duncan, D.J. (2002). Planning for future leadership in schools: An Australian study. *Journal of Educational Administration, 40*(5), 468–485.

D'Arbon, T. (2003, November–December). *Career aspirations of potential applicants for principals of Catholic schools: An Australian perspective.* Paper presented at the joint Australian Association for Research in Education Conference (AARE) and New Zealand Association for Research in Education (NZARE), Auckland.

Department for Education and Skills. (2004). *National standards for headteachers.* Retrieved November 2, 2008, from http://www.ncsl.org.uk/leadership_development/entry_to_headship/ldev-entry-nationalstandards.cfm

Dorman, J., & D'Arbon, T. (2003). Assessing impediments to leadership succession in Australian Catholic schools. *School Leadership & Management, 23*(1), 25–40.

Draper, J., & McMichael, P. (2003). The rocky road to headship. *Australian Journal of Education, 47*(2), 185–207.

Earley, P., Evans, J., Collarbone, P., Gold, A., & Halpin, D. (2002). *Establishing the current state of school leadership in England.* London: Department of Education & Skills.

Fitzgerald, T. (2004). Gender matters within/in middle management. *New Zealand Journal of Educational Leadership, 19*(2), 45–56.

Garrett, V., & McGeachie, B. (1999). Preparation for headship? The role of the deputy head in the primary school. *School Leadership & Management, 19*(1), 67–81.

Golanda, E.L. (1991). Preparing tomorrow's educational leaders: An enquiry regarding the wisdom of utilizing the position of assistant principal as an internship or apprenticeship to prepare future principals. *Journal of School Leadership*, *1*, 266–283.

Gronn, P. (2000). Distributed properties: A new architect for leadership. *Educational, Management and Administration, 28*(3), 317–338.

Gronn, P. (2003). *The new work of educational leaders: Changing leadership practice in an era of school reform*. London: Sage.

Gronn, P., & Lacey, K. (2004). Positioning oneself for leadership: Feelings of vulnerability among spirant school principals. *School Leadership & Management, 24*(4), 405–424.

Harvey, M.J. (1994). The deputy principalship: Retrospect and prospect. *International Journal of Educational Management, 8*, 15–25.

Harvey, M., & Sheridan, B. (1995). Measuring the perception of the primary school deputy principal's responsibilities. *Journal of Educational Administration, 33*(4), 69–91.

Hausman, C., Nebrasker, A., McCreary, J., & Donaldson, G., Jr. (2002). The work-life of the assistant principal. *Journal of Educational Administration, 40*(2/3), 136–157.

Healey, J. (2003). *Our aging world*. Thirroul, New South Wales, Australia: Spinney.

Hopkins, D. (2001). *'Think Tank'*. [Report to Governing Council]. United Kingdom: National College for School Leadership. Retrieved October 10, 2005, from http://forms.ncsl.org.uk/mediastore/ldthinktank.pdf

James, C., & Whiting, D. (1998). Headship? No thanks! A study of factors influencing career progression to headship. *Management in Education, 12*(2), 12–14.

Johnson, R. (2000). Other duties as assigned: Four rules for surviving the assistant principalship. *NASSP Bulletin, 84*(612), 85–87

Kaplan, L.S., & Owings, W.A. (1999). Assistant principals: The case for shared instructional leadership. *NASSP Bulletin, 83*(610), 80–94.

Katzenmeyer, M., & Moller, G. (1996). *Awakening the sleeping giant: Helping teachers develop as leaders*. Thousand Oaks, CA: Corwin Press.

Kerlinger, F., & Lee, H. (2000). *Foundations of behavioural research* (4th ed.). Fort Worth, TX: Hartcourt College.

Lacey, K. (2002). *Understanding principal class leadership aspirations: Policy and planning implications*. Report prepared for the Department of Education & Training (School Leadership Development Unit). Melbourne, Australia: Department of Education & Training.

Leithwood, K., Jantzi, D., Early. L., Watson, N., Levin, B., & Fullan, M. (2004). Leadership for large scale reform: The case of England's national literacy and numeracy strategy. *School Leadership and Management, 24*(1), 57–79.

Limerick, D., Cunnington, B., & Crowther, F. (2002). *Managing the new organisation: Collaboration and sustainability in the post-corporate world*. Sydney, Australia: Allen & Unwin.

Morrison, K. (1997). The deputy headteacher as the leader of the curriculum in primary schools. *School Organisation, 15*(1), 65–76.

NAESP. (2003). *Fact Sheet on principal shortage.* Retrieved May 3, 2006, from http://www.naesp.org/ContentLoad.do?contentId=1097

National College for School Leadership. (2003). *Deputy and assistant heads: Building leadership potential.* United Kingdom: Author.

New South Wales Department of Education and Training: Professional Support and Curriculum. (2004). *School leadership development: The school leadership capability framework.* Retrieved May 23, 2007, from http://www.curriculumsupport.nsw. edu.au/leadership/

Porter, J.J. (1996). What is the role of the middle level assistant principal, and how should it change? *NASSP Bulletin, 80*(578), 25.

Preston, B. (2002, December). *Tracking trends in principal and teacher demand and supply.* Paper presented at the Australian Association for Research in Education Conference (AARE). Brisbane.

Ribbins, P. (1997). Heads on deputy principalship: Impossible roles for invisible role holders? *Educational Management and Administration, 15,* 53–64.

Rutherford, D. (2002). Changing times and changing roles: The perspectives of primary headteachers on their senior management teams. *Educational Management and Administration, 30*(4), 447–459.

Southworth, G. (1995). *Looking into primary headship.* London: Falmer.

Thomson, P., Blackmore, J., Sachs, J. & Tregenza, K. (2003) High stakes principal-ship-Sleepless nights, heart attacks and sudden death accountabilities: Reading media representations of the United States principal shortage. *Australian Journal of Education, 47*(2), 118–133.

Webb, B.R., & Vulliamy, G. (1996). The changing role of the primary school head-teacher. *Educational Leadership and Management, 24*(3), 301–315.

Weller, D., & Weller, S.J. (2002). *The assistant principal: Essentials for effective leader-ship.* Thousand Oaks, CA: Corwin Press.

West, N. (1992). *Primary headship, management and the pursuit of excellence.* Harlow: Longman.

Williams, T.R. (2003). Ontario's principal scarcity: Yesterday's abdicated policy responsibility: Today's unrecognised challenge. *Australian Journal of Education, 47*(2), 159–172.

▶▶▶◀◀◀

CHAPTER 11

Technology and the Principal: Implications for Leadership

Michael Hough

This chapter will provide some recommended guidelines and action frameworks for principals to deal with the challenges created in working more effectively with technology. These guidelines and frameworks are based on the following seven concepts and understandings:

1. Effective schools and organisations are actually those that adapt to change and concentrate on developing their staff (i.e., teachers/ employees). Technology can help or hinder this process, but a concentration on technology, by itself, is not a proven success strategy.

2. The change pressures influencing schools and learning are actually on all organisations and their practices, and are created by the change pressures accompanying the development of an information and service-based global economy.

3. Situational leadership advises that different techniques may be required for each different specific leadership and management setting(s).

4. Principals need to act from an informed perspective of the impact(s) of Information and Communication Technologies (ICT) on current learning and schooling practices. In so doing, principals will need to understand:
   - the change pressures created by ICT are transformative technologies, which enable new style learning and schooling practices;
   - that new learning technologies are focused on creating and improving the intellectual mind tools of both individuals and groups;
   - that emerging mindsets such as wellness and preventative learning based as positive psychology are offering new ways of working with staff and students.

5. Some school pressures are created by the capabilities of digital native younger generations interacting with digital immigrant older generations.

6. There is a need to select or discard technology options by working out whether the technology will add value in improving the practices and approaches required by principals as they lead futures-oriented schools.

7. The research on effective schools clearly indicates that effective school improvement is premised on developing effective teachers. Studies such as the Organisation for Economic Co-operation and Development (OECD) Report on competitive school systems (2007) and the most recent PISA results (OECD, 2006) have identified the country with the highest achieving students as Finland, which uses national strategies that concentrate on developing and supporting highly qualified teachers in an environment of stable curriculum and very little national testing.

Before developing these concepts with more useful levels of detail, it is helpful to be clear on what is meant by the term 'new technologies'.

Emerging (New) Technologies and Their Influences

It is often assumed that ICT-based technologies are the current major change drivers of societal practices, and although this chapter will concentrate on ICT-based change, it is important to acknowledge that a much wider range of knowledge-based change drivers will also have major impact on schools and learning. For example, Ellyard (2001, 2004, 2007) identified the following drivers of societal change, coming from the knowledge revolutions based around:

- the ICT (Information and Communication Technologies) revolution;
- the biological revolution;
- the ecological revolution;
- the smart materials revolution;
- the long-cycle systems revolution; and,
- the nano-technology revolution.

A more detailed treatment of these can be found in Hough (2007a, 2007b).

Having acknowledged there are other technology-based changes that will radically influence schools and learning, this chapter will now concentrate on ICT-based technologies and their impact(s). These ICT-related concepts and understandings will be explained from the viewpoint that an effective educational leader should apply them to develop a school that deals with the future needs of its students, parents, staff and community. The term, futures-oriented school, will be used as a descriptor for this ideal outcome.

Each of the seven key concepts noted above are now explored to justify the action statements recommended from them, which together with some practical examples will be provided as the concluding section of this chapter.

Concept 1: Staff Are the Key to Successful, Adaptive Organisations

One of the more pragmatic definitions of curriculum in traditional schooling concerns 'what happens when the teacher shuts the classroom door, and the act of observing it changes it'. In short, the attitudes and behaviour(s) of teachers are the critical factors, and the outcomes of quality schooling have long been linked to the quality of teaching. In that sense, nothing has changed in providing advice on leading ICT-based futures-oriented schools, except that this same reality is now being accepted in business organisations as well. For example, in the 2008 Australian Boyer lecture series Murdoch (2008, p. 25) stated:

> I believe that technology is ushering in a new golden age for mankind. I also believe that technology is making the human side of the business equation-skills and knowledge- more valuable than ever … As technology levels the playing field, the human factor becomes more important, if you run a business. In plain English you need good people more than ever. That's because computers will never substitute for common sense and good judgment. They will never have empathy either. To be successful, a business needs good people who can see the big picture, who can think critically and have strong character.

When the thinking of one of the world's leading business persons converges with the research on effective schools — see Concept 7 below — it is important to understand that the major leadership tasks related to an effective understanding and use of technology are first, how to harness its potential to assist people to maximise the relevance of the school to current and future societal needs. The next task relates to how to gain the commitment of teachers to the benefits of ICT-based learning, and then how to support staff members to develop them as effective users of ICT as possible.

Concept 2: The Societal Setting for a Futures-Oriented School

It is helpful to remind educational leaders that many change pressures on a school are derived from socioeconomic–political dynamics. This section summarises the pressures exerted by a modern service economy on its organisations and social structures (which include but are more than schools), to emphasise that schools, learning and leadership are essentially societal constructs and need to change and evolve with their society. An excellent commentary on these changes is provided by the series of books by Handy (see for example Handy, 2001). Figure 1 following summarises how at least three different societal eras (agrarian, manufacturing/industrial and information/service economies) have created different needs and formats in learning, teaching and schooling, as well as different requirements for leadership and management. (This figure has been developed by the writer to illustrate the complex inter-relationships created by societal change that include, but are wider than, educational and school-based changes.)

The comparisons in Figure 11.1 on pp. 246–247 illustrate the dilemmas, pressures and problems facing many older teachers (and many principals) in that many were trained in non-ICT-based learning and teaching methodologies, delivered by teacher training institutions established to produce teachers for a quite different society and employment context. (A more detailed expansion of these ideas is presented in a summary table format in Hough, 2008, p. 20.)

The argument here is that principals need to incorporate into their educational leadership thinking the deep understandings that derive from accepting that a major task in developing effective ICT-based schools is to assist (many) teachers to successfully adapt to change by developing in them new mindsets and techniques in which they were not initially trained. Failure to recognise and react professionally (and empathetically) to these staff development challenges can result in increasingly irrelevant schooling practices being defended by teachers who do not regard ICT-based learning systems as a positive development/opportunity, and in fact, may see them as a threat.

Concept 3: A Changing View of Leadership — Situational Leadership

As the manufacturing era developed, it created new types and categories of work, including the emergence of the professional classes and new forms of jobs such as professional managers. These evolved

Key Factor (S) and the Spectrum of Change			
	Socioeconomic from Agrarian era (V1)	**Eras created through Manufacturing era (V2)**	**Different choices to Information/ service era (V3)**
FACTOR	↓ V1	↓ V2	↓ V3
Status of workforce	Low expectations of worker(s) — Low education levels Low training investment Low labour costs	⟶ Emergence of Skilled/Professional Classes	High expectations of worker(s) High education levels High training investment High labour costs
Status of capital	Small size of investment 'pool' — Capital held by elite few	⟶ Development of capitalism	Large, global investment 'pool' Capital held through formal, identifiable structures
Attitude of government	Poorly developed ⟶ government structures Focus on a few key functions (e.g., Defence, Treasury) Nonsophisticated government measures	Restricted ⟶ ownership Government domination Protected markets (tariffs, quotas) Simple regulatory systems	Open ownership Transparent government frameworks Global markets Sophisticated regulatory systems
Management measures	Simple relationships, ⟶ often not formalised into organisations Low levels of need for formal management, Management theory or management training (except for Church or Army)	Authoritarian ⟶ Downward imposed rules Hierarchical structures Quality by inspection Low levels of freedom/ choice for workforce Responsibility directed upwards Quality as defined by supervisors	Shared authority Rules developed by agreement 'Flat' structures Total quality for all activities High levels of freedom/ choice for workforce Responsibility vested with those who need to make the decision Quality for customer(s) specifications
Purpose and style of supervision	Poorly developed ⟶ concept Only required in narrow usage areas (e.g. specific skill development for relatively simple, usually physical tasks. E.g. craft guilds)	Supervision ⟶ emerged as a body of knowledge to gain more effective performance from persons performing skilled, often cognitive tasks, in a hierarchical environment	Concept of supervision radically changed Team or self direction, with supervision as a supportive coaching function, in non hierarchical environments
Probable basis of power	[Force – Physical ⟶ or Religious]	[Wealth/Capital] ⟶	[Knowledge/ Information]

Key Factor (S) and the Spectrum of Change			
	Socioeconomic from Agrarian era (V1)	Eras created through Manufacturing era (V2)	Different choices to Information/ service era (V3)
FACTOR	↓ V1	↓ V2	↓ V3
Status and role of schools	Very few schools, Mostly for training 'Elite few' for Church or Army	Schools and school systems started to evolve, main role was to produce and sort labour for manufacturing era	Work IS learning and traditional schools challenged by growth in 24/7 ICT-based learning. 'We all need learning, we may not need schools'
Learning	Learning occurred in informal/ small group settings, usually for survival skills	Formal learning and teaching evolved, learning concerned with preparing to work	Work is based on learning; learning becoming independent of teaching; knowledge is a valuable short-term asset
Technology	Technology was directed at SURVIVAL and responded to identified local needs	Technology was directed at PRODUCTION and reacted with needs and wants	Technology has begun to create LIFESTYLE options and often creates options before they are understood or agreed to
ICT and learning	Very little use of technology in learning and teaching	Limited use of technology in assisting traditional classroom based learning and teaching.	ICT offers 24/7 access to learning and the ability to change the role of teachers, learners and classrooms
Environmental	Little concern about the environment, as it dominated available choices	Little understanding or concern about the unlimited use of resources and the impact on the environment	Growing understanding of, and real concern about, preserving the environment
Toffler view of societal 'wave' structure (1)	↑ V1 (1st Wave Society) LABOUR INTENSIVE	↑ V2 (2nd Wave Society) CAPITAL INTENSIVE	↑ V3 (3rd Wave Society) KNOWLEDGE INTENSIVE

FIGURE 11.1

Labour (V1)/Capital (V2)/Knowledge (V3) Intensive Organisations

Note: The Key Factors summarising different aspects of change are presented in the vertical axis, and the choices created by different socioeconomic eras are provided horizontally for each factor.

  1. These concepts of societal change as 'Waves' and 'Eras' were introduced into the literature initially by Toffler (1985)
  2. It is important for principals making future-oriented choices to realise how many of their current schooling and learning practices are based in, or are derived from, past societies.

in parallel with the emergence of legal constructs such as companies and organisations with shareholders. The profession of management emerged, together with formal qualification and training systems and the distinction between leadership and management began to emerge.

For some, leadership is now simplistically seen as setting directions and inspiring others, while management is more about setting up appropriate systems and ensuring that established processes are implemented by the people working on them. In an emerging information society, the increasing influence of ICT on the practices of schools as organisations is a major change driver in the ways that schooling, learning, leadership and management are perceived and practiced.

There has been no shortage of reviews about leadership and school leadership in particular — see for example Cranston (2007), Gurr (2008a, 2008b) — and there have been many attempts to develop a generic set of leadership guidelines. A contemporary graduate level business text by Murray, Poole and Jones (2006) reviewed leadership and stated:

> [t]here are a number of ways of thinking about leadership. Recently leadership writers have emphasised the processes of leadership rather than the leader or person perspective. Studies have suggested that the processes of leadership highlight the interactive approach between leaders and the context in which they operate. (p. 276)

For this writer, one useful approach is that of situational leadership, an explanatory paradigm that essentially advises leaders to develop and match/adapt appropriate leadership and management capabilities for a range of specific situations and required outcomes. An example of how to use this approach is provided in the concluding section of this chapter.

One of the challenges for Australian educational leaders is dealing with the pressures created a wide ranging set of influences. Included here are issues such as:

- fewer student enrolments as a result of lowered birth rates, accompanied by more attentive parents who are much more concerned about the progress of each child (i.e., *greater scrutiny*)
- younger staff (and students) who are more competent with new technologies; more willing to be independent and are unresponsive to 'older' methods of supervision (i.e., *greater employee independence*)

- greater scrutiny of all activities due to the combined factors of an active press; 'Whistleblower'/Freedom of Information and privacy legislation; web-based information systems such as *Facebook,* and intrusive technologies based on camera equipped mobile phones (i.e., *increased reporting*)
- greater abilities of governments and organisations to track and measure selected activities and outcomes (i.e., *increased monitoring*)
- leaders holding responsibility while having less ability to directly control (i.e., *authority* has been delegated or diluted, while *responsibility* has been retained)
- the impact of ICT-based systems creating a sense of immediacy and urgency in decision-making and communication (i.e., *less reflection time*).

What emerges from the complexities of these factors is the realisation that old ways of leading and managing are increasingly less appropriate and less effective, and that many situations arise in which a response is the only choice for a leader as they are reacting to events that have already occurred. In reviewing the current leadership literature the following trends emerged:

- the research on effective school leadership does not identify ICT as a major direct factor in effective leadership of schools (see for example Cranston, 2007; Gurr, 2008b; Mulford, 2007)
- we have searched for universal theories of effective leadership without real success (see for example the reviews of Burns, 2002; Clawson, 2006; Robinson, 2007)
- Emotional Intelligence (EI) is an emerging concept that actually provides some research-based findings that relate abilities (EI-based abilities) to effective and ineffective leadership (see the work of Gardner, 2007; Goleman, 1995, 1998; Lennick & Kiel, 2005)
- situational leadership is an explanatory approach that uses the ideas of matching leadership style to the particular requirements of the leadership situation (for a clearly developed Australian-based model of situational leadership see Cacciope, 2004).

In making informed decisions about future schools, educational leaders will find it useful to develop strong insights into the emerging opportunities created by two parallel sets of intellectual capabilities, together with the increasing importance of intellectual property. The first of these is the learning capabilities opened up by ICT-based learning, together with the personal capabilities created through building these ICT-based mindsets. The second includes preventative behaviours associated with mindsets of wellness, and personal and professional wellbeing. Educational leaders also need to understand that schools and learning based on effective use of wisely selected ICT are equipping students to enter the emerging social era where intellectual property (IP) is one of the major assets of modern organisations. One (learning-based) IP trend is the emergence of intellectual (mind) tools designed to leverage and improve our mind capabilities, in the same way that in earlier eras, physical tools leveraged and improved our physical capability.

As an example of how technology can assist, these ideas have been leveraged further using the power of ICT-based organisational systems to become whole-of-organisation level tools for the mind and, increasingly, can be regarded as a set of intellectual tools for organisations. These organisational mind tools are becoming the intellectual property (IP) assets of organisations. In a modern economy they are analogous to the physical assets of successful organisations in the manufacturing era (Hough, 2004b). IP is now often closely protected as a core asset. These concepts were reviewed by Hough (2004a, 2004b), with Evans and Lindsay (2005) providing a more general reference.

There are also emerging mindsets such as prevention and wellness/happiness-based strategies for health and education, which are creating new ways of approaching human services. This recently emerging mindset is analogous to the mindset change in the health industry where the skills and professional tasks associated with an illness model of health (which essentially waits for symptoms/problems to emerge and then they are dealt with), is being challenged and replaced by the emerging skills and professional tasks associated with a wellness model based on prevention and anticipatory intervention. Following are some initial concepts derived from the Positive Psychology work of Martin Seligman (2008). (His ideas can be explored elsewhere; e.g., see http://www.authentichappiness.org). They are useful in a discussion about the ICT influences on the principalship because ICT-based learning provides the 'foundation stones' for ease of accessing, learning and using these new mindsets. Further, wellness-based learning can provide a constructive way forward in dealing with the major pressures on schools and their leaders.

As already noted, ICT-based learning technologies are creating new ways of learning that are challenging the roles and structures of traditional schools and teachers to remain relevant. Different terminology has emerged to describe people at different stages of development and understanding about ICT. *Digital natives* is a term introduced by Prensky (2005) to describe the natural familiarity and comfort with ICT in younger generations plus the observable reality that they learn and process information in quite new ways. *Digital immigrants* is a term used to describe (usually) the older generations who learned ICT-based capabilities as an add-on to existing learning methods and processing capabilities.

Preventative mindsets in education are also emerging in student-centred areas such as the work of Orpinas and Horne (2006) and Horne et al. (2008) in preventing bullying in which preventative strategies are strongly emphasised as the most effective long-term strategies for minimising bullying in schools. In brief, attempting to deal with situations before they can actually occur is emerging as a recommended strategy across a range of educational fields such as classroom discipline, as well as in school leadership.

Similarly, the research on effective schools strongly suggests that those schools and school systems that invest in teacher–staff development are the most successful in producing improved student achievements (see e.g., Gurr, 2008a, 2008b; Robinson, 2007). This focus on staff development is another way of conceiving and implementing preventative leadership.

In the final section of this chapter the work of Cacciope (2004) will be used to illustrate how a situational leadership model can be used to apply ICT as a value-adding tool in making leadership in schools more effective.

Concept 4: The Impact of ICT on Learning and Schooling

Spender (2007) reviewed the emerging differences between digital native as ICT-based learners and identified the subsequent gaps that are emerging between what our schools are actually offering to, and expecting from, these learners — compared with the outcomes inherently achievable if schools actually accepted and used students' ICT-based learning capabilities, which are mostly gained by experiences outside of school.

A recent Australian ACER sponsored publication (Lee & Gaffney, 2008) extensively reviewed the issues connected with effective and ineffective ICT-based learning in Australian schools. It provides many useful ideas, principles and practices for leading a digital school.

While ICT, in itself, has not be shown by research to create more effective schools, the subtle but important distinction for principals to note is that ICT must be evaluated in terms of its ability to assist (or prevent!) the direct factors that lead to effective schools and improved student outcomes. Black (2008, p. 32) reviewed the recent Australian research on teachers' use of technology across three Australian education sectors. He noted that:

> Technology is still an 'innovation' rather than a mainstream activity; the most important additional investment needs to be in teachers to provide the support and professional learning that enables teachers to embed technology into their practices ... Time to learn is the greatest barrier.

The futures-oriented school will, in part, be based on the shared acceptance by all involved that learners using ICT create new ways of learning and new ways of solving and dealing with issues and opportunities.

The initial uses of ICT-based digital technologies are sustaining — in that the technology enables one to carry out existing practices and systems in smarter/quicker/less costly ways. However, as users become more confident and immersed in the digital technologies, the usage becomes disruptive in that new ways of working and viewing issues emerge, for example, the technology has actually changed the ways that people learn, think and work — this is the disruptive use of ICT. As it is the disruptive aspects of ICT that probably threaten traditional teacher roles and comfort zones the most, the challenge for school leaders is to provide roadmaps or future outcomes as much as possible, so that wary teachers can see that the future is at least envisaged and probably not as threatening as they might originally have thought.

As an example of a simple roadmap, the following section provides a sample set of output and outcome characteristics towards which ICT-based activities should be encouraged.

A FUTURES FORMAT APPROACH

Principals should consider encouraging and supporting ICT-based options, which would assist the move towards desired learning output characteristics as illustrated by:

Successful learners. Successful people — both individually and collectively — will thrive in our future society by developing a set of human learning characteristics such as being flexible; being adaptive; developing to a high degree the set of knowledge, skills and understanding that are relevant to the current context; anticipating and coping with change; being skilled in information technologies; and being willing to continue learning across a lifetime. Ellyard (2004) called this set of characteristics *thrival,* the ability to both thrive and survive in a rapid change-based, electronic global community. Adapted to a school setting, they could be stated as summarised in Table 11.1.

TABLE 11.1
Learning Characteristics for the Future

Students in our I.C.T. based school community will learn in the following ways. They will:

- access through their own password protected web portal (tailored for their needs);
- access their daily schedules by speaking to a computer. This is mainly their own PDA, but for "large file" issues it will be a laptop or desktop;
- access through broad band (rather than narrow band) access to the web;
- have 24/7 access capability because they can access through web based systems into the school intranet;
- use expert systems to create proposed answers to complex problems eg. simulations, 'webquests', 'second world/life' websites;
- use computers as the basis for a problem-centred rather than a subject-centred curriculum;
- learn from anywhere in the school environment- because they will be wireless-connected rather than hardwire-connected;
- routinely voice-mail to their team problem-solving groups using voice recognition software, and will do this on a 24 hour access capability system;
- use synchronous (chat) and asynchronous (discussion) web-based learning systems;
- control their own learning pathways through a series of mutually agreed topics and tasks;
- have strong personal skills emphases in their technology-based learning;
- value and use teachers as a valuable resource available on a 24/7 basis;
- see teacher–student face to face time as an enrichment tool to provide human value-adding to the basic learning gained by technology-based delivery;
- develop electronic codes of conduct to deal with new privacy and confidentiality concerns e.g. video phones/e-morality and values. They are aware of social protocols and implications of the impact of their e-behaviours on others;
- be aware of their legal and social responsibilities when they access and use emails, websites and related ICT based activities;
- be aware of the financial costs and responsibility/implications of web based and mobile phone based behaviour(s).

Note: This table is derived from Hough (2008, Chapter 2)

Concept 5: Some Features of Our Younger Generations

It is becoming clear that our younger generations are very different in terms of their ICT awareness and that many of their interests, attributes and characteristics are premised on constant and instant access to ICT capabilities. (See for example the Ito et al., 2008, report on the *Digital Youth* project.) It is clear from the emerging evidence from sources such as Mackay (2005), McCrindle (2003) and Sheehan (2005), that members of this digital native younger generation are very different in their capacities as workers, consumers and parents. The challenges of developing and maintaining creativity, innovation and learning will be affected by these new characteristics and so to will schools and those who are leading them, as they meet these younger generations as parents, teachers and students.

These generational differences are exacerbated in importance by the fact that the changing demographics of Australia (reduced birthrates and lower workforce numbers together with longer-living older generations) mean that there is a looming skill shortage at the very time that the collective leadership of most Australian-based school systems will be replaced by these younger generations in the next decade or so. Generational research (see Hough & Bhindi, 2006, 2007; Hough, 2007c) also indicates that that the younger elements of schools (students, staff and parents) are very ready to embrace ICT-based technologies and resultant changes, but regard the (many) existing schools run by older staff and leaders as sterile, anti-ICT-based, and places of great irrelevance to their out of school real world experiences of *Face Book/ My Space/Second Life* and the constant use of SMS and web-based technologies to interact and learn. Paradoxically, this same generational research indicates a great unmet need in these same younger generations for social meaning (see for example, Mackay, 2005, 2007).

In brief, the major generational differences and pressures on schools are created by the capabilities and attitudes of younger students, teachers and parents (Generations X, Y and Z) who are digital natives, most of whom have innate capabilities in learning and living using ICT that older generations do not have. However, it should be noted that at the same time they may require (and welcome) much greater investment into moral and ethical capability development. These interesting and complex pressures have resulted in many school leaders feeling pressured for change, but largely unaware of what the changes should be.

Yet there is growing acceptance that working harder on the old model of schooling is not a solution.

Concept 6: Select or Discard Technology: Is it Value-Adding?

There is little doubt that many schools are becoming very active users of ICT. However, for many, this raises a number of questions and dilemmas for educational leaders. Among these are matters such as:

- How can I keep up with the constant new developments in ICT?
- Does increased ICT-based activity bring positive benefits to the school, as decided by the school governance structures and/or the funding authorities?
- Which ICT-based activities are contributing to value-adding in learning and which ones are not?
- Is it necessary or desirable that all staff and students are equally involved in ICT-based activities?
- How do we know which ICT-based proposals are worth investing in, both financially and in staff effort?

In reflecting on these questions, it is useful to explore any available evidence that links ICT directly to more effective leadership and/or school outcomes. Gurr (2008b, p. 7) reviewed the research on effective leaders and summarised the key factors as: 'Successful school leadership involves building vision and setting direction/understanding and developing people/redesigning the organisation/managing the teaching and learning program.'

Robinson (2007) reviewed 26 research studies that link school leadership and student learning outcomes and summarised the key factors as (2007, p. 8):

- establishing goals and expectations
- strategic resourcing
- planning coordinating and evaluating teaching and the curriculum
- promoting and participating in teacher learning and development
- ensuring an orderly and supportive environment.

It is clear that ICT can have an important impact on many of these student learning factors (e.g., strategic resourcing/aspects of curriculum delivery/teacher learning/supportive environment). But a key message for principals appears to be that ICT in itself is not (as yet) necessarily a success factor. The key issue to be considered is the ability of ICT to support or contribute to the actual key success factors selected for the school.

In the final section, the model of situational leadership developed illustrates how ICT can be used in this 'value-adding' way.

Concept 7: Effective Schools are Premised on Developing Effective Teachers

Horin (2008, p. 33) notes that: 'A plethora of recent studies have examined the world's successful school systems and all reach the same conclusion: first class teachers are the drivers of school improvement, not constant testing and league tables.'

This quote highlights much of the current debate in education in Australia at the moment as to the best ways to improve schools, with the federal government favouring the US-based practice of investing in systems of pupil achievement, testing and school league tables. However, the McKinsey Report (McKinsey & Company, 2007), the OECD (2007) study on improving school leadership and recent work by Caldwell and Harris (2008), all refute this approach and argue for developing high quality teachers as a key to successful schools. O'Keefe (2008, p. 20) also refutes the league table reporting approach and supports the views of Caldwell and others that investing in teachers is the key to long-term school effectiveness. Gurr (2008b, pp. 7–10) also reviewed the series of studies by Leithwood and colleagues on school effectiveness, the first of which was reported by Leithwood and Reihl in 2004. Gurr summarised nine policies and practices that promote student learning. Importantly, none of these improvement policies involved the use of external testing and evaluation by league tables.

An important conclusion to be drawn from all of these findings for school leaders is that if they wish to use ICT more effectively in promoting school effectiveness, then they need to evaluate any ICT-based proposals against the criterion of whether it assists the identified school success factors identified above, the paramount one being the development of higher quality teachers.

Some Concluding Advice

This final section provides some recommended leadership and management approaches based on a school's full acceptance of ICT capabilities and the use of leadership techniques, such as situational leadership and the use of Crosby Grids to chart the future progress of the school.

The recommended approach adopted in this concluding section essentially advises the educational leader to undertake two leadership tasks. The first of these is to activate and practise a series of leadership roles appropriate to differing outcomes using ICT-based systems to assist in the achievement of these roles (an example of this approach using situational leadership thinking will be provided). Secondly, to set up realistic ways of describing the likely characteristics of how the school will/should look when successful change has occurred. One way to do this is to use educational versions of Crosby Grids, as will be explained later in the chapter. A useful construct for implementing these two sets of leadership tasks is the concept of *preferred* and *probable* futures. The distinction between these two concepts was codified into the Australian literature by Ellyard (1998b) and offers the following futures mindset:

- *a preferred future* is the future that we aim to create or influence to some degree. This implies developing deliberate actions that are aimed at improving the likelihood of positive things occurring and reducing the likelihood of negative things occurring. It incorporates the concept of 'we control our own destiny'; and

- *a probable future* is the future that we can expect to encounter if we do not attempt to create or influence, and is created substantially by others. Among other things, it incorporates the concepts of helplessness; reacting to events and control by others.

Situational Leadership: Strategies and Approaches

It is acknowledged that there is a range of possible leadership action approaches that might be taken (see Murray et al., 2006). It is the opinion of this writer that all of these explanations are variations of the basic approach often labelled as situational leadership. The writer has found this overall label/approach a useful one that gains acceptance in workshop or conference settings with practising teachers. A fuller discussion is provided in the work of Cacciope (2004). In brief, the approach is referred to as *integral leadership* and includes a four-quadrant model of recommended roles, mindsets and actions for leaders within four situational contexts *'spirit' (values), 'head' (logic), 'hands' (skills) and 'heart' (feelings)*. In essence, each of these four quadrants identifies the underlying leadership challenges/tasks and roles in terms of the values and guiding logic that should apply to effective leadership within that specific context.

It should be noted that the actual leadership approach recommended is situational in that each specific ICT-based proposal should be assessed by leaders against the desired outcomes and that, in general, the intended effect of all such decisions should cumulate (i.e., they should build the desired futures-oriented school features that have been described in the preceding sections).

Stating a Preferred Future

Through use of knowledge creation strategies associated with preferred futures, such as simulating the future in a range of practical scenarios, school leaders can begin to recognise key positive features that one might want to work towards or create, as well as identify the important negative features that one might want to avoid or discourage from occurring. One useful method for planning, describing and tracking a futures-oriented school is the use of Crosby Grids, a method of describing a preferred future first suggested by Crosby (1980). A Crosby Grid is an improvement grid, and provides a way of describing the preferred future in concrete terms that can be easily understood, and can describe the predicted stages in the journey in achieving that future, in useful and usable terms.

Its development involves generating a matrix of two complementary logics:

- the key processes/features selected for improvement drivers for change
- a graded series of statements ranging from 'don't know about or have this feature' through to 'fully have/fully developed for this feature'.

There is an extensive treatment of the use of Crosby Grids for school planning and usage provided elsewhere (see in Hough, 2008), providing specific examples of actual school improvement grids. The important features of a school improvement grid are actually achieved by school staff and communities working their way through possible action options, either suggested to them or developed through their own thinking and discussions. One of the features of leadership required by Crosby Grid-based approaches is the emphasis on achieved outcomes and selected improvement processes, leaving considerable freedom for staff to interpret the best way to achieve these characteristics.

This leadership approach means the leader sets agreed boundaries and broad guidelines, and accepts that actual techniques to achieve these are the professional responsibility of well-trained staff. In addition, this grid-based approach describes the preferred outcome characteristics for both educational products and processes. For example, it does not attempt to proscribe which specific ICT aspect should be selected or how it should be implemented.

The real questions for staff as they travel this journey with ever changing ICT options are:

- How does the selected ICT contribute positively to our agreed school requirements? and
- How does use if ICT lead to a more effective school?

Final Comments

Finally, in considering the seven basic concepts established earlier, a number of key advice ideas can be synthesised in the form of some action guidelines as follows:

- Staff are the key to a successful school and developing their (positive) attitudes to ICT will be a key success factor (Concept 1).
- Many of the educational practices in which many current teachers and schools are skilled are non-ICT based, were derived to meet the needs of a previous society, and are needed less and less by current and future societies (Concept 2).
- Traditional or 'older' methods of leadership are less and less effective with younger generations and in meeting the needs of a postindustrial society (Concept 3).
- ICT-based learning will initially be based on existing practices, but over time will create interest and capabilities to move to new ways of working in schools (Concept 4).
- Younger generations are extremely comfortable and confident with ICT-based learning, and will welcome its greater usage in schools and learning (Concept 5).
- Technology in itself is not the primary issue — the leadership criterion applied to selecting and using technology should be: does it add value to the key processes and outcomes we have selected as important for the success of this school? (Concept 6).
- Effective schools that maximise student learning are those schools that focus on making their staff as professional and confident as possible in the value-adding usage of ICT (Concept 7).

The role of a futures-oriented leader is to essentially set boundaries, develop statements of acceptable outcomes, allocate resources, train and support staff and exchange delegated authority for timely information so they can remain accountable as the leader of the school. How ICT can be part of meeting those challenges requires careful thought and planning and is an ongoing challenge to school leaders.

Web Sites for Positive Psychology

- http://www.refectivehappiness.com (source for interventions)
- http://www.positivepsychology.org (source for literature)
- http://www.psych.upenn.edu/seligman (source for literature and manuals)
- http://www.authentichappiness.org (source for questionnaires)
- e-mail seligman@psych.upenn.edu (source for Questions and answers).

References and Further Reading

Beare, H. (2001). *Creating the future school.* Melbourne, Australia: Falmer Press.

Black, G. (2008). Embedding technology: How far have we come? *The Australian Educational Leader, 30*(4), 32.

British Education Communications and Technology Association. (2005). Evidence on the progress of ICT in education. *The Becta Review.* Retrieved September 2, 2006, from http://www.schools.becta.org.uk

Brown, J. (2000, April). Growing up digital: How the web changes work, education and the ways that people learn, *Change,* 11–20.

Burns. K. (2002). *Leadership.* New York: Methuen.

Cacciope, R. (2004, September). *Integral leadership: A 4 quadrant model of spirit, head, hands and heart.* Paper Presented at the ACEA National Conference, Perth Western Australia.

Caldwell, B., & Harris, J. (2008). *Why not the best schools?* Melbourne, Australia: ACER.

Clawson, J. (2006). *Level three leadership: Getting below the surface* (3rd ed.). New York: Pearson.

Cranston, N. (Ed.). (2007). Future school leaders: Images and challenges. *Leading and Managing*[Special Edition], *13*(2).

Crosby, P. (1980). *Quality is free.* New York: Mentor.

Ellyard, P. (1998a). From cowboy to cosmonaut. *Principal Matters, 9*(3), 15–18.

Ellyard, P. (1998b). *Ideas for the new millennium.* Melbourne, Australia: Melbourne University Press.

Ellyard, P (2001). Imagining the future and getting to it first. In C. Barker (Ed.), *Innovation and imagination at work* (Australia Management Today Series, pp. 152–173). Sydney, Australia: Australian Institute of Management.

Ellyard, P. (2004). Becoming a leader first of self, then of others. In J. Marsden (Ed.), *I believe this: 100 eminent Australians face life's biggest questions* (pp. 86–88). Sydney, Australia: Random House.

Ellyard, P. (2007). *Designing 2050: Pathways to sustainable prosperity on spaceship earth.* Melbourne, Australia: TPNTXT.

Evans, J., & Lindsay, W. (2005). *The management and control of quality* (6th ed.). New York: South Western/Thomson.

Gardner, H (2007). *Five minds for the future.* Boston: Harvard Business School Press.

Gliddon, J. (2006, October 17). Get smarter. *Bulletin,* 37–42.

Goleman, D. (1995). *Emotional intelligence: Why it can matter more than I.Q.* New York: Bantam Books.

Goleman, D. (1998). *Working with emotional intelligence.* New York: Bantam Books.

Gurr, D. (2008a). *Principal leadership: What does it do, what does it look like, and how might it evolve?* (Monograph Series No 42). Melbourne, Australia: ACEL.

Gurr, D. (2008b). Improving schools in challenging circumstances. *The Australian Educational Leader, 30(4),* 7–10

Handy, C. (2001). *The Elephant and the flea.* London: Penguin.

Horne, A., Stoddard, J., & Bell, C. (2008). *A parent's guide to understanding and responding to bullying.* Champaign, IL: Research Press.

Horin, A. (2008, November, 1–2). We know how schools get better: It's not league tables. *Sydney Morning Herald,* p. 33.

Hough, M. (2000). *Leadership of electronically capable schools.* (Monograph No 21). Melbourne, Australia: ACEA

Hough, M. (2004a). *New technologies and their impact on educators* (Hot Topic Series). Melbourne, Australia: ACEA.

Hough, M. (2004b). Updating our TQM thinking for a knowledge and service economy. *Total Quality Management, 13(5/6),* 763–801.

Hough, M. (2006a, March). *Developing moral leadership capabilities.* Hong Kong: Seminar to Academy of Management Consultancy.

Hough, M. (2006b, April). *Moral values: The bottom line.* Wanchai, Hong Kong: Public Sector Reform Conference.

Hough, M. (2007a, July). *Leading a digital school: The challenges* and *the next stage.* Keynote address to Conference of School Leaders, Sunshine Coast, Australia.

Hough, M. (2007b, September). *Teachers as leaders: What is the world we are preparing them for?* and *Leading a futures-oriented school.* Keynote address, QSite Conference, Moreton Bay College Queensland, Australia.

Hough, M. (2007c, November). *Managing upwards: Advice to generations X and Y for dealing more effectively with work situations.* Presentation to Sydney Chapter, Australian Computer Society, Australia

Hough, M. (2008). Educating for a digital world. In M. Lee & M. Gaffney (Eds.), *Leading a digital school: Principles and practice* (pp. 14–30). Melbourne, Australia: ACER Press.

Hough, M., & Bhindi, N. (2006, November). *Working more effectively with generations X and Y within a school environment.* Seminar to National Conference of Australian Council for Educational Leaders, Canberra, Australia.

Hough, M., & Bhindi, N. (2007, September). *Working more effectively with generations X and Y within a school environment.* NSW State Schools Secondary Principals' Conference, Sydney, Australia.

Ito, M., Horst, H.A., Bittanti, M., Boyd, D., Herr-Stephenson, B., Lange, P.G., Pascoe, C.J., & Robinson, L. (2008). *Living and learning with new media: Summary of findings from the digital youth project.* Macarthur Foundation. Retrieved September 2008, from http://www.digitallearning.macfound.org/ethnography

Lee, M., & Gaffney, M. (Eds.). (2008). *Leading a digital school: Principles and practice.* Melbourne, Australia: ACER Press.

Leithwood, K., & Riehl, C. (2004). What we know about successful leadership. *The Practising Administrator, 4,* 4–7.

Lennick, D., & Kiel, F. (2005). *Moral intelligence: Enhancing business performance and leadership success.* Boston: Wharton Business School.

Long, D. (2000). *Learner managed learning.* Sydney, Australia: Ashton.

Mackay, H., (1993). *Reinventing Australia: The mind and mood of Australia in the 90s.* Sydney, Australia: Angus & Robertson.

Mackay, H. (2004–2008). *The ipsos Mackay Report.* Regular 2 weekly reports on the issues and viewpoints of Australian Society as revealed by focus groups

Mackay, H. (2005, July). *Generations X and Y.* Presentation to AHISA Chairs Conference. Melbourne.

Mackay, H. (2007). *Advance Australia where?* Melbourne, Australia: Hatchette Books.

Marzano, R.J. (2003). *What works in schools: Translating research into action.* Washington: ASCD Publications.

McCrindle. M. (2003 onwards). *Understanding generation Y* (Series of Commentaries). Australian Leadership Foundation .

McKinsey & Company. (2007). *How the world's best school systems come out on top.* London: McKinsey & Company.

Metiri Group. (2005). *enGuage: 21st century skills for 21st century learners.* Washington: NCREL. Available at www.ncrel.org/engauge

Mulford, W. (2007). *Overview of research on Australian educational leadership: 2001—2005.* (Monograph 40). Melbourne, Australia: ACEL.

Murdoch, R. (2008). *New forces from this maelstrom.* Second Lecture in Boyer Series, *The Golden Age of Freedom*, Australian Broadcasting Corporation. Available at www.abc.net.au/m/boyerlectures. Reported in *Weekend Australian Inquirer,* 8–9 November, 2008.

Murray, P., Poole, D., & Jones, G. (2006). *Contemporary issues in management and organisational behaviour.* Melbourne, Australia: Thomson/Nelson.

O'Keefe, D. (2008). More international heavyweights slam reporting. *Education Review, 18*(8), 1, 20.

Organisation for Economic Co-operation and Development. (2006). *Program of international student assessment.* Paris: Author.

Organisation for Economic Co-operation and Development. (2007). *Improving school leadership.* Paris: Author.

Orpinas, P., & Horne, A. (2006). *Bullying prevention: Creating a positive school environment and developing social competence.* New York: American Psychological Association.

Philpson, G. (2008, December 9). Ten prophecies for the digital millennium. *Sydney Morning Herald,* p. 30.

Prensky, M. (2005). Listen to the natives. *Educational Leadership, 63*(4), 8–13.

Robinson, V. (2007). *School leadership and student outcomes: Identifying what works and why.* (Monograph 41). Melbourne, Australia: ACEL.

Seligman, M. (2008). *Happiness at work: Creating personal and professional wellbeing* (Australian Institute of Management Seminar). Sydney, Australia: Australian Institute of Management.

Sheehan, P. (2005). *Generation Y: Thriving and surviving with generation Y at work.* Melbourne, Australia: Hardie Grant.

Spender, D. (2007, May 19–20). Digi-kids and a new way of learning, *Sydney Morning Herald* (Weekend Edition), p. 32.

Toffler, A., & Toffler, H. (1970). *Future shock.* New York: Bantam.

Toffler, A., & Toffler, H. (1985). *The third wave.* New York: Bantam.

Toffler, A., & Toffler, H. (1995). *Creating a new civilisation: The politics of the 3rd wave.* New York: Futura.

▶▶▶◀◀◀

SECTION THREE
Professional Development
and Learning for Leaders

CHAPTER 12

The Preparation of Principals of Small Schools: Learning From the Debutantes

Helen Wildy and Simon Clarke

We have been researching the broad theme of the principalship for two decades (see, e.g., Wildy & Dimmock, 1993; Wildy, Forster, Louden, & Wallace, 2004; Wildy & Louden, 2000; Wildy & Wallace, 1995). Our research has recently focused on the work of principals of small schools (Clarke & Stevens, 2004; Clarke & Wildy, 2004; Clarke, Wildy, & Pepper, 2007; Clarke, Stevens, & Wildy, 2006; Wildy, 2004; Wildy & Clarke, 2005; Wildy, Clarke, & Slater, 2007; Wildy & Clarke, 2008a, 2008b), and our latest area of interest has been on the preparation of principals. By preparation, we mean the learning opportunities and experiences principals engage in prior to taking up their appointment. This chapter presents an account of the research approach we have used to study the preparation of principals of small schools and the outcomes of using this approach.

We draw on research with colleagues in 12 countries — The International Study of Principal Preparation (ISPP; http://www.ucalgary.ca/~cwebber/ISPP/index.htm) — to develop a framework for conceptualising principal preparation. From this research we show that there are distinctive features of small schools that make them particularly challenging for the novice principal, and more so today than previously. Although these challenges are not peculiar to the principal of the small school, we believe they are likely to be most taxing in this context.

The principal of a small school offers rich opportunities for investigation. In the next section we elaborate on three key issues associated with the principals' work in small schools that make such research worthwhile: the context of the small school, the role of the principal and implications of both for principal preparation. We then describe our research approach and the findings of our study of the challenges facing novice principals of small schools. We propose a conceptualisation of these challenges and we illustrate these challenges using narratives derived from several years of research. We conclude the chapter by locating the elements of the framework within the wider literature relating to principals' work and we make a case for a program of principal preparation that supports 'contextual literacy' (National College for School Leadership, 2007) among its participants.

THE CONTEXT OF THE SMALL SCHOOL

Studying the principal of the small school is worthwhile because of the numerical significance of small schools in the Australian setting.[1] In an earlier study (Wildy & Clarke, 2005), we reported that a quarter of all schools in each government education system in the Australian states cater for fewer than 100 students. In the Northern Territory 45% of government schools cater for fewer than 100 students and 7.5% of schools in the Australian Capital Territory are small schools, reflecting the relative concentration of population. Small schools account for a substantial proportion of the educational provision in Australia and it is important to understand the difficulties faced by principals in these school contexts.

The context of the small school — the small rural or remote community — is characterised by features that distinguish it from urban settings. Not only is the small community often geographically isolated either in agricultural areas or desert regions, but the culture of the small community is likely to be conservative (Clarke, Stevens, & Wildy, 2006; Nolan, 1998). It is not unusual for a small number of families to adopt a variety of key roles in such communities, including being a parent or grandparent of a student, and working as teacher, gardener, registrar, bus driver or cleaner at the local school. The principal interacts with community members in their various roles. Knowing that principals of small schools are also pivotal public people in their communities afforded high visibility but, needing high credibility, also suggests that the small-school context is worthy of study (Clarke, 2002a; Mohr, 2000; Nolan, 1998; Southworth, 1999).

A particular feature of the small school is that typically these schools are led by novice principals; that is, principals at the beginning of their career in the principalship. Historically, young teachers are often appointed to their first postings in small schools with the expectation that they will learn their craft in settings that are thought to be less complex than large urban schools. In the same way as novice teachers are usually 'sent bush', novice principals take up their first postings in the rural or remote small schools, many expecting that they will progress from there to larger and more urban school locations, just as Wilson (2007) and Wilson and McPake (2000) found in their studies of small schools in Scotland. However, while Scottish small schools have up to 50 students, Western Australian schools are classified as small if their enrolments are fewer than 100 students. Such schools are located in small communities, in sparsely populated and sometimes relatively inaccessible regions.

A further feature of the context of the small school is that the principal is likely to be female, single and, to an increasing extent, young. The principal who is female and single faces a particular challenge in the small rural community. Traditionally, school principals have been male and they have been welcomed into the social and sporting life of the town. Furthermore, when the male principal brings a wife and young children, the community is doubly blessed with increased school enrolments (Wildy, 2004). Perhaps because of these expectations, some communities are not inclined to welcome principals who do not fit this image (Clarke, 2002b; Clarke & Stevens, 2004). However, there is evidence that this is the profile of many novice primary principals (Department of Education and Training, Western Australia, 2007).

We have so far identified features of the context of the small school that make the small school a worthy site for research. However, the role of the principal in such settings makes the novice principal of the small school an even more fruitful subject for investigation.

THE ROLE OF THE SMALL-SCHOOL PRINCIPAL

Perhaps the most distinctive characteristic of the role of the principal of the small school that invites study is that the principal also tends to be a teacher. Principals of small schools have a teaching role in addition to their principal responsibilities and so their time, and commitment, is fragmented between the classroom and the office. The 'double load' has implications not only for their workload (Clarke, 2003) but also for their sense of efficacy. Typically, novice principals have some years of experience in the classroom but no experience as principals and the contrast between their confidence and skill in the two settings, often within the same day, is noticeable (Wildy & Clarke, 2008a).

The teaching principal is expected to meet shifting curricular expectations, including dealing with the changing nature of student learners, the expansion of new technologies, the need for appropriate pedagogy and additional demands made of teachers in a turbulent educational environment (Australian College of Education, 2001). However, as in schooling contexts everywhere, the work of the principal is also changing. The shift towards school-based management places new demands of autonomy, efficiency and accountability on the principal (Wildy & Louden, 2000) requiring sophisticated interpersonal skills to deal with their day-to-day encounters (Louden & Wildy, 1999a, 1999b). The personal resilience to handle interactions on a daily basis with a wide range of constituent groups such as staff, parents, department personnel and the community entails a good deal of 'emotional labour'.

In addition, the novice principal is also expected to be the leader of learning. That principals influence student achievement is long acknowledged (Rutter, Maughan, Mortimore, Ouston, & Smith, 1979). Lists of characteristics of effective schools and associated quality indicators are convincing in their endorsement of the importance of leadership (Christie & Lingard, 2001). The particular challenge principals of small schools face is to introduce and sustain improvement processes, when teachers are likely to be also high profile community members (Wildy & Clarke, 2008b).

Finally, principals of small schools are required to attend to the same system policies and procedures as their peers in larger schools but without the assistance of deputy principals or other support staff (Dunning, 1993). Contemporary models of distributed leadership (Crowther, 2002) are not always applicable in schools with small numbers of professional staff, particularly when these teachers are long-term members of both the school staff and the local community. Here, we have argued that the role of the small-school principal makes the principal of these schools worthy of research and now we turn to the implications of both context and role for principal preparation.

IMPLICATIONS FOR PRINCIPAL PREPARATION
Given the increasing complexity of principals' work it is hardly surprising that applications for the principalship are declining in Australia as elsewhere (D'Arbon, Duignan, & Duncan, 2002), especially for small rural and remote locations. Moreover, in light of projected shortfalls in numbers of teachers across Australia, the pool of future principals may diminish further (Preston, 2000). Knowing how best to prepare principals to survive, at the least, must be of national interest.

However, Australian principals in many state education jurisdictions take up their positions without formal preparation, expecting to learn on the job. Furthermore, such a journey to the principalship, although depicted in the literature (Su, Gamage, & Mininberg, 2003) as an 'apprenticeship model' with associated on-the-job theoretical and practical learning, is often characterised by variety, novelty and serendipity (Wildy, Clarke, & Slater, 2007), without a grounding in leadership theory, practice or reflection. As a result, we argue that leadership within our educational community is confused with narrow, technicist models of management that are inappropriate for connecting principals with the complexity and challenges of contemporary school leadership. Our current research derives from a concern that this on-the-job approach to preparing principals does not develop the level of leadership acumen needed to deal with the circumstances that are integral to the contemporary educational environment. This concern is accentuated in the small-school context which we have discussed earlier.

Approach

Our study of principals of small schools began by focusing on principals' perceptions of the complexity of their work. Specifically we asked: What issues do principals of small schools face in their day-to-day work? What is the nature of the context within which these issues arise? What strategies do principals of small schools adopt to deal with the complexities of their work and why do they adopt these strategies? In the Western Australian setting, small schools are those with fewer than 100 students and most of these schools cater for primary aged students. In remote areas, such schools are likely to cater also for a small number of secondary students.

We extended this research to align with the aims of the International Study of Principal Preparation (ISPP), a three-phase project in which we have engaged since 2004. The ISPP is a 12-country study designed to address the question: *How useful are principal preparation programs to novice principals?* In *Phase One*, each research partner conducted a mapping exercise of principal preparation programs provided in each local context. The mapping exercise showed that for aspiring and in-post government principals in Western Australia, leadership programs are provided by a Leadership Centre, a collaborative venture between relevant professional associations and the Department of Education and Training. Other programs offered by the five Western Australian universities are the Master of Education by coursework and the Master of Education by research, as well as the Doctorate in Education. All are undertaken on a voluntary basis by aspirants and principals in-post and none is considered by the employer to privilege the participant. *Phase Two* of the ISPP project is designed to identify, through the experiences of principals in their first year of appointment, those challenges for which they would benefit from improved preparation. Drawing on the findings of *Phase Two*, *Phase Three* is a large scale, cross-cultural survey of preparation for principals administered across the participating countries.

This chapter presents the approach and findings of the work we have done in Phase Two of the ISPP. The guiding research question was: To what extent do novice principals of primary schools perceive their preparation to align with their professional needs in their first year of appointment? Specifically, we sought to know:

- What challenges do novice principals experience and how do they deal with them?
- How do novice principals perceive the usefulness of components of their preparation?
- What knowledge and skills do novice principals think should have been included in their preparation?

Building on our previous research involving 200 principals in four education districts in Western Australia (Louden & Wildy, 1999a, 1999b) and principals of small schools in Western Australia and Queensland (Clarke & Stevens, 2004; Wildy, 2004), we selected five schools in remote and rural locations of the southern half of Western Australia within a day's travel from Perth. The selection process involved senior Department of Education and Training staffing personnel and the research team. We selected principals who were in their first year as a principal and their first year in the school. Hence, we focused on the experiences of the novice principal.

We adopted an interpretive orientation to capture the perspectives of principals in their first year in the job. Qualitative data were collected using a responsive and flexible approach, employing multiple data sources and inductive analysis (Taylor, Bogdan, & Racino, 1991). Data were gathered during site visits by two researchers in the first term of 2006. The researchers spent two evenings with the principal and one and a half days in the school and community, recording data from interviews, observations and school documents. Data were also collected during a half-day focus group in the middle of the year and follow-up phone interviews at the end of the year.

DATA REPRESENTATION

Data representation has been problematised in debates emerging from ethnography and phenomenology and applied in educational research (Richardson, 1994). Within this debate, the narrative has become an established way of revealing the human face of teaching (Connelly & Clandinin, 1990). Narrative is also an effective means of showing how school principals' work is characterised by dealing with dilemmas (Wildy, 1999, 2004; Wildy & Clarke, 2005, 2008a, 2008b; Wildy & Louden, 2000).

We argue that the narrative integrates and contextualises complex and multifaceted information. Our narratives are written in the first person, from the principal's perspective, to convey the rich texture of principals' experiences, without the researchers' explicit interpretation. Although the narratives contain factual information, each tells a story using the devices of storytelling. For example, each account has a title, a theme and some dramatic action over time (Clandinin & Connelly, 1991). Such storytelling is a creative act by the narrative writer. The narratives were constructed at the time of data collection, in the school setting using multiple sources of data.

Although information about the principals and school and community contexts is accurate, the narratives are subsequently *fictionalised*. Not only does this process provide anonymity for the principal and the community, it also serves to make general the particular, without losing the richness of the contextual detail. Noddings and Witherell (1991) argue that the strength of the narrative lies in portraying the abstract so that it is particularised and accessible. We use two strategies to fictionalise our narratives. We made general, rather than particular, statements in some instances. For example, when principals refer to places and people by their proper names we use the generic names, such as the gardener or the District Director. We also include distractors without altering the verisimilitude of the data, to confuse a reader who tries to identify the principal. For example, the school, depicted as 60 km from the nearest neighbouring school, might be 72 km or 53 km from its neighbour.

Narrative writing provides a lifelike account grounded in the principal's practice. Other principals who read the narratives often relate to the information, for example, by stating: 'I didn't know you had visited my school'. This level of vicarious experience promotes the capacity of the narrative to build on the reader's tacit professional knowledge by contributing to theory for both understanding and improvement (Clarke, Wildy, & Pepper, 2007). Furthermore, such features of narratives demonstrate that this mode of data representation has reader resonance or generalisability (Lincoln & Guba, 1986).

DATA ANALYSIS

Narrative writing is a form of analysis. Data were examined by the two researchers during site visits. Key themes and illustrations were identified. The themes were drawn from frameworks derived from the literature and applied in our earlier work. One framework was the impact of accountability, isolation and community (Clarke & Wildy, 2004). We also conceptualised the complexity of principals' work by means of dilemmas such as efficiency, autonomy and accountability (Wildy & Louden, 2000). As themes emerged, we constructed narratives, using verbatim text from the source documents and interview material. We used tape recordings to confirm accuracy of data and gave the narratives to principals for checking. In these ways we sought trustworthiness in matching the constructed realities of the principals with the reconstructions we attributed to them (Connelly & Clandinin, 1990; Lincoln & Guba, 1986).

Findings

We analysed 15 narratives generated in Phase 2 of the International Study of Principal Preparation (ISPP), as well as our earlier case studies of principals of small schools in Western Australia and Queensland. Our analysis revealed challenges facing novice principals in exercising their roles for which they believe they should have been better prepared. The challenges are conceptualised as a set of four foci: *place, people, system* and *self* (Wildy & Clarke, 2008a). While we conceptualise these as distinct foci, we recognise that they overlap and are intrinsically intertwined.

Place is described first because we have come to understand through our research that for novice principals in the settings investigated, it is *place* that has the most profound impact. Having the knowledge and understanding of place means that school leaders are able to read the complexities of their context. Sensitivity to context is exceptionally important for, though not restricted to, principals in small, isolated, rural or remote settings. These communities tend to be distinguished by a distinctive sense of place because they are imbued with particular societal and cultural values, some of which may appear unusual from the urban perspective that many principals acquire before appointment.

People is described next. Having the knowledge, understanding and skill to deal with people means that school leaders are able to handle a range of complex interactions on a day-to-day basis with diverse constituent groups, such as staff, parents, department personnel and community members. These interactions highlight the importance of the interpersonal dimension of the principal's role. Indeed, the heavily people-centred nature of the principals' work occupies a large amount of their daily time and creates an assortment of dilemmas and tensions. Compounding the challenge of dealing with people in small rural communities is the likelihood that teachers who are colleagues are also parents and members of the school community for whom the school provides a pivotal social function and whose goodwill is critical for the success of novice principals' school improvement efforts.

The third focus is *system*. Having the knowledge, understanding and skill to deal with the education authority, or system in our Australian setting, means that school leaders are able to find their way through complex and often quite baffling bureaucratic regulations, policies and protocols. That these are usually unique to the local educational system, but are likely to change dramatically in response to political intervention, adds to the complexity of dealing with the system for novice principals. Working skilfully within the system also entails judgment about what matters, distinguishing among the myriad paper and electronic correspondences, what needs immediate attention and what can be left. Dealing with the system, therefore, takes not only knowledge, understanding and skill but also confidence, determination and political sophistication.

The fourth focus is *self*. Looking after the self means having the personal resilience for the job. More than any other factor, novice principals face the challenge of their new appointment in terms of the cost to their confidence, self-efficacy and ability to manage competing pressures. The level of personal resilience required is widely underestimated by novice principals. Dealing with interpersonal interactions as well as dilemmas and tensions on a daily basis entails unanticipated levels of emotional labour. Self-knowledge and the ability to contextualise, understand, accept and deal with the emotional demands of the job is a key focus of our framework for principal preparation.

ILLUSTRATIONS

To illustrate both the distinctiveness and the interrelatedness of the four foci of our framework for principal preparation, we present four narratives. Each appears below, together with a brief analysis. The first of the four narratives, entitled *Kangaroo tails*, is set in a small remote school catering for both primary and secondary students. This narrative shows the importance of place.

Kangaroo tails

The new Vocational Education teacher took his five students to the local rock hole. The water hole was empty and lying in the hole, dead, was a camel. They pulled out the carcass using the four-wheel drive vehicle. As they cleaned the rock hole they realised they could prevent the wandering camels damaging the water hole by putting a fence around the area. Over the next months, they designed and welded a fence, complete with a handsome set of gates.

I was pleased to see this teacher having some success. He was a secondary teacher and expected our students to achieve what secondary students in other schools could do. He had no skills to deal with students whose achievements were low and his classroom management skills were inappropriate. As a primary teacher I was at a loss to help him.

The District Education Office awarded the school a certificate for Enterprise and Vocational Education for the project. We celebrated with a kangaroo tail barbeque for the families at the rock hole. Some of the men and women painted themselves and danced. When we ran out of kangaroo tails I drove back to school to get more, a trip of 30 kms. One family came to me for some more tails so I gave them to the elder. Then I realised that this family had already eaten. The two families who had not eaten were still without food. I couldn't intercede: this was a matter for the men to negotiate. To my horror our young female teacher stood up and walked across and asked the family with the extra tails to share them between the other two families.

There was shame all round. Those who were without tails were shamed; those who were asked to share were also shamed. The celebration disintegrated. People left. One family took the four-wheel drive vehicle and rammed the new fence, damaging the vehicle. Later one of the women told the teacher how she should have behaved. This was a learning experience for the teacher, and one that was not easy for me to handle.

The key issues for principal preparation from this narrative relate to the geographical and social isolation of the place characterised by an Aboriginal culture with distinct relationships and protocols, and methods of expression. Novice principals would rarely have experienced such a setting. We have selected an extreme example of place; not all novice principals begin their careers in such an unfamiliar environment. However, we found that, for novice principals, small farming communities were often as unfamiliar to them as the desert community was to the principal portrayed in *Kangaroo tails*.

The primary aspect of *place* that we considered worthy of attention in principal preparation programs is understanding the culture of the community in which the school is located. Understanding culture includes knowledge of local traditions, history, the geography of the area and its productivity, connections with wider communities, as well as local politics and social orders.

Nevertheless, the narrative *Kangaroo tails* illustrates more than the challenge of the cultural and physical contexts. Supporting teachers in their classroom management or to fine-tune their teaching strategies for the needs of their students, takes time and patience and a deep understanding of the complexities of initiating, implementing and sustaining change. Guiding teachers through the cultural expectations of the local community also takes considerable aptitude and novice principals do not always have these skills and understandings (Wildy, 2004). Such skills and understandings take time to develop and leaving such development to chance, to take place on the job, without preparation, is a risky business (Wildy, Clarke, & Slater, 2007).

While *Kangaroo tails* was chosen to illustrate the importance of place, this narrative also illustrates the connection between place and people in the building of relationships with the community members; and between place and self in the challenges to the principal's self-efficacy.

The next narrative, *The Gardener*, shows the importance of the second of the focal points of the framework: *people*.

The Gardener

My first year as principal was clouded by troubles with the gardener. In the first week I had to deal with his punctuality. He was used to coming and going whenever he pleased. I had to stop that quickly. He grumbled but made some effort to stay in the grounds during his work hours. In second term I had to speak to him again about his performance. He exploded when I started speaking to him. I lost my temper too. The argument lasted about 10 minutes. Unfortunately, we were in the playground and students were coming out to lunch.

In third term, he prepared the lines for the running track for our sports day. When I thanked him he was off-hand. I asked him what was wrong. He said I had been heavy handed over a minor classroom issue involving his wife who also works at the school. He demanded an apology. I told him the situation was resolved and I need not apologise. The next week some playground equipment was being repaired. I asked the gardener to seal off the area while the work was in progress. He refused. A parent erected the fence herself.

I was angry but waited two days before asking him to come to my office. He refused. He would speak to me only with a union representative present. The union representative was his wife. I sought advice from the District Education Office. It turned out I was also entitled to an observer at our meeting. I gave the gardener a letter outlining the purpose and timing of the meeting. He threw the letter on the ground and swore at me. The next day my observer arrived for the meeting but the gardener refused to cooperate.

After the term holidays, I received an e-mail from the gardener saying he was taking indefinite leave because I had been harassing him. Two days later, he resigned and I was relieved. Now at last I could concentrate on the students and their learning — the business of being a principal.

The key issues for principal preparation from this narrative relate to dealing with the relationship with the gardener. Handling conflict is not easy, especially when the principal's confidence is low. However, the issues for this novice principal are more complex because teachers in small communities are frequently parents in the school community, and they can wield considerable social pressure among their peers. Further, as members of the community, teachers tend to have long histories and will have witnessed numerous novice principals struggling to learn the job.

We illustrate the challenges of dealing with staff like the gardener not because these challenges are unique to novice principals or to principals of small schools. Such issues, though commonly faced by principals in a range of contexts, are particularly challenging for novice principals whose training and experience has prepared them to work as teachers, with students rather than with adults.

The primary aspect of people that we consider worthy of attention in principal preparation programs is the set of interpersonal skills to work constructively and productively with adults from a range of backgrounds. Building relationships with members of the school community, enhancing teachers' capacity, handling conflict between adults, dealing with the demands of parents and teachers and working with poorly functioning staff to improve performance are aspects of dealing with people that it would be desirable to include in a principal preparation program.

While *The Gardener* illustrates the focus on people in our conceptual framework, this narrative also illustrates other concepts that are interrelated to people. Place is important here: in small schools staff are also members of the community. *Self* is important too: principals in small schools do many jobs, such as supervising all staff, a responsibility that could be delegated in larger schools. Here, as in the previous narrative, learning how to balance the management aspects of the job with the leadership aspects is critical for principal preparation.

The third of the four narratives, entitled *You're on your own* shows the importance of the third of the focal points of the framework: *system.*

> *You're on your own*
>
> In a small school with low enrolment and few teachers I can keep on top of running the school. However, I never know whether I'm doing the right things, day-by-day and week-by-week.
>
> You're on your own. The school is 60 kilometres from the nearest town. It took me some time to get used to the physical isolation. There are four other schools like mine in the district but those principals are in the same position as I am, new and just getting by. I do notice the professional isolation. Previously, as a teacher in a large regional centre, I used to grumble about all the meetings I had to attend. Now I feel disconnected from the department. The District Director only comes down here when it is time to review the school. I try to go to network meetings with fellow principals. I don't have a Deputy Principal to give me advice about the school's policies and practices. I rely heavily on my Registrar, a local resident who has been at the school for 10 years. She is married into one of the three original families in the district and her own children and grandchildren attended the school. She knows everything about the community. Apart from the Registrar, no one gives me guidance. This was not a problem because everything seemed to be going fine. I started to relax and even enjoy the job until out of the blue I received a memo from District Director asking 'What are you doing about the [new reporting policy]?' I had not heard of this policy. Maybe I overlooked that e-mail. Perhaps it was discussed at a principals'

meeting I missed when our relief teacher was not available. I started to worry that I might be missing other matters.

I need a good mentor, someone who will respond to my calls when I need help. I want someone to help me when I have to act quickly.

For this novice principal, the remoteness of the school creates both physical and professional isolation causing the principal to feel unsupported and anxious. When asked by the line manager for a response to a new directive, the principal is caught off-guard, which makes him feel exposed and vulnerable.

The key issues for principal preparation from this narrative relate to the principal's relationship with the education authority. In the Australian context, the government education authority is highly centralised in each state, with a central office in the capital city and regional offices spread across the jurisdiction. In a sparsely populated state like Western Australia, with 0.5 million of its 2 million population located mainly around the coast of an area one third the size of China, the regional offices are widely dispersed and each services up to 50 schools. It is not surprising that principals like this novice principal feel professionally alone. Keeping abreast of policy shifts in a distant bureaucracy may not figure prominently in the awareness of a novice principal located in a remote part of the state.

The primary aspect of system that we consider worthy of attention in principal preparation programs is understanding the nature and role of the system in relation to the principalship. Such understanding implies knowing system policies, relations, processes and protocols; networking among system personnel; balancing system imperatives with local needs; and developing the skills and knowledge to acquire the resources needed in a small and isolated school.

The narrative *You're on your own* demonstrates more than the challenge of keeping connected to the system. Place is clearly important and so too is building relationships with significant people in the community such as the Registrar who is the keeper of the school and community culture. Equally important is the effect of isolation on this principal's self, when messages from the District Director serve not to support but to undermine the principal's confidence. The principal has yet to develop both the skill to seek the support that is required and the knowledge to identify and locate the source of such support.

The last of the four narratives, entitled *For the long haul,* shows the importance of the fourth focal point of the framework: *self.*

> *For the long haul*
>
> I plan to stay here as principal. The teaching side of my work is rewarding but I spend a great deal of time and energy learning about being a principal. I am learning many things, not only about the school and the community but also about myself.
>
> My priorities are my teachers, then parents, then the students. Learning about my teachers and supporting them is critical for me as a principal. I spend time each day talking with the two teachers to find out what they do in their classrooms and how they teach. I need to know about their teaching so I can lead the team. At the start of the year I had to learn much that is now routine. I had no prior experience of staffing, budgeting, timetabling and resource allocation. I worked hard every night to learn about the Regulatory Framework and the key policies that underpin our work in schools. I had to study the Duty of Care policy and the Excursions Policy when we had the school evacuation during first term.
>
> I attended five professional development days for my teaching during the year. However, I attended every available principal conference, meeting and workshop. I was out of the school for 24 days learning about the principal's work. Being out of the school so often meant that I had to work hard on weekends to catch up. However, next year I won't need to attend so many skill development sessions.
>
> I thought I was tolerant and respectful, listening and taking account of different perspectives. However, a parent complained to the District Director about my lack of tolerance and respect for her family. I was shocked and began to wonder how others perceive me. For a few months I went downhill, losing my confidence and feeling very vulnerable. There was no one to turn to. Then I thought, 'I have at least another year ahead of me in this school. I'll show the parents that I am sensitive and respectful'. I want to be here, as a good principal, for the long haul.

Unlike the principal in *You're on your own,* the novice principal in *For the long haul* is energetically fostering her professional engagement and development as a principal. The key issues for principal preparation from this narrative relate to the variety and magnitude of what is to be learned in the first year of the appointment. Despite spending long hours at school, in the evenings and on weekends to become informed and adept, this principal's sense of confidence is challenged after receiving criticism from a parent.

The primary aspect of self that we consider worthy of attention in principal preparation programs is developing personal resilience. Included in the development of personal resilience is balancing professional work and personal life needs, coping with the high visibility of the position, building confidence as a leader and coping with professional and physical isolation.

We believe that Goleman's (1995) concept of emotional intelligence (Goleman 1995) is related to our notion of self. Being mindful of one's own emotions as well as being able to manage them is necessary to be resilient and confident in often demanding circumstances. We argue that leadership in small schools is fundamentally about building relationships with the community. As a result, this concept should be acknowledged fully in the preparation of novice principals. It would also be beneficial for emotional intelligence to be acknowledged in the ongoing professional learning of small-school leaders by emphasising the value and use of emotional development for nurturing effective relationships.

However, the narrative *For the long haul* demonstrates more than the challenge of personal resilience. The traditions of place together with the social and political linkages of the people compound this principal's discomfort. The narrative also illustrates the influence of system personnel on the expectations that the principal brings to the job. As in the discussion of the previous narrative, the system appears to provide limited support for this novice principal and the principal has little knowledge or skill to acquire such support.

Discussion

The narrative accounts presented in this chapter capture the tenor of novice principals' voices to portray some of the issues faced by novice principals in small schools in Western Australia. From these and other narratives gathered over two decades we propose a framework for principals' preparation — place, people, system and self — that seems to support the view expressed by Day and colleagues (2001) that the experience of being a leader arises from a complex interplay of personal ideologies, relationships with staff [and significant others] and the demands of the school situation.

The emphasis on the interpersonal and contextual aspects of leadership is deliberate. It seems that principals in their first years need to have been prepared in matters beyond dealing with routine management and administrative tasks. Although we have no doubt that such a narrower approach is suitable for providing functional knowledge and skills to undertake their responsibilities within the *system* (Dempster, 2001). However, to accommodate the challenges of place, people and self, programs need to prepare principals for the challenges of dealing with the complexity of their roles as contemporary school leaders. Programs designed to support novice principals are unlikely to be effective if they are pursued haphazardly and episodically. Rather, it is desirable for leadership knowledge, dispositions and skills to be acquired according to long-term, iterative and reflective learning and, we argue, prior to taking up their first principal positions.

Our emphasis on place highlights the need for school leaders to be 'contextually literate' (National College for School Leadership, 2007). Contextual literacy involves understanding the culture of the community in which the school is located, and having the interpersonal skills to build relationships with, and among, members of the school and its community. Most importantly, though, contextual literacy requires knowledge of distinctive contextual features such as those applying to small communities located in rural and remote environments.

We acknowledge that novice principals will resort to on-the-job learning. However, it should not be necessary for them to rely exclusively on trial and error to acquaint themselves with the role, as is the tendency in the Australian settings we have studied. We believe that their preparation should involve both theory and practical leadership skill development, as well as rich local contextual knowledge; that they deserve to be well supported by their system colleagues and line managers; and that not only do they need the confidence in themselves, they also need to be nurtured by high expectations of success from their system personnel.

Concluding Comments

Approaching the preparation of principals from the perspective of their own experiences of the challenges they face in their first years provides a sound basis for a grounded, valid and relevant professional program to prepare principals to understand how they should be doing their work in the present and the future. While the preparation phase of a novice principal's learning is critical, there are ongoing learning needs equally important as principals develop into more experienced school leaders.

Finally, as a postscript to this chapter, we consider the future of school leadership development in this country. On the one hand, it seems fair to say that circumstances are favourable to the enhancement of processes for developing the capacity of school leaders, including their preparation for the principalship. For some time there has been a productive dialogue taking place across the professional community that seems to have sharpened understandings of the complexity of school leadership, the knowledge, skills and dispositions required to perform the role effectively and the ways in which school leaders can best be assisted to develop the kind of leadership capacity that contemporary schools increasingly demand (Clarke, 2006). This new and powerful thinking about leadership practice in schools presents a persuasive case for principalship preparation programs that are more systematic and specialised than the ad hoc nature of current approaches and could, therefore, encourage changes in policy.

That said, and on a more cautionary note, speculation about the future of school leadership development is a risky venture at the best of times as arrangements tend to be so varied. In a vast and politically complex country like Australia, this is particularly true because of the potential for disparate approaches to building the capacity of school leaders. We hope that this tendency towards fragmentation does not undermine the national sense of collaboration that will be required to provide aspiring (and practising) school leaders with the leadership development they deserve. At the very least, this will involve aligning their professional learning with the kinds of experiences and challenges of modern school leadership that debutante principals have portrayed in our research.

Endnotes

1   The proportions reported in this paper are based on 2003 enrolments provided by Data Management Officers responsible for collecting and collating government school information in each state.

References

Australian College of Education. (2001). *Excellence in school leadership*, Background paper. Developed by Australian College of Education for the Australian Secondary Principals Association. Retrieved May 19, 2008, from http://www.austcolled.com.au

Christie, P., & Lingard, B. (2001, April). *Capturing complexity in educational leadership*. Paper presented at the American Educational Research Association, Seattle, WA.

Clandinin, D.J., & Connelly, F.M. (1991). Narrative and story in practice and research. In D. Schon (Ed.), *The reflective turn: Case studies in and on educational practice* (pp. 258–281). New York: Teachers College Press.

Clarke, S.R.P. (2003). *Mastering the art of extreme juggling: An examination of the contemporary role of the Queensland teaching principal.* Unpublished report prepared for the Queensland Association of State School Principals.

Clarke, S. (2002a). The teaching principal: From the shadowlands to a place in the sun. *The Queensland Journal of Educational Research, 189*(1), 23–37.

Clarke, S. (2002b). Understanding small school leadership: Listening to the practitioners. *The Practising Administrator, 24*(3), 28–32.

Clarke, S. (2006). From fragmentation to convergence: Shaping an Australian agenda for quality school leadership. *School Leadership and Management, 26*(2), 169–182.

Clarke, S., & Wildy, H. (2004). Context counts: Viewing small school leadership from the inside out. *Journal of Educational Administration, 42*(5), 555–572.

Clarke, S., & Stevens, E. (2004). *Small schools leadership study. Leading and teaching in small schools: Confronting contextual complexity in work practices.* Unpublished report prepared for Education Queensland.

Clarke, S., Stevens, E., & Wildy, H. (2006). Rural rides in Queensland: Travels with novice teaching principals. *International Journal of Leadership in Education, 9*(1), 75–88.

Clarke, S., Wildy, H., & Pepper, C. (2007). Connecting preparation with reality: Primary principals' experiences of their first year out in Western Australia. *Leading & Managing, 13*(1), 81–90.

Connelly, F.M., & Clandinin, D.J. (1990). Stories of experience and narrative inquiry. *Educational Researcher, 19*(4), 2–14.

Crowther, F. (2002). Big change question: Is the role of the principal in creating school improvement over-rated? *Journal of Educational Change, 3*(2), 167–173.

D'Arbon, T., Duignan P., & Duncan, D. (2002). Planning for future leadership of schools: An Australian study. *Journal of Educational Administration, 40*(5), 468–485.

Day, C., Harris, A., & Hadfield, M. (2001). Grounding knowledge of schools in stakeholder realities: A multiperspective study of effective school leaders. *School Leadership & Management, 21*(1), 19–42.

Department of Education and Training, Western Australia. (2004). *If you think education is expensive* (Education Workforce Initiatives Report). Perth, Australia: Author.

Dempster, N. (2001, May). *The professional development of school principals: A fine balance.* Professorial lecture, Griffith Public Lecture Series, 24 May, Griffith University, Brisbane, Australia.

Dunning, G. (1993). Managing the small primary school: The problem role of the teaching head. *Educational Management and Administration, 21*(2), 79–89.

Goleman, D. (1995). *Emotional intelligence: Why it can matter more than IQ.* London: Bloomsbury.

Lincoln, Y., & Guba, E. (1986). But is it rigorous? Trustworthiness and authenticity in naturalistic evaluation. In D.D. Williams (Ed.), *Naturalistic evaluation* (pp. 73–84). San Francisco: Jossey-Bass.

Louden, W., & Wildy, H. (1999a). 'Circumstance and proper timing': Context and the construction of a standards framework for school principals' performance. *Educational Administration Quarterly, 35*(3), 399–422.

Louden, W., & Wildy, H. (1999b). Short shrift to long lists: An alternative approach to the development of performance standards for school principals. *Journal of Educational Administration, 37*(2), 99–120.

Mohr, N. (2000). Small schools are not miniature large schools: Potential pitfalls and implications for leadership. In W. Ayers, M. Klonsky & G. Lyon (Eds.), *A simple justice: The challenge of small schools* (pp. 139–158). New York: Teachers College Press.

National College for School Leadership. (2007). *What we know about school leadership.* Retrieved January 25, 2008, from http://www.ncsl.org.uk/publications

Noddings, N., & Witherell, C. (1991). Epilogue. Themes remembered and foreseen, In C. Witherell & N. Noddings (Eds.), *Stories lives tell: Narrative and dialogue in Education* (pp. 279–280). New York: Teachers College Press.

Nolan, B. (1998). Implementing departmental policy changes in one-teacher schools. *Journal of Educational Administration, 36*(3–4), 262–285.

Preston, B. (2000). *Teacher supply and demand to 2005: Projections and issues.* A report commissioned by the Australian Council of Deans of Education. Canberra. Retrieved May 19, 2008, from http://acde.edu.au/publications.htm

Richardson, L. (1994). Writing: A method of inquiry. In N.K. Denzin & Y.S. Lincoln (Eds.), *Handbook of qualitative research* (pp. 516–529). Thousand Oaks, CA: Sage.

Rutter, M., Maughan, B., Mortimore, P., Ouston, J., & Smith, A. (1979). *Fifteen thousand hours: Secondary schools and their effects.* London: Open Books.

Southworth, G. (1999). *A teacher training agency report into successful heads of small primary schools.* Reading, MA: University of Reading School of Education.

Su, Z., Gamage, D., & Mininberg, E. (2003). Professional preparation and development of school leaders in Australia and the USA. *International Education Journal, 4*(1), 42–59.

Taylor, S., Bogdan, R., & Racino, J.A. (1991), *Life in the community. Case studies of organisations supporting people with disabilities.* Baltimore, MD: Paul H. Brookes Publishing Co.

Wildy, H. (1999). Statues, lenses and crystals: Looking at qualitative research. *Educational Research and Perspectives, 26*(2), 61–72.

Wildy, H. (2004). *Small schools leadership study. Leading and teaching in small schools: Confronting contextual complexity in work practices.* Report prepared for the Western Australian Department of Education and Training. Retrieved May 19, 2008, from http://www.eddept.wa.edu.au/cpr/publications.htm

Wildy, H., & Clarke, S.R.P. (2005). Leading the small rural school: The case of the novice principal, *Leading & Managing, 11*(1), 43–56.

Wildy, H., & Clarke, S. (2008a). Charting an arid landscape: The preparation of novice primary principals in Western Australia. *School Leadership & Management, 28*(5), 469–487.

Wildy, H., & Clarke, S. (2008b, March). *L-plate drivers in the principal's office: Reflections through the rear view mirror.* Paper presented at the annual meeting of the American Education Research Association, New York.

Wildy, H., Clarke, S., & Slater, C. (2007). International perspectives of principal preparation: How does Australia fare? *Leading & Managing* Special Edition, *13*(2), 1–14.

Wildy, H., & Dimmock, C. (1993). Instructional leadership in Western Australian primary and secondary schools. *Journal of Educational Administration, 31*(2), 43–62.

Wildy, H., Forster, P., Louden, W., & Wallace, J. (2004). The International Study of Leadership in Education: Monitoring decision-making by school leaders. *Journal of Educational Administration, 42*(4), 416–430.

Wildy, H., & Louden, W. (2000). School restructuring and the dilemmas of principals' work. *Educational Management and Administration, 28*(3), 173–184.

Wildy, H., & Wallace, J. (1995). School leadership development in Western Australia: An impact study. *Journal of School Leadership, 5*(3), 248–271.

Wilson, V., & McPake, J. (2000). Managing change in small Scottish primary schools. *Educational Management and Administration, 28*(2), 119–132.

Wilson, V. (2007). *Leadership in small Scottish primary schools.* Report prepared for the Education Information and Analytical Services Division of the Scottish Government. Retrieved May 19, 2008, from http://www.scotland.gov.uk/Publications/2007/09/06091416/0

▷▷▷◁◁◁

CHAPTER 13

Preparing Aspiring Leaders Within Faith-Based Education Systems: Two Models

Tony d'Arbon, Annette Cunliffe, Kelvin Canavan and Adrienne Jericho

This chapter reports on two projects developed to stimulate interest in future leadership positions in education and to prepare future leaders for Catholic and Lutheran schools. Both projects were initiated in response to the need to address leadership succession and succession planning issues in these systems of education. This need emerged with the impending shortage of teachers, not only in specialist areas but also in general, and the attendant critical need for an ongoing supply of suitably qualified and highly motivated persons to apply for vacant principal positions in the future (Fenwick, 2000).

The projects described in this chapter represent different ways of identifying and supporting the leadership talent of the young contender. Nightingale (2006) points out that identifying and developing aspiring leaders is emerging as a way to tackle the challenge of recruiting enough leaders for the future, but spotting talent is not traditionally a school's strong point. In the case of the programs in this chapter, the two systems (Catholic and Lutheran) have taken the initiative to identify and nurture young teachers for future leadership positions — the Catholic education model by a process of self-nomination and the Lutheran model by system identification and system nomination.

Catholic and Lutheran schools in Australia operate predominantly as systems. Both systems are faith-based or faith-inspired in the Christian tradition, and while there are historical and theological differences, there is an overall unity of purpose in both groupings of schools. Inevitably there will be local variations in structures, leadership, management, administration and strategic planning in each system, brought about by location, history and other contextual factors. However, overall there are significant similarities and parallels between the Catholic and Lutheran systems of schools, especially in the areas of leadership succession and succession planning.

In relationship to the role of school principal, some of the special features of leaders in both systems include the principal being required to have the administrative background, experience and knowledge of curriculum, but also the confidence of the respective Church community. The community expects that the principal will have the necessary motivation and commitment to ensure that the doctrine and values of the Church are faithfully transmitted, and that a supportive ethos is encouraged and nurtured for all pupils and staff within the school. A similar set of expectations would apply to any body of faith-based or faith-inspired schools, where there is an intentional purpose to carry out a mandate of education within a specific religious tradition espoused by the governing bodies of those schools. Hence it is logical and valid to explore and compare the effectiveness of the two models of leadership planning and development within two comparable faith-based systems of education.

Taken as a whole, both Catholic and Lutheran systems of education are significant contributors to the national educational enterprise in Australia. In the Catholic system, there are over 1,700 schools, 690,000 students (approximately 20% of the total school population of the country) and over 46,000 teachers in 28 dioceses. Similarly, for Lutheran Education Australia (LEA) there are 83 schools with over 34,000 students and 3,000 teachers. As principals in both systems are generally employed on contracts of about 5 years these two systems will potentially experience a significant turnover of principals every 5 to 10 years. Although many principals would have their contracts renewed or move to other principal positions, there are significant numbers of principals to be replaced each year. Hence a need for a continuing supply of well-prepared teachers and future leaders for these schools is a matter of ongoing concern for planners in both systems of nongovernment education.

The leadership development program reported in this chapter conducted by the Catholic Education Office, Sydney (CEO) was titled *Leaders for the Future* (LFF). For Lutheran Education Australia (LEA), cohorts of aspiring leaders were enrolled in two separate projects, the *Millennial Principals Project* (MPP) of 2001–2004 and the subsequent *Leadership Development Program* (LDP) of 2005–2008. The LFF involved over 250 young teachers under the age of 30 years in a 12-month program in 2005–2006, while MPP and LDP together involved a total of 132 participants drawn mainly from Queensland and South Australia. These projects are detailed and discussed below.

The recent Pastoral Letter of the Bishops of NSW and the ACT — *Catholic Schools at a Crossroads* (2007) — addressed a number of major concerns including that of leadership. In the section entitled 'Leading and Staffing our Schools in this New Era' the *Crossroads* document states that:

> there are many reasons why the Church remains concerned to ensure that there is a 'critical mass' of Catholic leaders and staff in our schools ... The formation of our Catholic school leaders and teachers is crucial for the achievement of the goals of this Pastoral Letter ... We invite all those involved in Catholic education to join us in choosing and supporting leaders and staff for our schools who will effectively embrace the mission embraced in this Pastoral Letter. Particular attention must be given to succession planning, leadership formation and the preparation of Catholic teachers. (p. 16)

This statement emphasises the concern of Church leaders for the future leadership of Catholic schools. It is part of an ongoing stimulus to ensure that Catholic schools continue to succeed and flourish in their mission.

Similarly for LEA, in developing MPP and LDP, the concern was for a project to nurture and develop potential leaders for the future of Lutheran schooling in Australia. There was recognition of an urgent need to act systematically and intentionally to develop and grow leadership so that there would be an increased pool of leaders available for Lutheran schools.

Church statements define the mission of the Lutheran school as offering to Church 'members and to others in the community a formal education in which the gospel of Jesus Christ informs all learning and teaching, all human relationships, and all activities' (LCA, 1999). Its schools are one of the more successful ways in which the church has related to Australian communities. To ensure the ethos integrity of the Lutheran school and to maintain a vital school–church relationship, all principals in Lutheran schools are required to be Lutheran. The trebling of enrolments in Lutheran schools over the past 25 years, at a time when church membership has declined significantly, has created the need for great care in choosing future leaders from a shrinking pool.

Both CEO and LEA projects reflect the six-step process for leadership talent development described by the National College of School Leadership (Hartle & Thomas, 2003). The steps are:

- create a culture for growth
- benchmark current practice
- define leadership qualities you want
- identify the leadership talent pool
- assess individual talent
- grow leadership talent.

In LFF, MPP and LDP, both systems have independently and individually implemented these steps in the two systems with significant results that are discussed below.

Description of the Two Leadership Development Projects

Catholic Education Office Sydney Project

Leadership preparation programs in the past were generally focused on administrative aspects of the role but, more recently, leadership became the major focus (Caldwell, 2006; Earley & Weindling, 2004). Programs have generally targeted persons approaching or immediately following a career move or promotion. The program may be employer-initiated or sought by individuals who anticipate or seek a leadership or promotional opportunity. The initiative of the CEO Sydney represents a departure from this approach.

This major innovative response to the leadership succession issue was made though CEO Sydney, with a program entitled *Leaders for the Future* (LFF), which was conducted over a 12-month period in 2006–2007. The program was a direct response to the:

- shortage of suitable applicants for principalship
- ageing of the present cohort of principals
- practice of not appointing principals before the age of 40
- need to stem the loss of young teachers from the profession within 5 years of graduation
- development of leadership potential in enthusiastic young teachers interested in advancement
- need to focus the attention of future leaders on the mission of the Catholic Church in education
- growing realisation that unless more leaders are developed the future of Catholic schooling in Sydney will be at risk. (Canavan, 2007)

A full description of LFF and its evaluation are reported elsewhere (see for example, Canavan, 2007; d'Arbon & Cunliffe, 2007).

In brief, the program set out to provide a stimulus to young aspiring educational leaders who were under 30 years of age, in the prepromotional stage of their careers, by introducing them to a series of well-known persons and figures in leadership roles or positions in society, from a variety of situations or organisations and hearing their stories. The presenters included an Olympic medallist, a former leader of a political party, a professional football team motivator, leading Church and Church educational figures, an industrial negotiator, a psychologist, as well as leading teaching and curriculum specialists. Topics included leadership styles and personality, strategic leadership, leadership and management in the Catholic school, Catholic schooling and social issues, developing leadership capacity, as well as leadership and relationships. The evaluation of the program reported:

> LFF was found to be innovative, was perceived positively by the young teachers who participated and it contributed to an increased sense of loyalty, to confidence in their own abilities as aspiring leaders and to their seeking future leadership roles within their schools. Participants reported that some skills and knowledge gained from the program could be immediately applied to their current contexts. Longer term outcomes will become evident over time, but early indications are that such a generalist leadership program offers hope in retaining young teachers and possible encouraging more of them to recognise their own potential to take on future leadership roles. (d'Arbon & Cunliffe, 2007, p. 79)

Of the LFF program, Canavan (2007) reported:
- a high completion rate among the participants; 265 attended the original induction session in October 2006 and 242 graduated 12 months later having completed 30 hours of the program
- a practical application of skills and learning
- positive attitudes to the CEO
- empowerment and positive attitude to future leadership
- commitment to the ongoing journey of leadership.

The graduates' reports and interviews for an initial evaluation of the project and in the follow-up, online survey included some personal reflections on the program and what it achieved. Key points made included:

- there was an increased awareness of the need for quality in human interactions
- participants gained increased confidence in relating to people, especially in terms of conflict and delegation, as well as dealing with difficult situations
- the importance of role modelling was highlighted
- there was increased awareness as a potential young leader
- there was a greater awareness of strengths and areas for development
- most importantly, the course has given young leaders the vision and ability to strive for leadership positions in schools.

These positive outcomes from LFF have affirmed the CEO, which is now planning a similar program in the near future and acted as a stimulus and as a role model for other Catholic education systems in Australia such as CEO South Australia, which is currently developing a similar program entitled *Looking at Leadership*, with a focus on teachers under 35 years of age. The key points will be compared with those of the LEA programs.

Lutheran Education Australia Projects

At about the same time, the system of schools operated by Lutheran Education Australia (LEA) partnered with the Australian Catholic University (ACU) Flagship for Creative and Authentic Leadership (CAL) to develop programs that would assist it in identifying, nurturing and developing potential leaders for the future of Lutheran schools in Australia. These were the *Millennial Principals Project* (MPP) that commenced in 2001. A revised program was repeated in 2005 with modifications based on an evaluation of the MPP under the banner of *Leadership Development Project* (LDP) with 55 participants presently in the program. Though more traditional in targeting those identified as potential leaders, this program was distinctive in being based on a clearly articulated leadership framework based on a Lutheran vision for educational leadership.

The projects were driven by a realisation that the growth of Lutheran schools needed to be accompanied by an intentional fostering and nurturing of leadership. There was compelling evidence that the number of applicants for leadership positions was shrinking. The demographics of those holding principal positions indicated that there was an urgent need to plan for the future (Jericho, 2005). Furthermore, there was a need to address the gender imbalance in these positions, with only 11% of principals in LEA schools being female (Jericho, 2007).

LEA leadership development has been based on the following principles:

- Leadership development is a joint responsibility of the individual, the school, Lutheran state systems and the national LEA network.
- As a group of schools, significant resources have to be allocated for leadership development.
- Contemporary principals are the best people to model, mentor and nurture prospective principals.
- The formation/development activities need to be underpinned by good theory, reflection, access to best practice and related to the aspirants' practical experiences.

The key features of LEA's leadership development initiatives have been the development of a leadership framework, leadership profiling, formal study, mentoring and regional networking workshops.

Considerable effort was given to developing a leadership framework for Lutheran schools. The *Leadership Framework for Lutheran Schools* (LEA, 2005) is based on the mission and values of the Lutheran school and identifies five leadership capability clusters (ministry, personal, relational, professional, managerial and strategic) that are exercised in five educational areas (spiritual, authentic, educative, organisational and community). This framework has provided a focus for leadership development activities and has given a language for reflection and conversation on leadership.

Participants for the projects were either identified by their school leaders or system-nominated; they then participated in a leadership profiling activity. They were required to complete a portfolio and develop responses to two case studies. The portfolio invited participants to reflect on their leadership experiences in education and beyond in relation to key indicators from the leadership framework. The portfolio was supported by commentary from their principal. The portfolios and responses to the case studies were evaluated by teams comprising a member of LEA and a member of the Flagship, after which a report was forwarded to LEA proposing a professional development or academic program that would further the capabilities of the aspiring leader. It should be noted that the process was not an assessment of the candidate, but rather an appraisal of what would best advance their leadership prospects. System personnel met with each participant to discuss the report and develop an agreed action plan for the future, which included formal study for some.

Participants who were selected to be part of the formal study program were supported with a 50% subsidy from their system to complete a Postgraduate Certificate in Educational Leadership at ACU. Those who already had a postgraduate degree in leadership went into the next component of the program. The MPP commenced in 2001 with 104 participants, 77 of whom graduated from the formal study program; they are still in Lutheran schools.

Mentoring was an important component of both LEA leadership development programs and it sought to establish a supportive and facilitative relationship for reflection and growth. In MPP the mentee was assigned a principal from another school but, based on this experience, in LDP the mentee has chosen his/her own mentor who was to be in a formal leadership position in a Lutheran school or had been in one. Once mentors were selected, mentors and mentees were brought together for training on mentoring.

The final component of LDP, which was not part of MPP, was regional networking workshops. Networking was an important feature of the program and participants were generally brought together on a state basis every term over the 2 years of the program. Specifically, there was discussion and consideration relating to specific Lutheran education system issues. This camaraderie developed into a support network and issues that emerged among program participants could be discussed and worked through.

Evaluation of the Programs

Initially, there were individual evaluations for the LFF and MPP projects conducted by the respective systems on their conclusion. In the case of LFF, the evaluation was conducted by the Flagship for Creative and Authentic Leadership at ACU.

The LFF evaluation used:

- focus group interviews conducted for separate groups of primary and secondary teacher-participants to provide feedback twice: at the midpoint and the conclusion of the program
- written feedback from the participants, provided to the CEO
- impressions gathered during conversations by the evaluators during the program and informal interaction with participants, and CEO staff.

One recommendation of the initial evaluation of LFF was that further surveys be conducted to evaluate the longer term effects of the program.

In the light of this recommendation a meeting was held in 2007 that included representatives of the CEO Sydney, participants in the LFF and the original evaluators to discuss both the format of any such survey and the areas that should be explored. Suggestions from this meeting became the basis on which the further surveys reported here were based.

The MPP program was initially reviewed internally and the review was based on three documents:

- an audit of those involved in the project
- a report based on group reflections during a participant retreat in the Queensland region of LEA
- in other regions, feedback based on a written survey of participants, mentors and principals.

One recommendation of this review was that 'there be a similar leadership development process', which resulted in the LDP program being commenced 2005. In light of the proposed ongoing evaluation of the LFF, the LEA was approached about the possibility of using a similar survey. The LEA agreed to use such a survey as an external review of the LDP and to gauge the ongoing impact of MPP for its participants.

Evaluation Process

To enable suitable comparisons to be made across the Catholic and Lutheran contexts, a questionnaire with appropriate slight language and content modification for the two systems was developed and made available electronically to all graduates of all programs. The anonymous returns were collated, with the demographic questions providing a basis for comparison of the two groups. These questions sought information about age, gender and professional background and experience.

The two sets of programs had obvious contextual and methodological differences and the questionnaire sought to provide comparable information concerning outcomes, both by way of fixed responses and through open-ended questions. The survey sought information about:

- new roles undertaken since starting the program, changes in place of employment to further leadership aspirations
- formal study or in-service opportunities to further leadership aspirations

- perceived impact of the program on participants and their careers in education
- perceived impact of any aspect of the program
- any suggestions to improve the program if it were offered again.

Questions were designed by the original evaluators of LFF, an expert from the CEO Sydney and teams from the CEO and LEA. Ethics approval was managed through the Research Services Office of ACU.

The online survey used the 'LimeSurvey®' tool, from mid-June 2008 to mid-August 2008. The LEA and CEO Sydney issued the invitations to their participants and a total of 51 participants in the LFF and 41 of those who undertook the MPP or LDP completed the survey. The quantitative and qualitative responses have been analysed below.

Results

The response rates for the two groups represented 22.9% (CEO group) and 31.1% (LEA groups). As shown in Table 13.1, 2 years after completing the program, 86% of the LFF graduates were 31 years old or younger and completed their professional qualifications less than 10 years ago. For the Lutheran respondents, 95% were, at the time of the survey, 32 years or older and 78% had qualified more than 10 years ago, with correspondingly more years' teaching experience.

The gender distribution showed important differences with 78% female in LFF compared with 49% in the Lutheran programs. The percentage of females in the Lutheran project was significant in light of a deliberate attempt by LEA to redress the gender balance in leadership in schools of the Lutheran system. Table 13.1 provides a snapshot of the two groups of respondents.

Findings of the Evaluation of the Two Programs
CATHOLIC EDUCATION OFFICE, SYDNEY (CEO) PROJECT

The LFF Program was constructed to engage those teachers in Catholic schools in the Archdiocese of Sydney who were under 30 years of age in a formal program requiring participation in a minimum of ten 3-hour sessions, at monthly intervals. A further attraction of the program was that it was given accreditation by ACU to allow one unit of credit towards a Master of Education degree, on completion of an appropriate assignment.

One of the original premises of this program was that participation be governed by self-nomination at every stage. This gave the 'Generation

TABLE 13.1
Characteristics of the Groups

Characteristic	LFF group (%)	MPP/LDP group (%)
Aged up to 31	86	5
Aged 32+	14	95
Qualified up to 11 years ago	96	22
Qualified longer than 11 years	4	78
Years of experience up to 11	98	22
Years of experience over 11	2	78
Male	22	51
Female	78	49
Primary teacher	74	35
Middle school teacher	0	10
Secondary teacher	26	55

Y' target group opportunities for self-determination and choice, one of their age group's generally recognised preferences. On that basis, participants commenced the program in October 2005. The completion rate was 87%, made all the more impressive by the fact that participation was voluntary and all sessions conducted out of work hours.

The first key finding was that participants generally responded very positively to the program. They said they were made to feel special, that the CEO appreciated and responded to them and they appreciated the opportunity to be helped to see the broader picture of leadership and to make connections.

The evaluation stated that LFF should be considered a creative, groundbreaking attempt to address a major problem facing the future of Catholic education in Australia, with the potential to be applied to other systems of education.

LFF was recognised by participants as a practical, positive, creative and innovative response to the challenges identified by the Executive Director when initiating LFF and his desire to increase the pool of talented aspirants to school leadership positions in the future. A typical testimony was: 'To see the support of the CEO staff and Regional Director and Executive Director was great! I would love to be involved again.'

Second, the LFF program has been an effective catalyst in promoting further formal study at the master's level. Almost 40 participants (18%) have elected to use this unit towards a master's degree. This has had the added benefit of fostering a practical application of theory in the setting of their own school, through completion of the assignment and harnessing the support of their principal. It has awakened their professional appetite. In addition, many participants noted aspects of the program itself that increased their knowledge and skills in leadership.

The third aspect, undoubtedly the short-term highlight of the LFF, has been the development of leadership capacity among young teachers to the point where many now consider the option of lodging an expression of interest for advertised promotion positions within their school or other system schools. Just 2 years since program graduation, almost 48% of those who participated have been appointed to a new formal leadership role, as seen in Table 13.2.

Some typical comments about this aspect included:

> I would say that LFF enhanced my expectation rather than changed them. It empowered and skilled me to be a better leader and apply for promotion positions more confidently.

> I think that the program gave me the confidence to apply for leadership positions that I don't think I would have applied for if I hadn't completed the course.

Fourthly, one of the most significant strengths of the LFF program was its ability to draw on leaders from a diverse range of sectors and industry as keynote speakers. Although most keynote speakers were not drawn from the educational sector, participants valued the opportunity to see leadership models through the lenses of sport, politics, the corporate world, community services, communications and mediation services. Some commented:

> The range of leaders who presented was inspiring and from all different lines of work. They all had something amazing to contribute which we could apply as teachers in our experience. I would say that this was one of the most motivating and inspiring courses I have done.

TABLE 13.2
New Appointed Positions Since Graduation From LFF Program

Appointed position	Number of respondents	Percentage of respondents
Coordinator roles:	72	37.6
Rel. ed coordinators:	16	8.3
Assistant principals:	3	1.5
Project officers:	1	0.5

Continue to engage influential leaders both within and beyond the field of education (e.g., politicians, and corporate executives etc).

Continue to focus on practical leadership skills (e.g., communication).

I think that the variety of presenters was extremely valuable as it allowed the young leaders to see leadership from other perspectives.

An important outcome was the decreased numbers of young teachers 'lost' to the profession. Current experience in education across Australia is marked by a high attrition rate of teachers within the first 5 years of entry. Of 1,351 respondents to a national survey of primary and secondary teachers in their first 3 years of teaching, conducted in October 2006 by the Australian Joint Principals' Associations, 25% indicated that they would leave teaching within their first 5 years of teaching (2007). This is consistent with the cited figure for the western world of between 25% and 40% of new teachers who resign or burnout in their first 3 to 5 years (Ewing & Smith, 2003). In contrast, the attrition rate among *Leaders for the Future* participants is just 8.1%. Thus the program appears to have had a powerful effect in maintaining an extremely high retention rate of 91.9%.

From the viewpoint of a school system with a strong interest in succession planning, the LFF has been remarkable. Participants commented that they have a strong 'connection' with their school executives and regional consultants on professional matters. For example, one commented:

The opportunity to develop collegiality with my current school leaders and system leaders was invaluable. I no longer feel that there is a chasm between us. In fact the bridge is so strong that I have the confidence to use them in a mentoring capacity.

LUTHERAN EDUCATION AUSTRALIA (LEA) GROUPS

One highlight of the LEA programs has been that the 77 MPP participants have provided Lutheran schools with 33 persons who are now in senior leadership positions, and already ten of the 55 LDP participants have assumed senior leadership positions. Table 13.3 summarises the responses from the combined MPP and LDP projects.

The fact that LEA moved directly from MPP to LDP was indicative of the support for the project from participants, principals and system leaders. Indeed, there are regular enquiries of system offices about what happens when the current LDP has concluded and the plan is for

TABLE 13.3
New Appointed Positions Since Beginning MPP and LDP

Option/new role undertaken	Number of respondents	Percentage of respondents
No answer	10	24.39
Principal (a)	8	19.51
Deputy principal (b)	4	9.76
Head of sub-school (c)	7	17.07
Director in school (d)	4	9.76
Head of department (e)	6	14.63
Key teacher (f)	2	4.88
Classroom teacher (g)	0	0

another profiling activity to begin in 2009 with a further cohort in formal study in 2010. The change in focus from principalship (MPP) to the broader range of leadership roles in the LDP was a significant one, supporting the realisation that school leadership development needs to focus on a broader range of roles than only that of the principal.

While in 2000 only 11% of LEA principals were female, 50% of the leadership program participants were female. This figure is now reflected in a greater number of females applying and being successful in attaining senior leadership positions. Furthermore, in 2008, 30% of principals in Lutheran schools are now female, a significant increase.

A review of the online survey responses of LEA respondents suggested five key findings about the leadership development programs. These findings are now identified and illustrated with comments from the respondents.

First, participants were overwhelmingly positive towards MPP and LDP, reporting that they had experienced very valuable professional learning that had impacted their lives in important ways. In particular, respondents reported growing confidence in themselves and discovering things about themselves that they wanted to explore and try out. Some also learnt that leadership was not for them. Some representative comments were: '[The program} has affirmed me as a leader and given me the confidence to engage professionally in that role.' 'I now consider roles that I previously felt I wasn't qualified for.'

Second, when asked to identify what aspect of the leadership development program had had the most impact on them, participants reported a wide variety of influences, including academic study, theological insights, networking and mentoring. In relation to the impact of academic study, each formal unit studied was identified as significant by at least one participant. The availability of a range of experiences with options within a clear framework was an important feature of both MPP and LDP and appears to have contributed towards its positive outcomes.

Thirdly, academic study emerged as important in providing a framework for participants' learning. Key concepts encountered in the academic study, such as authentic leadership, distributed leadership and servant leadership were reflected in evaluation comments. The rigour of academic study helped participants make sense of leadership, as evidenced by these comments: 'Provided the framework for decision making and structural organisation required for the principal.' 'Better understanding of the complexities of leadership.'

Fourthly, although mentoring was seen as the weak link in the program, where it worked there was a powerful response. The 'busyness' of school life and the lack of regular contact militated against the success of mentoring. Thus respondents reported:

> The mentoring is essential and very rewarding.

> The mentoring process is critical to the journey, and in my experience this was not done well with the MPP.

> The mentoring process that was encouraged is just so important — in my case — life changing.

Finally participants reported that they enjoyed being together and found this collegiality a vital component of the program. The networking experience of studying in a cohort was valued highly. Comments illustrating this included:

> Continue to allow the participants plenty of opportunities to talk. (As a piece of advice for the future.)

> The opportunity to meet and network with other potential leaders. (Seen as a highlight.)

> Mentoring occurred between the participants in the program rather than the outside contacts that were required. (Advice for the future was to re-think the process.)

The evaluation of the LEA leadership development programs indicates that they have achieved key goals in terms of increasing the pool of leaders available for Lutheran schools. They have also created an interest in leadership, provoking thinking about leadership. The response of participants has been very encouraging.

Major Themes from the Evaluations

Seven major themes emerged from the evaluation of the responses of the combined group of participants to the on-line survey:

Positive Impact of Programs

There was a generally positive response from respondents about the programs. In addition, both system authorities have been asked when their project is likely to be offered again. These general responses indicate the positive reactions and experiences of participants in LFF, LDP and MPP.

One question asked of participants in the LFF was, 'How would you rate the effectiveness of the LFF to stimulate your interest in pursuing a role in educational leadership in Catholic schools?' The responses indicated that 45% believed the program had been very effective, and a further 45% rated it as having medium to high effectiveness, while none rated it as having no effect.

For the MPP and LDP the parallel question was phrased, 'Several years after its conclusion how would you now rate the effectiveness of the MPP or LDP to stimulate your interest in a role in educational leadership in a Lutheran school?' In this case 37% believed the program had 'a great deal of effect', while 39% rated it as 'somewhat effective' while 7.32% chose 'not at all effective'.

The surveys also asked either 'Did the LFF program help you change your expectations about becoming an educational leader?' or 'Have your expectations about your own future as an educational leader changed since beginning the MPP or LDP program?'

Responses are shown in Tables 13.4 and 13.5 and indicate that for both groups, a large majority reported that they were influenced by the programs.

One respondent suggested: 'It helped me to be more prepared rather than change my expectations.' In contrast one LFF participant who responded 'Yes' to the question said: 'My expectations about becoming an educational leader changed entirely.'

From the Lutheran groups the only obvious comment linked to a negative response to the question was: 'Unfortunately, no direct impact. Perhaps just the encouragement from being accepted into the LDP.'

A typical comment from one who believed that the program had caused a change was: 'It has made me realise that I am leadership material and that it is a challenge that I would be able to undertake.'

TABLE 13.4
Sydney LFF group: Changed Expectations About Leadership?

Answer	Count	Percentage
Yes (1)	33	64.71
No (2)	18	35.29

TABLE 13.5
MPP and LDP groups: Changed Expectations About Leadership?

Answer	Count	Percentage
Yes (a)	30	73.17
No (b)	11	26.83

Development of Confidence

Respondents generally reported growing in confidence in their current roles and in their abilities and skills for leadership. Many of the comments related to their response to whether the program had any effect on their leadership expectations referred to this, for groups from both systems.

Options and Variety

Many comments in response to the request to provide advice if the program were to be offered again related to the importance of providing options and variety in such a program, though the different style of the LFF compared with the Lutheran programs meant that these comments differed in their content. Some further comments in this vein from the LFF participants suggested that it was important:

> To provide a range of dynamic and interesting presenters that inspire and support our drive to become leaders with Catholic Education.

> The most beneficial part of the course was that although it was offered through CEO it organised for outside speakers to talk.

Of those who had completed the MDP and LDP one participant commented: 'I was happy with the variety of options provided for study. It was a good balance.'

The LFF participants appreciated the variety of presenters, with another commenting:

> It is very useful and helpful to work with people from a range of organisations, that is, outside of the educational arena as well as

those involved in education — this helps give the bigger picture and provides a wider understanding of the complexity of management, leadership and a range of views and approaches.

Academic Study

Many indicated the importance of academic study in providing a framework for undertaking leadership with confidence and competence. Some comments from LFF participants stated:

> By undertaking the LFF program I completed the assignment and gained one unit of credit towards a master's degree in Educational Leadership. This has contributed to my decision to continue my studies. The LFF program has encouraged me to further my professional development and given me the confidence to become a leader.

> [It} gave me theoretical knowledge about leadership that I didn't realise was essential to being a good leader.

Those who undertook the MPP or LDP, which included formal study opportunities, commented quite specifically:

> The MPP provided an opportunity to view leadership in a different light. It also provided the framework for decision making and structural organisation required for the principalship.

> The studies have enabled me to learn more about authentic leadership and leading schools in the 21st century.

They also commented on specifics of the courses that have influenced them:

> My reading of writers like Sergiovanni and Fullan and Hargreaves during my master's course.

> The focus on being authentic. This one has permeated throughout my whole life, and has given me the basis for all my decision-making.

Leadership Appointments

An important practical outcome of both programs was the actual number of participants who applied for, and were appointed to, more senior leadership roles within education. As illustrated above in Tables 13.2 and 13.3, 47% of the participants in the *Leaders for the Future* project had been appointed to a more senior role within 2 years of the conclusion of the project, while all respondents from the MPP and LDP programs had taken on some more senior role. It needs to be noted that the first of these programs began 9 years earlier, with participants identified by their schools and system as potential leaders. In contrast, the LFF participants had accepted an invitation to self-nominate into the program, though some had been encouraged in this by leaders in their schools.

Mentoring
Though formal mentoring was not a feature of the LFF program, in the LDP and MDP programs there were indications that mentoring was a weak link, but where it worked it was found to be valuable. Some commented specifically related to mentoring were provided earlier.

Sense of Community
One aspect of all programs was that they created sense of community within the group of participants, but also with the system representatives involved. Indeed one LFF participant suggested: 'I wished that there was more opportunity to meet up with the people involved in the course.'

Participants from LEA noted the importance of the group experiences, offering as advice: 'Continue to allow the participants plenty of opportunities to talk. I often found that what we talked about in small groups and at lunch time was almost as beneficial as the lecturer's notes.'

Discussion and Reflections
Both Catholic and Lutheran systems have invested considerable personnel and system resources, as well as time and energy, in these programs designed with to ensure an ongoing supply of well-prepared and highly motivated future leaders for the two systems of education. Both groups have adopted and developed these creative and innovative projects and the evaluation findings reported above are positive and show considerable promise for stimulating interest in future leadership positions.

The Organisation for Economic Development and Co-Operation (OECD) Report *Improving School Leadership Activity* (2007) has recognised that a key challenge for developers of school leadership programs is the identification of features that are central in the preparation of school leaders. Leadership standards and frameworks such as those developed by Spry (2004), LEA (2005), Cunliffe (2007), Australian Principals' Associations Professional Development Council (2006), Catholic Education Commission Victoria (CECV, 2007) and that being developed by Teaching Australia (2008) are seen to play a significant role in the development of future leaders 'so long as the frameworks draw on a strong evidence base and are subject to ongoing monitoring and evaluation of impact' (OECD, 2007, p. 71).

CEO and LEA had a different focus in terms of population target. Each of the programs operated within a different generation of the population — CEO focused on the prepromotion group of teachers under 30, while LEA addressed a population of teachers further along the professional experience continuum. Despite these differences and differences in content and delivery, the outcomes for the two programs were remarkably consistent. Reflecting on the process overall, there were a number of salient features which deserve comment.

Academic study. In today's school, the need for qualified leaders is becoming more and more critical, given the growing sophistication and demands of the communities in which they operate. There is no doubt that higher academic study and qualifications lead to greater confidence in the leaders themselves and provide intellectual frameworks from which they can articulate their own leadership activities and that they can use in the formation of future leaders. The development of a culture of quality leadership with a shared leadership language in a school setting is vital if future leaders are to have formal frameworks for making sense of leadership. These frameworks can lead to a greater rigour and professionalism, as well as opportunities for formal reflection in daily practice on the part of the educational leader. In this respect, it was interesting to note the data indicating the number of graduates of the programs who had gone on to further study.

Partnership in leadership. One thing that became obvious from the study of the programs was the willingness of the participants to engage in their current roles as a partnership in the leadership activities of the school. This did not necessarily mean undertaking a formal role, but did lead to taking the opportunity to engage in professional dialogue with the formal leadership and mentor figures at the school and system levels. The following comment illuminates this point: 'It provided me with insights into others who have leadership roles and the demands it may place on my life. It also increased my understanding of the different roles leaders have'. This partnership was seen as a 'two-way' process and helped the participants become aware of how their system worked and how their systems looked at the need for future leadership. A number of participants reported a greater awareness of the demands of leadership in terms such as this: '(It) gave me a greater indication of some of the issues associated with leadership that I hadn't thought of. It showed me some of the potential challenges and how I could best use my skills to deal with school-based situations.'

Connecting. The ability to connect and network with peers and colleagues was a pleasant and professionally rewarding experience for the participants. In the CEO program, the regular monthly meetings for input broadened their experiences. 'The chance to meet CEO staff was excellent.' The opportunities to network for the LEA programs came when they took on more formal studies as a cohort of peers in postgraduate studies and these were favourably reported. The special role of the mentoring in the LEA programs was a feature of the respondents from this program. One asked for 'more regular group meetings so that mentors and mentees can share experiences.' Both systems have networks that enable them to provide aspiring leaders with experiences of wider education systems through exchanges and study visits. Regular secondments to the management teams of schools provide aspiring leaders with a sound grasp of whole school issues and help them realise their leadership potential. One person reported that the experience helped refine her view of leadership and had an impact on her leadership style. Identifying people very early in their career seems to be very important and working on a key area together means they develop team work (Nightingale, 2006)

Personal impact. From the respondents' reports, there is no doubt that both sets of programs had significant personal impact on improving their perceptions and understandings of leadership and their willingness to engage in career development activities. The following responses illustrate this: 'affirmed me as a leader', 'helped me to reflect on and develop my awareness of my leadership potential', 'I became more confident about personal qualities that could be effective in school leadership.' Such comments abound in the written responses. They also reflect the ability to celebrate their participation and achievements through the programs and open new leadership horizons. From the system point of view, comments indicating that participation had increased (their) loyalty to the system were noteworthy.

Tangible outcomes. As well as the personal impacts noted above, the respondents reported taking up promotion positions in their schools and systems (Tables 13.2 and 13.3), which were encouraging to the course sponsors and developers as tangible signs of ongoing commitment to the systems. Further evidence of this included the number of respondents who had undertaken further studies at postgraduate level and who had used the opportunities provided by the programs for academic credit at ACU.

Managing outcomes. The challenge now, for both systems, is how to maintain the momentum and enthusiasm generated by the various programs. The CEO program focused on a group identified as Generation Y, a characteristic of which has been identified as preference for short-term commitment; whereas LEA addresses an older cohort with different generational characteristics. Strategies such as graduates presenting at conferences, engaging them in future leadership planning programs and as 'critical friends' in ongoing projects, newsletters and personal encouragement, are being actively pursued.

Expectations for the future. Participants were invited to provide advice for future projects and this was readily forthcoming. The continuation of the mentoring program was strongly urged by the LEA graduates with suggestions about how the process might be made more effective — 'same school', 'on-site learning', 'mentor training', 'matching mentors and mentees'. The structure of the CEO program provided the basis for comments on future speakers and structure. There was overwhelming support for conducting similar programs in the future.

Conclusions

'We can't imagine the school of the future, so how can we prepare principals and leaders for it?' — is a question being asked of system leaders of both Catholic and Lutheran education. Beare (2006) examines this question from the point of view of schooling as networked organisations and interactive communities dealing with the creation of new knowledge through the curriculum. Such a situation will require a new kind of leader and leadership, an issue explored by d'Arbon (2004) and others.

Future leadership and succession planning for schools and schooling have been the subject of ongoing interest and concern at the research, policy, administration and management levels. The OECD (2001) developed a number of compelling scenarios for the future of schooling worldwide. In Australia, national bodies such as Teaching Australia (2008), the Australian Principals Associations Professional Development Council (2006), the Australian Education Union (2004) have reflected on future educational leadership and supply of leaders in the 21st century, while for the Catholic and Lutheran systems of education there has been ongoing reflection and research (Carlin, d'Arbon, Dorman, Duignan, & Neidhart, 2003; d'Arbon, 2008; d'Arbon, Duignan, & Duncan, 2002; Jericho, 2007).

Any attempt at redesigning the principalship will now focus on at least two major aspects of talent identification and development for future school leadership — recognition that everyone is a leader and focus on the development of the person of the future leader through the development of leadership capabilities (Duignan, 2004) and through the strategic implementation of the leadership or system frameworks for system leadership (Cunliffe, 2007; Spry, 2004).

The changing role of the principalship is closely aligned with the changing nature and challenges of 21st century schools and schooling. The recent publication *Leading Australia's Schools* (Duignan & Gurr, 2007) presents case studies of 17 principals highly regarded within the profession and by their school and communities who were recommended by peers. Key themes such as those distilled from the principals' stories provide a valuable framework on which to base a talent identification and development strategy within any school or network of schools.

The recent OECD Report *Improving School Leadership Activity* (OECD, 2007) notes that 'much of the available research (about school leadership) is largely focused on the principalship and pays limited attention to prospective leaders and to those who exercise school leadership in a variety of formal and informal ways' (p. 72). In some sectors, explicit succession planning strategies are being developed, some of which rely on encouragement and persuasion rather than control and direction (Bush, 2008). As reported here, both CEO and LEA have responded and addressed the issues by development of a pool of potential leaders in a positive, imaginative and scholarly manner.

This chapter set out to consider these creative initiatives for developing aspiring leaders for the future within the two faith-based systems of education and schooling. Both systems have approached the same problem, that of leadership succession and succession planning, but they have used different models of talent identification and development. Both initiatives have successfully stimulated and inspired future leaders to consider a future in educational leadership in those systems — a positive and satisfying outcome for the system leaders and planner.

This comment from one of the participants sums up the experience:

My expectations about becoming an educational leader changed entirely. I am in the fourth year of teaching (primary). As my principal has said, the program gave me 'wings' and my confidence as a teacher and as a leader has soared. I feel more than ever that I am worthy of a leadership position. I feel that even after I have had a family that I am very likely to return to teaching and pursue a leadership role. ... The program has encouraged me to further my professional development and given me the confidence to become a leader.

Acknowledgment

The authors wish to express their appreciation and thanks to the staff of Catholic Education Office, Sydney and Lutheran Education Australia for their contributions and support to the writing of this chapter. Mr John Edwards and Mr Peter Ireland from CEO Sydney, provided important opinions and access to the IT resources and assistance in organising the electronic data collection for this project. Mrs Joan Scriven at LEA, provided significant infrastructure support and advice which were highly valued.

References

Anderson, M., Gronn, P., Ingvarson, L., Jackson, A., Kleinhenz, E., McKenzie, P., et al. (2007). *The Australian country background report for the OECD's Improving School Leadership Activity* (A report prepared for the Australian Government, Department of Education, Science and Training). Melbourne, Australia: ACER.

Australian Education Union. (2004). *Educational leadership and teaching for the twenty-first century*: Project discussion paper. Retrieved from http://www.aeufederal.org.au/Debates/elat21pap.pdf

Australian Joint Principals' Associations. (2007). *2007 survey: Beginning teachers*. Accessed October 23, 2008, from http://www.aspa.asn.au/images/surveys/2007beginning teachersreport.pdf

Australian Principals' Associations Professional Development Council (2006). The L5 Frame. In *Leaders lead*. Retrieved September 23, 2008, from http://www.beecoswebengine.org/servlet/Web?s=157573&p=LLS_FRAMEWORK

Beare, H. (2006). *How we envisage schooling in the 21st century: Applying the new 'imaginary'*. Sydney, Australia: Australian Council for Educational Leaders.

Bishops of NSW and the ACT. (2007). *Catholic schools at a crossroads: Pastoral letter of the Bishops of New South Wales and the ACT.* Sydney, Australia: Catholic Schools Office.

Bush, T. (2008). Developing educational leaders: Don't leave it to chance. *Educational Management Administration and Leadership, 36*(3), 307–309.

Caldwell, B.J. (2006). *Reimagining educational leadership*. Camberwell, Victoria, Australia: ACER Press.

Canavan, K. (2007). Preparing leaders for the future: A systemic perspective. *Leading and Managing, 13*(2), 66–78.

Carlin, P., d'Arbon, T., Dorman, J, Duignan, P., & Neidhart, H. (2003, April). *Leadership succession for Catholic schools in Victoria, South Australia and Tasmania (VSAT). Final Report*. Sydney, Australia: Australian Catholic University.

Catholic Education Commission Victoria. (2007). *Leadership in Catholic schools: Development framework and standards of practice*. Retrieved September 23, 2008, from http://www.lsf.vic.catholic.edu.au

Cunliffe, A. (2007). *Framework for system leadership in Catholic Education in Australia*. Sydney, Australia: Australian Catholic University.

D'Arbon, T. (2008, August). *Principal succession and succession planning in Catholic schools: Strategic lessons for future planning*. Paper presented at the Christian Schools Australia National Conference, Melbourne. Retrieved September 21, 2008, from http://www.csa.edu.au

D'Arbon, T. (2004). Future principals for schools of the future. *The Practising Administrator, 28*(1), 4–44.

D'Arbon, T., & Cunliffe, A. (2007). Evaluation of a leadership succession initiative in a postmodern context, *Leading and Managing, 13*(2), 79–89.

D'Arbon, T., Duignan, P., & Duncan. D.J. (2002). Planning for the future leadership in schools: An Australian study. *Journal of Educational Administration, 40*(5), 468–485.

Duignan, P. (2004). Forming capable leaders: From competencies to capabilities. *New Zealand Journal of Educational Administration, 19*(2), 5–12.

Duignan, P., & Gurr, D. (2007). *Leading Australia's schools*. Sydney, Australia: Australian Council for Educational Leaders.

Earley, P., & Weindling, D. (2004). *Understanding school leadership*. London: Paul Chapman Publishing.

Ewing, R.A., & Smith, D.L. (2003). Retaining quality beginning teachers in the profession. *English Teaching: Practice and Critique, 2*(1), 15–32.

Fenwick L.T. (2000). *The principal shortage: Who will lead?* Cambridge, MA: The Principal's Center, Harvard Graduate School of Education.

Hartle, F., & Thomas, K. (2003). *Growing tomorrow's school leaders: The challenge*. Nottingham, England: National College for School Leadership.

Jericho. A. (2005). *Leaders who are ready*. Paper presented at the Lutheran Education Association Convocation, Indianapolis. Retrieved September 20, 2008, from http://www.lutheran.edu.au/tools/getFile.aspx?tbl=tblContentItem&id=1433

Jericho, A. (2007). Leadership and succession planning: A Lutheran Education Australia perspective. In *College Year Book 2007. The Treasure within: leadership and succession planning* (pp. 52–62). Geelong, Australia: Australian College of Educators.

LCA. (1999). *The LCA and its schools*. Unpublished policy statement. Retrieved September 21, 2008, from http://www.lutheran.edu.au/tools/getFile.aspx?tbl= tblContentItem&id=65

Lutheran Education Australia. (2005). *Leadership framework for Lutheran Schools*. Retrieved September 20, 2008, from http://www.lutheran.edu.au/tools/getFile. aspx?tbl=tblContentItem&id=75

LimeSurvey. (n.d.). [An open source survey application] Retrieved from http://www. limesurvey.org

Nightingale, J. (2006). Looking for the young contenders. *ldr — the online magazine for school leaders*. Retrieved September 26, 2006, from http://www.ldr-magazine.co.uk/viewstory.php?id=516

Organisation for Economic Development and Co-operation. (2001). *What school for the future?* Paris: Author.

Spry, G. (2004). *A framework for leadership in Catholic schools*. Project conducted for the Queensland Catholic Education Commission, Sydney: Flagship for Creative & Authentic Leadership, Australian Catholic University.

Teaching Australia. (2008, May). *National professional standards for advanced teaching and for principals: Second consultation paper*. Retrieved September 23, 2008, from http://www.teachingaustralia.edu.au/

▶▶▶◀◀◀

Professional Learning for Experienced Educational Leaders: Research and Practice

Neil Dempster, Jan Alen and Ruth Gatehouse

Much has been written over the last decade about the recruitment and retention of school leaders, as well as about their needs in professional development and how they can sustain themselves physically and psychologically over lengthy careers (Gronn, 2007; MacBeath, 2006; Reeves & Dempster, 1998). This chapter concentrates on the latter two issues, arguing they are linked. In other words, timely and targeted professional learning is essential if school leaders are to manage themselves and their leadership journeys productively over extended periods. While this statement seems obvious, it begs two questions: (1) what type of professional learning is needed; and (2) when and to whom should it be available? Before we address these questions, we undertake a scan of literature related to the professional learning agenda for school leaders in order to highlight its scope and recent emphases, particularly as they relate to the needs of experienced leaders. We follow this with a description of a program for experienced school leaders in Queensland, Australia, titled the Strategic Leaders' Program (SLP); first, to ascertain the extent to which the emphases found in the literature are put into practical effect in this program, and second, to describe and analyse some of the effects of that program drawing on evaluation data over a 5-year period. Finally, we put forward a justification for concentrating professional development for experienced leaders on the personal and interpersonal learning critical in building resilience and in sustaining them over time.

Principals' Learning Needs

There is a wealth of material on the knowledge and skills principals need to lead and manage their schools effectively. In a comprehensive compendium on leadership theories, Macbeath (2004) described some 25 theoretical explanations of leadership, each having a particular emphasis which, when followed, requires a concentration on different aspects of the principal's role. Moreover, recent reviews of research findings (see below) have produced syntheses identifying critical leadership components to which professional learning should be dedicated. We analyse four of these reviews that use a range of analytical techniques, to show what is common in school leadership and therefore in need of continuing professional learning.

Four Recent Reviews

The research reviews on which we draw come from educational researchers in the United Kingdom, Australia and New Zealand, and from international corporate consulting specialists, McKinsey and Company.

'TEACHING AUSTRALIA' REVIEW

The Australian review commissioned by Teaching Australia (2007a) used standard literature searches to undertake an analysis of what constituted 'quality school leadership'. Its authors produced three overlapping analytical categories or 'key domains' containing practices for which there was an abundance of evidence.

The *first category* focused on the need for leaders to understand global and local contexts. In other words, knowledge of global economic, political and technological change and their impact on educational policy were seen as central to a school leader's repertoire. This needed to be supplemented by knowledge of the school's local external and internal contexts. Prominent in the former are school location, size, socioeconomic status, cultural and language mix and parental aspirations; for the latter, teacher morale, capacity and efficacy, coupled with student background, motivation and student achievement were identified as priorities.

The *second category* was labelled 'professional practice'. Critical among the leadership practices the review recorded were the ability of school leaders to develop a school mission and values, to promote a culture of trust and collaboration, to facilitate shared decision-making, to design the structures that enable this to occur and to be able to draw upon a wide range of well-documented leadership strategies. Among these, the review mentions some of the theoretical work we noted above in the MacBeath (2004) inventory, as sources of practical help. In short, school leaders need to know and understand when it is appropriate to employ *transactional* as opposed to *transformational* leadership tactics, when it is timely to shift into *strategic* leadership mode, and how to ensure that *distributive, participative* or *parallel* leadership flourishes, all the while being conscious of their actions as *moral* leaders.

The *third category* identified the kind of personal attributes and capabilities considered essential for successful school leadership: *personal, relational, organisational* and *professional.* A summary of each of these shows that:

- *personal attributes and capabilities* include a passion and commitment in the school leader for education, what the school stands for, its staff and its students, as well as a capacity for personal reflection and learning from others
- *relational attributes and capabilities* define abilities such as the provision of professional support and mentorship for staff members, and the emotional intelligence, interpersonal care and integrity to become trusted by staff members, students and the school community as a whole
- *organisational attributes and capabilities* signal the need for school leaders to be 'contextually aware', and able to employ strategic thinking, sound problem solving, and effective change management
- *professional attributes and capabilities* are linked to a knowledge and understanding of standards for school leadership and a range of professional development approaches to ensure standards can and are being met across a leadership career.

Overall, the Teaching Australia (2007a) review documented a comprehensive profile of the knowledge, attributes and capabilities required for quality leadership. Such is the scope of the findings that it is abundantly clear that leadership in school settings needs to be recast, not as the preserve of a single agent, but as an activity requiring collective agency. The implications of this finding are at the heart of our argument about the significance of relationships in the professional development of school leaders.

UNITED KINGDOM NATIONAL COLLEGE FOR SCHOOL LEADERSHIP REVIEW

The United Kingdom Review, undertaken by Leithwood, Day, Sammons, Harris, and Hopkins (2006) for the National College for School Leadership and involving the analysis of over 60 research articles from around the world, was circumspect in its synthesis of the leadership research literature. Its authors were prepared to assert the importance of leadership or the significance of particular leadership practices only if there was strong research evidence behind them — hence the title of the review: *Seven Strong Claims about Successful School Leadership*. Those claims and some of the circumstances surrounding them (pp. 4–14) are summarised below:

1. *Leadership is second only to classroom teaching as an influence on students' learning.* While it accounts for only 5–7% of the difference in student learning and achievement across schools, the effects of transformational school leadership have been shown in the research to be significantly positive. In undertaking the review, the authors were not able to find a single case of improvement in student achievement in the absence of talented leadership. Finally, there is convincing evidence that unplanned leadership succession is a common source of a school's failure to progress (p. 4).

2. *Almost all successful leaders draw on the same repertoire of basic leadership practices.* From the review, the National College for School Leadership identified a verifiable set of four basic leadership practices:
   - building vision and setting directions
   - understanding and developing people
   - redesigning the organisation
   - managing the teaching and learning program.

3. The ways in which leaders apply these practices — not the practices themselves — demonstrate responsiveness to, rather than dictation by, the contexts in which they work. This claim implies that the context should not be allowed to render a leader powerless to make changes. Gone, therefore, is recourse to the often automatic excuses used by leaders for a failure to act: laying blame on the limiting effects of government policy, community aspirations, parental support, or anything else that seems to be active or inactive in the school's environment. What is suggested is the need for school leaders to know the contexts in which they are working, to be sensitive to what they find and then use that knowledge to design strategies to maximise the chances of success in what they are wanting to do.

4. *School leaders improve teaching and learning indirectly and most powerfully through their influence on staff motivation, commitment, and working conditions.* The review shows that school leaders influence teachers' pedagogical capacity least, but that they have a strong influence on working conditions and a moderate influence on motivation

or commitment. While teachers' capacity has most bearing on altering classroom practices that directly affect learning, motivation and commitment and working conditions do make a contribution in this direction. The key point here is that school leaders working alone are unlikely to improve the figures quoted in 1 above. It is the next claim that holds out hope to the busy school leader.

5. *School leadership has a greater influence on schools and pupils when it is widely distributed.* We have said that this claim 'holds out hope' to school leaders because, as yet, the NCSL reviewers are not willing to say that there is sufficient research evidence of the effects of distributing leadership across an organisation to say that it always works. However, they refer to some results from work by Leithwood and Mascall (2008) related to the effects of 'total leadership' defined as 'the combined influence of leadership from all sources' (p. 12) on teachers' capacity, motivation, commitment and working conditions. This they say accounted for 27% of the variation in student achievement across schools. This is much higher than the 5–7% reported consistently for the effects of individual leaders. The implication of this claim puts the spotlight on leaders learning to work with others using collaborative leadership strategies.

6. *Some patterns of distribution are more effective than others.* While a strong inference about the superiority of collective leadership over that of the single person has been put forward by the reviewers, the National College authors were unable to find studies that demonstrate the effects of different patterns of leadership distribution. Nevertheless, three conclusions were drawn from their analysis:
   (a) there is no loss of a leader's power and influence when the power and influence of others increases
   (b) there is consistent evidence about the ineffectiveness of laissez-faire leadership
   (c) there is emerging evidence about the need for coordinated patterns of leadership practice (p. 13).

7. *A small handful of personal traits explain a high proportion of the variation in leadership effectiveness.* The reviewers found a substantial body of research into leadership traits, personal characteristics and qualities outside education in the worlds of business, industry and commerce, sufficient to support the claim. Indeed they found that the most successful school leaders are:

- open-minded
- ready to learn from others
- flexible in their thinking within a set of core values
- persistent in the pursuit of the school's purpose
- resilient
- optimistic. (p. 14)

These personal traits or qualities are similar to the *personal attributes and capabilities* identified by the Teaching Australia reviewers. They point to a focus in professional development on the self, or the leader within, as the Australian Council for Educational Leaders implies (Teaching Australia, 2007b). Encouraging school leaders to learn and apply the reflective processes that produce realistic assessments of their personal characteristics, both strengths and weaknesses, is therefore an important professional responsibility.

NEW ZEALAND ITERATIVE BEST EVIDENCE SYNTHESIS

In New Zealand, the review strategy employed in the 'Best Evidence Synthesis' as reported by Robinson (2007) began with a focused selection of research studies on the tasks undertaken by school leaders that had most impact in schools. Their analysis of these studies yielded five leadership 'dimensions' describing essential tasks, drawn from 198 spreadsheet entries on leadership — entries such as questionnaire items taken from the selected studies or entries describing leadership constructs. Effect sizes were calculated for each of the dimensions. Robinson (2007) argues that an effect size of more than 0.6 has a 'large and educationally significant impact' (p. 9). The five dimensions with their average effect sizes are:

- Establishing Goals and Expectations (average effect size = 0.35)
- Strategic Resourcing (average effect sizee = 0.34)
- Planning, Coordinating, and Evaluating Teaching and the Curriculum (average effect size = 0.42)
- Promoting and Participating in Teacher Learning and Development (average effect size = 0.84)
- Ensuring an Orderly and Supportive Environment (average effect size = 0.27).

The figures above point to two conclusions from her analysis: (a) the most important aspect of leadership for a principal is 'promoting and participating in professional learning' (p.15); and (b) 'the more leadership is focused on the core business of teaching and learning, the greater its impact' (p. 9). These conclusions might suggest to some that therefore, school leaders should concentrate their professional learning and their daily efforts on how they might get as close to their teachers' practice as possible. Doing so, however, would be impractical, particularly in large schools. Personally undertaking the promotion of all professional development programs and participating shoulder-to-shoulder in seminars and workshops with teachers across a range of disciplines is not feasible. This suggests that committing a leader to carry out such tasks as those in Robinson's five dimensions, in person, is not a viable option.

Robinson (2007) highlights the need to acknowledge the importance of relationships in leadership, pointing out their apparent omission from the five leadership dimensions she produced. In her own words she says:

> The task–relationship distinction has been eschewed here because relationship skills are embedded in every dimension. In goal-setting, for example, effective leadership involves not only determining the goal content (task focus) but doing so in a manner that enables staff to understand and become committed to the goal (relationships). What works, it seems, is careful integration of staff considerations with task requirements. Effective leaders do not get the relationships right and then tackle educational challenges — they incorporate both sets of constraints into their problem-solving. (p. 9)

To sum up, the New Zealand Iterative Best Evidence Synthesis of leadership research suggests to us that principals require plans and strategies for the creation of professional learning communities within their schools. What they need to know and are able to do to ensures that they and others are well prepared to contribute to this most significant task should constitute a major component of their ongoing professional development.

MCKINSEY AND COMPANY REVIEW

The approach taken by Barber and Mourshed (2007) for the McKinsey and Company review began with a desire to assemble evidence about the world's best performing school systems. They did this through recourse to comparative cross-country reports by agencies such as the Organisation for Economic Development and Co-operation (OECD) and by examining the results of international testing programs such as the Program for International Student Assessment (PISA). Part of the review included a discussion of school leadership practices and their links with effective student learning.

In summary, the authors of the report conclude that the best performing school systems in the world achieve the strongest student outcomes by focusing on teacher quality. This, for them, is first and foremost. They contend that focusing on quality is done best in systems with a culture of high expectations of teachers and students and a climate in which all are striving for improvement. Creating both of these conditions, culture and climate, is seen by McKinsey and Company as an important task for school leaders. Indeed, from their perspective, systems and schools will improve outcomes for students only when they focus their leadership on improving instruction, that is, improving the actions of classroom teachers aimed at student learning.

Barber and Mourshed (2007) also refer to and reinforce the four common leadership practices promoted by the National College for School Leadership (listed earlier) as tried and tested leadership tools or tasks. Thus, the McKinsey and Company review emphasises, as does the Teaching Australia Review, that effective school leaders create the circumstances in which teachers are able to learn from each other. Both agree that fostering a professional learning community, rich in conversations about classroom pedagogy and effective learning, gives school leaders confidence that student achievement will be maximised.

Finally, McKinsey and Company pick up a theme that has been emerging as we have travelled over the leadership review terrain, that is, school principals alone cannot improve their schools; they must create the circumstances that help themselves and the adults around them learn. In other words, to get greater purchase on student learning, efforts must be directed to the most important learners in the school — the teachers. The implications of this conclusion for the professional learning of school leaders have already been raised above, that is, school leaders need to have recourse to knowledge and skills that enable them to create collaborative professional learning communities in their schools.

SUMMARY

In the research reviews we have consulted, different emphases have suggested different professional learning priorities. For example, the New Zealand Iterative Best Evidence Synthesis could be used to justify a narrowing of school leaders' learning to a concentration on instruction. Doing so is not realistic, particularly when school principals are being called on increasingly to implement government mandates, connect with their communities, model professionalism and accept new accountabilities. While deeper knowledge of instruction is directly related to improved student achievement, it is not the principal alone we argue, on whom the focus should be placed. Indeed, the New Zealand Review concedes that there is a necessary relational component of each of the five leadership dimensions their analysis produced.

The Teaching Australia (2007a) Review could be used to sanction a broadening of professional learning to ensure that leaders 'covered' everything under the banners of 'global and local contexts', 'professional practice', and 'personal attributes and capabilities'. Doing so would automatically reduce professional development to shallow or 'surface' learning because of the unrealistic time demands necessary to achieve depth across such a broad agenda.

One reading of the McKinsey and Company review could be used to support a focus on a restrictive 'performativity' agenda in leadership learning (performativity generally refers to a preference for the measurement of those aspects of student performance amenable to testing). This would match the New Zealand concentration on instruction outlined above and highlight the use of student performance evidence as the basis for leadership decisions. However, schools are about more than achievement tests and the positional leader's use of them. A closer reading of the work for McKinsey and Company by Barber and Mourshed (2007) warrants a call for leaders' professional development to be directed towards collaborative activity and how and why it should be fostered so that a more comprehensive view of achievement is shared and pursued by leaders and teachers together.

The review by the United Kingdom's National College for School Leaders leans heavily towards learning about and implementing new patterns of distributive leadership. It highlights significant gains to be made when the locus of power and influence in the school is spread, downplaying, but not neglecting, the individual role played by the appointed school head.

Overall, the four reviews have documented much of the state of our present understanding by mapping the learning terrain across which school leaders need to travel, not as 'lone explorers' but as members of expeditions. We sum up the scope of school leadership thus portrayed by the reviewers as five 'knowledges': knowing the purpose of leadership, knowing oneself, knowing others, knowing the context and knowing the job. While purpose, context and tasks beckon seductively to those responsible for leadership development, it is our opinion that 'knowing self' and 'knowing others' are fundamental to effective leadership practice, especially as leaders become more experienced and move into larger and larger schools. We say this because as Leithwood and Riehl (2003, p. 7) argue: 'leaders mobilise and work with others to articulate and achieve shared intentions.'

The conclusions produced by the four reviews show that school leadership is so multifaceted that one person alone would be hard-pressed to develop such a comprehensive knowledge and skill set over a lifetime. The spreading of knowledge and skills to others and encouraging their effective use are key tasks for leaders because it is through combined human agency that successful school leadership is possible.

We turn now to the second part of this chapter to describe a Queensland approach to professional development for experienced principals — the Strategic Leaders' Program.

Education Queensland Strategic Leaders' Program (SLP)

Our purpose in presenting a description of the SLP is threefold: (a) to outline its focus and delivery; (b) to highlight the professional learning on which it concentrates, explaining how this is related to the leadership learning needs reported in the research literature in the first part of the chapter and (c) to report on the effects of the SLP for its participants, drawing on evaluative data obtained over the last 5 years.

The SLP Focus and Delivery

The Strategic Leaders' Program has been run since 2001 by Education Queensland (EQ). It therefore preceded the reviews that have constituted the first part of this chapter. In the first instance the program was designed for experienced people in leadership positions from schools, central and regional offices, and later, for experienced principals only. The program is residential, requiring an initial commitment of 5 days for intensive introductory work, followed by the use of 3 days for further task-related meetings over a 6-month period. To date, there have been a total of 26 programs with an average of 26 participants in each. There have been several formal and informal evaluations of the SLP, the most recent occurring in 2007. While the SLP has always been aligned with EQ leadership expectations, it is now intended to reflect the current leadership framework — *Leadership Matters: Capabilities for Education Queensland Principals* (Education Queensland, 2007). This framework defines five sets of capabilities: educational, personal, relational, intellectual and organisational, more about which is added later in the chapter.

In 2007 the stated aims of the SLP were:

- to develop the professional capabilities of leaders in driving educational reform that supports students in Queensland schools
- to develop the skills and knowledge required for people to work in more collaborative ways across the department and with communities.

While these general objectives describe the corporate focus of the SLP, they do not indicate the matters on which leaders' learning is centred nor the learning experiences they encounter in the 5-day residential and follow-up meetings. Right from the outset, the program designers felt that for mature leaders, an opportunity was needed for reflection on the 'person within' to examine personal strengths, weaknesses, motivations and aspirations as individuals and educational leaders. They also wanted to put the interpersonal attitudes and skills of the participants under scrutiny with a view to assisting them to redefine their approaches to leading and working with others. This was a bold step in the face of the government's reform agenda, which had been demanding changes in the system to emphasise school performance and student outcomes accountabilities for several years. We say this because there is a tendency for two of the 'knowledges' referred to above to dominate in times of change: knowledge of the reform *context* and knowledge of the *tasks* required. Yet, in the face of ongoing change, within both the organisation and its schools, the original design basis has continued this decade. So in the 2007 SLP, seven enduring fundamentals from research findings in adult learning are reflected in the program design. These were:

- approximately 75% of professional learning occurs on the job
- over 90% of that learning takes months and sometimes years
- more than 50% of what professionals learn is from peers and colleagues (McCauley & Brutus, Centre for Creative Leadership, 1998)
- over 95% of behaviour transfer after professional learning is achieved through on-the-job coaching with feedback (Joyce & Showers, 1982)

- effective professional learning is structured around business or organisational objectives (Australian Public Service Commission, 1998) and personal motivations
- engaging professional learning processes are created through challenge, novelty, relationships and responsibility.

These enduring fundamentals of professional learning underscore the importance of personal experience and the capacity of individuals to learn from it, but not necessarily alone. Van Velsor and McCauley (2004) in the second edition of the *Handbook for Leadership Development* observe that:

> developing the individual capacities needed for effective leadership — such as self-management, social skills, and work facilitation capabilities — is synonymous with what is often labelled personal development. This development unfolds over time. It is maximized by a variety of experiences that challenge people, support them, and provide them with understanding of how they are doing. It also depends on their having an ability and willingness to learn from experience (p. 25).

Taking this view into account, the design and methodologies employed in the SLP are:

- *integrated*: to include organisational and personal outcome priorities and accountabilities
- *blended*: to include a flexible mixture of mediums such as personal coaching, online e-facilitation, peer-learning networks, personal readings and reflection processes, group forums and face-to-face professional development workshops, and school-linked action learning projects
- *relational*: to connect participants with partnerships and networks of learning relationships to support and challenge them as well as to provide working models of the relationships and cultures they wish to create and influence
- *experiential*: to create learning-by-doing and merge cognitive and social–relational learning experiences such as challenge, repeated interpersonal feedback, and skill building
- *longitudinal*: to conduct planned interventions over enough time to accommodate experiential and rich reflective learning.

In practical terms, the design elements were incorporated into the following eight-step sequence:

1. Self-nominated participants were subject to a selection process managed by their supervisors (usually an Executive Directors of Schools).
2. Participants experienced 6 to 8 weeks of e-facilitated/online preparatory work requiring up to 1 hour of interaction per week.
3. Objective-setting interviews were conducted by program facilitators with participants with input from their supervisors.
4. Individual experiential assignments were set during the interview to focus participants' objective-specific learning (these objectives were 'signed-off' as agreements by participants and supervisors).
5. A 5-day residential workshop followed, focusing on the personal and relational capabilities necessary for the kind of leadership required to achieve the identified organisational and personal priorities.
6. On-the-job applications of particular learning from the program material were confirmed after the residential component, agreed with supervisors, reported online, and supported by participant partnerships created at the residential program.
7. Preparation for the second workshop commenced 6 months later, facilitated online, to gather feedback from participants on evidence of impact on their leadership behaviours.
8. The second residential program for 3 days provided an opportunity to report on performance, including individual learning stories and judgments of the value of the effects of on-the-job applications.

The SLP and Leadership Learning Needs

Space does not allow for a full elaboration of the learning experiences encountered in the SLP by participants at the residential programs and in their places of work. However, the brief description we have provided of the content and processes employed are sufficient for us to say that of the five 'knowledges' to which the leadership research literature points, a bias towards knowledge of *self* and knowledge of *others* is evident, particularly in the first 5-day residential component and its 3-day follow up 6 months later. It would be fair to say that participants were encouraged to harness these two areas of knowledge in their pursuit of specific tasks meant to address organisational and personal priorities. Indeed the program, in its use of participant partnerships, models the collective human agency described in the literature as an essential companion of effective leadership in schools. Concern with the other three knowledges, *'purpose'*, *'context'*, and *'tasks'* remained 'backstage' until participants returned to school where on-the-job applications were to be implemented. With its clear leaning towards knowing *self* and knowing *others*, the SLP was likely to bypass some of the components of the Leadership Matters: Capabilities for Education Queensland Principals framework (Education Queensland, 2007) to which it was meant to contribute. We move now in the final part of the chapter to discuss some of the program's effects, well documented in evaluations conducted after each offering.

Effects of the SLP

In the 2007 evaluation of the SLP, we sought responses on the Leadership Capabilities from the 2007 Leadership Matters framework addressed in the program. We did this as part of a survey of the 210 participants since 2003. Our purpose was to ascertain present emphases and areas on which future leadership learning programs might be focused. We received responses from 100 principals clustered around the five sets of capabilities referred to earlier, namely, *educational, personal, relational, intellectual,* and *organisational*. We used a 4-point Likert Scale to elicit judgments about the extent to which the SLP's content and processes strengthened each of the five capabilities for the participants. The scale, which included the response options of *thoroughly, reasonably, a little,* or *not at all* was used across 49 items clustered around each of the capabilities. Examples are offered below.
To what extent did the SLP include content or processes aimed at strengthening your ability to:
   • create high expectation for others;
   • create high expectations for yourself (***Educational Capabilities***).

To what extent did the SLP include content and processes that contributed to strengthening:
   • the awareness of you own values and beliefs;
   • your awareness of others' values and beliefs (***Personal Capabilities***).

To what extent did the SLP include content or processes that strengthened your ability to:
- interact with others with sensitivity and dignity;
- be honest and authentic (***Relational Capabilities***).

To what extent did the SLP include content and processes that strengthened your ability to:
- understand and influence the strategic agenda;
- recognise local, national and international trends (***Intellectual Capabilities***).

To what extent did the SLP include content and processes that strengthened your:
- planning skills;
- skills to measure outcomes (***Organisational Capabilities***).

In our analysis, we found that 8 out of every 10 participants reported that their *personal* and *relational* capabilities were strengthened. Against some items, the figures were above 9 out of every 10. Overall, the survey showed that the SLP had its strongest effect on *personal* and *relational* capabilities, a limited effect on *educational* capabilities, and little effect on *intellectual* and *organisational* capabilities. Some critics reading the results of the literature review we presented earlier might suggest that these results are not defensible or, at least, sufficient. They might argue that school leaders should be concentrating on educational, organisational and intellectual capabilities. Are not these closer to the instructional imperative contained in the McKinsey and New Zealand reviews? And after all, aren't schools about student learning and should not professional learning be committed to doing everything possible to keep this focus 'centrestage'? While this is an understandable argument, we believe that it is not defensible in large schools where experienced leaders practise their craft. The effects of the SLP reported by participants justify a commitment to *personal* and *relational* capabilities for experienced leaders in complex settings. To illustrate this claim, we now provide graphic examples from principals' reports about the effects of the SLP on them some 6 months after its completion.

The SLP and its Effects

Principals were asked before the second residential program to write a report about the effects of the SLP on their leadership practice. This included making judgments about the value they placed on the outcomes of the on-the-job applications they worked to implement. Our analysis of these reports suggests that there were at least two kinds of effects, namely, a rethinking of personal approaches to leadership and new and more confident ways of working with others to achieve common goals. We include samples of typical personal statements provided by participants to illustrate these outcomes.

RETHINKING PERSONAL APPROACHES TO LEADERSHIP

I learned lots about my own behaviour and this has helped me to better understand the behaviour of others. I now have an improved ability to actively support the development of strong, trusting and positive workplace relationships. I have learned to trust my judgment in knowing when, and how best to support, challenge or intervene.

I learnt to use 'self-talk' more effectively to challenge negative messages and beliefs about self, especially in situations of difficult interactions with others. I have learnt to use self-talk as these interactions are taking place in order to remain calm and handle the situation more effectively, and to be gentler on myself. I have learnt to have more effective conversations and workplace communications, particularly in meeting situations.

I learned that some people actually appreciate feedback, even that which is negative, as long as they then feel supported in ensuring a positive outcome. I also learned that certain people have difficulty in accepting feedback. In those cases, I have learned that I need to have a clear agenda, strategy and evidence to back up my concern/s. I have also learned that the difficult conversations and the other processes which followed are not as difficult as I had envisaged. I realise now that my need to be liked has resulted in some of the much-needed conversations being delayed. This does not help, as often the issues get worse — they don't go away without intervention of some form. However, the conversations have proven easier (with practice) and my confidence has grown as a result.

I am greatly affected by emotive statements and emotional pressure and sometimes I need time to be able to separate my feelings from the decision that should be made. I recognise the emotions within me when this occurs and ensure that I take action not to make decisions in this context.

NEW WAYS OF WORKING WITH OTHERS

I learned that an increase in recognition of other people's skills and abilities has impacted my overall management style/abilities, including: staff personal development, increased parent involvement; positive management of change within the school, greater student interaction with the curriculum and interest in the curriculum, stronger partnerships within the school community and external agencies, and a new and challenging focus for myself and the school staff and students. Survey results show that team unity has increased from 80 to 95%. The acknowledgment of and utilisation of staff personal skills, has increased by 15% and staff alignment to the school vision has improved from 65% to 95%.

Principalship and leadership are not necessarily the same thing. The person who is the principal must display considered leadership to be effective. The principal has some positional authority but has to have personal credibility and professional respect and knowledge before people will follow.

I have reviewed my strategy of stepping back to encourage others to step up and have continued to role model this.

Leadership is about winning the hearts and minds of the staff to effect sustainable learning cultures. Teachers are the change agents and the pedagogical decision-makers. I don't have to be as task-orientated as I thought. I am letting ideas flow and people run with ideas. I have to be more open to constructive criticism. I am more prepared to accept the advice of others and act on that advice. I don't let intellectual arrogance get in the way.

As the examples above show, the effects of the SLP have been profound with participants who are all very experienced people. What is clearly evident is the depth of feeling that has been provoked by the opportunity for a self-reflective re-examination of professional work and the heightened aspirations aroused for a renewed leadership partnership with others.

Conclusion

In concluding this chapter, we restate that our purpose was to examine the scope and nature of learning necessary for school leaders well into their careers. We did this by first summarising the results of a number of reviews of relevant research literature to help us define the parameters of leadership learning. We underscored five related areas of knowledge to which principals' professional development should be directed.

Our analysis of the Strategic Leaders' Program in Queensland, Australia, suggests to us that leaders should encounter the five areas of knowledge at different times in their careers. Aspirants and new appointees are likely to need a heavier emphasis than experienced leaders on knowledge of the job, that is, *task* knowledge as well as *context* knowledge. All need reinforcement about the *purpose* of schooling from time to time, but experienced leaders responsible for larger and more complex schools need a realistic knowledge of *self* and *others* that is essential if they are to sustain themselves over extended service. Our most experienced leaders should be open to learning about the long-term *purpose* of education and the strategic issues being encountered or likely to be encountered in the future. Using Education Queensland's Leadership Capabilities Framework, we suggest that people need a good 'dose' of educational and organisational capabilities on entry to leadership, personal and relational capabilities should dominate experienced leaders' learning, and those most experienced in complex environments should have their learning focused on intellectual capabilities, particularly futures, strategic directions, challenge and change. We think that herein lies a blueprint for ongoing action by policymakers, administrators and school leaders themselves.

References

Australian Public Service Commission. (1998). *Leadership development: Good practice guide.* Canberra, Australia: Author.

Barber, M., & Mourshed, M. (2007). *How the world's best-performing school systems come out on top.* London: McKinsey and Company.

Education Queensland. (2007). *Leadership matters: Capabilities for Education Queensland principals.* Brisbane, Queensland, Australia: Department of Education, Training and the Arts.

Gronn, P. (2007). Grooming next generation school leaders. In N. Dempster (Ed.), *The treasure within: Leadership and succession planning* (pp. 5–19). Canberra, Australia: The Australian College of Educators.

Joyce, B., & Showers, B. (1982). The coaching of teaching. *Educational Leadership, 40,* 4–10.

Leithwood. K., Day, C., Sammons, P., Harris, A., & Hopkins, D. (2006). *Seven strong claims about successful school leadership.* Nottingham, England: National College for School Leadership.

Leithwood, K., & Riehl, C. (2003). *What do we already know about successful school leadership?* Philadelphia: Temple University.

Leithwood, K., & Mascall, B. (2008). Collective leadership effects on student achievement. *Educational Administration Quarterly, 44*(4), 529–561.

MacBeath, J. (2004). *The Leadership File.* Glasgow, Scotland: Learning Files Scotland.

MacBeath, J. (2006). The talent enigma. *International Journal of Leadership in Educational, 9*(3), 183–204.

McCauley, C., & Brutus, S. (1998). *Management development through job experiences: An annotated bibliography.* Greensborough, NC: Centre for Creative Leadership.

Reeves, J., & Dempster, N. (1998). Developing effective school leaders. In J. MacBeath (Ed.), *Effective school leadership: Responding to change* (pp. 153–165). London: Paul Chapman Publishing Ltd.

Robinson, V.M.J. (2007). *School leadership and student outcomes: Identifying what works.* Winmalee, Victoria, Australia: Australian Council for Educational Leaders.

Teaching Australia. (2007a). *Teaching and leading for quality Australian schools: A review and synthesis of research-based knowledge.* Canberra, Australia: The Australian Institute for Teaching and School Leadership.

Teaching Australia. (2007b). *National professional standards for advanced teaching and school leadership: A consultation paper.* Canberra, Australia: The Australian Institute for Teaching and School Leadership.

Van Velsor, C., & McCauley, C.D. (Eds.). (2004). *Handbook for leadership development.* Colorado Springs, CO: Center for Creative Leadership.

▶▶▶◀◀◀

CHAPTER 15

Principals as Architects of Formal Mentoring Programs in Schools

Lisa C. Ehrich

An important responsibility of principals in schools is fostering a healthy learning-rich environment for both staff and students. Previous research (Duignan & Gurr, 2008; Ehrich, 1998; Leithwood & Day, 2007; Nias, Southworth, & Campbell, 1992) has shown that effective principals create opportunities for teachers to learn with and from each other. For instance, they are involved in establishing supportive structures and creating environments for collaboration and learning to take place (Leithwood & Day, 2007). They do this in a variety of ways such as by providing resources and professional development opportunities, structuring time for staff to learn and work together, and establishing a host of other conditions to facilitate learning and sharing. Beck and Murphy (1993) refer to this role as 'organisational architect' (p. 191) since it harnesses the expertise of teachers who then work with other teachers to help them improve their skills and abilities. This role sees the principal as a facilitative leader who encourages teachers to exercise leadership by leading, teaching and supporting others. The argument in this chapter is that because principals are key architects of staff development and learning within schools, they have a role and responsibility to initiate, support and facilitate a variety of learning activities (both formal and informal) that build a sense of community. The focus of this chapter, then, lies with one type of formal learning approach that principals might like to consider introducing in their schools as a way of enhancing learning and growth for staff. This approach is a formal mentoring program. Although it is more than likely that most schools have some type of mentoring arrangement or buddy scheme operating for staff, particularly new staff, it is argued here that planners of mentoring programs, such as school principals, would do well to be cognisant of the extant research in the field and, where possible, minimise potential difficulties from arising from these programs.

The chapter begins by exploring the meaning of mentoring and formal mentoring programs and identifies their advantages and drawbacks based on structured reviews of the literature. The final part of the chapter identifies a set of critical issues emerging from the mentoring research and literature that are worthy of consideration when planning and implementing a formal mentoring program in schools.

Mentoring

While the original meaning of 'mentor' deriving from Homer's epic, 'Odyssey' is a father figure who guides, supports and develops another, its meaning today has broadened. Mentors are seen to play a multitude of roles from role model to coach to critical friend and can be found in a variety of professional contexts and fields. Due to the widespread usage of the term, 'mentoring', a number of authors claim it is a vague and ill-defined concept (see for example, Gibb, 1999; Healy & Welchart, 1990; Jacobi, 1991).

For the purposes of this chapter, mentoring has been defined as an interpersonal and developmental relationship between a mentor (who is usually a more experienced person) and a mentee that is characterised by support and learning (Hansford, Tennent, & Ehrich, 2003). Hansford et al. (2003) derived this definition from an analysis of 159 research-based papers that examined mentoring for educators. Implicit in the definition are four key assumptions about mentoring that come from a number of theoretical perspectives. Firstly, mentoring is an important interpersonal relationship and developmental phase in the life of a mentor and mentee (Levinson, Darrow, Klein, Levinson, & McPhee, 1978). Secondly, mentors are those persons who are more experienced than those whom they mentor (Ehrich & Hansford, 1999). Thirdly, mentoring is characterised by support (Kram, 1985) or psychosocial supportive functions played by a mentor that include listening, providing advice and friendship and being a sounding board (Kram, 1985). Finally, learning is central to mentoring (Daloz, 1986). For example, Daloz (1986) argues that learning occurs in a mentoring relationship when two key constructs are said to be in operation — these are challenge and support. Challenge refers to challenging assignments and opportunities for the mentored person to grow, be stretched and re-evaluate his or her assumptions, beliefs and practices. Support, is said to be necessary in a mentoring relationship, since it provides an interpersonal context in which the learning, sharing and challenging can take place.

Formal Mentoring Programs

Over the past 3 decades, organisations in many countries around the world have introduced mentoring programs as a means of fostering the learning and growth of graduates and new staff, new and aspiring leaders and members of target groups, including women. In effect, formal mentoring programs are organisational intervention strategies since they are initiated by the organisation to meet organisational goals such as inducting new staff into the culture or developing competencies for new leaders or members of minority groups. Because these programs are organisationally driven, they tend to be structured and set within specific time frames (Ragins & Cotton, 1991). In most organisations, a coordinator is usually responsible for overseeing and implementing the program. Formal programs lie in contrast to informal mentoring, which is unplanned, ad hoc and simply evolves due to the interest of either party.

Formal mentoring programs have been used by systems for both principal and teacher development across many countries. For instance, three commonly cited approaches to principal development include (1) mentoring programs that are part of induction programs for new principals, (2) mentoring programs that constitute some aspect of principal training within the context of a professional qualifications and (3) systemwide mentoring programs that form part of leadership development programs targeting both novice and aspiring principals alike (Hansford & Ehrich, 2006). An example of this latter approach is a program entitled, 'Enhancing Leadership for the Future', recently conducted by the Department of Education, Training and the Arts for aspiring school leaders in Queensland schools.

In terms of teacher development, using mentors to support beginning teachers' careers has come to be seen as common practice in Australia, the United States and the United Kingdom (Carter & Francis, 2000; Ganser, 1995). Central to these programs are mentors who play a critical role in developing novices' skills, competencies, understandings and requisite knowledge required for effective practice. Mentoring has often been hailed as a means by which systems can retain beginning teachers (Carr, Herman, & Harris, 2005). Not surprisingly, education systems across the world have instituted mentoring programs within districts and regions.

School-Based Mentoring Programs

While there has been much writing and research exploring systemwide mentoring programs for teachers in the United States and United Kingdom (Bower & Yarger, 1989; Feiman-Nemser, 1996; Kane & Campbell, 1993), there have been fewer research studies that have explored the introduction and implementation of mentoring programs developed by schools for schools. From my experience of working in schools (both government and nongovernment), it seems that they do have some semiformal mentoring arrangements in place for teachers and these are especially apparent for beginning teachers. In many of these schools, the mentoring program is part of the school's induction program for new staff. For instance, graduates who begin their first year of teaching often participate in a school's induction program (lasting between 6–12 months) and a key part of it will be a mentoring component where the new teacher works with a more experienced teacher. Some schools have fairly formal mentoring guidelines while others have no guidelines. As Ganser (1995) states, there are discernible differences among programs and these differences can be found in terms of goals and structure. For instance, some schools have clear guidelines that cover matters such as the goals and purposes of the mentoring program, expectations of both parties, roles and responsibilities, requisite training for mentors who are involved in the program and time lines. Others, however, approach mentoring in a less structured manner so that roles and expectations may not be articulated formally. Here, for example, a member of the school's management team may simply assign a new teacher to a more senior teacher and expect that mentoring will take place, leaving the mentor to determine what and how he or she will proceed. The danger with this ad hoc and more laid-back approach is that there can be misunderstandings and miscommunication about the nature, purpose and outcomes of the mentoring experience. It is argued, therefore, that principals as organisational architects who initiate or oversee mentoring programs or support others to oversee or coordinate these programs, be pro-active in establishing ones where there are clear roles, responsibilities and expectations that are known and resources set aside to ensure the program is going to succeed.

Why Mentoring?

A cursory examination of the writing in the field of mentoring suggests that it holds a myriad of benefits for those who are mentored, those who mentor others and the organisations in which the mentoring occurs. Douglas (1997) summarises the benefits of mentoring for mentors as career advancement, personal support, learning and development and increased confidence. According to Douglas, mentors are said to benefit also by assistance on projects, increased confidence and a revitalised interest in work. For the organisation, mentoring provides a means through which staff can be developed. Furthermore, organisational commitment and increased communication are benefits for organisations. Organisation communication is said to occur because of the sharing of information that takes place between the mentor and mentee (Antal, 1993). Yet, mentoring is not without its dilemmas and problems. A number of writers (e.g., Douglas 1997; Long, 1997; Murray & Owen, 1991) have identified a variety of drawbacks associated with mentoring. For example, for the mentor these include lack of time to do the mentoring, lack of perceived benefits, lack of skills needed for the role and pressure to take on the role (Douglas, 1997). For mentees, unrealistic and negative experiences, overdependence on the relationship, neglect of core job and conflict that can arise between the boss and the mentor were among the drawbacks (Douglas, 1997). For the organisation, lack of organisational commitment/support (Douglas, 1997; Murray & Owen, 1991) was seen to be a problem, as well as difficulties in coordinating programs and the costs and resources required to administer the programs (Douglas, 1997).

In order to identify more precisely the benefits and drawbacks of mentoring, Hansford et al. (2003) undertook a structured review of the literature that involved analysing a sizeable body of research-based papers on mentoring programs for educators. To do this, the authors searched several education databases and identified 159 research papers. Each of these papers was coded according to factual data (i.e., the year of publication, the publication type, the sample size, methodology of the study and so on) and descriptive data (i.e., positive and negative outcomes of mentoring for the parties concerned). A key finding within the factual data was that two-thirds of the research-based studies focused on preservice or beginning teachers. This was not a surprising finding given that many programs target novice teachers and are designed to help them transfer the knowledge and skills they

TABLE 15.1
Positive Outcomes of Mentoring

Mentors	Mentees	Organisation
Collegiality, cross-fertilisation of ideas	Support, empathy, encouragement	Improved education/ grades/attendance
Reflection	Help with teaching strategies	Support/funds for the school
Professional development	Discussion/sharing ideas	Contributes to good of the profession
Personal satisfaction	Feedback/positive reinforcement	Less work for principals/ staff
Interpersonal skill development	Increased self-confidence	Retention/continuity of teachers

Note: Adapted from Hansford et al., 2003.

learned at university into the classroom environment. Ninety per cent of the studies coded by Hansford et al. reported at least one positive outcome associated with mentoring, which highlights the point that mentoring does provide benefits for those who are involved in mentoring relationships.

The discussion that follows considers the five most frequently cited outcomes for the mentor, mentee and the organisation based on the Hansford et al.'s (2003) structured review. The positive outcomes are discussed followed by the negative outcomes.

Positive Outcomes of Mentoring

The most frequently cited positive outcome of mentoring for mentors was collegiality/collaboration. This outcome refers to the opportunity that mentoring provides for mentors to be collegial and exchange ideas. Reflection referred to the reappraisal and reconsideration of previously held ideas, practices and beliefs that helped mentors come to new understandings and self-awareness. The generic category of professional development referred to being able to learn from mentees as well as learning from the mentoring relationship itself. Personal satisfaction/ reward referred to the satisfaction of helping another to learn and achieve his/her goals. Mentoring enabled mentors to improve their interpersonal skills since they were engaged in listening, giving feedback and advice and responding to another person.

Given that mentoring is said to be a helpful type of relationship that fulfils a psychosocial function (Kram, 1985), it was not surprising that the most frequently cited positive outcome for mentees was support/encouragement/friendship. Help with teaching strategies appeared as the second most frequently cited outcome. This can be explained by the predominance of research-based papers that focused on novice teachers. As with the mentors, the outcome of sharing ideas/ discussion was found. Receiving feedback/positive reinforcement referred to mentors who provided mentees with constructive feedback based on their teaching performance. Finally, increased confidence due to the mentoring relationship and its associated activities was said to be a benefit of mentoring for mentees.

Only a small percentage of the research-based papers referred to one or more positive outcomes that impacted upon the organisation (Hansford et al., 2003). Of these, the most frequently mentioned was improved education/attendance/grades. This category referred to the effects of mentoring on students either in school or university. Increased support/funds for schools referred to the additional funds that schools receive when they take on preservice teachers. Other positives included how mentoring contributes to the good of the profession; it means less work for principals/staff since mentees provide an extra set of hands and retention/continuity of mentored teachers.

Negative Outcomes of Mentoring

As alluded to earlier, the vast majority of the studies in Hansford et al.'s (2003) review reported at least one positive outcome associated with mentoring. However, over half of them (54.1%) reported a mixture of both positive and negative outcomes. Table 15.2 summarises the five most frequently cited negative outcomes of mentoring as experienced by mentors, mentees and the organisation.

TABLE 15.2
Negative Outcomes of Mentoring [refer to original layout]

Mentors	Mentees	Organisation
Lack of time	Lack of mentor time	Cost
Professional expertise/ personality mismatch	Professional expertise/ personality mismatch	Lack of partnership between schools and other organisations
Lack of training/understanding of goals	Mentors critical/out of touch	
Extra burden	Difficulty of meeting/ observation	
Frustration with mentee performance	Lack of mentor support/ guidance	

Note: Adapted from Hansford et al., 2003.

As can be seen from Table 15.2, the two most frequently cited negative outcomes of mentoring for both mentors and mentees were lack of time and personality/professional incompatibility. Lack of time often signalled a mentoring relationship destined for failure since mentoring is so dependent on time to share, work and communicate. Professional/personal incompatibility was the second most frequently cited negative. This referred to mentors and mentees who were ill-matched in either personality or professional outlook. For mentors, the third most frequently cited negative was a lack of training/understanding of goals. It is not surprising that mentors who do not receive training may feel overwhelmed by the mentoring function. Many researchers in the field argue, therefore, that mentors should undergo some type of training to better prepare them for their role, as not everyone has the requisite skills to be a good mentor. An extra burden was seen to be another frequently cited outcome for mentors. This referred to mentors who saw that mentoring was one more job on top of their already increasing workload. Finally, a frequently cited outcome was frustration with mentee performance. Performance also included the mentees' attitude or level of commitment.

For mentees, two of the negative outcomes: mentors who were critical or out of touch and lack of mentor support/guidance referred to aspects of their mentor's behaviour that was deemed unhelpful. The final negative outcome for mentees identified in Table 15.2 was the difficulty of meeting/being observed. In the research studies reviewed by Hansford et al. (2003), this problem occurred because of timetable clashes or limited time available on weekly schedules. This negative outcome reinforces the need for time to be made available within the weekly schedule for mentoring to take place.

For the organisation, the two most frequently cited problems of mentoring that impacted upon the organisation were costs of mentoring and lack of partnership. Mentoring was said to be a costly exercise. As Hansford et al. (2003) state, lack of time for mentoring may have been attributed to the lack of funds available to release staff to mentor. Lack of partnerships referred to mentoring programs for preservice teachers where there was limited communication between the parties, such as schools and universities.

What the aforementioned discussion on the positive and negative outcomes of mentoring points to is that mentoring can and does work and all parties — mentors, mentees and the organisation at large — can benefit. However, mentoring is not without its 'dark side' (Long,

1997) and, for this reason, there are certain issues that should be considered carefully during the planning and implementation stages of a formal mentoring program in order to minimise potential difficulties from arising. The final part of the chapter identifies a set of important issues for principals to consider to assist them in establishing successful school-based mentoring programs.

Issues to Consider in Establishing a Mentoring Program
Support by Senior Management
It has been strongly recommended in the literature that senior managers in organisations be supportive of mentoring programs that are implemented (Douglas, 1997). The same applies to schools. It is argued here that school principals and members of the senior management team need to actively promote, encourage and support the purpose and place of mentoring programs to give them the best chance possible of success. One critical way in which support can be demonstrated is by principals allocating time in the school's timetable for mentoring to take place. This allocation then signals how important mentoring is to the learning in the school. Another way support can be given is by acknowledging the work of mentors. In some organisations, mentors are given extra pay in acknowledgment of the work they do. While this may not be a feasible option, other forms of recognition could be afforded to those who participate in mentoring programs.

Appointment of a Coordinator
The school principal, as formal school leader, does not necessarily need to be *the* coordinator or implementer of a mentoring program. What is important is that the principal, like an organisational architect, has a basic understanding of the design of the mentoring program (i.e., its purpose and focus, and goals, roles and expectations of the various parties) and is able to work with and/or through others who will be responsible for its development and implementation. It is possible that other personnel in the school, either members of the administrative team or teacher leaders, could exercise leadership by taking on the role of the coordinator. It is anticipated that the coordinator would perform a variety of activities such as organising the training, helping to identify a potential pool of mentors, facilitating the matching process, monitoring and evaluating the program, and being the first port of call for either party if there are concerns or difficulties arising from any aspect

of the mentoring relationship. If this role were taken up by a teacher, then there would be some expectation that this person would receive recognition, such as a reduced workload, for doing so.

Purpose and Focus of the Mentoring Program

A key decision when designing a program is to articulate the purpose of the mentoring program. Is it to develop competence in beginning teachers? Is it to improve midcareer teachers' pedagogical skills? Is it to develop leadership capacity in members of the senior management team? It is essential that the purpose be known and understood so that a clear and well-thought through plan can be developed.

Goals, Roles and Expectations

As alluded to earlier in the discussion, there is a need to articulate the goals of the program and the roles that mentors and mentees are to perform so that expectations will be known and can be agreed upon. In Hansford et al. study (2003), lack of understanding about the goals of the program was seen as one of the frequently cited negative outcomes reported in the research-based papers. It makes good sense, then, to communicate the goals so that all parties have an understanding of them. Douglas (1997) goes as far as suggesting that the programs goals should be communicated to all parties — not only those participating but others in the organisation so they are aware of the program.

Training

Much writing in the field of mentoring advocates the training of mentors in order to help them understand the goals of the program, their role within it and as a means of developing their skills so they can mentor another person effectively. While the focus of the training program would depend on the goals and nature of the program, it is likely that topics covered would include 'clinical supervision, research on effective teaching, beginning teacher concerns, and theories of adult learning' (Feiman-Nemser, 1996, p. 3). Feiman-Nemser states also that opportunities within the training for mentors to analyse their own beliefs and teaching practices would be valuable. Tovey (1998) claims that a training program for mentors should teach them about the need to 'scaffold' their mentee's skills and knowledge level ,as well as knowing when they need to 'fade' by gradually removing the scaffolding. Clutterbuck (2004) argues that an important issue that needs to be understood in mentoring is power and how it is used in a mentoring relationship. He maintains that mentors and mentees should negotiate issues of power and, ideally, the mentor should allow the mentee to set the agenda and manage the relationship. It is anticipated that the goal of any mentoring experience should enable the mentee to move from dependence to independence and this can be achieved by a mentor who understands that mentoring is 'a relationship that is both power dependent and helping' (Elmes & Smith, 2006, p. 484). A final consideration regarding training is the choice of a suitably qualified trainer. External consultants can and often play this role.

Selection of Mentors

For mentoring to work it require commitment on the part of those involved. Mentoring needs to be approached as a two-way learning opportunity for both parties, not just a benefit for mentees. It becomes problematic when mentoring is seen as a burden by mentors (Hansford et al., 2003). It is possible that not all experienced staff in a school (or a department or an organisation) would necessarily wish to become involved in a mentoring scheme. Nor should they be. It is argued here that participation in mentoring programs should be voluntary. As Douglas (1997) rightly says, 'the effectiveness of the initiative [mentoring] will be diminished by participant resistance' (p. 96–97). Antal (1993) outlines a number of ways in which mentors can be identified and these include self-nomination and nomination by senior managers or the coordinator. Willing acceptance on the part of mentors to participate is vital. It is anticipated that mentees (particularly new teachers) would in most cases welcome an opportunity to be mentored.

A related concern to selection is the potential difficulties that can emerge when the mentor is also a person's line manager. In other words, a new teacher is being mentored by the school principal. Cohen (1999) notes that this situation can be problematic because the principal is playing the role of developer and appraiser at the same time. He suggests that another party, such as another teacher, should be the 'mentor' to eliminate this role conflict. Furthermore, Kochan (2002) notes that a mentee might not feel comfortable to share concerns and show vulnerability to his/her immediate manager (i.e., principal) because of fear of an unfavourable staff appraisal. In her review of the literature on mentoring in schools, Feiman-Nemser (1996) concurs when she says, 'mentors should assist not assess' (p. 3).

Matching Process

Once mentors have been identified and have agreed to participate, the next step is matching. As indicated earlier, professional/personal incompatibility between the mentoring dyad can yield unproductive mentoring outcomes (Hansford et al., 2003). For this reason, it is argued that the coordinator of the program considers some effective ways to facilitate the matching approach. In a small school where there might be one new member of staff requiring mentoring, the matching process would be simpler than in a large school where there could be 10 new graduates. In larger programs, the coordinator might ask mentors and mentees to complete a profile on themselves and then he/she would proceed to match according to similar interests/foci. Another way of approaching the matching could be for the coordinator to organise a social function whereby mentors and mentees could get to know each other and select a suitable partner.

Time Scheduled Into the Timetable

Time to work together, share and discuss is crucial if mentoring is to work. Lack of time, as Hansford et al. (2003) discovered, was the greatest impediment identified by mentors and mentees. Ideally, time should be structured into the school's timetable so that both parties have an opportunity to observe each other in action. Allocated time shows commitment by senior management to the value of the program. It seems that time is required particularly in the early stages of the relationship where both parties are getting to know each other. Feedback and discussion are key parts of mentoring, so time needs to be allocated for both parties to engage in conversations for and about learning. The time necessary for meetings will depend on a number of matters. However, in a study by McNally and Martin (1998) of a mentoring program for beginning teachers, mentors and their mentees met one hour per week. It is anticipated that both parties would negotiate where they would meet, when they would meet and the specific focus of their meetings (within the overall goals of the program).

Monitoring and Evaluation

In any mentoring program, there is a need for ongoing monitoring and an evaluation of the process and the program. Kram and Brager (1991) suggest strategies such as focus group interviews and surveys to be distributed to participants to gain their feedback about the mentoring experience at different times during the program. This type of information can assist with refining the existing program and maximising the benefits for all (Hansford et al., 2003). Obtaining valuable information about the process is also necessary from the point of view of the school as an organisation. If schools are going to invest time and other resources into mentoring programs, then it is not an unreasonable expectation for data to be collected that reveals the extent to which the program has met its goals and has made a contribution to the overall learning in the school.

Conclusion

This chapter has presented the view that mentoring programs are an important planned and structured learning activity in schools. Some key planning and implementation issues emerging from the research were identified and discussed. It was argued that consideration of these issues should help to minimise difficulties that can sometimes arise when orchestrating these programs. It is important to point out that mentoring is not a panacea; it alone is not going to transform schools into learning communities. However, it is one activity that principals as organisational architects might like to consider exploring as a way of encouraging staff learning, talk and working.

References

Antal, A.B. (1993). Odysseus' legacy to management development: Mentoring. *European Management Journal, 11*(4), 448–454.

Beck, L.G., & Murphy, J. (1993). *Understanding the principalship: Metaphorical themes 1920s–1990s.* New York: Teachers College Press.

Bower, A., & Yarger, G. (1989). Mentor–intern relationships in New York state's formal program: Beginnings. *Action in Teacher Education*, xi(2), 60–65.

Carr, J.F., Herman, N., & Harris, D.E. (2005). *Creating dynamic schools through mentoring, coaching, and collaboration.* Alexandria, VA: Association of Supervision and Curriculum Development.

Carter, M., & Francis, R. (2000, December). *Mentoring and beginning teachers' workplace learning.* Paper presented at the AARE Conference, Sydney, Australia.

Clutterbuck, D. (2004), *Everyone needs a mentor: fostering talent in your organisation* (4th ed.). London: Chartered Institute of Personnel and Development.

Cohen, N. (1999). *The mentee's guide to mentoring.* Amherst, MA: HRD Press.

Daloz, L. (1986) *Effective teaching and mentoring.* San Francisco: Jossey Bass.

Department of Education, Training and the Arts. (2006). *Enhancing leadership for the future*. Queensland Government. Retrieved December 22, 2008, from http://education.qld.gov.au/staff/development/employee/school_leaders/enhancing.html

Duignan, P., & Gurr, D. (2008). *Leading Australia's schools*. Sydney, Australia: ACEL and DEST.

Douglas, C.A., (1997). *Formal mentoring programs in organisations: An annotated bibliography*. Greensboro, NC: Centre for Creative Leadership.

Ehrich, L.C. (1998). Principals' experiences of the professional development of teachers. In L.C. Ehrich & J. Knight (Eds.), *Leadership in crisis: Restructuring principled practice* (pp. 96–104). Flaxton, Queensland, Australia: Post Pressed.

Ehrich, L.C., & Hansford, B. (1999). Mentoring: Pros and cons for HRM. *Asia Pacific Journal of Human Resources, 37*(3), 92–107.

Elmes, M.B., & Smith, C.H. (2006). Power, double binds, and transcendence in the mentoring relationship: A transpersonal perspective. *International Journal of learning and change, 1*(4), 484–498.

Feiman-Nemser, S. (1996). *Teacher mentoring: A critical Review*. Washington, DC. (Eric Clearinghouse on Teaching and Teacher Education, ED397060)

Ganser, T. (1995). What are the concerns of beginning and questions of mentors of teachers? *NASSP Bulletin, 70*, 83–91.

Gibb, S. (1999). The usefulness of theory: A case study in evaluating formal mentoring schemes. *Human Relations, 52*(8), 1055–1075.

Hansford, B., & Ehrich, L.C. (2006). The principalship: How significant is mentoring, *Journal of Educational Administration, 44*(1), 36–52.

Hansford, B.C., Tennent, L., & Ehrich, L.C. (2003). Educational mentoring: is it worth the effort? *Education Research & Perspectives, 30*(1), 42–75.

Healy, C.C., & Welchart, A.J. (1990). Mentoring relations: A definition to advance research and practice. *Educational Researcher, 19*(9), 17–21.

Jacobi, M. (1991). Mentoring and undergraduate academic success: A literature review. *Review of Educational Research, 61*, 505–532.

Kane, I., & Campbell, A. (1993). Mentor and mentor-training in the North West Articled teacher scheme. *Mentoring, 1*(1), 16–22.

Kochan, F. (Ed.). (2002). *The organisational and human dimensions of successful mentoring programs and relationships*. Charlotte, NC: Information Age Publishing Inc.

Kram, K.E. (1985). *Mentoring at work: Developmental relationships in organisational life*. Glenview, IL: Scott Foresman.

Kram, K.E., & Brager, M.C. (1991). Development through mentoring: A strategic approach. In D. Montross & C. Shinkman (Eds.), *Career development: Theory and practice*. Springfield, IL: Charles C., Thomas.

Leithwood, K., & Day, C. (2007) What we learned: A broad view. In C. Day & K. Leithwood (Eds.), *Successful principal leadership in times of change: An international perspective* (pp. 189–203). Dordrecht, the Netherlands: Springer.

Levinson, D.J., Darrow, C.N., Klein, E.B., Levinson, M.H., & McPhee, B. (1978). *The seasons of a man's life*. New York: Ballantine.

Long, J. (1997). The dark side of mentoring. *Australian Educational Research, 24,* 115–123.

McNally, P., & Martin, S. (1998). Support and challenge in learning to teach: the role of the mentor. *Asia Pacific Journal of Teacher Education, 26*(1), 39–50.

Murray, M., & Owen, M.A. (1991). *Beyond the myths and magic of mentoring: How to facilitate an effective mentoring programme*. San Francisco: Jossey Bass.

Nias, J., Southworth, G., & Campbell, P. (1992). *Whole school curriculum development in the primary and secondary school*. London: The Falmer Press.

Ragins, B.R., & Cotton, J.L. (1991). Easier said than done: Gender differences in perceived barriers to gaining a mentor. *Academy of Management Journal, 34*(4), 939–951.

Tovey, M.D. (1998). *Mentoring in the workplace: A guide for mentors and managers*. Sydney, Australia: Prentice-Hall.

▶▶▶◀◀◀

CHAPTER 16

Enhancing Leadership Density Through Effective Senior Management Teams (SMTs)

Neil C. Cranston and Lisa C. Ehrich

Increasingly, it has been argued that senior management teams, comprising principals, deputy heads and other personnel, play a critical role in the governance of schools. In recent years, researchers have drawn upon the tools of micropolitics to illuminate the relationships, dynamics and power plays between and among members of SMTs. This chapter examines two key questions about such bodies. First, it overviews some of the seminal literature available about SMTs and micropolitics and thus identifies important learnings about both the challenges facing members of SMTs and how these challenges might be addressed to make SMTs more effective. Second, it looks at one way that SMTS can review their current dynamics and practices and how such information might be used developmentally to make SMTs more effective. The *TEAM Development Questionnaire* and *TEAM Development Process* are key elements of this. The questionnaire presented here was especially devised to use with members of SMTs to help them (1) identify the dynamics among team members and (2) identify areas for the team to improve. A set of procedures for implementing the *TEAM Development Questionnaire* is provided to demonstrate its application to the field. While this instrument provides some guidance regarding the way SMTs can work towards more effective collaborative practices, it emphasises that teams need to regularly reflect critically on the relationships among, and dynamics of, such teams in schools if leadership synergies are to be achieved. The rapidly changing and challenging contexts now so evident in schools demand this.

Background and Context for Considering Senior Management Teams (SMTs)

There is little doubt that the roles and responsibilities of school leaders in most countries across the world have become more complex and challenging in recent years (Billot, Goddard, & Cranston, 2007; Cranston, 2007a; Gronn, 2003). In large part, this has resulted from the discontinuously changing contexts and day-to-day dynamics within which school leaders now operate. Indeed, principals are now faced with having to make a plethora of decisions in an environment of competing priorities and with consideration for the interests of students, teachers, parents and the school and wider community. Increasingly, principals now share many of their decision-making responsibilities among members of their senior team; deputy principals, assistant principals, associate principals (Cardno, 2002) — the nomenclature varies across various countries and systems. Cardno (1998) sees the use of teams as connected to collaborative management notions and that:

> Teamwork is important because it has both idealistic and practical dimensions. Ideally, it is connected to values of cooperation and collaboration, while on a practical level it provides the means for functional groups to carry out tasks in self-managed school structure. (p. 47).

Such teams, where the focus is on groups of designated school leaders (such as the principal, deputy principals and so on), and often referred to as Senior Management Teams (SMTs), have increasingly become the focus of researchers and writers (Bennett, Woods, Wise, & Newton, 2007; Cranston & Ehrich, 2005; Ehrich & Cranston, 2004; Gronn, 1998; Hall & Wallace, 1996; Wallace, 2002). Several researchers have examined such teams through the lens of 'micropolitics' (Blase, 1991; Blase & Anderson, 1995).

In part, this increasing, and some would argue overdue, attention has paralleled developing interests in notions of distributive leadership emerging in recent years (see, e.g., Gronn, 2002; Harris, 2005). While the rationale for such notions is contested because of 'greater managerial complexity in school administration (i.e., have to) ... to an explicit commitment to collaboration (i.e., want to)' (Gronn, 2003, p. 111), there is now strong evidence that an approach of working with and through others is much more likely to characterise principals' work than earlier individualistic 'great man' approaches or 'lone leadership' (Southworth, 2002). Indeed, developing leadership synergies through already established bodies such as SMTS provides opportunities for distributing leadership in an operational context in which the 'the task of transforming schools is too complex to expect one person to accomplish single handedly' (Lashway, 2003, p. 1). In many ways, the workings of SMTs can be considered as one element of distributive leadership notions. They might also be seen as offering the potential to 'unleash' the leadership capacities among team members, given that many principals and deputy principals report their roles being characterised by a dominance of management over leadership (see Cranston, Ehrich, & Billot, 2003; Cranston, Tromans, & Reugebrink, 2004). But there remain questions and challenges as to what is going on in SMTs (i.e., their dynamics) and how might we use such understandings for improving their effectiveness. These two questions provide the focus of this chapter.

The chapter now moves to overviewing some of the key literature into SMTs. The earlier work of writers such as Blase (1991) in the United States and Hall and Wallace (1996) in the United Kingdom and others is examined along with more recent writings by Cardno (2002) and Cranston and Ehrich (2005). The chapter then synthesises from such literature a number of common and powerful themes about the underlying principles and characteristics of effective Senior Management Teams in schools. Discussion then moves to the development of the *TEAM Development Process,* central to which is the *TEAM Development Questionnaire,* an instrument developed from the synthesis of the literature. The characteristics of the questionnaire (items, format) are also briefly be discussed. Of key interest is the *TEAM Development Process* — that is how the questionnaire is used in practice with SMTs as a means of examining their dynamics and identifying areas for development. Notions of action research are evident here. Central to the process is the challenge offered through the questionnaire for SMT members to 'describe' how their team currently operates (what is termed the *real*) and then how they would like to see their team operate in a preferred situation (what is termed the *ideal*). It is an examination of the alignment, or more importantly the lack of alignment, between the *real* and *ideal* where critical reflections and key developmental conversations can be generated. Not surprisingly, sound facilitation of such conversations are required to take the SMT forward by building on any positives identified via the questionnaire (e.g., where there is alignment between the *real* and *ideal*) as well addressing any areas for improvement (e.g., where there is a lack of alignment between the *real* and *ideal*).

The chapter concludes by offering some reflective learnings (Cranston, 2007b) from the application of the TEAM process with SMTs. These reflections have been documented as the process has been used in a number of different situations (state and nonstate schools) and different types of teams. In sum, what these learnings suggest is that the TEAM process as discussed offers a useful means for SMTs to both reflect on their dynamics and the effectiveness of these, as well as identify areas for attention and development. Of note is that the process and learnings have wider applicability beyond just SMTs and are equally applicable to, and suitable for use with, schools' teams of a variety of types, such as curriculum teams and school councils and boards.

Earlier Research as Framing an Interest in SMTs

The findings of two surveys of senior management team (SMT) members in Queensland (and New Zealand) secondary schools revealed that teamwork and leadership characteristics of a school's SMT were key determinants of respondents' levels of role satisfaction (Cranston et al., 2003, 2004). Specifically, respondents' levels of satisfaction and self-efficacy as school leaders and managers were significantly correlated with the goodness of fit between how their SMT actually functioned and how they would ideally like it to function. This suggested that SMT dynamics were a critical factor in supporting, maintaining and promoting the leadership and management skills and aspirations of SMT members. Analysis of the qualitative data collected in the surveys pointed to micropolitical theory as a useful conceptual framework for understanding and managing those dynamics.

In response to these findings, a research project aimed at developing a strategy (instrument and process) to examine the characteristics, dynamics and effectiveness of SMTs was initiated. The background, current developments and future directions of that research are explored elsewhere in detail (Cranston & Ehrich, 2005). What is critical about this research is that it has high relevance for schools across all education systems, nationally and internationally, which have been subjected to school-based management and similar reforms and restructurings in recent times. It is these operational contexts where such reforms intensify the need for enhanced and collaborative decision-making at the school level, making the effectiveness of key groups, such as SMTS, engaged in such decision-making, of high importance. More recent developments in distributed, shared and multiple leadership, as noted above, are also relevant. In short, Southworth (2002) argues today there is much more talk about shared leadership, leadership teams and distributed leadership than ever before.

Analysis of the qualitative data of the research survey noted above highlighted interpersonal relations, participatory and transparent decision-making, delegation of authority and responsibility, and leadership style as key themes for delineating SMT dynamics (Cranston et al., 2004). The following quotes provided by secondary school deputy principal respondents illustrate some of these dynamics:

> I'm not satisfied in my role, because ... Our principal often calls important meetings at short notice so not all of us can get there. I'm made to feel like a troublemaker if I raise an objection to a decision made in my absence and I don't think my expertise is used or valued at all, except for dealing with behaviour problems and staff gripes.

> I'm more satisfied in my role now because ... Change of school to a place where my contribution is valued and I feel that my work is worthwhile; having a Principal who delegates without feeling the need to oversee; working with colleagues who share roles without power plays. (Cranston & Ehrich, 2005, p. 81)

The frequency and consistency of such comments in the survey data demonstrated the political nature of SMTs and their susceptibility to internal conflict, individual/group manipulation, defensive behaviour and power struggles. They also captured the quintessential nature of micropolitics, which is concerned with how strategies such as power, coercion, cooperation, cooption and influence can be applied in group settings to obtain resources and/or achieve goals.

As indicated earlier, it was this research finding that gave the impetus for further investigation of SMTs, the dynamics, quality and effectiveness of these and how some developmental gains might be made to assist SMTs reflect on their current status and identify areas for development. A review of the literature did indeed reveal that micropolitics could provide a useful lens for focusing this research.

Looking at SMTs Through the Lens of Micropolitics

Micropolitics has been described by Blase (1991, p.1) as:

> ... the use of formal and informal power by individuals and groups to achieve their goals in organizations. In large part, political actions result from perceived differences between individuals and groups, coupled with motivation to use power to influence and/or protect. Although such actions are consciously motivated, any action, consciously or unconsciously motivated, may have political 'significance'

in a given situation. Both cooperative and conflictive actions and processes are part of the realm of micropolitics.

It is not unusual for this description to evoke images of the divisive and self-promoting behaviours that characterise the 'negative' side of organisational life (Hoyle, 1999), which Hall and Wallace (1996, p. 7) refer to as the 'covert and illegitimate world of underhand manoeuvres and dirty tricks'. However, micropolitics also entails positive, cooperative and facilitative strategies that can promote and maintain collaboration and commitment among members of an organisation to achieve common goals (Blase & Anderson, 1995). These ideas become important in operational contexts such as in devolution and school-based management reforms, where SMTs, parents, teachers, and community members increasingly need to collaborate in decision-making processes affecting the school and its policies. Principals are under considerable pressure to ensure that the SMT functions effectively in this context, which places them in a critical position as both the leader and a member of the team. As Wallace and Hall (1994, p. 186) observed, 'if the team does not work, not only does the principal lose credibility but also the potential "synergy" which is often the result of working with others'.

So how might knowledge and understanding of micropolitics help? In brief, the literature and theory of micropolitics suggests that the effectiveness of a SMT is determined by its strengths across a number of important dimensions, including the following (a more detailed discussion is provided in Ehrich & Cranston, 2004):

THE CLARITY OF ITS ROLE AND OBJECTIVES
The research (see, e.g., Hughes & James, 1999; Wallace & Hall, 1994; Wallace & Huckman, 1996) strongly supports the notion that central to achieving clarity of role and expectations requires a willingness to engage in ongoing discussion to negotiate roles and responsibilities as tasks and new issues emerge.

THE COMPETENCE AND CREDIBILITY OF ITS MEMBERS
For effective team functioning, each member of the SMT needs to be competent and credible in the eyes of the other team members. Researchers such as Evans (1998) and Wallace (2002) identify these characteristics of competent and credible as vital also in developing positive perceptions among teachers towards the SMT.

THE UNIFORMITY OF MEMBERS' VALUES
AND THEIR COMMITMENT TO TEAM WORK
The need to develop a shared culture among the SMT and to work effectively together to achieve consensus and avoid conflict are identified as important requirements for effective SMT operation as is the role of the principal or head and other administrators in achieving this (Evans, 1998; Hall & Wallace, 1996; Wallace, 2002; Wallace & Huckman, 1996). Central to the achievement of a shared culture are positive working relationships where all members participate fully and communicate openly with one another (Wallace, 2002).

INTERPERSONAL RELATIONSHIPS AND COMMUNICATION
AMONG MEMBERS AND BETWEEN MEMBERS AND OTHER STAFF
Not surprisingly, the research (see writers as above) has also shown that these characteristics are vital to achieving an effective and positively acknowledged SMT. Communication within SMTs and between SMTs and other members of staff are key elements in enabling meaningful decision-making to proceed. Importantly, Evans (1998) found that SMTs' practices potentially could have detrimental repercussions on teacher morale and teacher quality of life, noting 'how easy it is for SMTs to reduce rather than increase, democratization' (p. 427).

ACCESSIBILITY OF PROFESSIONAL DEVELOPMENT OPPORTUNITIES
FOR THE TEAM AND FOR ITS INDIVIDUAL MEMBERS
Hall and Wallace (1996) referred to two different types of learning opportunities for SMTs: first, a planned induction into the SMT was seen as particularly important for assisting new members of the team to be socialised and integrated into the workings of the team; and second, individual members of the team as well as whole team attendance at structured development activities provided training to support team development. Other research (Bell, 1992; Cardno, 1999, 2002) suggests that teams need to participate in ongoing learning and reflection if they are to improve their overall effectiveness as a unit. Participation in critical reflection requires a certain type of openness to what is working, as well as areas that need to be addressed (Cardno, 2002). Cardno maintains that the challenge in team learning 'lies at the point where people collectively interact to overcome the forces that work against honest communication, especially in situations fraught with conflict' (p. 220). Thus it becomes important for teams to learn how to overcome defensiveness and other barriers so that open communication among

members of the team can result. However, it is not just barriers within the SMT that need to be broken down; barriers between the SMT and staff must be reduced. Shared values between the managers and the rest of the staff are also important in determining SMT success (Evans, 1998). The *Team Process* discussed below addresses many of the issues identified.

Perhaps part of the learning journey for SMTs should begin with some systematic critical reflection of staff's perceptions of the SMT's performance. Such feedback has the potential to provide valuable information for SMTs and contribute to their ongoing learning and development as a team. Cardno (2002) sees that leaders need to 'take the lead' in providing ongoing learning opportunities for team members and team members need to be open to such learning. She cautions, however, that if team learning and development are not seen as critical areas for SMTs to pursue, then the potential for teams to learn may well go unrealised.

A recent comprehensive review of the (school) team literature (Cranston & Ehrich, 2008) synthesised a number of important issues to be noted when considering teams generally, and senior management teams in particular. Many of these reinforce the ideas already raised above, as well as providing some wide contextual matters for consideration. These are included with commentary below:

Other Key Issues to Consider Regarding SMTs
THE IMPORTANCE OF TEAM WORK
For some years, there has been a strong argument that sharing leadership in teams is not only empowering for its members and an inclusive activity, but also more effective since it is unlikely that one person can act alone effectively in all circumstances. This is particularly the case now in schools where responsibilities and accountabilities have increased in recent years. In brief, it is argued that teamwork can be empowering and is inclusive and morally just since it gives voice to all members. It can also be more effective than working on one's own, engendering greater commitment and support. Finally, it has idealistic and practical dimensions.

CHARACTERISTICS OF EFFECTIVE TEAMS
Effective teams are those that are said to demonstrate particular characteristics. These characteristics relate to the dynamics of the team, its

purposes and practices, the relationships among team members and the relationships it has with others in the organisation. These characteristics include that the team has common purpose and clear vision, with clear roles, commitment and communication. The team ought to comprise people who have a range of personal attributes and demonstrate positive team modelling. Members need to hold clear expectations, resolving disagreements openly by discussion and being committed to the readiness for change as necessary. It is also argued for the inclusion of wider staff in the processes, and that integrity must be evident as a key element of teamwork. Integrity includes notions such as trust, collegiality, respect and partnership among members. Finally, there needs to be a demonstrated commitment to reflecting on, and improving team dynamics and practices.

CHALLENGING ROLE OF THE FORMAL LEADER

Some writers argue that it is the formal leader of the school (i.e., the headteacher or principal) who, in most cases, sets the parameters and culture or tone for the type, extent and quality of teamwork that is enacted. Key matters to highlight about the principal in SMTS include the importance of the formal leader in influencing and shaping team dynamics and promoting a culture of teamwork. To be noted is that this leader occupies a unique position: that of leader and member of the team. The formal leader also determines largely the extent to which teams are collegial or hierarchical as well as determining the degrees of sharing and tasks undertaken. They may also be influential in providing ongoing learning opportunities for team members.

TENSIONS FACED BY FORMAL LEADER

Because of the dual location of the formal leader as both leader and team member, teamwork can be perceived as a risky activity. Formal leaders may be reluctant to share their decision-making with other members of the team for fear of costly mistakes being made; mistakes for which they must bear the consequences. Sharing decision-making in this way may also bring into question issues of power, such as power over, power with, power through. Past practices and culture are important here. The formal leader(s) may face tensions and dilemmas between exercising formal authority versus desire for collegiality, the need to maintain control and hierarchy versus equal contribution for members, and empowering others versus responsibility for decisions made.

CHALLENGES FACING TEAMS AND TEAM EFFICACY

Teamwork does not occur automatically or by chance. It requires sensitive and proactive leadership to facilitate it. There are many challenges facing teams and a range of barriers impacting upon team efficacy. Among these are the lack of clarity and expectations among team members, the presence of defensive patterns of behaviour by members and operational matters such as time constraints and limited or no provision of resources. Perhaps more significant are issues such as team members' disagreement over goals, intragroup competition, domination by one or more players, and personal attacks.

MICROPOLITICS AS A LENS FOR UNDERSTANDING TEAM DYNAMICS

Micropolitics, as noted above, has been described as a powerful analytical tool to illuminate how members of teams use a variety of strategies such as coercion, cooperation and influence to obtain resources and achieve goals. Central to micropolitical activity is an analysis of influence and power. For some writers, understanding micropolitics and how it relates to team functioning is at the heart of effective team development. Key notions central to understanding micropolitics include cooperation, coercion, collaboration, cooption; power utilisation and power sharing; negotiation and conflict resolution; covert and overt actions and goals; facilitative actions; favouritism and manipulation; positive and respectful interpersonal relationships among members. These are the very essences of micropolitics in action.

TEAM LEARNING AND EFFECTIVENESS

Effective teams do not simply happen; they require training and development and ongoing reflection if they are to be successful. Matters to be considered here, and acted upon, include the requirement that teams must be accountable and able to evaluate their performance and that they need to learn together. In practice, they may use a variety of tools (e.g., brainstorming, SWOT analysis, Appreciative Inquiry) to assist them to work together, in this way developing their particular goals and visions together. Importantly, new members of teams can benefit by an induction process whereby they are 'socialised' into the team. Subsequently, structured developmental activities can support team learning. Finally, it is argued that teams should reflect constantly on their performance.

The key messages about the dynamics and effective operation of SMTs outlined in these reviews provide important pointers to what needed to be examined in our research to better understand the dynamics of SMTs. Further, they emphasised the importance of focusing that research in an attempt to make some contribution, in a developmental way, to potentially enhancing SMT operations in schools. A pilot study was undertaken to explore the possibility of stimulating and promoting learning among SMTs through a systematic process of self-analysis and critical reflection grounded in micropolitical theory. The *TEAM Development Questionnaire* [TEAMS IN EDUCATIONAL ADMINISTRATION AND MANAGEMENT©], was subsequently developed from this research and emerged as an effective tool for this purpose.

Development of the TEAM Development Questionnaire

The following discussion provides some insights into how SMTs (and team members) can critically and constructively reflect on their current dynamics and practices with a view to developing and improving these with the ultimate intention of enhancing the leadership capacity and density in the school. While there are other means by which this might be achieved, the *Team* process provides both a practical and challenging way of doing this, as well as an effective way for teams to remain mindful of what the literature argues are the critical elements of team effectiveness.

Further details about the development of the instrument are provided elsewhere (see Cranston & Ehrich, 2005). In summary, the *TEAM Development Questionnaire* was formulated 'from the ground up' in a variety of ways. Importantly, the questionnaire items drew on the perceptions and experiences of SMT members (e.g., principals, deputy principals) across a range of contexts, including their responses to surveys regarding their roles, workloads and leadership and management experiences; their advice on the scope and detail of the questionnaire; and their feedback on the acceptability and relevance of questionnaire items as they were progressively drafted. Because of its potential to offer a unique and valuable perspective on the workings and effectiveness of SMTs, the micropolitical literature in education also contributed significantly to the formulation of the questionnaire items.

The TEAM Development Questionnaire in Action

The *TEAM Development Questionnaire* has been refined such that it now comprises 32 core items, and five biographical and background items. The structure of the questionnaire takes account of the desire to achieve an instrument design to reflect the strong developmental focus derived from the notion of alignment of team dynamics (real versus ideal) as discussed below. It is these latter aspects as to how the instrument might be used in practice by SMTs that is of greatest interest here.

With regard to the notion of alignment, and to enable SMT members to profile their current SMT dynamics and those of a potentially more desired state, the instrument has now been designed to elicit two focused sets of responses:

- first, respondents are asked to complete the items for how their team functions now (i.e., the real team); then,
- second, respondents are asked to complete the same items for how they would prefer their team to function (i.e., the ideal team).

Hence, two sets of TEAM profile data are available, viz. the *real* and the *ideal*. With such data, SMTs are able to analyse and profile both individual items as well as scales/domains (i.e., sets of items) to ascertain where *real* and *ideal* alignment is high as well as low. This provides a powerful developmental tool to identify the strengths and weaknesses/areas for development of SMTs. For example, areas where there is a lack of alignment can be used to target strategies (e.g., professional development) to move to the more desired state. Additionally, areas indicating high alignment can generally be considered as team strengths and used in positive supportive ways.

The following process can be used by SMTs to investigate their effectiveness and dynamics. Ideally, it is considered that an external facilitator might best oversee the process which entails:

- each member of the SMT team completing the TEAM Development Questionnaire — this includes both real and ideal responses for each of the items
- real and ideal responses are analysed for alignment and lack of alignment
- the external facilitator provides feedback on the alignment to individuals and the team as a whole — this is by way of a summary report, with simple figures highlighting important findings
- under the coordination of the external facilitator, developmental strategies to address team weaknesses are identified, agreed upon and prioritised for addressing.

PREPARATION FOR ENGAGING IN THE TEAM PROCESS

Consistent with the arguments of Cardno (2002) noted earlier, for such a process to be successful and truly developmental there are risks involved. SMT members need to be willing, honest, trusting and constructive in participating in the process. There is, not surprisingly, the potential for revelation of highly challenging and sensitive data. To assist teams reflect on their readiness for involvement in such a process a simple *TEAM Readiness Tool* has been developed — see Figure 16.1. It is suggested that all team members complete the checklist (which takes about 5 to 10 minutes) then discuss their respective responses as a whole team together. That discussion should conclude with a team

TEAM Readiness Tool

To be completed by all team members individually—THEN responses shared across team members—THEN a collective decision made as to whole team readiness for professional development. Respondents simply indicate whether they AGREE, DISAGREE or are UNSURE with the following five statements.

Statement	Agree (✔)	Disagree (✔)	Unsure (✔)
1. As a team member, I am keen to look at ways of improving my contribution to the 'performance' of the team.			
2. As a team member, I am keen to look at ways of improving the overall 'performance' of the team.			
3. We can always improve the way we 'do business', both as a team and as individuals.			
4. This team plays an important role in the school and it is vital that we regularly reflect on our practices and processes to ensure they are helping to maximise our contributions to schools goals.			
5. This team plays an important role in the school and it is vital that we regularly reflect on our relationships to ensure they are helping to maximise our contributions to schools goals.			
Share responses ☐ discuss ☐ decide on readiness (or otherwise) to proceed with professional development.			

Source: Cranston & Ehrich, 2008.

FIGURE 16.1
TEAM Readiness Tool.

decision as to whether they are ready to embark on a particular team professional development activity.

IMPLEMENTING THE PROCESS: SOME GENERAL PRINCIPLES, COMMENTS

A number of important principles need to be attended to, both before and during the process. These include that all data, participants' names, school name and so on are treated in the strictest confidence throughout the process and by all participants. Participants must be assured the intent of the process is constructive and developmental in so far as the outcomes are about team strengths as well as areas for development. As part of this, the focus must be on the team, not individuals, although individuals are able to reflect on their own data. Finally, participants need to commit to overall outcomes that are about better understanding their team and the development of an action plan for strengthening the team in the future.

A TYPICAL PROCESS AND MEETINGS

The flow chart in Figure 16.2 summarises the *TEAM Process* in action. It is possible that there may be variations to this depending on the school context and other factors, but generally, these elements are seen to provide an effective approach for school teams. Building confidence and trust to begin with, for example, is a critical first and fundamental step in the *TEAM Process*.

Not surprisingly, how effective this process might be relies heavily on some of the key findings of the micropolitical literature as discussed earlier. For example, for the process to be effective there needs to be a shared commitment to teamwork among SMT members, sound interpersonal relationships among members and most importantly, a willingness to learn and change as a result of the process. These are essential dynamics underpinning effective SMTs. However, in reality, they are not always evident or readily achievable. The *TEAM Readiness Tool* provides some 'facilitation' of deepening understandings of what might be involved in the process as well as preparing participants for the potential challenges ahead.

Feedback From the TEAM Process

The *TEAM* instrument and process has now been used in a number of schools. Feedback from participants has been positive. In brief, the learnings to date (Cranston, 2007b) indicate that the process is challenging for team members. Team members must be committed — risk

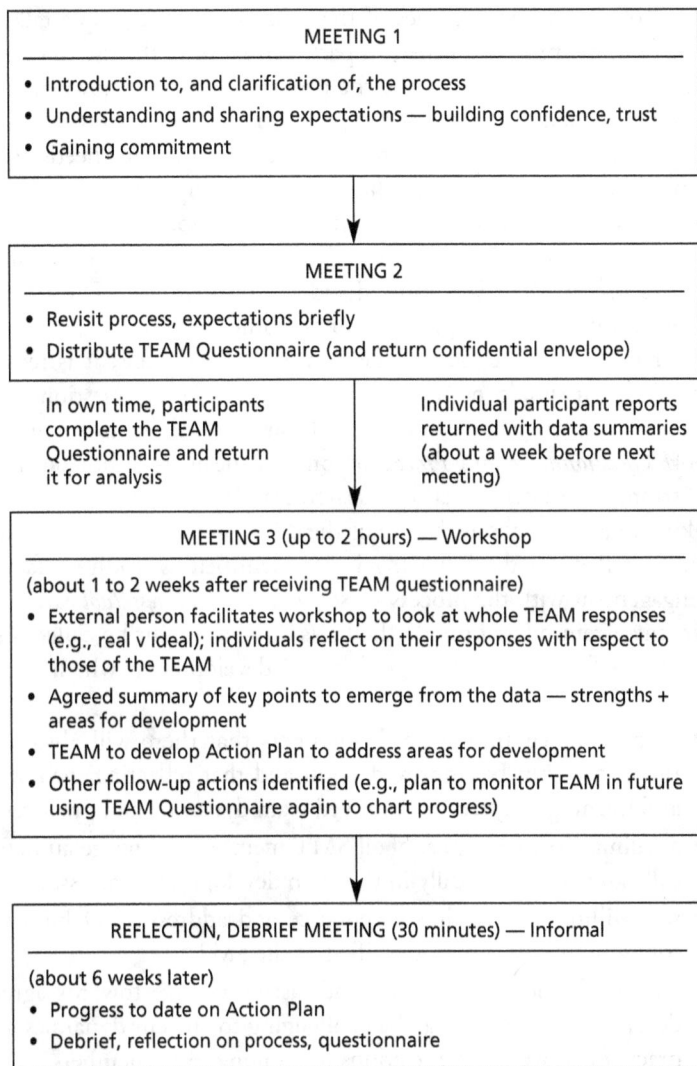

MEETING 1

- Introduction to, and clarification of, the process
- Understanding and sharing expectations — building confidence, trust
- Gaining commitment

⬇

MEETING 2

- Revisit process, expectations briefly
- Distribute TEAM Questionnaire (and return confidential envelope)

| In own time, participants complete the TEAM Questionnaire and return it for analysis | Individual participant reports returned with data summaries (about a week before next meeting) |

⬇

MEETING 3 (up to 2 hours) — Workshop

(about 1 to 2 weeks after receiving TEAM questionnaire)

- External person facilitates workshop to look at whole TEAM responses (e.g., real v ideal); individuals reflect on their responses with respect to those of the TEAM
- Agreed summary of key points to emerge from the data — strengths + areas for development
- TEAM to develop Action Plan to address areas for development
- Other follow-up actions identified (e.g., plan to monitor TEAM in future using TEAM Questionnaire again to chart progress)

⬇

REFLECTION, DEBRIEF MEETING (30 minutes) — Informal

(about 6 weeks later)

- Progress to date on Action Plan
- Debrief, reflection on process, questionnaire

FIGURE 2
Flow chart of TEAM process in action.
Note: Adapted from Cranston & Ehrich, 2005, p. 88.

takers — to making things better in their team. This requires that the data from questionnaire must be accepted as a conversation starter, and the start of a developmental journey.

One of the major outcomes of the process is to get people talking, sharing and trusting each other. In part, this requires the use of quality facilitation to manage and shape the process, and an acknowledgment that 'slow' is good. The pace of the process must be determined by the team members, not the facilitators such that each team needs to be 'taken' from where they are'. In this regard, it is important that there is time for the facilitator to develop trust with group. Participants must have confidence in the facilitator and the process. Finally, it is critical that as a group, the team must decide to be involved. The process cannot be imposed by the principal or any other person.

To reinforce the developmental nature of the process, it is recommended that it should be revisited over time — to ask questions such as 'are we doing what we agreed to do as a team?' In this way, the *TEAM Questionnaire* and *Process* becomes a means to a broader goal, with strong overtones of action research learning processes evident. In thinking practically about the use of the questionnaire and process, it is useful to reflect on the following issues identified as readiness factors for engagement with the process — see *TEAM Readiness Tool* earlier. In short, these reminders provide the basis of what might be called a set of readiness factors for SMT professional development, which would include:

- an acceptance among SMT members that there will always be things that can be improved upon and that reflecting, reviewing and learning can lead to improved team dynamics and practices
- a willingness on the part of all SMT members to engage authentically and enthusiastically in the team development processes
- this willingness requires acceptance and addressing of both the strengths and weakness identified of the SMT
- an understanding that deep and lasting change towards agreed developmental goals may be challenging to current dynamics and practices, as well as the relationships among team members
- an understanding that changes to the SMT dynamics and practices will take time and will require ongoing monitoring of progress towards team agreed developmental goals
- acceptance of external facilitation of any whole team development professional learning activities.

Discussion and Conclusions

There is no doubt that senior teams in schools, such as SMTS, and other teams are now part and parcel of the leadership and decision-making arms of schools. An understanding of micropolitics has been suggested as a powerful lens by which greater insight into the effectiveness and dynamics of such school management teams (SMTs) can be achieved. The team instrument and process reported here represent major progress in generating a strategy for using that lens to reflect on the dynamics of SMT and better understand their effectiveness and identify ways forward to enhance that effectiveness. This is a critically reflective process that is not without its complexities, as it may fundamentally challenge the micropolitics of the SMT itself. The *TEAM Readiness Tool* is offered as one way to ascertain whether a particular team is ready to engage in the process. The benefit of the *TEAM Development Questionnaire* lies in its developmental potential to assist SMTs to move from current realities to future possibilities resulting in more effective team functioning and better relationships — in short, to enhance the leadership capacity and density of the school. Thus, the questionnaire is a potentially useful tool for SMTs as they take on increasingly enhanced decision-making and accountability responsibilities under current school restructuring and reform processes.

References

Bell, L. (1992). *Managing teams in secondary schools.* London: Routledge.

Bennett, N., Woods, P., Wise, C., & Newton, W. (2007). Understanding of middle leadership in secondary schools: A review of empirical leadership. *School Leadership & Management, 27*(5), 453–470.

Billot, J., Goddard, T., & Cranston, N. (2007). How principals manage ethnocultural diversity: Learnings from three countries. *International Studies in Educational Administration, 35*(2), 13–19.

Blase, J. (1991). The micropolitical perspective. In J. Blase (Ed), *The politics of life in schools: Power, conflict and cooperation* (pp 1–18). Newbury Park: Sage.

Blase, J., & Anderson, G. (1995).*The micropolitics of educational leadership: From control to empowerment.* London: Cassell.

Cardno, C. (1998). Teams in New Zealand schools. *Leading & Managing, 4*(1), 47–60.

Cardno, C. (1999, November–December). *Taking the team by the tail: An examination of the potency and demands of team contribution to an organisational learning culture.* Paper presented at the joint Australian Association for Research in Education (AARE) and New Zealand Association for Research in Education (NZARE) Conference. Melbourne.

Cardno, C. (2002). Team learning: Opportunities and challenges for school leaders. *School Leadership & Management, 22(2)*, 211–223.

Cranston, N. (2007a). Through the eyes of potential aspirants: Another view of the principalship. *School Leadership & Management, 27(2)*, 109–128.

Cranston, N. (2007b, November). *Developing quality senior teams in schools: A 'case study' of a Queensland secondary school*. Symposium Paper presented at the Australian Association for Research in Education (AARE) Conference, Fremantle, Australia.

Cranston, N., & Ehrich, L. (2008). *Characteristics and development of best practice leadership teams in schools: Technical paper*. Unpublished paper prepared for Education Queensland.

Cranston, N., & Ehrich, L. (2005). Enhancing the effectiveness of senior management teams in schools. *International Studies in Educational Administration, 33(1)*, 79–91.

Cranston, N., Ehrich, L., & Billot, J. (2003). The secondary school principalship in Australia and New Zealand: An investigation of changing roles. *Leadership & Policy Studies in Schools, 2(3)*, 159–188.

Cranston, N., Tromans, C., & Reugebrink, M. (2004). Forgotten leaders? The role and workload of deputy principals in Queensland government secondary schools. *International Journal for Leadership in Education, 7(3)*, 225–242.

Ehrich, L., & Cranston, N. (2004). Developing senior management teams in schools: Can micropolitics help? *International Studies in Educational Administration, 32(1)*, 1–31.

Evans, L. (1998). The effects of senior management teams on teacher morale and job satisfaction: A case study of Rockville county primary school. *Educational Management & Administration, 26(4)*, 417–428.

Gronn, P. (1998). *Life in teams: Collaborative leadership and learning in autonomous work units*. (ACEA Monograph Series No. 24). Melbourne, Australia: Australian Council for Educational Administration.

Gronn, P. (2002). Distributed leadership. In K. Leithwood & P. Hallinger (Eds.), *Second international handbook on educational leadership & administration*. Dordrecht: Kluwer.

Gronn, P. (2003). *The new work of educational leaders: Changing leadership practice in an era of school reform*. London: Paul Chapman.

Hall, V., & Wallace, M. (1996). Let the team take the strain: Lessons from research into senior management teams in secondary schools. *School Organization, 16(3)*, 297–309.

Harris, A. (2005). Distributed leadership. In B. Davies (Ed.), *The essentials of school leadership* (pp. 160–172). London: Sage.

Hoyle, E. (1999). The two faces of micropolitics. *School Leadership & Management, 19(2)*, 213–222.

Hughes, M., & James, C. (1999). The relationship between the head and the deputy head in primary schools. *School Leadership & Management, 19(1)*, 83–95.

Lashway, L (2003). Distributed leadership. *Clearing House on Educational Management, 19,* 4.

Southworth, G. (2002). *Evidenced-based management and leadership in primary school.* London: Falmer.

Wallace, M. (2002). Modelling distributed leadership and management effectiveness: Primary school senior management teams in England and Wales. *School Effectiveness and School Improvement, 13(2),* 163–186.

Wallace, M., & Hall, V. (1994). *Inside the SMT: Teamwork in secondary school management.* London: Paul Chapman.

Wallace, M., & Huckman, L. (1996). Senior management teams in large primary schools: A headteacher's solution to the complexities of post-reform management. *School Organization, 19(3),* 309–324.

▷▷▷◁◁◁

SECTION FOUR

**Leading in and for
Successful Schools**

CHAPTER 17

Successful School Leadership in Australia

David Gurr

This chapter explores some of the Australian literature on successful school leadership. It is not a critique of the research and so discussion of the arguments about what constitutes success are largely ignored. [It can be noted, however, that Mulford (2008) and Mulford, Kendall, Edmunds, Kendall, Ewington, & Silins (2007) argue for use of broad indicators of success along with the more traditional indicators such as literacy and numeracy test scores]. The chapter draws on some important reviews of the area from outside Australia to indicate how much is known about successful school leadership, and then delves into selected Australian research to show the contributions to the broader view. It draws in part on two earlier papers that explored this area of interest — Gurr (2008); Gurr and Drysdale (2008) — and explores a model of successful school leadership developed by Gurr, Drysdale and Mulford (2006) as part of a large international project, the International Successful School Principalship Project (ISSPP).

What We Know: International Evidence

The study of successful school leadership has attracted significant interest this decade as is evident in several important reviews of the field (see, for example Leithwood, Day, Sammons, Harris, & Hopkins, 2006; Leithwood & Riehl, 2003, 2005; Leithwood, Seahshore Louis, Anderson, & Wahlstrom, 2004; Robinson, 2007), and in the ongoing work of the ISSPP (Leithwood & Day, 2007a). Leithwood and Riehl (2003, 2005) support the argument that the impact of educational leadership is mainly indirect because leadership is essentially a process of influence where educational leaders are mostly working through, or influencing others to accomplish goals. While the effect is indirect, it is nevertheless significant (Leithwood, Day, Sammons, Harris, & Hopkins, 2006, p. 5). In their review of research on how leadership influences student learning, Leithwood et al. (2004, p. 70) conclude that 'leadership is second in strength only to classroom instruction' in terms of factors that influence student learning. Leithwood et al. (2006) provide a concise and useful definition of leadership in schools. They see leadership involving:

- building vision and setting direction
- understanding and developing people
- redesigning the organisation
- managing the teaching and learning program.

Despite criticism of the leadership field (see, for example Lakomski, 2005), this list is a useful statement of the core aspects involved in leading a school.

The reviews of Leithwood and colleagues (Leithwood et al., 2006; Leithwood & Riehl, 2003, 2005; Leithwood et al., 2004) tend to preclude certain types of research, such as the more qualitative approaches and those that can not provide clear evidence of leadership impacting on student outcomes. They also tend to rely on research from North America, and to a lesser extent the United Kingdom, and on principal perceptions of success, often involving narrow definitions of success. The ISSPP was developed to address some of these limitations. In particular, it includes a wide range of countries (initially western in orientation, but more recently including Middle-East, Eastern European, African and further Asian countries), and the voices of teachers, parents, students and school council members. The ISSPP is a large and important body of research that currently contains more than 75 case studies and several thousand survey responses across eight countries, and has produced two books (Leithwood & Day, 2007a; Møller & Fuglestad, 2006) an additional seven book chapters, two special journal issues (*Journal of Educational Administration*, 43(6), 2005; *International Studies in Educational Administration*, 35(3), 2007), and more than 60 refereed journal papers. Its focus is on the knowledge, skills and dispositions that successful school principals use for implementing leadership practices across a range of successful schools in different countries. Success measures varied across countries, but always included peer recommendation, and often included student performance on external examinations and school review reports. In analysing the case studies across the countries, Leithwood and Day (2007b, p. 189) found evidence for additional practices to be added to those of Leithwood et al. (2006), indicating that the principals in the ISSPP were: concerned about ensuring there was a safe environment; had clearly articulated core values; constructed context-sensitive improvement plans; established trust; ensured they were visible in the school; influenced the instructional program either directly or, more often, indirectly, and were good at working with the broader context through the building of productive coalitions. The initial focus on principal leadership is being expanded in the next phase of the ISSPP to include a more distributed perspective. In this phase the original principals and schools are being revisited to explore the sustainability of success. Later in this chapter, the findings from the Australian contribution to the ISSPP are noted.

What We Know: Some Australian Evidence

Mulford (2007a) recently reviewed the quantity and quality of Australian educational leadership research through an examination of articles published between 2001 and 2005 in the four leading Australian-based educational journals (*Australian Journal of Education*, *Australian Educational Researcher, Leading and Managing*, and the *Journal of Educational Administration*). Reliable, evidence-based conclusions were provided in the areas of leadership, transformational leadership, distributed leadership, school organisation and student outcomes, job satisfaction/stress and leader supply/demand, system and community issues, and survey instruments. Of significance for the discussion here, Mulford was troubled by the small number of papers on educational leadership — in both absolute (64 articles) and relative (14% of all articles published) terms — and the quality of the research. For example, he argued many were too local in nature, not strongly connected to previous research, with questionable capacity for the research to be extrapolated to larger populations, policy and practice. Despite criticisms of Mulford's review (Wildy & Clarke, 2008) it does indicate some of the limitations of Australian educational leadership research.

Although Mulford promotes a rather pessimistic outlook for educational leadership research in Australia, it is possible to get a sense of the available Australian research on successful school leadership through a circuitous and sometimes surprising journey, as there is material available in this area. For this chapter, a broad-based review of the evidence for successful school leadership in Australia was conducted. This involved searching electronic journals and theses using the key words: successful school leadership, successful principalship, successful schools, good schools, effective school leaders, educational administration in Australian schools.

One source of information about successful school leadership emerges from descriptions of the work of principals, principal groups, and schools. Walker (1966) edited a book of 26 case studies of educational administration at both the school and system level across all school types. It was a pioneering book in Australian educational administration, bringing to Australia a relatively new technique for improving the work of those leading schools. Mostly the case studies were focused on technical (*George Brent's Toilets*), student (*Second Best for Anthony*), teacher (*Mrs Davis Loses Her Temper*), supervisory (*Inspectorial Enquiry*) or policy (*The Archbishop Closes His Schools*) issues, with none seemingly concerned with the idea of improving school performance directly. This work was published in between the publication of the two editions of *Headmasters for Better Schools* by Bassett, Crane and Walker (1963, 1967). These books were, in many ways, ahead of their time and a product of a partnership between the two pioneering institutes for educational administration in Australia, The University of Queensland through Bassett and the University of New England through Walker. The 1967 edition had chapters on *Characteristics of Good Schools*, *The Meaning of Leadership*, and *The Headmaster as Leader*. The remaining seven chapters were concerned with the details of educational administration, such as running staff meetings, or the relationships a headmaster will have with different members of the school community. The view of school leadership was that it resided in the male head of the school. The chapter on the characteristics of good schools did not reference one research report and included such advice as, '[a] good school has good staff ... Given a reasonable basis on which to work, the headmaster can *create* a good staff.' (p. 3). The chapter exploring the meaning of leadership had stronger connections to the research literature and even had a contemporary feel to it in that it acknowledged that there might be leaders other than principals in schools (those who 'take the lead in volunteering to organise a swimming carnival'; p. 16), and ended with the often used quote from Lao-tzu about the invisible leader. The definition of leadership used was: 'leadership is accomplished by changing the goals of others or by providing ways for others to achieve their goals' (p. 17). This was further expanded upon in the chapter that explored the headmaster as leader. Leadership was largely seen as individualistic and positional, something that was done to groups of people, but, importantly, something which mattered: '[e]ven if he [the Headmaster] (sic) already has a good school, he can look forward to leading an infinitely better one' (p. 32).

In the decades that followed there was little indication that leadership was considered broadly and studies were generally firmly focused on principals, sometimes on deputy principals (Simpkins, Thomas, & Thomas, 1982), with only a few exceptions that considered more complex leadership arrangements. For example, Badcock (1977) explored the effectiveness of various task/relationship orientations of principals and deputy principals in Victorian state high schools and found that task orientation in one or both, lead to more favourable perceptions of effectiveness by teachers, and that, in schools with unfavourable group atmospheres, task-oriented leadership may be more effective. It was research that was clearly a product of its time, focused on the now classic task/relationship dichotomy, at the same time acknowledging that context influenced the impact of leadership. While clearly there had been studies on principal leadership, there seemed to be little that explored in detail how leadership mattered, something that Hallinger and Heck (1998) were arguing for in the 1990s. The 1980s however, was a period of change, and an emerging research interest focused on how to improve schools.

In a book edited by Simpkins, Thomas and Thomas, entitled *Principal and Task*, and coming in 1982 from the University of New England, Simpkins provided a chapter, 'The Principal: A Bibliographic Guide to the Recent Australian Literature', that documented the literature on principals under the headings: role, management, authority and decisions, style, principals and teachers, supervision, community relations and complementary administrative roles. Inspection of the more than 200 titles suggests that few, if any, can be construed as having a focus on successful leadership. There were several titles that mentioned the impact of leadership on staff, but none that had any indication of the impact of leadership on school success. The index to this book had no references to success or effectiveness, although chapters on the position of the principal, and the principal and staff development, provide good information that would help to increase the impact of the work of principals on school success.

At the time of the publication of this book a major study on the work of principals was being conducted by the Australian Commonwealth Schools Commission. The project, *The Australian School Principal: A National Study* (Duignan et al., 1985), involved interviews with principals, parents, teachers and students from government and nongovernment schools in all Australian states and territories, a survey to 1600 principals, and 14 case studies of highly effective schools from across Australia. This project explored the role of principals (both the actual role, and the expectations of principals and other school community members), the professional development needs of principals, the factors which impinge on the role, and the relationship between principal role and school effectiveness. This was the first major study in Australia to explore school leadership and effectiveness. A model relating principal role to goal achievement was presented. This model described principals in terms of personal (confidence, willingness to accept criticism, sensitivity, tolerance, honesty, integrity, consistency, approachability, intellectual acuity, good judgement, tough mindedness, resilience, a sense of perspective and a sense of humour) and professional qualities (leadership, effective communication, effective relationships, knowledge of learning processes and instructional design, initiating change and innovation), and the nature of their work in terms of the role complexity and ambiguity evident. Through focusing on task, process and function strategies, principal work was divided between school (e.g., stimulating and motivating staff), classroom (e.g., monitoring programs and instructional processes) and out-of-school (e.g., facilitating parent and community involvement) factors to influence directly the improvement of teaching and, ultimately and indirectly, the improvement of student learning. It remains a model that helps to understand the work of principals, but is somewhat unsophisticated compared to later ideas in that it does not acknowledge the full complexity of schools, and, in particular in the current context, the more team-based nature of work in schools.

Five years after their earlier book, Simpkins, Thomas and Thomas (1987) provided another edited collection, this time entitled *Principal and Change: The Australian Experience*. Influenced by the earlier book, as well as the *Australian School Principal* study, and the research from effective schools and school improvement movements in North American and England, there were chapters that specifically explored how school leadership could lead to improved student learning outcomes. For example, Duignan wrote a chapter, 'The Culture of School Effectiveness', which drew on the work of North American school effectiveness researchers such as Deal and Kennedy (1983), Lipham (1981), and Purkey and Smith (1983), and the influential corporate study of successful organisations, *In Search of Excellence*, by Peters and Waterman (1982). There was also a chapter by Caldwell and Spinks, 'A Model for Policy-Making and Change Management' that heralded their soon to be released book, *The Self-Managing School* (Caldwell & Spinks, 1988), which built upon earlier research on effective resource allocation in schools led by Caldwell (1986). *The Self-Managing School* was the first in what was to become a trilogy of books focused on improving schools (Caldwell & Spinks, 1988, 1992, 1999), and drawing upon Australian and overseas research. The trilogy included a volume that was devoted to leadership issues, entitled *Leading the Self-Managing School* (Caldwell & Spinks, 1992), which used cultural, strategic, educational and responsive leadership categories. Soon after the publication of *Principal and Change: The Australian Experience,* and *The Self-Managing School,* Beare, Caldwell and Millikan (1989) produced an important synthesis of the school effectiveness and improvement literature, *Creating an Excellent School.* Here, in a volume written by three academics who had all been excellent practitioners at school or school system level, was a treatise that connected both educational and noneducational literature on organisational success, and that provided the signposts for those in schools to create successful schools. Leadership by principals and others in schools was a key component of this. Building upon the work of Beare, Caldwell and Millikan (1989), Caldwell and Spinks (1992, p. 50–55) suggested that leaders in the then rapidly emerging context of self-managing schools:

- have the capacity of work with others in the school community to formulate a vision for the school
- have a coherent personal 'educational platform', which shapes their actions
- communicate a vision for the school in a way which ensures commitment among staff, students and others in the community
- have a multifaceted leadership role which includes technical, human, educational, symbolic and cultural leadership
- keep abreast of trends and issues, threats and opportunities in the school environment and in society at large, nationally and internationally: they discern the 'megatrends' and anticipate their impact on education and in the school
- empower others, especially in respect to decision-making.

It was a view of leadership that foreshadowed the findings of later international reviews of successful school leadership by Leithwood and colleagues (Leithwood et al., 2006; Leithwood & Riehl, 2003, 2005; Leithwood et al., 2004) mentioned previously.

These and other scholarly writings set the scene for a deeper interest in exploring successful school leadership. For example, E.B Thomas and A.R. Thomas individually edited several issues of *The School Principal's Handbook* between 1994 to 2000. These handbooks, published by *The Professional Reading Guide for Educational Administrators*, provided concise summaries or full papers from leading researchers in Australia and overseas, together with some insightful editorials. There were three titles that are relevant to this paper:

- *What every principal needs to know about leadership skills.* (E.B. Thomas, Ed., 1994).
- *What every principal needs to know about good schools* (E.B. Thomas, Ed., 1995).
- *Challenges of the principalship.* (A.R. Thomas, Ed., 2000).

In these and the other Australian publications mentioned above, there was not a rich amount of Australian research to draw upon, with the writing mostly relying on overseas research (with the notable exceptions of *The Australian School Principal* study described previously, and the *Australian Effective Schools Project* discussed below). However, high-quality Australian research was starting to appear. What now follows is a discussion of some of the Australian literature over the past two decades that contributes to our understanding of successful school leadership.

Australian Effective Schools Project

The Australian Council for Educational Research (ACER) conducted a national survey of parents, students, teachers, principals, schools and community members on their views on effective schools (McGaw, Piper, Banks, & Evans, 1993a, 1993b). It remains as one of the most ambitious educational research projects conducted in Australia, and pioneered large-scale use of qualitative analysis software. From a distribution of more than 300,000 survey booklets, there were over 7,000 responses from nearly one-third of Australian schools to questions on areas identified as contributing to school effectiveness including: the important components of an effective-school curriculum, extent of parent and teacher roles and goals for student learning. Among the findings was that effective schools had: a central focus on learning and a conducive school climate; a concern for the learning and welfare of all students; a committed and professional staff; an organisational culture characterised by collaborative decision-making and effective educational leadership; a curriculum that is relevant, coherent, and inclusive; a focus on ongoing professional development and parent involvement. It is also interesting to note that academic achievement was only one of several outcomes identified as being important for effective schools; this view is supported by the later research of Mulford and colleagues (Mulford, 2008; Mulford, Kendall, Edmunds, Kendall, Ewington, & Silins, 2007). While this research was not specifically focused on school leadership, it was one of the elements identified, although it was not until later studies that its importance was more fully recognised (see Leithwood et al., 2004). What was needed at this stage was research to uncover in more detail how leadership might contribute to school success, and to focus more particularly on the role of school leadership in school success. Three such projects are discussed next, with each of these based on small numbers of intensive case studies that explore the principal leadership and school success.

Life History Portraits of Successful School Principals

Dimmock and O'Donoghue (1997) explored leadership using life history portraits of six successful secondary school principals who were regarded as being innovative, based on peer and community recommendation of principals who were known for 'attempting to promote adventurous change programmes to improve the quality of curriculum, teaching and learning in their schools' (Dimmock & O'Donoghue, 1997, p. 30). Elements of leadership that were important to school success included: personal vision, seizing opportunities, goal-setting, using the research literature, understanding their own values and having a clear sense of moral purpose, understanding and using symbolism, questioning the status quo, balancing vision and processes, maintaining pressure for change and including all the stakeholders.

Market-Centred Leadership

In linking marketing with leadership, Drysdale (2001, 2002) provides an unusual perspective on successful school leadership. Multiple perspective case studies of all seven government schools (a special school, a secondary school and five primary schools) in a clearly defined geographical and educational zone were conducted. The schools comprised some that were clearly successful and others that were not, including one that has subsequently closed as a result of its poor performance. It was found that there was a positive link between the degree of market orientation and school performance as measured by enrolments, resources, reputation, community support and growth. The degree of market orientation reflected the leadership of the principal. The most successful principal (outstanding school performance as evidenced by: a waiting list for, and growth in, enrolments; outstanding resources; excellent reputation; strong community support and outstanding school review report) had a compelling vision, harnessed necessary resources, gained commitment from the educational and business community to help improve her school, ensured there was excellent organisational alignment and was an educational leader who spent time building the individual and professional capacity of staff. (Later analysis of her continuing success as an educational leader can be found in Drysdale, 2007).

Successful Leadership in Christian Schools

Begun in 2000, Twelves (2005) reports on an intensive case study of one successful Christian school, utilising a multiple-perspective case study approach, and school review methodologies. The principal had a major influence in all of the seven features identified as contributing to the school's success: fostering Christian values, ethics and beliefs and displaying moral integrity; developing a clear school vision and fostering a predilection for change; care for and development of people; promoting distributed leadership; building a Christian community (students leading a worthwhile Christian life was an outcome as important as any measure of student learning); valuing and encouraging outstanding student learning outcomes; encouraging school leaders who are reflective and always learning. During the 15 years as principal of the school's 21-year history, the principal had overseen substantial growth and was seen as both the spiritual and educational leader, displaying a collaborative and visionary leadership style: 'The Principal's leadership of Sandford Christian College was probably the most significant contributory factor in the success of the school' (Twelves, 2005, p. 315).

Research of the type conducted by Dimmock and O'Donoghue (1997), Drysdale (2001, 2002) and Twelves (2005) provides wonderfully rich descriptions of how principals promote school success, but they are based on only six and seven case studies respectively, and hence suffer the limitations of this type of research, such as weaker external validity, and being less likely to contribute in a cumulative way to knowledge-building (Leithwood, 2005). However, there are also examples in the Australian successful school leadership literature of large-scale surveys, and high-number case study research, the type of research that Leithwood (2005) has called for to complement small-number case study research, to build a better understanding of school leadership effects. These studies differ from the earlier research of the ACER in that all of them specifically focus on school leadership.

LOLSO: Leadership for Organisational Learning and Student Outcomes

Mulford has an active research career spanning four decades in the areas of organisational development, educational leadership, school effectiveness and organisational learning (Mulford, 1986, 1994, 1996; Mulford, Conabere, & Keller, 1977; Mulford, Silins, & Leithwood, 2004). Throughout this time he has been a champion for the use of Australian educational research. For example, in 1977 Mulford, Conabere and Keller argued that the adoption of overseas initiatives, such as organisational development, without research on their applicability within the Australian context is fraught with danger. In the late 1990s, Mulford and Silins began an important research project to explore, on a large scale, the link between leadership and student outcomes (Mulford & Silins, 2003; Mulford et al., 2004), The *Leadership for Organisational Learning and Student Outcomes* (LOLSO) project involved surveys of 3,500 students and 2,500 teachers in 96 government secondary schools in two Australian states, South Australia and Tasmania (including all of the eight secondary schools in Tasmania at the time). The research demonstrated that leadership makes a difference in schools in an indirect manner — 'leadership contributes to organisational learning, which in turn influences what happens in the core business of school — the teaching and learning' (Mulford & Silins, 2003, p. 183). In the model developed from the survey analysis, 15 variables are included with principal leadership to show the indirect influence on student academic achievement. In the model, principal transformational leadership impacts on teacher leadership and administrative team leadership to influence organisational learning. Organisational learning influences teacher work, and through this, student participation and engagement, to ultimately impact on academic achievement. School size, home educational environment and socioeconomic status variously influenced the outcomes of this process. For example, larger school size negatively influenced principal transformational leadership, teacher leadership, and student participation, but positively influenced academic self-concept. Mulford (2008) notes that this model places much less emphasis on organisational, managerial and strategic elements, and more on dispersed leadership and organisational learning cultures; a marked contrast from the findings of *The Australian School Principal* study reported above.

AESOP (An Exceptional Schooling Outcomes Project)

Building on the growing interest in the importance of subject departments to the success of secondary schools (White, 2000, 2001), AESOP involved the study of 50 subject departments and cross-school programs (e.g., student welfare) across 38 secondary schools (Dinham, 2005, 2007). All were able to demonstrate outstanding educational outcomes over at least a 4-year period. Multiple-perspective interviews were used involving the principal, head teacher/leader of the outstanding department/program, staff group forum, student fora, parent forum, classroom observation and document analysis. While the focus of the research was on the outstanding faculties and teams, it found that principal leadership was a key to success. Principals promoted success through:

- external awareness and engagement with the wider environment
- a bias towards innovation and action
- high level interpersonal skills, and generally being well-liked and trusted
- having a clear vision, high expectations and fostering a culture of success
- encouraging teacher learning and responsibility, and showing trust
- promoting student support, developing common purpose and encouraging teacher collaboration
- having a core focus on students, learning and teaching.

This research highlighted the importance of the principal in 'providing the conditions where teachers can operate effectively and students can learn' (Dinham, 2005, p. 355). It is as Leithwood and colleagues stated in their review of the impact of school leadership on student outcomes: 'Educational leadership, our review also makes clear, comes from many sources, not just the "usual suspects" — superintendents and principals. But the usual suspects are likely still the most influential' (Leithwood et al., 2004, p. 70)

IDEAS (Initiating, Discovering, Envisioning, Actioning and Sustaining)

At the same time as the LOLSO and AESOP project were being conducted, a team from the University of Southern Queensland were refining school improvement ideas begun with a project in 1997 designed to explore how school-based management could be constructed to ensure it had a positive effect on classrooms (Andrews et al., 2004; Crowther, Kaagan, Ferguson, & Hann, 2002; Crowther, Ferguson, & Hann, 2009; Lewis & Andrews, 2007). In particular, the research has been concerned with establishing professional learning communities to improve school outcomes. IDEAS involves three components: a research-based framework for enhancing school outcomes that includes development of strategic foundations, cohesive community, appropriate infrastructure, schoolwide pedagogy, and professional learning; a five-phase school-based implementation strategy — initiating, discovering, envisioning, actioning and sustaining (IDEAS); and, parallel leadership in which the principal and teachers engage in mutualism (mutual trust and respect), a sense of shared purpose and an allowance of individual expression. IDEAS promotes teacher leadership, and defines the core roles of the principal to include: facilitating the development of a shared vision, creating cultural meaning through identity generation, supporting organisational alignment, distributing power and leadership and developing networks and external alliances. IDEAS has been shown to lead to improved school outcomes, although often this is more concerned with changes associated with teachers and teaching practice, rather than explicit evidence of improved student learning outcomes. For example, Lewis and Andrews (2007) describe the journey of one school, the 'dance of influence' that enabled the principal to fully develop a quality improvement model, and which led to increased teacher confidence, self-reflection and review, and the development of a professional learning community. Within the paper there is mention of improved student outcomes in terms of student exit outcomes (although no data were provided), but little further exploration of the impact of IDEAS on students. Lewis (2006) similarly describes the improvement journey of one school, but is again focused more on the changes to the work of teachers. There is reference to higher expectations by teachers of what students can achieve, and 'that improvements were evident in both behaviour levels and learning achievements' (Lewis, 2006, p. 113) but no evidence of this improvement was provided. Andrews et al. (2004) indicated that there is research that shows the effectiveness of IDEAS, although, again unfortunately, the detail of this evidence is scant. However, perhaps there is an explanation for this. IDEAS is essentially a framework for profound culture change in a school, and whether this impacts on student learning outcomes depends on what other aspects of a school change, For example, to improve literacy there needs to be appropriate teaching and learning, and there are many ways to do this. Implementing IDEAS will likely provide a leadership and professional learning environment that will allow changes in literacy teaching to have maximum impact.

Despite the lack of clarity in terms of the impact on student learning outcomes, IDEAS is a process that helps schools embark on major schoolwide change to teaching and learning. It works through the parallel leadership of teachers (focus on pedagogical development) and principals (focus on strategic development) combining to activate and integrate culture-building, organisationwide professional learning, and development of schoolwide pedagogy, which leads to school alignment and an enhanced school community capacity to improve school outcomes. In terms of understanding successful school leadership, its main contribution is to highlight the importance of principals in direction setting (as metastrategists), in supporting change and the work of teachers, and promoting a distributed view of leadership through the concept of teacher and parallel leadership.

The ISSPP in Australia

Drysdale, Gurr and Mulford have made an important contribution to the ISSPP through the production of nine case studies of Victorian schools (one independent K–12 school, four Catholic primary schools, two government primary schools, a government secondary school, and a government special school), five case studies of Tasmanian schools (all government primary or primary/lower secondary schools), and surveys of principals in Victoria and Tasmania. [Discussion of the case studies can be found in: Drysdale, 2007; Gurr, 2007a, 2008; Gurr & Drysdale, 2007, 2008; Gurr, Drysdale, & Mulford, 2006, 2007; Gurr et al., 2003; Gurr et al., 2006; Mulford & Johns, 2004. Tasmanian survey data have been reported in Ewington et al., (2008), and Mulford et al., 2008.] Across the eight countries that founded the ISSPP, it is the Australian group that has sought to use models to describe the findings (Gurr et al., 2003; Mulford & Johns, 2004), most notably through the model shown in Figure 17.1 and described more fully in Gurr, Drysdale & Mulford (2006).

In this model, principals exert an influence on broadly conceived student and school outcomes (Mulford, 2007a) through a focus on teaching and learning that is driven by their own values and vision, an agreed school vision, elements of transformational leadership (individual support and commitment, critical reflection, modelling of appropriate values, beliefs and behaviours), and increasing school capacity across four dimensions (personal, professional, organisational and community), taking into account and working within the school context, and using evidence-based monitoring and critical reflection to lead to change and transformation. The school capacities of level 2 each have four elements — what we have termed a four by four (4 × 4) approach to capacity building because a piece of 4 × 4 is a piece of wood that is used as a strong structural element in building:

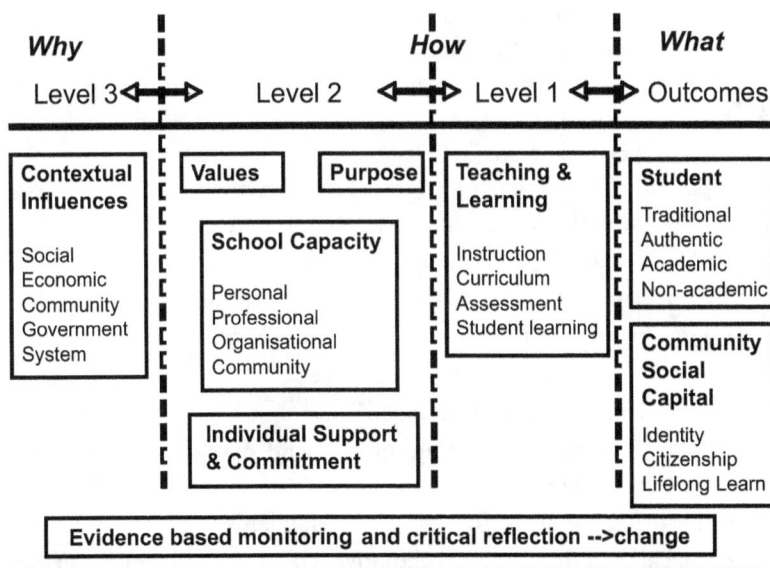

FIGURE 17.1
Simplified Australian model of successful principal leadership.

- *Personal capacity* — self-management,; professional networks, individual professional pedagogy, knowledge creation and construction
- *Professional capacity* — professional infrastructure, teachers as leaders, professional learning teams, schoolwide pedagogy
- *Organisational capacity* — distributed leadership, culture of organisational learning, organisational structures, building a safe environment
- *Community capacity* — social capital, community networks and alliances, parent–school partnerships, relationship marketing.

This model is complex but provides several useful conceptual frameworks to allow principals to locate their work. It indicates that principals can impact both directly and indirectly on student learning, but that the impact is mostly indirect in that they work with and through others to improve student and school outcomes.

Leading Australia's Schools

The principal stories from *Leading Australia's Schools* (Duignan & Gurr, 2007a) provide additional evidence of the qualities and characteristics of successful school leaders. While this book is not empirical research in the same sense as the previous writings, it is a rich collection of seventeen stories about the exhilaration of being a principal. A project of the Australian Council for Educational Leaders, it has been distributed in 2008 to every Australian school through the sponsorship of the Australian federal government. Principals were selected for inclusion based on a peer-review process.

Analysing the seventeen chapters, Duignan and Gurr (2007b, pp. 158–164) found that the principals seemed to have:

- a clearly articulated philosophy and deep moral purpose
- an unwavering focus on all students and their learning needs
- a passionate belief in the significance of what they do
- a commitment to making a difference
- a focus on, and valuing of, people
- strong support for learning, growth and development of themselves and others
- an expectation for high professional standards
- were able to develop a collaborative, collegial and inclusive school culture

- a view in which leadership was seen as service
- an attitude that hard work was accepted
- a 'can do' attitude to all that they did
- a high level of enjoyment and satisfaction from what they do.

It was also evident that these individuals had an orientation to life and work that helped them to be a principal (e.g., use of self-reflection, clear values, love of people), a love of and for learning, a strong sense of moral purpose for what they do, and an unwavering hope for a better future. These were aspects that we believed motivate the principals to love what they do.

Discussion and Conclusions

There is growing consensus about what successful school leadership looks like. We know from major international reviews of the field that the core elements are:

- building vision and setting direction
- understanding and developing people
- redesigning the organisation
- managing the teaching and learning program.

In addition, the ISSPP suggests that principals are good problem-solvers, can articulate worthwhile core values, build trust, focus on ensuring there is a safe and secure environment, are a visible part of the school, facilitate improvement in teaching practice, and they work well with the broader environment through coalition-building activities. *The Australian School Principal* study and the LOLSO project highlight the complexity of representing leadership, but they do so nearly 20 years apart. Comparing the two it becomes apparent that a contemporary view of school leadership is one where the leadership of the principal clearly remains important, a notion also confirmed by the AESOP and IDEAS projects. The personal and professional qualities required of principals, and the role complexity and ambiguity identified in the earlier study are still apparent in later research (e.g., Day, Harris, Hadfield, Tolley, & Beresford, 2000; Duignan, 2007). The research of Dimmock and O'Donoghue (1997), Drysdale (2001, 2002), Twelves (2005), the 14 Australian case studies of the ISSPP (and the more than 70 across the whole project), the case studies from the IDEAS project, and the 17 stories of principals in Duignan and Gurr (2007a), provide examples of outstanding principal leaders and the qualities and practices that they bring to their role.

But there are other dimensions that are important for school success. The LOLSO project promotes the leadership of the administrative team and teachers, and the concept of organisational learning. This combination of ideas is not dissimilar to the concept of professional learning communities promoted by Stoll and others (2007). The AESOP and IDEAS projects remind us that the focus in contemporary schools should not be only on principal leadership, as there are many other leaders in schools making significant contributions to school success (Crowther, Ferguson, & Hann, 2009; Crowther, Kaagan, Ferguson, & Hann, 2002; Dinham, 2005, 2007). The IDEAS project acknowledges the crucial role of principals in school improvement, but suggests that this must work in parallel with teacher leadership. Expanding this view of distributed leadership, all of the Australian principals in the ISSPP acknowledge the work of the teaching and non-teaching staff, the support of parents and the community, and the commitment of students in achieving extraordinary outcomes. A strength of the Australian model of successful school leadership from the ISSPP is that much of it can be used by those in other school leadership positions, especially those in middle-level student or teacher coordinating roles (White, 2001). For example, the 16 elements of the capacity-building section are relevant for most school leaders because an important aspect of leadership is working with people to help them to develop relevant capacities. In workshops with principals using the ideas drawn from the model in Figure 17.1, it has been found that the 4×4 aspect of the model is particularly useful to get a sense of where school resources are currently targeted to help staff improve, which areas need further development, and which areas school leaders think they can work with. (The research of White, 2001, clearly showed that work of middle-level school leaders is heavily dependent on how their roles are constructed; some are expected to be leaders while others have few expectations or opportunities to exercise leadership.)

In the next stage of the ISSPP, the original principals (where possible) will be revisited 5 years after the initial case study research to explore the sustainability of success. This will provide longitudinal and rich information about leadership and school success, and while the focus will still be on the principal, the original ISSPP research indicates that a broader view of leadership will be needed. Preliminary findings from the first of these case studies have indicated a very close relationship between the leadership of the principal and assistant principal, and development of strong teacher leadership teams (Goode, Drysdale, & Gurr, in press).

Figure 17.1 provides a sound base to conceptualise successful school leadership. By itself it is not sufficient, and the reviews of Leithwood and colleagues (Leithwood et al., 2006; Leithwood & Riehl, 2003, 2005; Leithwood et al., 2004), the complexity of the LOLSO model, and the contemporary ideas of professional learning communities and distributed leadership encapsulated in the work of the IDEAS project are needed to supplement it. It is also evident from the ongoing research of the ISSPP that it will be modified over time, and, in particular, developed further to account for different school situations. Nevertheless, the concern to engage with the context, the articulation of a range of capacities that can be developed in teachers by those in leadership roles, the focus on educational leadership and the use of broad outcome measures, supplemented by a focus on data literacy and transformational leadership, provides a complex yet manageable view of successful school leadership.

There are other avenues of productive research that may help our understanding of successful school leadership. Three areas of interest from the Australian literature are noted.

Australia is a country that is geographically large, with most of the relatively small population concentrated into eight major cities and coastal regions, and the remainder dispersed, often in small, rural and remote townships. This means that there are many small schools of fewer than 100 students in which the principal is also a teacher. There has been considerable interest in the past decade in researching about principals of small schools (e.g., Clarke & Wildy, 2004; Gilbert, Skinner, & Dempster, 2008; Jarzabkowski, 2003; Johns, Kilpatrick, Falk, & Mulford, 2001; Lester, 2003; Wildy & Clarke, 2005). This is an important context for school leadership, and one about which there is not enough known about how this context may alter conceptions of successful leadership (Leithwood, 2005). While there is research that has attempted to identify expectations of the characteristics and dispositions of principals that might lead to success in these settings (Ewington et al., 2008; Gilbert, Skinner, & Dempster, 2008), there is no study that has identified successful small schools and then sought to systematically explore how school leadership has contributed to this success.

At a systemic level, the now Victorian Department of Education and Early Childhood Development, has published both a review of system performance (Fraser & Petch, 2007) and a comprehensive and clearly articulated leadership framework (Office of Government School Education, 2007), within one of the most developed and developmental accountability frameworks in Australia (Gurr, 2007b; Office of Government School Education, 2008). It would be a relatively small step for this system to explore successful school leadership, as there is comprehensive data on school performance, and now there is an orientation to school leadership that can be 'measured' with a new 360-degree online survey tool (Department of Education and Early Childhood Development, 2008). While school systems do not often have the capacity to conduct the research required here, it is fascinating to witness this coalescing of a data-rich school environment, a developmental accountability framework, and a clearly articulated leadership framework and the temptation to explore the linkages (if any) across these.

And, of course, while exploring successful school leadership it is also worth considering what does not work. For example, Barnett, McCormick, and Connors (2001) argue that leadership does not always have a positive effect on student learning. Based on research in 12 randomly selected secondary schools in New South Wales, they found that visionary leadership resulted in more distractions from core tasks associated with the teaching and learning program, and therefore had the potential to suppress student learning outcomes. That leadership can have a negative impact is not new. For example, in experimental studies of anonymous groups in group support system environments (an example is an electronically mediated brainstorming activity) leadership results in lower outcomes (Avolio, Kahai, & Dodge, 2000). The lesson from these findings is that we should not automatically assume that our leadership models and ideas work well in all contexts.

It would be unfortunate to end this chapter on a negative note. There is a growing interest in successful school leadership in the Australian context. The Australian Council for Educational Research, for example, is producing a series of books in which they link an outstanding practitioner with an educational researcher (Anderson & Cawsey, 2008; Fleming & Kleinhenz, 2007), as well as several publications describing Australian and overseas research on outstanding educational practice (Caldwell & Harris, 2008; Dinham, 2008). The recent publication by Australian Council for Educational Leaders (ACEL) of

Leading Australia's Schools highlights the outstanding work of principals, and, importantly, suggests that this role is within the capabilities of many teachers in schools. The IDEAS project continues to develop as indicated by the 2009 book of Crowther, Ferguson and Hann. The continuing research of the ISSPP will be important, not only for understanding successful school leadership in Australia and attempting to conceptualise this in terms of models accessible to practitioners and policymakers, but also for the link with the more than fourteen countries currently involved (the project continues to grow and to attract more countries).

References

Anderson, M., & Cawsey, C. (2008). *Learning for leadership*. Melbourne, Australia: ACER.

Andrews, D., Conway, J., Dawson, M., Lewis, M., McMaster, J., Morgan, A., & Starr, H. (2004). School revitalisation the IDEAS way, *Monograph, 34*. Melbourne, Australia: Australian Council for Educational Leaders.

Avolio, B.J., Kahai, S., & Dodge, G.E. (2000). E-leadership: Implications for theory, research, and practice. *Leadership Quarterly, 11*(4), 615–668.

Badcock, A.M. (1977). *Combinations of Effective Leadership Styles as Related to the Two Task Areas of Principal and Deputy Principal in Victorian High Schools*. Unpublished doctoral dissertation, the University of Melbourne.

Barnett, K., McCormick, J., & Connors, R. (2001). Transformational leadership in schools, panacea, placebo or problem? *Journal of Educational Administration, 39*(1), 24–46.

Bassett, G.W., Crane, A.R., & Walker, W.G. (1963). *Headmasters for better schools*. St Lucia, Queensland: University of Queensland Press.

Bassett, G.W., Crane, A.R., & Walker, W.G. (1967). *Headmasters for better schools* (2nd ed.). St Lucia, Queensland: University of Queensland Press.

Beare, H., Caldwell B.J., & Millikan, R.H. (1989). *Creating an excellent school*. London: Routledge.

Caldwell, B.J. (1986). *Effective resource allocation in schools project: A summary of studies in Tasmania and South Australia*. Hobart, Australia: Centre for Education, University of Tasmania.

Caldwell, B.J., & Harris J. (2008). *Why not the best schools? What we have learned from outstanding schools around the world*. Melbourne, Victoria, Australia: ACER Press.

Caldwell, B.J., & Spinks, J.M. (1987). A model for policy-making and change management in schools. In W.S. Simpkins, A.R. Thomas & E.B. Thomas (Eds.), *Principal and change: The Australian experience*. Armidale, New South Wales, Australia: University of New England.

Caldwell, B.J., & Spinks, J.M. (1988). *The self-managing school*. London: The Falmer Press.

Caldwell, B.J., & Spinks J.M. (1992). *Leading the self-managing school.* London: The Falmer Press.

Caldwell, B.J., & Spinks J.M. (1999). *Beyond the self-managing school.* London: The Falmer Press.

Clarke, S., & Wildy, H. (2004). Context counts: Viewing small school leadership from the inside out. *Journal of Educational Administration, 42*(5), 555–572.

Crowther, F., Kaagan, S., Ferguson, M., & Hann, L. (2002). *Developing teacher leaders.* Thousand Oaks, CA: Corwin Press.

Crowther, F., Ferguson, M., & Hann, L. (2009). *Developing teacher leaders* (2nd ed.). Thousand Oaks, CA: Corwin Press.

Day, C., Harris, A., Hadfield, M., Tolley, H., & Beresford ,J. (2000). *Leading schools in times of change.* Buckingham, England: Open University Press.

Deal, T.E., & Kennedy, A.A. (1983). Culture and school performances, *Educational Leadership, 40*(5), 14–15.

Department of Education and Early Childhood Development. (2008). iLead 360 degree survey. Retrieved November 24, 2008, from www.education.vic.gov.au/proflearning/schoolleadership/Developmental_Learning_Framework.htm

Dimmock, C., & O'Donoghue, T. (1997). *Innovative school principals and restructuring. Life history portraits of successful managers of change.* London: Routledge.

Dinham, S. (2005). Principal leadership for outstanding educational outcomes. *Journal of Educational Administration, 43*(4), 338–356.

Dinham, S. (2007). The secondary head of department and the achievement of exceptional student outcomes. *Journal of Educational Administration, 45*(1), 62–79.

Dinham, S. (2008). *How to get your school moving and improving.* Melbourne, Australia: ACER Press.

Drysdale, L. (2001). Towards a model of market centred leadership. *Leading and Managing, 7*(1), 76–89.

Drysdale, L. (2002). A study of marketing and market orientation in selected Victorian Schools of the Future. Unpublished doctoral dissertation, the University of Melbourne.

Drysdale, L. (2007). Making a difference. In P. Duignan & D. Gurr (Eds.), *Leading Australia's schools* (pp. 132–138). Sydney, Australia: ACEL and DEST.

Drysdale, L., Goode, H., & Gurr, D. (in press). Successful school leadership: Moving from success to sustainability. *Journal of Educational Administration.*

Duignan, P. (1987). The culture of school effectiveness. In W.S. Simpkins, A.R. Thomas & E.B. Thomas, E.B. (Eds.), *Principal and change: The Australian experience.* Armidale, New South Wales: University of New England.

Duignan, P. (2007). *Educational leadership: Key challenges and ethical tensions.* Cambridge: Cambridge University Press.

Duignan, P., & Gurr, D. (Eds.). (2007a). *Leading Australia's schools.* Sydney, Australia: ACEL and DEST.

Duignan, P., & Gurr, D. (2007b). Hope for a better future. In P. Duignan & D. Gurr, *Leading Australia's Schools* (pp. 157–164). Sydney, Austarlia: ACEL and DEST.

Duignan, P., Marshall, A.R., Harrold, R.I., Phillipps, D.M., Thomas, E.B., & Lane, T.J. (1985). *The Australian school principal: A summary report.* Canberra, Australia: Commonwealth Schools Commission.

Ewington, J., Mulford, B., Kendall, D., Edmunds, B., Kendall, L., & Silins, H. (2008). Successful school principalship in small schools. *Journal of Educational Administration, 46*(5), 545–561.

Fleming, J., & Kleinhenz, E. (2007). *Towards a Moving School: Developing a professional learning and performance culture.* Melbourne, Australia: ACER Press.

Fraser D., & Petch J. (2007). *School improvement: A theory of action.* Melbourne, Australia: Office of School Education, Department of Education and Early Childhood Development.

Gilbert, C.C., Skinner, J., & Dempster, N. (2008). Expectations of successful female small school principals. *Leading and Managing, 14*(1), 72–91.

Gurr, D. (2007a). We can be the best. In P. Duignan & D. Gurr (Eds.), *Leading Australia's Schools* (pp. 124–131). Sydney, Australia: ACEL and DEST.

Gurr, D. (2007b). Diversity and progress in school accountability systems in Australia. *Educational Research for Policy and Practice, 6*(3), 165–186.

Gurr, D. (2008). Principal leadership: What does it do, what does it look like, and how might it evolve? *Monograph, 42.* Melbourne, Australia: Australian Council for Educational Leaders.

Gurr, D., & Drysdale, L. (2007). Models of successful school leadership: Victorian case studies. In K. Leithwood & C. Day (Eds.), *Successful school leadership in times of change* (pp. 39–58). Toronto, Canada: Springer.

Gurr, D., & Drysdale, L. (2008). Reflections on twelve years of studying the leadership of Victorian schools. *International Studies in Education Administration, 36*(2), 22–37.

Gurr, D., Drysdale, L., Di Natale, E., Ford, P., Hardy, R., & Swann, R. (2003). Successful school leadership in Victoria: Three case studies. *Leading and Managing, 9*(1), 18–37.

Gurr, D., Drysdale, L., & Mulford, B. (2006). Models of successful principal leadership. *School Leadership and Management, 26*(4), 371–395.

Gurr, D., Drysdale, L., & Mulford, B. (2007). Instructional leadership in three Australian schools. *International Studies in Educational Administration, 35*(3), 20–29.

Gurr D., Drysdale, L., Swann, R., Doherty, J., Ford, P., & Goode, H. (2006). The international successful school principalship project (ISSPP): Comparison across country case studies. In L. Smith & D. Riley (Eds.), *New waves of leadership* (pp. 36–50). Sydney, Australia: ACEL.

Gurr, D., & Duignan, P. (2007). Leading Australia's schools. In P. Duignan & D. Gurr (Eds.), *Leading Australia's schools* (pp. 5–12). Sydney, Austarlia: ACEL and DEST.

Hallinger, P., & Heck, R. H. (1998). Exploring the principals' contribution to school effectiveness: 1980–1995, *School Effectiveness and School Improvement, 9*(2), 157–191.

Jarzabkowski, L. (2003). Teacher collegiality in a remote Australian school. *Journal of Research in Rural Education, 18*(3), 139–144.

Johns, S., Kilpatrick, S., Falk, I., & Mulford, B. (2001). *School contribution to rural communities: Leadership issues.* Hobart, Australia: University of Tasmania.

Kilpatrick, S., Johns, S., Mulford, B., Falk. I., & Prescott, L. (2002). *More than an education: Leadership for rural school-community partnerships.* Launceston, Tasmania, Australia: Rural Industries Research and Development Corporation.

Lakomski, G. (2005). *Managing without leadership.* Oxford: Elsevier.

Leithwood, K. (2005). Understanding successful principal leadership: Progress on a broken front. *Journal of Educational Administration, 43*(6), 619–629.

Leithwood, K., & Day, C. (Eds.). (2007a). *Successful school leadership in times of change.* Toronto, Canada: Springer.

Leithwood, K., & Day, C. (2007b). What we learned: A broad view. In K. Leithwood & C. Day (Eds.), *Successful school leadership in times of change* (pp. 189–203). Toronto, Canada: Springer.

Leithwood, K., Day, C., Sammons, P., Harris, A., & Hopkins, D. (2006). *Seven strong claims about successful school leadership.* Nottingham, England: National College of School Leadership.

Leithwood, K., & Riehl, C. (2003). *What do we already know about successful school leadership?* Paper prepared for the AERA Division, a Task Force on Developing Research in Educational Leadership.

Leithwood, K., & Riehl, C. (2005). What we know about successful school leadership. In W. Firestone & C. Riehl (Eds.), *A new agenda: Directions for research on educational leadership* (pp. 22–47). New York: Teachers College Press.

Leithwood, K., Seashore Louis, K.A., Anderson, S., & Wahlstrom, K. (2004). *How leadership influences student learning.* New York: The Wallace Foundation.

Lester, N.C. (2003). Primary leadership in small rural school communities. *Leading & Managing, 9*(1), 85–99.

Lewis, M. (2006). It's a different place now: Teacher leadership and pedagogical change at Newlyn Public School. *Leading and Managing, 12*(1), 107–120.

Lewis, M., & Andrews, D. (2007). The dance of influence: Professional relationships evolve as teachers and administrators engage in whole school renewal. *Leading and Managing, 13*(1), 91–107.

Lipham, J.M. (1981). *Effective principal, effective school.* Reston, VA: National Association of Secondary Schools.

McGaw, B., Piper, K., Banks, D., & Evans, B. (1993a). *Improving Australia's schools: Executive summary of making schools more effective*. Melbourne, Australia: ACER.

McGaw, B., Piper, K., Banks, D., & Evans, B. (1993b). *Making schools more effective: Report of the Australian effective schools project*. Melbourne, Australia: ACER.

Møller, J., & Fuglestad, O.L. (Eds.). (2006). *Leadership in recognized schools*. Oslo, Norway: Universitetsforlaget.

Mulford, B. (1986). *Indicators of school effectiveness: A practical approach (Monograph, No. 2)*. Melbourne, Australia: Australian Council for Educational Administration.

Mulford, B. (1994). *Shaping tomorrow's schools* (Monograph No. 15). Melbourne: Australian Council for Educational Administration.

Mulford, B. (1996). Do principals make a difference? Recent evidence and implications. *Leading and Managing, 2*(3), 155–170.

Mulford, B. (2007a). *Overview of research on Australian educational leadership 2001– 2005*. (Monograph, 40). Melbourne, Australia: Australian Council for Educational Leaders.

Mulford, B. (2007b). Successful school leadership: What is it and who decides? *Australian Journal of Education, 51*(3), 228–246.

Mulford, B. (2008). The leadership challenge: Improving learning in schools. *Australian Education Review, 53*.

Mulford, B., Conabere, A., & Keller, J. (1977). Organisational development in schools: Early data on the Australian experience. *Journal of Educational Administration, 15*(2), 210–237.

Mulford, B., & Johns, S. (2004). Successful school principalship. *Leading and Managing, 10*(1), 45–76.

Mulford, B., Kendall, D., Edmunds, B., Kendall, L., Ewington, J., & Silins, H. (2007). Successful school leadership: What is it and who decides? *Australian Journal of Education, 51*(3), 228–246.

Mulford, B., Kendall, L., Kendall, D. Edmunds, B. Ewington, J., & Silins, H. (2008). Successful school principalship and decision-making. *Leading and Managing, 14*(1), 60–71.

Mulford, B., & Silins, H. (2003). Leadership for organisational learning and improved student outcomes. *Cambridge Journal of Education, 33*(2), 175–195.

Mulford, W., Silins, H., & Leithwood, K. (2004). *Educational leadership for organisational learning and improved student outcomes*. Dordrecht, Netherlands: Kluwer Academic.

Office of Government School Education. (2007). *The developmental learning framework for school leaders*. Melbourne, Australia: Department of Education and Early Childhood Development.

Office of Government School Education. (2008). *Accountability and improvement framework for Victorian government schools 2008*. Melbourne, Australia: Department of Education and Early Childhood Development.

Peters, T.J., & Waterman, R.H. (1982). *In search of excellence.* New York: Harper and Row.

Purkey, S.C. & Smith, M.S. (1983). Effective schools: A review. *The Elementary School Journal, 83*(3), 426–452.

Raihani, & Gurr, D. (2006). Value-driven school leadership: An Indonesian perspective. *Leading and Managing, 12*(1), 121–134.

Robinson, V. (2007). *School leadership and student outcomes: Identifying what works and why (Monograph No. 41).* Melbourne, Australia: Australian Council for Educational Leaders.

Simpkins, W.S., Thomas, A.R., & Thomas, E.B. (Eds.). (1982). *Principal & task: An Australian perspective.* Armidale, Australia: University of New England.

Simpkins, W.S., Thomas, A.R., & Thomas, E.B. (Eds.). (1987). *Principal and change: The Australian experience.* Armidale, Australia: University of New England.

Stoll, L., & Louis, K.S. (Eds.). (2007). *Professional learning communities: Divergence, depth and dilemmas.* Berkshire, England: Open University Press.

Thomas, E.B. (Ed.). (1994). *What every principal needs to know about leadership skills.* Point Lonsdale, Australia: Professional Reading Guide for School Administrators.

Thomas, E.B. (Ed.). (1995). *What every principal needs to know about good schools.* Point Lonsdale, Australia: Professional Reading Guide for School Administrators.

Thomas, A.R. (Ed.). (2000). *Challenges of the principalship.* Point Lonsdale, Australia: Professional Reading Guide for School Administrators.

Twelves, J.B. (2005). Putting them in the hands of god: A successful Christian school in Australia. Unpublished doctoral dissertation, the University of Melbourne.

Walker, W.G. (ed.). (1966). *The principal at work: Case studies in school administration.* St Lucia, Queensland, Australia: University of Queensland Press.

White, P.W. (2000). The leadership role of curriculum area middle managers in selected Victorian government secondary schools. Unpublished doctoral dissertation, the University of Melbourne.

White, P. (2001). The leadership of curriculum area middle managers in Victorian government secondary schools. *Leading and Managing, 7*(2), 131–150.

Wildy, H., & Clarke, S. (2005). Leading a small rural school: The case study of a novice principal. *Leading and Managing, 11*(1), 43–56.

Wildy, H., & Clarke, S. (2008). ACEL *Monograph No. 40*: What counts as evidence? It depends ... *Leading and Managing, 14*(1), 92–98.

▶▶▶◀◀◀

CHAPTER 18

Leadership for Student Achievement[1]

Steve Dinham

> Leadership matters and is changing ... School leadership needs to be smart; it needs to be evidence-based and shared. (Mulford, 2008, p. 69)

> Ask anyone who has had one or more years working in a school whether leadership has made a difference in their work and the answer will be an unhesitating 'Yes'. No matter who the respondent is ... they all seem to know good (and bad) leadership when they experience it. (Wahlstrom & Louis, 2008, p. 459)

> I ... advance the following three arguments. First, leadership matters ... Second, leadership is inclusive ... Third, leadership practices can be taught and learned. (Reeves, 2008, p. 3)

> The more leaders focus their influence, their learning, and their relationships with teachers on the core business of teaching and learning, the greater their influence on student outcomes. (Robinson, Lloyd & Rowe, 2008, p. 636)

Today, the prime focus for any educational leader must be on the academic, personal and social advancement of his or her students.[2] Everything done in a school should be geared to impact in some way on facilitating student achievement, the true core business of teachers and schools. This reality has been reflected in increased expectations and pressures placed on educational leaders to lift school, teacher and student performance, matters for which they are increasingly being held accountable.

However, this was not always the case, and for a long time the prevailing view was that schools made little difference to student achievement, which was believed to be largely the result of innate ability and socioeconomic background (Reynolds, Teddlie, Creemers, Scheerens, & Townsend, 2000). In other words, every student had his or her personal glass ceiling in respect to possible achievement and the best that schools could do was to help students reach this predetermined level. Today that view has been powerfully refuted. We know from comprehensive international research that while home, family and socioeconomic background factors are important influences — schools, and in particular, the classroom teacher, do have significant influence on student achievement (see Hattie, 2003, 2007; Marzano, 2003; Marzano, Pickering, & Pollock, 2005; Bransford et al., 2000).

This chapter briefly reviews the research evidence on student achievement, especially meta-analytic effect size research (see Glass, 1976), and what contributes most to student learning. Research evidence on successful teaching and effective school leadership is then examined. From this, a model outlining four fundamentals of student achievement and the implications of this for schools and educational leaders is provided.

While there are no recipes for instant success or 'quick fixes', and 'lifting up' and 'turning around' a school are not easy, the evidence shows that it can be done. Thus there are valuable lessons to be learned from the histories of successful schools, educational leaders and teachers.

What We Have Learned About Student Achievement

Following on from earlier views that student ability was largely innate and fixed and that schools make little difference to student achievement, there has been considerable research into effective schools and effective teachers and teaching, such that the evidence today is incontrovertible that schools and teachers do have a major influence on student learning and development.

Major international meta-analytic studies such as those led by Professor John Hattie at the University of Auckland (2003) have shown that around 50% of the variance in student achievement is attributable to what each student 'brings to the table', especially their prior achievement. Homes account for another 5 to 10% of the variance in student achievement, including factors such as expectations and encouragement over and above that 'feeding' into the initial 50% of variance. Schools account for another 5 to 10% of the variance. This includes matters such as school finances, buildings, resources and procedures. It is generally taken that the influence of school principals is largely indirect and accounted for by the school-level variance. Peer effects account for another 5 to 10% of the variance. Classroom teachers are, however, the major in-school influence on student achievement, accounting for about 30% of the variance. Wright, Horn and Sanders (1997, p. 63) have noted:

... the most important factor affecting student learning is the teacher ... the immediate and clear implication of this finding is that seemingly more can be done to improve education by improving the effectiveness of teachers than by any other single factor.

It is for this reason that there has been such a focus on quality teaching over the past two decades. However, research evidence is also clear on two related factors. Firstly, it takes time, learning and effort to develop from a 'novice' to an 'expert' teacher, and not all teachers become experts. Secondly, flowing from this, we also know that teacher expertise varies considerably, including within schools (see Berliner, 2004).

Thus, it is not socioeconomic background in terms of innate ability that we should concern ourselves with, but using leadership and quality teaching to overcome socioeconomic disadvantage. It is a telling, universal finding that overall, there is more variation in student achievement *within* schools than *between* schools. A quality teacher in every classroom is thus the major equity issue in education today. Education remains a powerful driver of individual learning, growth and development, opportunity and of individual and societal health and prosperity (Dinham, Ingvarson, & Kleinhenz, 2008).

The broad conclusions that can be drawn from extensive meta-analytic research on student achievement such as that by Hattie (2003, 2007) can be summarised as follows:

- The quality of the teacher and the quality of his or her teaching are major influences on student achievement, along with the individual student and his or her prior achievement (all have large effect sizes[3]).
- School-based influences (beyond the classroom) have weaker effects on student achievement than those within the classroom.
- Structural and organisational arrangements (e.g., 'open' versus 'traditional' classrooms, multi-age versus age-graded classes, ability grouping, gender, class size, mainstreaming) have negligible or small effects on student learning. It is the quality of teaching that occurs within these structural arrangements which is important.
- Examples of 'active teaching' (e.g., reciprocal teaching, feedback, teaching self-verbalisation, metacognition strategies, direct instruction, mastery learning, testing) have large to moderate effects on student achievement.

- Effect sizes are negligible or small for 'facilitory' teaching (e.g., simulations and games, inquiry-based teaching, individualised instruction, problem-based learning, differentiated teaching for boys and girls, web-based learning, whole language reading, inductive teaching).

- Literacy is the foundation of student achievement. Strategies to promote and remediate literacy figure prominently in Hattie's full list of 100 effects on student learning.

- While socioeconomic status and home environment do have effects on student achievement (each ranked 22nd on Hattie's list of 100 effect sizes, ES = .57), this influence is outweighed by the quality of teaching students receive in the classroom (ES = .77).

It must be recognised that there is not a level playing field in either education or life. Schooling still reflects and reinforces many social and economic divisions, and students, after all, spend less than 15% of their time in school. Socioeconomic status and family background still exert powerful influences, not, as noted, on innate student ability or capacity, but on advantage, expectations, role-modelling, support, opportunities and life choices.

In the highest performing nations, however, socioeconomic factors have less influence on student achievement than in Australia, once again pointing to the importance of quality teaching. In a paper for the Business Council of Australia, Lawrence Ingvarson, Elizabeth Kleinhenz and I noted (2008, p. 10):

> Although Australia performs well on international measures of student achievement such as PISA (the OECD's Programme for International Student Assessment involving 400,000 15-year-olds in 57 countries), there are concerns over equity. Many students in Australia continue to struggle, including Indigenous students, where the performance gap with non-Indigenous students remains wide. Students' social backgrounds have a greater influence on educational results in Australia than in higher performing countries such as Finland and Canada.

Leadership Makes a Difference

The crucial importance of the teacher to student learning has been confirmed. The challenge for any educational leader is to make things happen within individual classrooms. Wahlstrom and Louis have commented (2008, p. 459): 'In the current era of accountability, a principal's responsibility for the quality of teachers' work is simply a fact of life. How to achieve influence over work settings (classrooms) in which they rarely participate is a key dilemma.'

Despite the small measured effect sizes for school-based factors beyond the classroom (Hattie, 2007), research evidence has confirmed that 'school leaders can play major roles in creating the conditions in which teachers can teach effectively and students can learn' (Dinham, 2008a, p. 15).

Some, however, have suggested that because of its 'messy', indirect influences, the effect of leadership on student achievement has actually been underestimated (see Dinham, 2007a; Reeves, 2008). Leithwood, Louis, Anderson. and Wahlstrom (2004, p. 5), in reviewing the research literature on leadership and school achievement, found: '[t]he total (direct and indirect) effects of leadership on student learning account for about a quarter of total school effects', and that:

- Leadership is second only to classroom instruction among all school-related factors that contribute to what students learn at school.
- Leadership effects are usually largest where and when they are needed most [i.e., in the most challenging schools and circumstances].

Today, leadership is seen as central and essential to delivering the changes, improvement and performance that society increasingly expects of all organisations, including schools. What has become clear is that leadership, including educational leadership, is a more contentious, complex, situated and dynamic phenomenon than thought previously.

The study of leadership has been through many phases and fashions, with various idealistic, empirical, theoretical and ideological stances: trait versus process leadership, assigned versus emergent leadership, bureaucratic versus charismatic leadership, administration/management versus leadership, transactional versus transformation leadership, universal versus contextual/contingent leadership, 'born' versus 'learned' leadership, command versus relationships, line management versus distributed leadership and so forth (Dinham, 2007b).

Changes in how educational leadership has been conceptualised and enacted reflect a number of realities: that teaching and learning, rather than management, should be the prime focus of the school; that principals cannot bear all the burden of school management and leadership due to increasing pressures and demands being placed upon them and their schools, and that the contribution of 'other' (nonprincipal) leadership to school functioning and student achievement has tended to be overlooked or undervalued (see Gronn, 2002; Spillane, Halverson, & Diamond 2001). While the administrative and management functions of the school leader are important and are not going to go away — and many would argue are increasing due to increased responsibilities and accountability — leaders need to find the time and means to focus on improving the quality of teaching and learning within their schools.

There is also the issue of leadership succession, especially when leaders who have attempted to keep leadership power largely to themselves depart (see Hargreaves & Fink, 2004; Lambert, 1998). However, as will be seen later in this chapter, effective, 'authoritative' leaders cede leadership power to others and seek to develop mature, confident, autonomous professionals. In effect, they seek to make themselves redundant. In contrast, 'authoritarian' leaders tend to hold power closely and infantilise their subordinates, who can become dependent upon them, resulting in a leadership vacuum when such leaders leave (Dinham & Scott, 2008).

Today, it is widely recognised that while the principal is the *key* leader in a school, they are not the *only* leader, and there are real benefits from sharing, empowering and fostering the leadership of others, something which has come to be known as distributed leadership (see Gronn, 2002; Harris, 2004; Spillane, 2006). Rather than traditional line management with delegation of tasks and responsibilities, distributed leadership is about leaders recognising and acknowledging the capacities of others and encouraging and entrusting people to assume responsibility and to provide leadership in a particular area.

Distributive leadership should not be confused with distributing 'jobs'. It is less about this (formal leaders shedding responsibility) and more about releasing human potential (sharing power and developing capacity). While distributed leadership is often conceptualised as resulting from the actions of leaders ('top down'), distributed leadership can also arise from the spontaneous actions of those in various parts of the organisation taking the lead on a particular issue or problem ('bottom up'). However, most accounts of distributed leadership (and educational change generally) recognise the need for both 'top down' and 'bottom up' commitment and action if distributed leadership is to be successful.

Although the concept of distributed leadership can be traced back to social psychology in the 1950s, it is only in the last decade or so that the concept has achieved widespread prominence (see Gronn, 2002). With the growing enthusiasm for distributed leadership, which has intrinsic appeal, there have been concerns expressed over loose definition, varying approaches, measuring effects, and seeing distributed leadership as a 'quick fix' or panacea. Some have noted the need for questioning and evidence to temper enthusiasm and 'faddism' in this area (see Harris, 2004, 2005; Leithwood et al., 2004; Leithwood & Mascall, 2008; York-Barr & Duke, 2004).

Despite concerns over the effectiveness of various forms of distributed leadership mentioned above, overall, there is growing recognition that there is unreleased and unrealised leadership potential and capacity for improvement residing in educational organisations and that leaders can play a key role in unlocking this (Crowther, Kaagan, Ferguson, & Hann, 2002; York-Barr & Duke, 2004).

Later is this chapter it will be seen how leaders in successful schools and faculties help to create environments in which teachers can teach and students can learn, but first we need to briefly consider successful teaching and what lies behind it, if we are going to understand the links between leadership and student learning.

What Successful Teaching Looks Like in One Context

In the late 1990s, Paul Ayres, Wayne Sawyer and I undertook a study of successful teaching at the New South Wales Higher School Certificate (NSW HSC) on behalf of the NSW Department of Education and Training (DET) (see Ayres, Dinham, & Sawyer, 1998, 1999, 2000, 2004; Dinham & Sawyer, 2004; Sawyer, Ayres, & Dinham, 2001).

The full methodology and findings for the study are available elsewhere (see Ayres et al., 2000). In summary, teachers had been identified from confidential data because of their success in helping students perform in the top 1% in statewide HSC examinations over at least a 5-year period. These teachers (n = 25) were drawn from all subject areas across NSW government secondary (Years 7 to 12) and central schools (Years K to 12). Various external and internal mechanisms were used to select teachers who achieved success, both across the state and in comparison to other teachers in their school working with the same students.

Teachers were observed teaching senior classes and were interviewed, as were some of their students, faculty heads, other school executive and fellow teachers. We also spent time in staff rooms and were able to observe these teachers' actions and interactions with students and staff. We also examined various faculty documents and resources.

As a result of this process, seven broad factors were identified as contributing to HSC teaching success:

- school background
- subject faculty
- teachers' personal qualities
- relationships with students
- teachers' professional development.
- resources and planning
- teaching strategies.

In summary, these teachers were genuinely expert in their subject area(s), and clearly enjoyed teaching. Although a wide range of teaching strategies were observed, the key common factor was an emphasis on having students think, solve problems and apply knowledge. These teachers consciously built understanding and connected students' work to previous work, work that was yet to come and events in the broader environment. Frequent assessment and quality feedback were hallmarks of these teachers (Dinham, 2008b). Rather than teaching to the HSC, these teachers saw their role as challenging students beyond the demands of the HSC.

Mutual respect, confidence and high expectations were features of classroom lessons observed. Good relationships and positive classroom climate were also universally observed.

Assisted note-building, ownership of note-making and economic use of class time were other features of their teaching. Despite the competitive nature of the HSC, the use of group work and cooperative learning was more common than might have been expected.

While the HSC was a constant presence in the classrooms of these teachers, what was observed was broadly consistent with our understanding of quality teaching gained from other research. Consistent with the literature, quality teaching was found to be the major in-school factor in the success of these students, although other faculty and school factors were important.

Personal qualities, experience, deep content knowledge, strong pedagogic knowledge, understanding of the HSC and its requirements, and use of appropriate and effective teaching strategies all led to teacher effectiveness and student achievement. Again, these findings are consistent with the broader literatures on student achievement and effective or quality teaching.

We will now consider how leadership can be exercised to create a situation in which teacher learning, quality teaching and student success can occur.

School Leadership for Student Success

AESOP (*An Exceptional Schooling Outcomes Project*) grew from the previous successful HSC teaching project and was a much larger study funded by the Australian Research Council. It was carried out by staff from the University of Western Sydney, the University of New England and the NSW DET. Unlike the HSC study, where the focus was on individual teachers and the HSC (Years 11 and 12), AESOP focused on faculties and teams responsible for producing exceptional student outcomes in Years 7 to 10 in NSW public central schools (Years K to 10 and K to 12) and secondary schools (Years 7 to 12).

Rather than concentrating on academic achievement alone, the project defined exceptional educational achievement using the rubric of the three, interrelated domains or principles outlined in the *Adelaide Declaration on National Goals for Schooling in the Twenty-first Century* (Ministerial Council on Education, Employment, Training and Youth Affairs [MCEETYA], 1999). The domains are that schools should:

- 'develop fully the talents of all students'
- attain 'high standards of knowledge, skills and understanding through a comprehensive and balanced curriculum'
- be 'socially just'.

Once again, full details on methodology are provided elsewhere (see Dinham, 2007c) but briefly, research sites selected as possibly achieving exceptional student outcomes were of two types: faculties or departments responsible for teaching certain subjects in Years 7 to 10 (approximately 80% of sites), and teams responsible for certain cross-school programs in Years 7 to 10, such as Student Welfare (approximately 20%). Fifty sites were studied in a broadly representative sample of 38 secondary and central schools across the state.

There were surprises in the findings. The HSC study had revealed the importance of faculties and teams in individual teacher success. AESOP, a study of faculties and teams producing exceptional student outcomes, revealed the key influence of leadership inside — but also outside these faculties and teams — in creating an environment where teachers could teach and students could learn. While the AESOP study was not focused on the role of the principal, examination of the factors responsible for the success of faculties and teams revealed the key influence principals had made and were making to this achievement. (Heads of faculties and leaders of program teams, along with other school leaders, shared many of the characteristics and approaches detailed below, although the discussion here focuses on the principal.)

Principals possessed and demonstrated two broad characteristics: they were aware of and *responsive* to people and events around them and, through high standards and expectations, they were *demanding*, both of themselves and others: essentially, they 'give a lot, and expect a lot' (Dinham, 2005). Briefly (see Dinham, 2005, 2007c), these principals were able to foster exceptional educational achievement in Years 7 to 10 through a variety of means and as result of possessing certain attributes.

EXTERNAL AWARENESS AND ENGAGEMENT
These principals are open to change and opportunity and are outward- rather than inward-looking; they derive benefits for their school from being in the forefront of mandated change and develop productive external linkages inside and outside the educational system; they are entrepreneurial and efficiently mobilise community, financial and other support.

A BIAS TOWARDS INNOVATION AND ACTION
These principals fully use their discretionary powers and 'bend the rules' on occasion. They are often groundbreakers, some appearing to act on the dictum that 'it is easier to gain forgiveness than permission'. They exhibit a bias towards experimentation and risk-taking and are prepared to embrace change, even when things appear to be going well. They support others proposing initiatives and are willing to invest money and time while risking failure. They empower others, encapsulated in the expression 'let's give it a go'.

PERSONAL QUALITIES AND RELATIONSHIPS

These leaders have positive attitudes that are contagious and they motivate others through example. They realise negativity can be self-handicapping and their positive approach helps the school to keep moving and improving. They demonstrate a high degree of intellectual capacity and imagination, are astute, and are good judges of people. They balance the big picture with finer detail and can deal with many issues concurrently. They know when to consult and when to be decisive and courageous.

These principals are authentic leaders, exhibiting the values, professionalism and behaviour they expect of others. They are effective communicators and listen to and assist staff. They provide prompt and appropriate feedback, both good and bad. They treat staff professionally, provide (and demand) a professional working environment and expect a high degree of professionalism in return. Others 'don't want to let the boss down'. These leaders are generally liked, respected and trusted, although inevitably, not by all.

They demonstrate humour, empathy and compassion and are seen to work for the betterment of the school, teachers and students, rather than for themselves, while being unmistakeably in control.

VISION, EXPECTATIONS AND A CULTURE OF SUCCESS

These principals 'give a lot and expect a lot'. They communicate clear, agreed, high standards and take every opportunity to recognise students and staff. They relentlessly 'talk up the school' and reinforce where the school is attempting to go.

They espouse the power of education for social change and find ways for all students to experience success. Their beliefs and actions help create a culture of continuous improvement and doing one's best.

They pay attention to the physical environment of the school, provide pleasant, tidy facilities and ensure that all graffiti, rubbish and so forth are dealt with promptly. There are displays of student work and other school achievements, and teachers and students identify positively with the school, which has earned a good and often rising reputation in the community.

TEACHER LEARNING, RESPONSIBILITY AND TRUST

These principals place a high value on professional learning, both their own and that of other teachers. They encourage and support teacher learning and fund professional development inside and outside the school. They find ways and means to release staff for professional learning and bring others to the school for this purpose. They recognise that all teachers can be leaders and foster and acknowledge the leadership of others. They 'talent spot', encourage and 'coach' staff to assume responsibility. Trust is an important aspect of the mutual respect they enjoy with staff, students and the community.

STUDENT SUPPORT, COMMON PURPOSE AND COLLABORATION

Student welfare was found to be central in these schools and faculties, and seen as every staff member's responsibility. The purpose of student support and welfare is not about 'warm fuzzies' or 'boosting self-concept' but of 'getting students back into learning' (see Dinham & Scott, 2007). Support from school leaders for student welfare programs and procedures is essential and students clearly understand and support student welfare as something done *for* and not *to* them. Over time, there is an improvement in standards, behaviour and attitude that underpins academic success, personal growth and social cohesion.

Many of these principals have utilised a common purpose to unite the sometime disparate 'silos' of the secondary school (e.g., technology, assessment, literacy, pedagogy). Resources are diverted to this priority area and often a champion or team is empowered. Such projects serve to bring the school together. These principals are, however, pragmatic realists, knowing that all staff cannot be moved simultaneously — 'if one waits for everyone to get on the bus, it will never leave' — and thus they concentrate on interested and committed staff and provide them with encouragement, guidance, resources, learning opportunities and support. There is danger in this, in that one can be accused of playing favourites, and some staff can be left behind, but the hope is that success will have a contagious effect through the school and bring others 'on board' over time.

FOCUS ON STUDENTS, LEARNING AND TEACHING

This emerged as the core category from data analysis of the 38 school case study reports. Within faculties and the school there is concern for students as people, and teaching and learning are the prime considerations of the school.

There are commonly cross-school approaches to pedagogy, assessment, reporting and tracking of student achievement, with a particular focus on easing the Year 6 to 7 primary–secondary transition. There was a common emphasis on data-informed decision-making for improving teaching and learning.

There is consistency yet flexibility in policy implementation, with the simple, standard things done well. While some staff characterised this as 'zero tolerance', in reality this was found to be more a case of having clear guidelines and effective communication to ensure that everyone understands procedures and where he or she 'stands'. When needed, compassion and flexibility were evident.

While not all faculties and program teams in the study were confirmed as achieving exceptional outcomes, the vast majority were, and while not all principals were found to possess and exhibit the above qualities and approaches to the same high degree, once again, the majority did.

It needs to be noted that the schools in the study covered the socioeconomic and geographic spectrum of NSW and many were not in favoured or high socioeconomic areas. Rather than just surviving, these schools and faculties were thriving, often in difficult circumstances. In some cases, schools and faculties had been in decline until new principals, deputies and faculty heads had been appointed.

It also needs to be emphasised that the process of getting schools moving and improving is a challenging one, having taken 6 to 7 years in many of the schools and faculties investigated during the AESOP project. There are no quick fixes, and creating an environment where teachers can teach and students can learn takes time. These leaders were seen to build on what is there and they possessed a long-term agenda to turn their school around and take it to a higher level.

Within these schools exists a web of distributed leadership with the principal at the centre. This is not just a matter of spreading existing responsibility, but developing additional, dispersed leadership capacity. While principals do not usually teach, they identify and nurture the seeds for change and improvement, releasing latent individual and organisational energy that translates into improved performance in the classroom.

The quantitative data from external examinations and other measures, and the qualitative data obtained in the study revealed through the 50 site studies, clearly confirmed the dramatic change and renewal that had occurred in many of the faculties and schools. The most obvious evidence of this turning around and improving was in student numbers. Many of the schools had formerly been in decline but had now doubled enrolments, with the school having assumed de facto selective status, and with principals having to deal with the politics of turning away potential enrolments at a time when there is a general drift away from government schools across the state. Leadership by principals and other staff was found to be essential to this process of halting decline, initiating renewal and lifting performance.

In a recent review of research into the effects of leadership on student outcomes, Robinson, Lloyd and Rowe (2008, n.p.) concluded: 'The more leaders focus their influence, their learning, and their relationships with teachers on the core business of teaching and learning, the greater their influence on student outcomes.'

Their view resonated strongly with the findings of this study.

The Four Fundamentals of Student Achievement

We have confirmed the crucial importance of the teacher to student learning. The challenge for any educational leader, and the focus of this chapter, is to make things happen within individual classrooms. While the measured contribution of school leaders to student achievement is less than that of the teacher, it is clear that school leaders can have major influences, for good or bad, on matters such as school climate and culture, professional learning, school welfare programs and quality teaching. In reviewing a major examination of the effects of educational leadership on student achievement, published in the *Educational Administration Quarterly*, Wahlstrom (2008, p. 596) has noted:

> Although principals are not usually actively engaged in the moment-to-moment and day-to-day instructional decisions that teachers make in their classroom, their actions clearly have sometimes powerful and sometimes more diffuse effects on how teachers teach and what teachers know about effective instructional strategies.

Extensive research involving many teachers, many students and many schools in a variety of countries has led me to conclude that there are four, interdependent fundamentals to student achievement, and thus successful schools. These are illustrated in Figure 18.1 (Dinham, 2008a, pp. 139–140):

- Highly effective schools, faculties and individual teachers have a central focus on *students as learners* (every student can learn, concern for individual needs and progress) *and people* (the personal touch, student welfare, personal development and pastoral care).
- There is a constant effort to see and enhance *quality teaching* in every classroom.

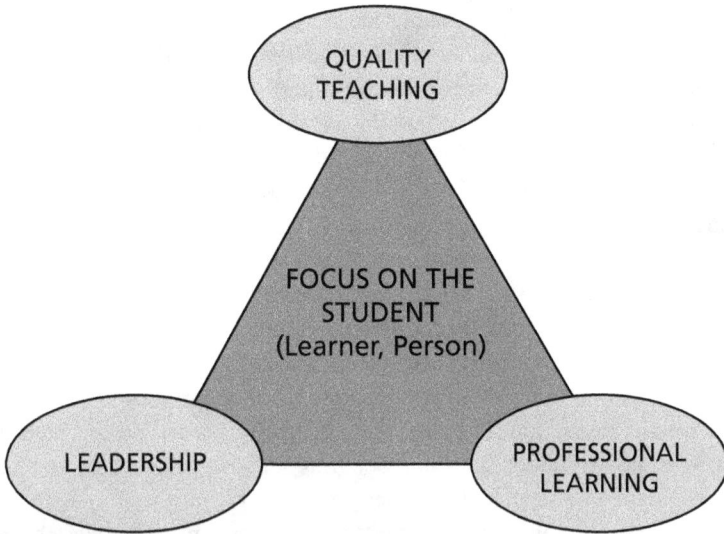

FIGURE 18.1
The four fundamentals of student achievement.

- These schools, leaders and individual teachers place a high value and priority on *professional learning*, both for themselves and others.
- *Leadership* (principal and distributed), is a key enabler of professional learning, quality teaching and thus student success.

Conclusion

As noted earlier, anyone who has taught in a school, or indeed has been a student, knows that leadership is important. However, we now have a much better understanding of why this is this the case and of that vital, yet somewhat elusive, link between leadership and learning.

We will probably never be able to measure with precision the actual effects of leadership on student learning, but does that really matter? Leadership is about human engagement, action and influence in social, dynamic contexts and to try to reduce it to some form of algorithm is probably a step too far. Education, teaching and learning will never be exact sciences in that sense. My strong suspicion informed by my research is that while some leaders may in fact have little influence on the quality of teaching and learning in their school, other leaders have a great influence.

As noted, leadership probably has most impact, and is needed most, in settings such as schools and faculties that are underperforming or 'coming off a low base'. It is probably equally true that poor leadership can have a quicker, greater effect than good leadership — it is easier to send an organisation such as a school into decline than it is to lift it up.

What *is* important is the growing recognition that educational leaders need to understand how students learn and what effective teaching looks like — leaders need to plan, act and evaluate on the basis of solid, empirical *evidence*, and not fad, fantasy, superstition or ideology.

They need to be instructional leaders more than managers and to place students at the centre of their school or part of the school. They need to do what is necessary to facilitate teachers' professional learning and quality teaching. They need to be able to work with others to create an environment in which teaching and learning are valued and where teachers can teach and students can learn.

Research has shown us what effective leadership looks like, as well as the attributes and actions of successful leaders. The challenge is to attract, select, prepare and support the next generation of educational leaders while offering similar support to those already in leadership positions.

Student accomplishment, however, through quality teaching, must be our ultimate aim.

Endnotes

1   This chapter draws upon Dinham, S. (2008a). *How to get your School moving and improving*. Melbourne, Australia: ACER Press.

2   While principals are important leaders, they are not the only leaders in schools. Other leaders, formal and informal, through distributed leadership, also play important roles in facilitating student learning. Unless stated otherwise, in this chapter, leadership and leaders refer to all those exercising leadership in schools, including teacher leadership.

3   'Effect size (ES) is a name given to a family of indices that measure the magnitude of a treatment effect (i.e., the size of the effect that A has on B). Unlike significance tests, these indices are independent of sample size. ES measures are the common currency of meta-analysis studies that summarise the findings from a specific area of research'. See http://web.uccs.edu/lbecker/Psy590/es.htm. An ES of 0.6 or above is usually considered large. See also Coe (2002).

References

Ayres, P., Dinham, S. & Sawyer, W. (1998). *The identification of successful teaching methodologies in the NSW Higher School Certificate: A research report for the NSW*

Department of Education and Training. Penrith, New South Wales, Australia: University of Western Sydney, Nepean.

Ayres, P., Dinham, S., & Sawyer, W. (1999*). Successful teaching in the NSW Higher School Certificate*. Sydney, Australia: NSW Department of Education and Training.

Ayres, P., Dinham, S., & Sawyer, W. (2000, September). Successful senior secondary teaching. *Quality Teaching Series, 1*, 1–20.

Ayres, P., Dinham, S., & Sawyer, W. (2004). Effective teaching in the context of a grade 12 high stakes external examination in New South Wales, Australia. *British Educational Research Journal, 30*(1), 141–165.

Berliner, D. (2004). Describing the behaviour and documenting the accomplishments of expert teachers. *Bulletin of Science, Technology & Society, 24*(3), 200–212.

Bransford, J., Brown, A., & Cocking, R. (Eds.). (2000). *How people learn*. Washington, DC: National Academy Press.

Coe, R. (2002, September). *It's the effect size, stupid*. Paper presented at the Annual Conference of the British Educational Research Association, University of Exeter, England. Retrieved November 10, 2008, from http://www.leeds.ac.uk/educol/documents/00002182.htm

Crowther, F., Kaagan, S., Ferguson, M., & Hann, L. (2002). *Developing teacher leaders*. Thousand Oaks, CA: Corwin.

Dinham, S. (2005). Principal leadership for outstanding educational outcomes. *Journal of Educational Administration, 43*(4), 338–356.

Dinham, S. (2007a). How schools get moving and keep improving: Leadership for teacher learning, student success and school renewal. *Australian Journal of Education, 51*(3), 263–275.

Dinham, S. (2007b). The waves of leadership. *The Australian Educational Leader, 29*(3), 20–21, 27.

Dinham, S. (2007c). *Leadership for exceptional educational outcomes*. Teneriffe, Queensland, Australia: Post Pressed.

Dinham, S. (2008a). *How to get your school moving and improving*. Melbourne, Australia: ACER Press.

Dinham, S. (2008b, May). Feedback on feedback. *Teacher*, 20–23.

Dinham, S., & Sawyer, W. (2004). Mobility and highly effective teachers: Re-visiting beliefs about 'Over-Stayers'. *Melbourne Studies in Education, 45*(2), 83–97.

Dinham, S., & Scott, C. (2007). Parenting, teaching and leadership styles. *Australian Educational Leader, 29*(1), 30–32; 45.

Dinham, S., & Scott, C. (2008, April). Responsive, demanding leadership. *Management Today*, 32–35.

Dinham, S., Ingvarson, L., & Kleinhenz, E. (2008). Investing in teacher quality: Doing what matters most. In *Teaching talent: The best teachers for Australia's classrooms* (pp. 5–53). Melbourne, Victoria, Australia: Business Council of Australia.

Glass, G.V (1976). Primary, secondary, and meta-analysis of research. *Educational Researcher, 5*(10), 3–8.

Australian School Leadership Today

Gronn, P. (2002). Distributed leadership. In K. Leithwood & P. Hallinger (Eds.), *Second international handbook of educational leadership and administration* (pp. 653–696). Dordrecht, Netherlands: Kluwer.

Hargreaves, A., & Fink, D. (2004). The seven principles of sustainable leadership. *Educational Leadership, 61*(7), 8–13.

Harris, A. (2004). Teacher leadership and distributed leadership: An exploration of the literature. *Leading and Managing, 10*(2), 1–9.

Harris, A. (2005). Distributed leadership. In B. Davies (Ed.), *The essentials of school leadership* (pp. 160–172). London: Paul Chapman.

Hattie, J. (2003, October). Teachers make a difference: What is the research evidence? Paper presented to ACER Annual Conference. Retrieved November 10, 2008, from http://www.leadspace.govt.nz/leadership/articles/teachers-make-a-difference.php

Hattie, J. (2007, August). Developing potentials for learning: Evidence, assessment, and progress. Paper presented at the EARLI Biennial Conference, Budapest, Hungary. Retrieved November 10, 2008, from http://www.education.auckland.ac.nz/ uoa/education/staff/j.hattie-conference

Lambert, L. (1998). *Building leadership capacity in schools*. Alexandria, VA: Association for Supervision and Curriculum Development.

Leithwood, K., & Mascall, B. (2008). Collective leadership effects on student achievement. *Educational Administration Quarterly, 44*(4), 529–561.

Leithwood, K., Louis, K., Anderson, S., & Wahlstrom, K. (2004). *Review of research: How leadership influences student learning*. New York: The Wallace Foundation.

Marzano, R. (2003). *What works in schools: Translating research into action*. Alexandria, VA: ASCD.

Marzano, R., Pickering, D., & Pollock, J. (2005). *Classroom instruction that works: Research-based strategies for increasing student achievement*. Upper Saddle River, NJ: Pearson.

Ministerial Council on Education, Employment, Training and Youth Affairs (MCEETYA). (1999). *Adelaide declaration on national goals for schooling in the twenty-first century*. Retrieved November 10, 2008, from http://www.mceetya.edu.au/mceetya/nationalgoalsindex.htm

Mulford, B. (2008). The leadership challenge: Improving learning in schools. *Australian Education Review, 53*, iii–21.l

Reeves, D. (2008). Leadership and learning. *ACEL Monograph Series, 43*, 3–21.

Reynolds. D., Teddlie, C., Creemers, B., Scheerens, J., & Townsend, T. (2000). An introduction to school effectiveness research. In C. Teddlie & D. Reynolds (Eds.), *The international handbook of school effectiveness research* (pp. 3–25). London: Falmer.

Robinson, V., Lloyd, C., & Rowe, K. (2008). The impact of leadership on student outcomes: An analysis of the differential effects of leadership types. *Educational Administration Quarterly, 44*(5) 635–674.

Sawyer, W., Ayres, P., & Dinham, S. (2001). What does an effective year 12 English teacher look like? *English in Australia, 129*(30), 51–63.

Spillane, J. (2006). *Distributed leadership*. San Francisco: Jossey-Bass.

Spillane, J., Halverson, R., & Diamond, J. (2001). Investigating school leadership practice: A distributed perspective. *Educational Researcher, 30*(3), 23–28.

Wahlstrom, K., & Louis, K. (2008). How teachers experience principal leadership: The roles of professional community, trust, efficacy, and shared responsibility. *Educational Administration Quarterly, 44*(4), 458–495.

Wahlstrom, K.L. (2008). Leadership and learning: What these articles tell us. *Educational Administration Quarterly, 44*(4), 593–597.

Wright, S., Horn, S., & Sanders, W. (1997). Teacher and classroom context effects on student achievement: Implications for teacher evaluation. *Journal of Personnel Evaluation in Education, 11*, 57–67.

York-Barr, J., & Duke, K. (2004). What do we know about teacher leadership? Findings from two decades of scholarship. *Review of Educational Research, 74*(3), 255–316.

▶▶▶ ◀◀◀

SECTION FIVE
Summary and Conclusions

CHAPTER 19

Australian School Leadership Today: Conclusions

Bill Mulford, Neil Cranston and Lisa Ehrich

The evidence provided in this book allows us to conclude that the context of 'new managerialism', which embraced managerial efficiency and effectiveness through bureaucracy and accountability as key levers for meeting higher community expectations and reforming schools, has failed. It also allows us to conclude that it is time that the professionals, the school leaders, ensure that what happens in schools, now and in the future, is what *they* want to happen. The professionals need to re-establish their individual and collective educational agency. The major professional challenge for any school leader is overcoming the gap between dependence on, or a feeling of, the inevitability of political, system or bureaucracies being the means of achieving what they want, and actively working to implement their preferred model of schools as social centres, learning organisations or professional learning communities (see chapters in this book and Mulford, 2008).

The major leadership challenge is for school leaders and their professional development programs to be able to understand and act on the context, organisation and leadership of the school, as well as the interrelationship between these three elements (see Figure 19.1).[1] Successful Australian school leadership will be contextually literate, organisationally savvy and leadership smart. In addition, successful school leadership is, by definition, the prime vehicle for linking all three elements (Mulford, 2008).

The Major Challenge: School Context, Organisation and Leadership

SCHOOL CONTEXT

Context matters. School leaders need to be contextually literate. They need to be aware of and responsive to the people and events around them. As the authors in this book have pointed out, this context involves on the one hand increased globalisation; increased, discontinuous and constant

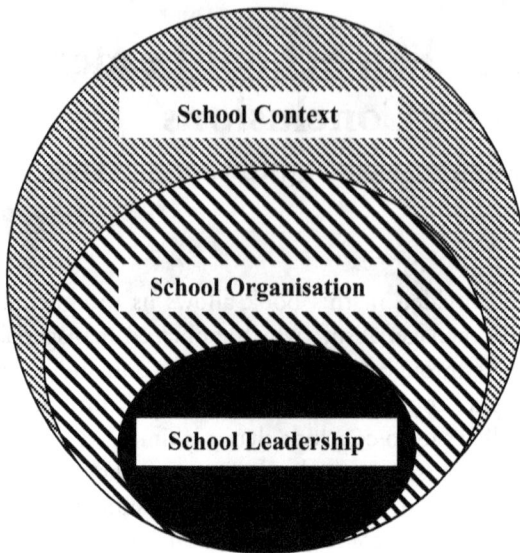

FIGURE 19.1
The major leadership challenge: The interrelationship of context, organisation and leadership.

change; increased complexity; increased uncertainty and insecurity; and an increase in ethical dilemmas; and on the other hand increased expectations and evaluation and accountability. To be successful, educational leaders will need to achieve balances between and/or choose between competing forces, broaden what counts for good schooling and broaden the ways schools are organised and run.

Choices between competing forces make the most sense when they foster stability in the form of a school's collective capacity to learn for change, independence rather than dependence, community rather than individualism and heterogeneity rather than homogeneity. Broadening what counts for good schooling needs to include excellence and equity and cognitive and noncognitive, especially personal and social skills. As authors in this book have pointed out, excellent education is not just about doing and having but also being and becoming. Understanding and being able to act in such a context will see school leadership that is intense, varied, accountable and rewarding (Mulford, 2008; National College for School Leadership [NCSL], 2007).

SCHOOL ORGANISATION

School organisation matters. School leaders need to be organisationally savvy. As the authors in this book reveal, they need to be able to build capacity. Broadening the way schools are organised and run would see a move from the mechanistic to organic, living systems (or social centres, learning organisations, professional learning communities) and from hierarchies to networks.

This broadening in the way schools are organised and run is best based on the development of a community of professional learners (see Figure 19.2 based on Mulford, 2007).

Successful school leaders will move their focus from the operational to the people agenda, to first develop community with, and leadership in, others. Awareness and skill development in group and organisational processes (understanding and developing people) is the first step in the development of school capacity-building. But it is only the first step. It needs to be followed by deciding where the school is going, building a vision and setting directions showing how it is going to get there (such as managing teaching and learning). This means being a community of professionals. A third stage in this developmental

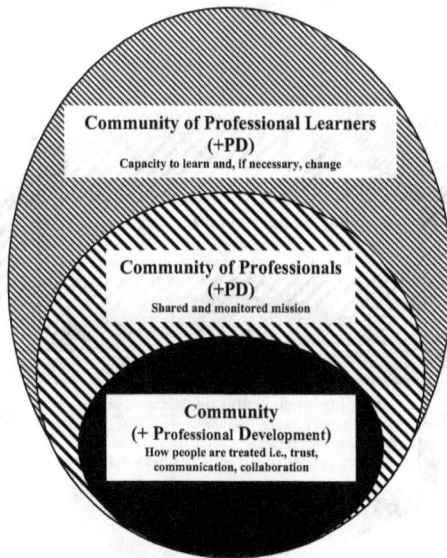

FIGURE 19.2
Community of professional learners.

journey is an ability to monitor success of both the outcomes and process employed, learn and, if necessary, make changes. This involves being a community of professional learners.

This developmental conceptualisation is consistent with Leithwood, Day, Sammons, Harris, and Hopkins' (2006) much used recent model, but adds an important sequence to their elements, that is, understanding and developing people, followed by building vision and setting direction, managing the teaching and learning program, and then, if necessary, redesigning the organisation.

Also adding to Leithwood et al.'s model is the argument that broadening what counts for good schooling and the way schools are organised and run would see an increased focus on social capital development, that is, not only bonding within schools but also bridging between schools and linking between schools and their communities (see Figure 19.3). Parent–school partnerships, for example, would be genuine rather than silent acquiescence. Social capital development at all three levels requires support, especially time.

'Linking' social capital operates across power differentials and thus is vertical in nature. It refers to ties to people in positions of authority. In other words, **ties between schools and their employer and other communities**.

'Bridging' social capital is also horizontal in nature referring to ties between people with more or less equal social standing. In other words, **ties between schools**.

'Bonding' social capital is horizontal in nature and refers to ties between people who are similar in terms of their demographic characteristics, such as family members and work colleagues. In other words, **ties within a school**.

FIGURE 19.3
Three forms of interrelated social capital.

This concept of a developmental journey, which involves tailoring action to an understanding of context, organisation and people, is demonstrated in this book in the chapters on school leader professional development. For example, more systematic and specialised programs are called for, especially for novice principals of small schools and the different knowledges have been identified for aspirant/novice (context, task, purposes of schooling) when compared with experienced (self, other, purposes of schooling) school leaders.

School leadership in the organisations we are advocating will be less lonely and more collaborative and professionally interactive (NCSL, 2007).

SCHOOL LEADERSHIP

The chapters in this book clearly demonstrate that Australian school leadership matters and is changing. In this situation school leadership needs to be smart; it needs to be evidence-based and shared. In fact, school leadership today is more evidence-based than ever before, but care is needed to ensure the evidence used is of high quality. Survey instruments such as that reported in this book on senior management teams (TEAM) will be valuable here. We need to encourage others to provide information about useful, valid, reliable, and short, easily administered evidence-gathering instruments for use by those in our nation's schools.

For example, academics and departmental officers represented in the 2005 (Volume 11, No. 2) edition of *Leading & Managing* have been part of a movement to encourage use of quality evidence-gathering instruments in schools and the reporting of the findings in the academic and professional literature. These people should be applauded, for it is only in this way that we can have an open, professional debate over evidence rather than, as seems to be the current norm, seeing it locked away in employers' files and being selectively used for accountability and control purposes, if used at all, rather than to improve schools and the children in them. It is also the only way to nip in the bud the growing use by schools of commercially available instruments accessed only by those willing to pay exorbitant amounts of money for the 'privilege'. The lack of validity and reliability of many of these instruments, as well as the spending of scarce resources by those in schools to line the pockets of the entrepreneurs who have jumped on this bandwagon, is reprehensible. This situation is especially so where those entrepreneurs have had the privilege of developing their surveys as members of publicly funded universities and/or research schemes.

Successful school leadership is not just about building organisational capacity but also about building personal leadership capacity (NCSL, 2007). The Australian evidence in this book demonstrates that leadership that makes a difference is both position-based and distributive. However, as others have shown (Mulford, 2008), positional and distributive leadership are only indirectly related to student outcomes. Leadership contributes to organisational capacity, which, in turn, influences what happens in the core business of the school: that is teaching and learning. It influences the way students perceive that teachers organise and conduct their instruction and their educational interactions with, and expectations of, their students. Students' positive perceptions of teachers' work directly promote a range of outcomes, such as their participation in school, academic self-concept, engagement with school and academic achievement (Mulford, 2008).

Emerging models of shared leadership and interactive professionalism highlight the need for different school leadership skills. Distributive leadership, emotional leadership and coordinated learning-centred patterns of distribution matter. However, there is enormous risk in us becoming too enamoured with the plethora of singular, simplistic, 'adjectival' leaderships now on offer (such as charismatic, heroic, instructional, transactional, transformational, sustainable, etc.).While one leadership style or approach may work well for some leaders, in practice most adopt a range of leadership styles. Successful leaders adapt and adopt their leadership practice to meet the changing needs of circumstances in which they find themselves (such as in the context and organisation of Australian small schools).

As schools develop and change, different leadership approaches will inevitably be required and different sources of leadership will be needed so that development work keeps moving. Any single 'one-size-fits-all' or adjectival approach to leadership, or checklists of leadership attributes, is superficially attractive but is likely to limit, restrict and distort leadership behaviour in ways not conducive to school development and improvement. For example, Barnett and colleagues' (Barnett, McCormick, & Connors, 2001) Australian research demonstrated that leadership does not always have a positive effect on student learning. They found that visionary leadership resulted in more distractions from core tasks associated with the teaching and learning program, and therefore had the potential to suppress student learning programs.

Despite the apparent singularity of much of the literature, in practice proponents of 'adjectival' leaderships in this book (such as Indigenous, spiritual, parallel, emotional, technology, distributed) have moved well away from the exclusivity of the one-size-fits-all models of school leadership. They incorporate an expanded understanding of leadership to include aspects of the context, of antecedent conditions and of the school mission and culture, structure and instructional program. All these leadership approaches have at their heart the development of leadership in others. No skill is currently more important than school leadership development and succession planning. Given the demographics of the profession in Australia, now is the right time to identify talent, fast-track those with potential, mentor and coach them, as well as take the opportunity to move from administration to strategic, educational and curriculum leadership. Well-functioning senior management teams are crucial here. We also need think more about change to traditional hierarchical-based career patterns in our schools and school systems (see Mulford, 2008).

Conclusion

Throughout this book there has been a reiteration of how a great deal of a school's success depends on its leaders and the model(s) of leadership that are implemented in the school. Its success also depends on which areas of school life the educational leader chooses to focus the time and attention of the school leadership team. As any single input by a leader can have multiple outcomes, so does the impact of multiple leaders have a still greater effect. An effective leader, acting either alone or as a leadership team leader, needs to be able to see and act with a whole-organisation perspective, as well as work on the individual elements, and the relationships between them (NCSL, 2005). As Dinham argues in his chapter in this book, school leaders need to be aware and responsive to people and events around them and, through high standards, an expectations they are demanding both of themselves (give a lot) and others (expect a lot). Given this complexity both in and around schools, it is little wonder that principals and their leadership teams find their work both exhausting and exhilarating.

As has been argued earlier, success in managing the three elements of context, organisation and leadership, especially in respect to the embedded interrelationships they contain, is perhaps the biggest current leadership challenge for Australian school leaders. Within this broad challenge, school leaders must be part of ongoing conversations about context and its implications for schools. Leaders then need to understand and be able to act on the evolving and preferred organisational models for schools with a clear priority to student learning and effective teaching.

Additionally, it is clear that leaders need to be able to understand and act on the quality evidence that is now accumulating on being a successful school leader. This book, by its existence and in its structure and substance, represents a plea for educational leaders to actually use the quality evidence thus presented. It is recognised that there is a need to move beyond mere technical competence. It bears repeating that there is a need to empower the professionals, providing the time for reflection on effective change and serious support for creativity. We believe this same argument should apply to the students and their leadership and empowerment. Only in these ways can Australian schools and school systems truly move forward.

Obviously there is a need to achieve better balances in our world, including between learning what the political and bureaucratic systems require of individual school leaders and what practicing professionals require of themselves and their colleagues. On the basis of the evidence in this book, it can be argued that this balance can best be achieved by groups of educational leaders, or professional collectives and alliances, negotiating and then setting and delivering their own agendas. After all, participation in context, organisation and leadership, including policymaking and the provision of professional development, not only enhances efficiency in implementation but also can contribute to the creation of more pluralistic and democratic educational systems (Lecomte & Smillie, 2004).

Finally, and to return to the points made in the introduction to this book, we believe what 'is good for the goose is also good for the gander'. What is 'good' for Australian school leaders is also 'good' for Australian school leadership scholars, both in terms of their research and the need to work more closely together.

First, there is a need for Australian school leadership scholars to avoid simplistic 'solutions', lists and adjectival leaderships. It makes no sense, for example, to apply the same leadership style all the time or to novice principals in small rural schools, experienced principals in large urban schools and faith-based religious schools. It is time to take up the comprehensive and developmental models we have promulgated and which are illustrated in Gurr's chapter in this book.

Second, practitioners and scholars cannot continue to overlook each others' contributions. As Bates and Eacott (2008, p. 159) state, 'Nobody, practitioner or scholar, benefits from a field that is littered with loosely related contributions that do not acknowledge [or build on] one another'. (p. 159). It is time for us to start talking to each other about our Australian scholarship.[2]

On the one hand, 'Australia is fighting above its weight in the international literature. ... [with] a core group of academics [who] have established a research track record ... [and] there are signs of a new group of scholars entering the dialogue' but, on the other hand, 'educational leadership does not get the attention in Australia that it does receive in other nations such as USA and UK' (Bates & Eacott, 2008, pp. 157–159). It is time for Australian scholars in the field to also show leadership through individual and collective professional agency. To start with, we would all 'benefit from listening and working with each other to further establish the unique Australian perspective within the global educational leadership field' (Bates & Eacott, 2008, p. 160).

Endnotes

1   This nested 'Russian dolls' pictorialisation, stressing the interrelationships between elements as clearly embedded within each other as well as suggesting a sense of development (starting in the middle and moving outwards), is deliberately employed for all three major concepts (the major leadership challenge, community of professional learners and social capital) in this chapter.

2   It is worth noting that a quick tally of references used in the chapters in this book found that on average 50% were from Australian sources with the range varying from 21 to 80%. There was also a sense that a start was being made in the cross-referencing of each others' work.

References

Barnett, K., McCormick, J., & Connors, R. (2001). Transformational leadership in schools: Panacea, placebo or problem? *Journal of Educational Administration, 39*(1), 24–46.

Bates, R., & Eacott, S. (2008).Teaching educational leadership and administration in Australia. *Journal of Educational Administration and History, 40*(2), 149–160.

Leithwood, K., Day, C., Sammons, P., Harris, A., & Hopkins, D. (2006). *Seven strong claims about successful school leadership*. Nottingham, England: National College for School Leadership.

Lecomte, H., & Smillie, I. (2004), *Ownership and partnership: What role for civil society in poverty reduction strategies?* Paris: Organisation for Economic Development and Co-operation.

Mulford. B. (2007). The challenge of building social capital in professional learning communities. In L. Stoll & K. Seashore Louis (Eds.), *Professional learning communities: Divergence, depth and dilemmas* (pp.166–180). London: Open University Press/McGraw Hill.

Mulford, B. (2008). The leadership challenge: Improving learning in schools. *Australian Education Review Series No. 53.* Melbourne, Australia: Australian Council for Educational Research. Available at http://www.acer.edu.au/research_reports/AER.html

National College for School Leadership. (2005). *Emerging lessons from NCSL research activity.* Nottingham, England: Author.

National College for School Leadership. (2007). *What we know about school leadership.* Nottingham, England: Author.

▶▶▶◀◀◀

www.ingramcontent.com/pod-product-compliance
Lightning Source LLC
Chambersburg PA
CBHW050558270326
41926CB00012B/2105